BEYOND THE
LOOKING GLASS

America's Beauty Culture

By Kathrin Perutz

BEYOND THE LOOKING GLASS
MOTHER IS A COUNTRY
THE GHOSTS
A HOUSE ON THE SOUND
THE GARDEN

BEYOND THE LOOKING GLASS

America's Beauty Culture

by KATHRIN PERUTZ

WILLIAM MORROW AND COMPANY, INC.

New York   1970

For Michael,
with love

Acknowledgments

In February, 1968, I read an article in Vogue on face lifting: five women told why they would do it again. The article was macabre, funny, pitiful and, mainly, hopeful. Each woman willingly bore the expense, pain and fear because she knew at the end of it she would look younger. From that article, this book was conceived.

It would not have issued without the labor and assistance of many people. George Greenfield and Sally Belfrage first helped give it shape. I would like to thank all who gave their time, knowledge and generous permission to use their words.

In particular, I thank Polly Devlin, who even took time off from Vogue to help me; Milton Luger, who gained me entrance to the New York Department of Corrections; Marten Brouwer, who gave me clippings and encouragement; Ray Sokolov; Jean Shrimpton; Dr. Donald Opdyke; Bill Mandel; Mary Lindsay; Kenneth Battelle; Margaret Mead; Norman Mailer; Oliver Swan, my equable and helpful agent; and James Landis, whose intimacy with the book made possible many necessary deletions and amendments, who gave the book its title and, as my editor, always provided encouragement.

In addition, I thank all the following: Albert Asenjo, Sam Badian, Ken Baker, Jacqui Brandwynne, Dr. Earle W. Brauer, Dr. James A. Brussel, David and Sarah Burnham, Mary Butler, Jessica Canne, Alma Cunningham, Ruth Downing, Henry Flower, Dr. Robert Alan Franklyn, Nancy Grace, Amy Greene, Elaine Grollman, Larry Gross, Elizabeth Hogen, Zofya Jastrzembska, Jean Kane, Dr. Jeffrey Kramer, Gloria MacFarland, Harold Melvin, Paul Mitchell, Robert Niedelman, Jean Nidetch, Michael and Ashley Pakenham, Dolly and Tino

Perutz, Norman Podhoretz, Anita Porter, Francesca Ruta, Vidal Sassoon, Janet Simon, Jerry Spallina, Gloria Steinem, Michael Studdert-Kennedy, Carola Trier, Howard Wagman, Dr. William Webb, Sol Worth, and the others who must remain anonymous.

My thanks to Kostya.

Contents

Introduction   1

MAKE UP, AMERICA

1. The Image and How It's Taught   7
2. The Business   22
3. Products and Services   49

HAIR

1. The Presentation of Hair   69
2. Hairdressers   90

WHAT A PIECE OF WORK IS MAN

1. The Man-Made Woman and the Man Who
   Made Her   109
   [1] THE WOMAN   109
   [2] THE MAN   116
2. Only Correct   126
3. Interview with a Star Surgeon   141

THE OUTSIDE OF THE INSIDE

1. Body Image   157
2. The Fat Are Different from Us (They Have More
    Flesh)   160
3. Outcasts and Outlooks   171
4. Inside   183
    [1] START   183
    [2] THE WOMEN'S HOUSE OF DETENTION   188

LIVING DOLLS

1. Models   199
2. Celebrities   216
3. Jean Shrimpton   228

UNISEX

1. Prettifying the Male   237
2. What Is Unisex?   247

BEAUTY RETREAT

    259

LIFE IN THE BEAUTY CULTURE

1. Prepare a Face to Meet the Faces That You Meet   295
2. The Real Unreal   318

NOTE

All dialogue in this book is actual, most of it transcribed from tapes. Some people asked me not to use their names; others didn't specify any restrictions but I felt real names might damage or expose them. These I refer to with generally descriptive phrases ("an eminent psychiatrist," "a New York plastic surgeon," "a prison official") or I give a substitute name (Susie, Dr. B.). All prisoners' names are invented. In the final chapter I use a few composites to represent a type of person, but even there, only actual words are used.

I am convinced that nothing has so marked an influence on the direction of a man's mind as his appearance, and not his appearance itself so much as his conviction that it is attractive or unattractive.

—TOLSTOY, *Childhood*

God mend thine ev'ry flaw . . .

—*America, the Beautiful*

Introduction

To write a book on personal beauty is to expose oneself, more than with any other subject, to those elaborations of vanity and doubt that people term their self-expression. We have all been warned to avoid discussion of politics and religion when we hope to charm; but an antipathetical credo is much more forgivable than reference to a sagging chin. There's no better way to make an enemy than by alluding to an unattractive feature, and of all topics persistent with man, none finds so little agreement as beauty. Each man has his type of woman, and each woman her type of man. Everyone has a model of beauty for himself. The truism that beauty is in the eye of the beholder is only half the story, since beauty is equally in the mind of the beheld. Most of us have been beautiful at times, ugly at others, or have seen ourselves that way. Though Beauty may be Truth, there is nothing true about beauty. It depends, like love, on a subtle form of communication, where both participants have received the Word or at least gotten the message.

As with beauty, so with its ritual. No two practitioners are alike. Making up, like practicing witchcraft, is a private system for casting spells. Beauty, like drugs, has been condemned for its power over rational faculties, and the means of achieving or maintaining beauty once were kept secret, so that only a valet knew his man and only a lady's maid knew her woman. Now, beauty is an open secret: as with most other forms of American life, it is conditioned by communications and lack of privacy. Now everyone can be beautiful, and the ways to beauty are well marked in print and on television.

Beauty is a seven-billion-dollar industry and the largest advertiser in America. As a theme, it goes from aesthetics to statistics and takes in almost every aspect of self-presentation. It is in the ground that makes up fields of anthropology, sociology, psychology, marketing, literature, art, psychoanalysis, fashion and more. In order to cultivate a fertile area, one must choose one's plot. This book leaves out much more than it includes, and fashion, for instance, beauty's sister, has no place here. Weight is treated superficially and fragrances are only occasionally mentioned. In trying to present the beauty culture— a society in which stereotyped images become models for a person's view of himself—I am more concerned with practices, attitudes and developments in beauty than I am with the products themselves or current fads. Everyone's involved in the beauty culture—the baby-powdered infant, long-haired hippy and dieting grandmother—and has learned to attribute redemptive powers to it. We judge ourselves through the image we have been taught to accept. The beauty culture provides a modern quest for youth and love, the hope of seeming what one has not become, and a chance to disappear into the fabled America of wealth and liberty.

By looking at the way an individual in a society presents himself to other members of society, one finds a measure of his values, his personal relations and his integration. Any particular American has a limited range in which to modify his appearance. Class, age, geography, profession, marital status and other factors condition his choices. But a guiding mystique rules us all, and emanates mainly from New York, where magazines, advertising agencies, cosmetics companies, models and hairdressers supply an image, which the rest of America must then be taught to demand.

My interest in the topic is rarely objective. I'm part of the beauty culture: it put lipstick on me when I was twelve, a tiny bra around my chest when I had nothing to fill it with and had me reaching for a hair lightener when I was thirteen. While writing this book, I retained my usual beauty habits, though I had expected they would change radically. Habitual visits to the hairdresser continued, each new issue of *Vogue* gave me the same delight as an uncracked, fat summer novel and I made up every day. When much-loved friends (male) from abroad arrived without warning, my pleasure in seeing them developed only after I had gone up to change, done my hair and face, put on perfume. My concern with this frippery is very serious, and when I show archness in this book it is usually directed toward myself. I dislike my dependence; I despise the abandonment I feel when I misplace my makeup kit, or my refusal to go even to a dark movie when my hair is awful. My hair, incidentally, is the only thing that changed during this book. It's been long, thick and wild since the age of thirteen; I clung to my unmanageable tresses as a sign (I hoped) of femininity, always seeing in the mind's eye a cascade of silken hair spilling down in the boudoir. At the beginning of summer, I had it all cut off and—perhaps a measure of health that the book gave me—suffered no trauma.

I stand to the beauty culture much as I do to America and have with it an uneasy, respectful, guilty, religious involvement from which I can't exile myself because there is nowhere to go that wouldn't remind me of what I had left. A Norwegian critic wrote generously of one of my novels that it shows "we are all Americans." If so, then we are all, too, part of the American beauty culture. America first; then follow all the nations that, by attaining our high standard, open Pandora's box: fear, competitiveness, social injustice and the absence of God fly out to make people afraid of confronting each other without ritualized disguise.

This culture made me. As a believer, I am appalled by heresy. I am alarmed by the abuses and implications, by morbid self-preoccupation and the substitution of concern with appearance over self-knowledge. The beauty culture has rescued me from self-hatred more often than poetry or philosophy; it is part of my growing up and Americanization.

MAKE UP,
AMERICA

My mistress' eyes are nothing like the sun;
Coral is far more red than her lips' red;
If snow be white, why then her breasts are dun;
If hair be wires, black wires grow on her head.
I have seen roses damask'd, red and white,
But no such roses see I in her cheeks;
And in some perfumes is there more delight
Than in the breath that from my mistress reeks.
I love to hear her speak; yet well I know
That music hath a far more pleasing sound.
I grant I never saw a goddess go:
My mistress, when she walks, treads on the ground.
  And yet, by heaven, I think my love as rare
  As any she belied with false compare.

—SHAKESPEARE, *Sonnet CXXX*

1

The Image and How It's Taught

"Thing is," said the actress with cropped, frosted hair, "he's got to believe he's got eighty percent, or even more. Men are so insecure, they've got to think they have you."

Her friend, a former actress and now novelist, purred. A light coating of smile covered her pretty, middle-aged face and she agreed. "Yes, but never let him have more than twenty percent. That's the rule—give him twenty and he'll think it's eighty. He'll still be wanting more. . . ."

"Because he's got to have challenge. He has to keep on, wanting more." The lady, who kept her body in perfect condition and was addicted to affairs with the near-famous, smiled at me. I shrugged. "And," she continued her instruction, "you've got to get at least eighty percent of him—"

"At least," the novelist interjected sagely.

"—even though he thinks he's holding out. Not all, though, if you want to keep the affair going. Get all of him and that's it. Too boring."

"Boring," intoned her friend.

Both women looked younger than they were. Both had been through marriages and children and emerged remarkably unscarred by maturity. I argued that intimacy might be nice; that, after all, you knew yourself and didn't get bored. Maybe the trick was to get to know someone so well that you could be surprised by him, not merely jolted.

They disagreed. Love, America's favorite game, had rules like any other and all contributed to the glory of power. I remembered an English friend interrupting a diatribe of mine with, "That's not interesting. I don't care about your feelings and all, I'm only interested in your facade. Everyone's alike in their souls, everyone has the same emotions. It's simply not interesting to talk about them." I was angry until I realized he meant only that self-pity was incurable, contagious and flourished under attention. The ladies in their talk of love meant something else: the obliteration of a private self through a conscious game played on the board of possible true emotions. The Englishman was talking about a front, a disguise that came in aid of social situations. The Americans hoped to remove the distinction between public and private, allowing a constant trickle of emotion to whet the appetite for play before being absorbed. They believed they could make up their lives.

A magazine article by a woman who had never allowed her husband to see her naked face in three years of marriage instructed readers in her methods. When showering with your lover, make sure you remain in position farthest from the spray. In bed with him, always remember to take your makeup kit for repair work under the covers. For optimum results, hide kit and a magnifying mirror under the bed so that waking up at night, you can secretly restore whatever passion has undone. When about to give birth, ignore labor, put on your face and hold off as long as possible the dash to the hospital. Once there, resist any attempt by nurses or aides to wash your face; become hysterical or have a temper tantrum (have two) if necessary. If you're late enough, the child will issue immediately and you are prepared for doctors, interns and visitors.

The scheme is beautiful, but possibly not flawless: your man might become suspicious. Most men, the author reminds us, say they don't like makeup, though most men—sweet little things—are really too naïve to know when it's in front of their faces. However, should your man begin to doubt (or think), there are steps you can take: cut down the time of your makeup routine to seven minutes (no more) and, when going off to the ladies' room, announce that you must "powder your nose." He will never suspect, nature being what it is, that you have time for more. Whenever you see an obviously made-up woman, denounce her. Say artifice is terrible, that you would never do more than put on lipstick and powder. If these and other ruses fail to remove all doubt from his mind, then prepare for the Moment of Truth: he sees your "naked" face.

This requires time and patience. Instead of the usual hour spent in making up, you need two. Everything must be done lightly, naturally. No thick fringe of lashes; each lash is applied individually. Every item—foundation, blusher, highlighter, shadow, eyeliner, mascara, eyebrow color, lipstick—must be used sparingly, must sink invisibly into the skin. The moment comes. Your freshly washed and set hair is loose and unsprayed. He enters. Your hands move up to cover your face (carefully) and you murmur, "You're so early! I haven't even had time to put on lipstick." He approaches, gently draws both hands away from the cherished face, contemplates a moment, then jubilantly announces, "Baby, you look great!"

The article was not meant as satire. Deceit is serious and lucrative business. Disguise is essential, the game must be played and love's in the service of masquerade. A person who exists only on the level of physical attraction is the Image as presented most spectacularly by *Playboy* (for men) and *Cosmopolitan* (for women). The outside is not the inside, perhaps, but it is all that matters. People are flattened into characters and their reality is only what one sees. Like Potemkin villages, the cosmopolitan girl and the playboy exist only externally. Behind the facade is either nothing or squalor and in either case isn't recognized. When the Empress Catherine toured her country and saw the gleaming model villages her lover had constructed, she was pleased and never thought to question the life behind the stucco. The social and economic unreality of a Potemkin village corresponds to the psychological unreality of the image presented in these magazines, both of which stand on the premise that members of our own sex are real people, while members of the other are playthings. The prospect of living with a cosmopolitan girl or playboy is as hospitable as moving into a Hollywood set.

To accept the Image at twenty-five, one must be trained. The child must learn to accept the authority of magazines and to think of itself as an object. From *Jack and Jill* and *Child Life*, American children progress to magazines of adventure and love, movie magazines and pop music glossies. Nubile girls read *Teen Miss, Sixteen, American Girl* and *Ingenue* before graduating into the beauty and fashion gospel for teen-agers, *Seventeen*. Their early reading has prepared them for the message and moral of this *Vogue* for adolescents; they are eager to consume, to find their individual stereotype, to smell sweet, be in fashion and observe daily rituals of beauty.

"The care you take of your looks is an authentic indication of your self-esteem," pronounces *Seventeen* and berates the current trend of "personal negligence." Self-esteeming readers, mainly high school girls, are encouraged to take part in the beauty cult, to shave legs and underarms (even if they are thirteen-year-old blondes), shampoo and deodorize daily, own many makeup products and "experiment" with them in ways outlined by the magazine; to spend money at beauty shops (they start going at age ten) and on those "nice little extras" that make their daily bath a luxury. This message is easily taught to girls who received their first toy makeup kit at five and a year or two later were playing with Barbie dolls: miniature effigies of superconsuming teen-agers that are models (instead of babies) for the children who own them.

In a Philadelphia toy shop, I asked to see makeup kits. Two were fake, costing 88 cents and 89 cents. The items were plastic or paper and included lipstick, nail polish, comb, other beauty aids and play money. The real kits were Prettykins for $1.99, a meager assortment that would cost a quarter of the price if bought separately at Woolworth's, and Betsy McCall's Pretty Pak for $4.49, a pink plastic hatbox filled with Pond's toiletries. "How old is the little girl?" asked the pretty black saleslady.

"Eight . . . nine," I improvised. She looked amused. "Isn't that the right age?" I inquired.

"Well, mostly we sell them for five- and six-year-olds. I remember I got one of these when I was about six. Of course you *can* buy them for older girls, but by the time a girl's ten, she'll buy the real thing."

A slightly more mature gift would have been the platinum dynel wig for fifteen dollars, to be worn by a doll and set by its owner. Of course Barbie-doll accessories would have been best. My eight–nine-year-old would certainly own Barbie and probably some of her friends. She would have read their stories, have accepted their preoccupation with power and know that Barbie holds sexual sway through her appearance (a bland prettiness), reinforced by a wardrobe of many hundred items. I could have bought a wig, fall and ribbon-pleated braid for Barbie, or even better, false lashes. Since the lashes are too small to be applied by anyone but a watchmaker, they come already fastened to a head, and children are invited to "put this new head on your doll." After this, how pedestrian are organ transplants.

I thought about my invented child and read about her. In Boston, a buyer announced that four- and five-year-olds are aware of fashion trends and "are interested in the waistline look and the return of belts." Another buyer reported that the Nehru look "is hot." Even in infant wear, the Mao and military looks were catching on.

In New Orleans, girls between seven and fourteen were choosing the Bonnie-and-Clyde look; in Milwaukee they liked pant-dresses and culottes, while their brothers chose turtlenecks and double-breasted jackets. In Los Angeles, "real fashion awareness" was reported: "Style-conscious kids are leading their mothers to fashion." (Milne's poem takes on new meaning:

> James James
> Morrison Morrison
> Weatherby George Dupree
> Took great
> Care of his Mother
> Though he was only three.)

And in the country as a whole, *Women's Wear Daily* reports, "It is generally felt that high-fashion influence had the most impact at the 10 year old and older level, where children are making their own decisions. However, younger children, shopping with their parents, also are decision-makers in more and more instances."

The instances are upon us. Little girls of ten pose for bra ads, wearing a Teencharm bra—a bandeau of almost flat white material stretched across the thorax, which in the fifties was known as a button bra because nothing larger than a button could fit into the cup— and underneath, the advertiser asks: "Have you seen this little girl?"

You have. Dressed in her mother's clothes beside her tiny dressing table, she is trying to make up her mind which Tinkerbell cosmetic to put on next. She's using "The Fashion Grooming Line for Children" and can then wear her fake fur from the Archie Baby Line, whose designer says, "Children basically don't like to look like children. And I feel they need a little help."

All over the country, people are helping them. At the airport in Los Angeles, I chatted with a fellow passenger. She was subtly made up, her platinum-streaked hair well groomed, wearing a mini fur coat over imitation broadtail trousers with Persian lamb cuffs and leading a white toy poodle. She was approximately eight. She and her friends are the inspiration for fashion absurdities: "Little girls love to show off their tans in sundresses that expose a lot of skin. The bare look for spring is not just for the ladies." We see "the almost topless swimsuit" on a fourth-grade model and sundresses "in a sexy yellow and navy cotton" to "keep spring dolls cool."

Children have not been deprived of nude advertising, and my eight–nine-year-old can be seen draped with corduroy, genitals covered but her nudity made prurient by a naked shoulder, naked leg exposed to the waist. The five-to-ten-year-olds who compete in the Little Miss America Contest, and audiences of the same age who watch them, are being shown it's never too early. Affluence reaches further and further down the age ladder; when teen-agers have close to sixty billion dollars, younger siblings clamor to own or at least control their fair share. I asked a magazine editor, "When does a child become a consumer?" and she told me, "From the minute it can talk and watch television and say, 'I want a Mattell toy or a Remco toy,' or, 'Get me Post Toasties.'"

As part of the economy, children can be appealed to and exploited. With teen-agers, you try for direct sales. With young children, you try for influence. Get the brand name in the child's head and the mother will buy the product. Superconsumption can start at any age, and we will assume that all citizens are equal. The good selling gimmicks, principally status and sex, work for any age. An advertiser, giving the anatomy of the American girl, defines sex: "It's her affair. And a lot of your business."

By the time a girl turns to *Seventeen*, she knows the rules of the game. The magazine's statistics show that only 2 percent of its readers dare go without deodorant, while only 6 percent refrain from removing body hairs. The girls are independent, will color their hair for whatever reason (but not to please their boyfriends), or won't (but not because their parents object). For beauty ideas, the girls turn to magazines (78 percent), occasionally to friends and mothers, but not to their own inspiration. Self-reliant and individualistic, readers of *Seventeen* learn to augment these qualities by following the magazine's advice.

At this moment in fashion, when beauty means to look very young and being young means doing your own thing, the pattern becomes difficult. Formerly, little girls tried to look like their mothers. Now the fashion authority of *Vogue* and *Harper's Bazaar* (and behind them, the éminence grise of *Women's Wear Daily*) dictates the natural, kooky look of sixteen-year-olds, and *Seventeen* carries on the message. Though it has been an American quirk since at least De Tocqueville's time to make everyone the same age, and place that age somewhere in adolescence, the modern variation has been to change values from conservative and rigid to existential and frivolous. The woman with blue rinse in her hair always wanted to look young, but was aware that society placed limitations on her behavior. Now, ads to "cover up gray" show a nineteen-year-old model and the implied message is, "Get with it, remove your antisocial gray, hike up your skirts and get thee to a discotheque." Teen-agers have become guardians of our culture. "The child is father to the man" has commercial meaning. If Tom wears his hair shoulder length, Dad will grow (or buy) sideburns. If Janie is wearing boots up to her crotch, they will be available at Bergdorf Goodman's and Neiman Marcus. When Tom clutters the bathroom with cosmetics, Dad might try powder to cover his beard; and Janie's natural look causes Mom to buy Yardley and remove the emerald green from her eyelids.

Paul Mitchell of Bendel's Beauty Salon opened The Crimpers* for young New Yorkers. "Young can start with a switched-on kid of eight or nine," Mr. Mitchell said. They, and older children, come to the salon alone. "They can go there, have loud music playing, *their* kind of music. If they'd like a tune, they just tell the girl at the desk and we try and play it or we get it. It's *their* place, where they can sit around, meet their boyfriends." Paul Mitchell is a tall, mustachioed man in his early thirties whose blue eyes focus on a woman with warning and flattery. "And young doesn't mean just teen-agers," he pointed out. "It means young people, hip people and forty-year-old people—if you're sixteen and you want your hair teased up and rollers put into it, then you're not welcome."

Seventeen carries the message of *Vogue* to its readers, but educating the whole young world "out there" (beyond New York's East Fifties) must be done gradually. A few false lashes can be shown, but the credo of ritual grooming is paramount: daily bathing, mouth washing, deodorizing, shampoo, manicure, shaving a few times a week. The essentials (skin, hair, face) must be made perfect, the girl

---

* *Crimper* is the Cockney term for hairdresser that Vidal Sassoon applies to himself in his book, *sorry to keep you waiting, madam.*

given her life lesson, before present fashion can be introduced. The *Seventeen* image is America's sweetheart: marvelously young, full of vitality, smells sweet as a baby, with a dusting of information; she's Daddy's Little Girl, a real honeybun who's young enough not to care.

At college, the little girl changes and learns how to be herself through *Glamour* and *Mademoiselle*. *Mademoiselle* is more sophisticated, more *Vog*uish; *Glamour* has the largest readership of any fashion magazine and sees its readers as undiscovered princesses. Make-overs, the most popular feature in the magazine, show how any girl in America can be transformed through makeup, hair style and clothes into someone beautiful, charming and, most important, successful. College girls, secretaries, lab assistants or bank clerks, all are ordinary girls with the special dream of looking like Cheryl Tiegs (blond) or Lisa Palmer (brunette), *Glamour*'s two favorite cover girls. To fulfill this dream, editors, hairdressers and makeup men work in front of a photographer on someone who, ostensibly made in the image of God, is now made over in the image of *Glamour*. "I gave them instant class," said Amy Greene, former beauty editor. "The good haircut and the shiny hair and lots of makeup, but yet nobody knew they had lots. . . . Every girl that passed through my hands uses a night cream," she said proudly. "Why do they want to be made over? Well, it's a fairy tale—that she would get a prince, or that she would get a better job or that she would just look better. Kids are very realistic, by the way."

Amy Greene, now at *McCall's*, appropriate in apple-green shirt, skirt and tights, wearing a wide blue necktie held down by a coral snail to match her blue eyes, so thickly mascaraed that each lash stood alone, said that she often saw the girls later. "I would say that ninety percent were completely changed—in my image. And they kept it up. No adaption. They liked themselves and they were afraid to try anything else. They became ultraconservative, and they wouldn't veer from that specific thing I wrote down for them to do every day."

Though theoretically the girls come from all parts of America, most actually live in big cities. "Environment has a lot to do with it," said Miss Greene, pointing out that in some places a make-over would be inappropriate. "I did three girls from Brooklyn, through the years. And they loved themselves, but they couldn't keep it up. Because their girlfriends, or their aunts, or their mothers, or somebody would say, 'Listen, Mary, you look terrible. You don't look like everybody else on the block.' " Make-overs are not adapted to surroundings and some girls "have to fight the entire neighborhood, they have to fight everybody."

But a large bank in Kansas City, deciding to change its image, asked *Glamour* to renovate the female staff. *Glamour* obliged, and part of the bank was transformed into a beauty salon while hair-dressers and makeup men worked. The result, according to the features editor, was "a miracle." By New York standards, the girls at the bank had looked ghastly—old-fashioned and overdone. The make-over gave them *chic*, "class," and the editors of *Glamour* felt they had redesigned a little neighborhood store into Saks Fifth Avenue.

The success of make-overs depends on the image one chooses, and though the girls certainly become more glamorous, worthy of being photographed on glossy paper, their facial expressions are often obscured or even extinguished. Makeup conceals a multitude of sins, and if they are more heinous than having acne or crow's feet, if they are sins of commission, one regrets their concealment. To apply class, it seems, one must remove all quirks.

"Instant class" doesn't stop with beauty. The *Glamour* reader is given snippets of "culture" to make her Instantly Interesting. She can read about books, music, movies and men's opinions. Occasionally, she is fed some politics and is always given advice on how to get a man and avoid skin trouble. Like any magazine with primarily female readership, *Glamour* is a little club, which makes allusions to itself and assumes fidelity in its reader. The quality of most columns again suggests a Potemkin person: bright and glittering on the outside, the *Glamour*ous young woman has a brain undefiled by maturity, with a simple directness tolerating neither wit nor thought.

Mademoiselle shows a higher quality of writing, and its fashions are close to *Vogue*. It is a better, more professional and more boring magazine than *Glamour*. Its image is similar but more understated. The big-city career-girl look of *Glamour* has been adapted to the tennis-playing campus look. *Glamour* is read on subways and in the nurses' quarters of hospitals; *Mademoiselle* is read on bunk beds and the New Haven Railroad.

With *Cosmopolitan*, distinctions end. Like *Playboy*, it appeals to all readers dedicated to the proposition. Sex, tough-minded and embellished with status symbols, is the essence. People of our sex are the only ones to be taken seriously and our most serious quest is the hunt for sexual trophies. The *Playboy* approach, amusing and offensive, carries on the he-man tradition popular in America and some Latin countries that makes a fetish of the male ability to penetrate a woman and ejaculate. Endowed with such a stunning trait, man is superior to woman—stronger, more intelligent, and free of the social and moral rules that naturally bind her. The world turns on the tip of the penis and it is woman's duty to keep the world looking up. She's a function, and is pleasurable. The amount of pleasure she offers can often be measured by the size of her breasts or if not, then by her willingness to perform. Sex is liberating; a man must be free to play the game and he displays his freedom through symbols of virility: money, fast sports cars, yachts and hard liquor.

This well-entrenched attitude has provided decades of arguments about double standards and pseudomasculinity. *Cosmopolitan* is original in simply standing this approach on its head. American Amazons, of slight build and double breasted, stalk their men in black negligee and gold chains. The men should be handsome and rich, but when they aren't, anything will do. Because a woman is able to open her thighs or keep them closed, she must be revered. Pleasure and procreation are within her power entirely. Woman has been freed economically, biologically (The Pill) and socially to become the master race. And *Cosmopolitan,* whose editor, Helen Gurley Brown, wrote *Sex and the Single Girl*—a rule book for female power maniacs—so appropriates the double standard that it can tell its readers not to mind about their own infidelities. A woman needs many men in her life, says the authority, but a man is naturally monogamous. The husband has enough to do, making money, watching television and all his other boyish pastimes, but the wife, needing occupation, is free to have affairs. This the husband should accept. (There is even a slight suggestion that he should be a virgin at marriage.)

"What sort of man reads *Playboy*?" asks the ad. Answer: "A *now* breed of man who takes to today's handsome new breed of cars. Sporty makes and spirited models are just his speed." Or: "An insider. The kind of guy who knows where to find what he wants—from the loveliest playmates to the liveliest parties." The ads for *Cosmopolitan* are more subtle. An image is created to take in the whole woman. A beautiful, flamboyant girl fills the page. At the side of her head, typewritten, appear her thoughts: "Do you know what Clyde (that's *my*

Clyde, not Bonnie's Clyde) said to me the other night? He said, 'Sharon, I'm so glad you don't wear a lot of makeup like other girls!' I kissed him, of course . . . after I picked myself up off the floor. You see Clyde is a trifle naïve—even if he does run a management consulting firm and have a master's degree from Yale. I wear a *lot* of makeup . . . eyeshadow, eyeliner, lashes, foundation, blusher, lip gloss . . . the works! But the trick is to do it so subtly that nobody notices. . . . Do you know who my strongest ally is in the art of beautiful camouflage? A magazine, of course. . . . I guess you could say I'm That COSMOPOLITAN Girl."

Women who believe love is the game of making twenty percent appear the whole hog are the natural audience for *Cosmo*. In another ad, the girl says: "Last night Allen said something very intelligent, I thought. (He does that all the time!) He said he loved me because there was some intrigue about me . . . because I *wasn't* as simple as Cream of Wheat. I think what he was talking about is that one night I'm a long-haired island girl (with dewy makeup to match) and next night I'm an East Sixties hostess (with two rows of fake lashes and glitter-gold on my eyelids)." Another girl proclaims: "I've been through *several* images . . . from French Doll (silken shifts and sexy black) to cool, cool intellectual (separates, understated, from wall to wall!). Right now I'm in my Real Girl phase . . ." Another announces that a girl should have a lot of vanity, that it's right to set aside time for exclusive attention to one's body because, "even my *soul* is more radiant when I know I *look* good!" In case anyone has missed the point of what a *Cosmopolitan* Girl is, one more ad gives the summary: "What does a girl like me think about all day long . . . men? Clothes? How to look prettier? The party I'm going to Saturday night? I think about *all* those things, but it's not quite as simple as that. I'd say in the last hour I also wondered when they're going to do something about Biafra and get more of the food to the kids, if there's anybody *else* I could write to about getting out of Vietnam, if psychiatry is dead (and what's going to replace it), why Mayor Lindsay doesn't tow away a few *more* cars on Seventh Avenue (that's where I work) and whether Truffaut is ever going to make it as big as Hitchcock?"

She is (not to overlook the fact) an Instant Person: Money Maker, Concerned Citizen, Cultured Human Being, Somebody with Soul, Money, Looks, whose psyche is as subtle and private as a billboard.

She is a meal of leftovers, a hash garni to look like tournedo Rossini. Her Real Girl act is going great this season, and *Cosmo* supplies the script with lines extracted from the consciences and deliberation of other people. Her stupid sister still reads the *Ladies' Home Journal* or *McCall's* or *Family Circle*, getting hints on how to prepare the meal and how to prepare herself for her husband, who should be her lover too. The *Cosmo* girl scorns this. Husbands appear in her magazine only after divorce or infidelity; children don't come near the pages. The sentimental stuff of women's magazines is not for her. The editor-in-chief's column describes activities that serve as checklist for the reader: weekend in Paris for a party at Maxim's; writing a best seller; marrying a millionaire. The column is written in a breathless, almost incoherent style that suggests Helen Gurley Brown is really much too busy and successful to be writing this. (When I phoned Miss Brown for an interview, she told me that she would not consider taking time out for anything but a television appearance.) She ends with the promise of what an issue holds: "Oh, you know . . . making it . . . making good . . . making love . . .'

The *Cosmopolitan* Girl and her swinging *Playboy* friend prowl the streets in their Unisex outfits and matching sports cars, Don Juan and Donna Juana, seeking prey to find their power, forgetting Biafra, Culture and the rest of it as they plot how to extract a confession of love.

Cosmopolitan, read by more married than single women, reflects a dream life. The *Cosmopolitan* Girl and the *Playboy* are archetypal creatures whom no one really recognizes, though all readers sense that something in themselves corresponds to one of these figures. The Image is not meant for distribution or adaption throughout America; it is not used to educate the country in fashion or style. Static, the Image relies for acceptance on fears of sexual impotence or frigidity.

There is only one authority, one throne, shared a bit unequally by *Vogue* and *Harper's Bazaar*. Every beauty and fashion editor in the country reads those two, reads them as a mandate and tries to adapt and deliver The Message to their readers. Diana Vreeland of *Vogue* and Nancy White of *Harper's Bazaar* are the monarchs of the fashion world, sometimes widening their office to a triumvirate where Eugenia Sheppard (formerly of *Women's Wear Daily*) also rules. "I adore

Vogue . . . and *Vogue* to me is an illusion," says Amy Greene. Of course she passes on The Message to readers of *McCall's*.

The beauty editor of *Vogue*, Jessica Canne, said that her magazine is read by all the retail trade, "by people who do make fashion." When *Vogue* reports on a product, it's picked up by other magazines, by women and by the industry. "We may write an editorial which says, to the effect, that we believe skin foundation should really perform two things: it should give coverage and it should give sheen and transparency. And that perhaps one is not enough, perhaps you need two. Well, we will find that eventually—it'll be about a year—some company will do that very thing. They will bring out two products. . . . It's *Vogue* magazine that's greatly responsible for the growth of the eye makeup business."

Mary Butler, beauty editor of *Harper's Bazaar*, didn't, but could have, put forth similar claims. These magazines are the superglossies, directed to women like the editors themselves, the fashion leaders and trend setters who belong to the group of Beautiful People or are on its fringes, as businesswomen or professionals. A market report shows that twenty-five percent of *Vogue* families have incomes of $25,000 or more (compared to seven percent of U.S. families), that seventy-three percent of the women who read *Vogue* have attended college (compared to sixteen percent of American women) and that in seventy percent of *Vogue* households stock is owned (twelve percent of U.S. adults own stock). *Vogue* readers belong to many clubs, travel an average of forty-four days a year and spend seven times as much as the average U.S. traveling family. They love to entertain, drink, go to the theater and read. *Vogue* articles and features assume a sophisticated reader and, instead of offering a quickie look at contemporary civilization—as do *Glamour* and *Cosmopolitan*—they are frankly diversionary, to give the busy woman a chance to relax in her scented bath with gossip and anecdotes.

The fashion world operates through a whispering campaign or by that party game where a phrase is passed along the line until it becomes garbled. *Vogue*, taking careful note of what *Women's Wear Daily* has written (and that newspaper keeps a steady gaze on Paris and other international fashion centers), proclaims the year or month of the eyelash. Elegant department stores display lashes—"as seen in Vogue"—then drugstores show them and finally, the lashes sell two pairs for a dollar at Woolworth's, supermarkets or variety stores. The

Word has gone from *Vogue* to *Glamour* to *Seventeen,* and women's and family magazines have been listening in. What is first in *Vogue* appears months later in Sears Roebuck catalogs. Sometimes the message takes years to reach the whole country, sometimes it falls on deaf ears (body paint, for instance) and sometimes it is misunderstood. Minis must be worn with boots to retain aesthetic proportions. Thick fur lashes are for evening only. Though black is in, it must be enlivened by white. But everywhere, women who have heard the word obliquely wear minis with sandals, sleep in their fur lashes to be ready for breakfast and come to their offices in somber mourning.

It's not the fault of *Vogue* and *Harper's Bazaar.* They are trailblazers, the encyclopedias of whatever is current. They're more interested in aesthetics than in practical application. Models appear in fantastic settings, in faraway lands or lunar scapes. Models can be bizarre, in poses no ordinary human could keep. They can fly, stretch limbs higher than houses, bask naked at the Parthenon, sit cross-legged in Turkey wearing only golden skin and pearls; their hair can be made of fur, gold shavings or peacock feathers and their makeup can represent any style of modern art: futuristic, cubistic, abstract, op or pop. Suspension of disbelief is required of all readers as they enter a fantasy world where dreams, in professional hands, come true with more detail and attention than the dreamer could ever have incurred himself.

The "class" that *Glamour* tries to give its readers is here so rarefied that it goes beyond class into something worshipful, a religion perhaps, of aesthetic perfection where humans lose all ties with their humanity and become material for artists to work on. Sexuality is blurred by artistic photographs of naked women, rendering them as nudes, and by frozen stances, irreproachable tableaux formed by two women touching each other or indicating the other's genitals. The language of *Vogue* has reference only to itself, a self-perpetuating litany that lulls and soothes the reader into belief that beauty is possible and within reach. "The deliciousness of it—hair all pulled back, tight to the skull, and two precious little pigtails looped behind each ear. . . . Handkerchiefs of every size and length, pulled bias and straight, wrapping the head, wrapping the waist, wrapping the throat. The throat. The throat. As though every girl had perpetual unending laryngitis." (Because this is *Vogue,* the reader must not picture a lifetime of discomfort and ice-cream eating, but instead see the incarnation of fragility, a Camille reclining on the brink of expiration, each cough a signal for her lover to smother her with kisses.) The article continues: "Never have the gaieties of the world been more deliciously projected. . . ."

Caressed by such a song, suspended from all fear and doubt by an ethereal massage repeated twice a month, one is placed within Keats's transport: "To cease upon the midnight with no pain/While thou art pouring forth thy soul abroad/In such an ecstasy." And in central Manhattan, where Beautiful Heads are styled, where words of copy run like liquid love through Madison Avenue corridors, bronzers transform executives to Olympian gods and skin is burned off the face to reveal youth and beauty, there offices, lobbies and salons receive *Vogue* and *Harper's Bazaar*, the monthly or bimonthly installment of The Word.

Mary Butler said: "Beauty isn't a separate thing, it's part of the whole. It has to do with the way women live. . . . When we talk about beauty, it's that quality that attracts others. . . . It depends on what your taste has been educated to accept as beautiful."

Jessica Canne said: "The whole beauty mystique . . . is our cultural background, it's the health syndrome that we're all involved in. . . . It's a sensual kind of thing, the fun and pleasure of doing. . . . Makeup lets every woman become an artist. With makeup, you can do what you want to yourself to change yourself."

Those images that yet/Fresh images beget . . .

Both women are missionaries, bringing the good news to the people of America: everyone can be, if not beautiful, attractive anyway. Through cosmetics, you learn who you are and how to project that self. Cosmetics teach joy in oneself. "I think if I were running a country," said Jessica Canne, whose skin is obviously aging but whose subdued makeup, well-cut suit and loose hairdo give her aristocratic mien, "if I were a dictator, I would have somebody in charge of aesthetics as a department. [He] would teach people how to dress and comb their hair—I'd certainly give them scope for individuality, but I do think that we do have certain norms of taste that they should adhere to."

2

The Business

"We compete with *everybody*," said the young woman at Revlon publicity, checking the mirror to make sure her Sassoon cut had not been rearranged by the emphatic toss of her handsome head. "I think we bring out a new product a week. There's a market for practically everything."

A market, but no mercy. Up to 80 percent of a company's budget is spent on advertising, a necessarily high percentage, since the product will be bought only if a consuming psychological need for it has been created. All cosmetic companies copy each other and the "originality" of a product is generally only the packaging. Ingredients of any cosmetic usually remain the same, though their proportions vary slightly. A new ingredient requires many years of testing for safety, and only the largest companies can afford to do this, since the average research budget of major cosmetic companies is .5 percent to 1 percent of sales. (No drug company spends less than 10 percent of its sales on research.)

Congressmen or journalists occasionally express outrage at the lack of adequate safety regulations in cosmetics or at what they consider excessive markup on all products, but the crusade is never popular. Though control is necessary to prevent illegal or preposterous claims by cosmetics manufacturers, though deaths and mutilations through the use of cosmetics occur, though many people know that the cost of ingredients in a two-dollar lipstick may be less than ten cents, the American consumer is basically uninterested. Commenting on a book by Toni Stabile, *Cosmetics: Trick or Treat?*, which exposed the dangers of cosmetics, Dr. Earle Brauer, at the Revlon Lab, accused the author of "wanting to create sensationalism. Certainly she picked up mistakes, but not in the proper perspective." To keep perspective, he went on, one must remember that "penicillin has killed hundreds of people . . . but thousands owe their lives to it. So you must weigh both sides. The good must be emphasized—this product got her a husband or lifted her out of a depression."

Dr. Donald Opdyke, director of basic research at Revlon, added: "The things we are doing are such that if there were FDA legislation tomorrow, we wouldn't do anything different." At a meeting of the Toilet Goods Association, Dr. Opdyke had warned that adequate testing must be done on cosmetics to avoid the disaster brought by thalidomide.

Consumers aren't interested in dissecting the cosmetics industry. Nothing is bought through physical necessity; no one is dependent on cosmetics, as on food and drugs, for the continuation of life. Almost every product exists at different price levels, and there are few women in America who can't afford a lipstick. When people pay five dollars or fifty dollars for a cream, they don't want to hear that the same cream is available for one dollar, and they don't want to know the cost of making it. Elizabeth Arden has a subsidiary company's inexpensive line selling at Woolworth's; but, though many people know that exactly the same products are sold in different packaging, they insist on buying the more expensive variety.

They pay "the high price of hope," according to Dr. Joseph Kalish, technical editor of *Drugs and Cosmetics Industry*. The individual, he says, creates worth in the product, and he asks, "Who could put value on the oils in a Rembrandt?" Because cosmetics are nonutilitarian, they must be sold as intangibles. They bring glamour, beauty, youth—even love. They raise the status of the wearer, allow him to act out his dreams and nourish hopes that he can approach his image of success, perfection or attractiveness. The price is kept intentionally and artificially high. Psychoanalyst Erika Freeman explained on a television report (NET) of the beauty industry: "An item that promises a fantasy by definition must be priced fantastically. . . . If a cream begins to sell at fifty cents it will not sell as well nor will it be considered as potentially miraculous as a cream that sells at thirty dollars." And a department-store owner explained: "If a product sold for fifteen cents, a face cream, we could not give it away, we certainly couldn't sell it for fifteen cents. At a dollar, there'd be a certain group of customers, at a dollar fifty maybe a little more. At three dollars an even wider number of customers. . . ."

Price creates value. Some years ago, an American woman in Paris sat facing the mirror while Dior concocted a hat for her in a twinkling. "Voilà! Five hundred dollars, madame."

The lady was indignant. "Five hundred dollars! Why, it's just a piece of ribbon!"

The great couturier bent, unraveled the hat and handed it to her with magnanimity. "The ribbon, madame, is free."

The cost and reputation of a product or line may explain why a consumer chooses it over another but won't explain why any are bought at all. Evan William Mandel, executive vice-president of Revlon, told new employees: "What you are now faced with in this business is the innermost, mysterious essence of woman—Freudian, if you will—her ideas—her dreams—her fears—her fantasies—her hopes —her sex life—her youth. The nature of this industry is dames—and the key to success in it lies in understanding them." Mr. Mandel goes on to say that "every single product [in the Revlon line] stems from a deep-seated need," and the products are all "necessary luxuries."

To sell this dreamlike stuff you develop an image, an alter ego the consumer can recognize and you send out the message: that a book is judged by its cover and a person will be judged by his looks. If he wants to participate in the American dream, if he wants success, money and women, then he must join the beauty culture. No one can love or hire someone whose perspiration he smells. No man will choose a naked face when around him irridescent lids blink welcome-ingly and gleaming soft mouths invite kisses. The woman you want will run away from you in the direction of the man whose cologne excites her or whose bronze skin she yearns to lie beside. If your "maturity" shows in crow's feet and sagging chin, your job will be given to someone with more "dynamic appeal"; and if you're a little girl or boy, you're missing out on life's goodies if you try growing up any which way.

Bill Mandel, probably the beauty culture's most eloquent spokes-man, explained in another speech, "Cosmetics is ever so much more serious and solemn than it is gay or frivolous. . . . We really market Eve's alter ego—the being that she wants to be—the being that she really likes to be." He continued, to the Philadelphia Fashion Group, "There are some who would call our business 'a comedy of

Eros'—because the yearning for youth—and sex—are interwoven in no other business like it is in ours. . . . We become a twenty-four-hour-a-day part of a woman's body. . . . What we must give her in our products is an exquisite compound of the *functional* and the *romantic.*"

To accomplish this, a campaign is launched within the battle of the sexes, the fight against death and the war on poverty. Bill Mandel or Charles Revson, commander-in-chief of Revlon, gets an idea for a new product. Their note is sent to chemists in the Bronx, who begin mixing and testing. "Ad people are already working on the words and pictures; packaging people are already working on packaging—while the product is being made," explained the publicity girl in the bright metallic jersey. "And finally, after death, sweat and tears, the product is ready, the advertising is right, the words are right, the pictures are right." To reach this blissful state has usually taken six months to a year. The advertising, which offers reassurance, depends on which of the lines within Revlon is carrying the product.

Because Revlon is so vast, there are companies within companies. Ultima II is the "Cadillac line—our couture cosmetic collection geared towards a fashionable woman, who may be in advertising. . . . She wears it for prestige—she wants to be a fashion leader. She's the first to buy jeweled belts, she wears pants to the El Morocco. But she wants to be safe—her bags are Gucci and her underclothes are Pucci."

Moon Drops is the "General Motors line, for the twenty- to thirty-five-year-old market, career girls and young mothers. It's for the person who tries new things, isn't worried about being safe. There's an emphasis on moisture—this age group is very concerned about staying young." The girl, who looked eighteen but must have been at least twenty-six, paused to catch her eye in the mirror and automatically stroked back a wayward bit of hair. The mirror, a round, feminine object properly belonging on a piece of furniture called vanity and not on a desk, kept a watchful eye over our interview. Not more than three sentences could pass before it sought out its mistress and blindly, reassuringly, caressed her face a moment.

Natural Wonder, which for ten years was sold only in drugstores and given little advertising, is the "Chevrolet line . . . geared towards the young swingers." When the teen-age market began to expand and Revlon's youth line got more competition from other companies (especially Yardley), Natural Wonder was elaborated. The image was "very young, very kicky. We put the lipsticks in very kicky cases and there was something for everyone, for every teen-age image."

For blacks, no special line—each of the others carries two dark foundations, and dark body makeup. "Negroes don't want to be different—they want to use the same products as everyone else," the girl explained. But Negroes have been a problem, she indicated, because they tend to have oily skin, and most makeups look gray on them. Her voice dropped to a whisper as we talked about this vaguely forbidden, far-out subject. Though Revlon has tried to bring Negroes into its national image, the press is not yet willing to go along. As an example, she spoke of the Moon Drops launching in 1966, when Revlon gave a press party and had two makeup consultants, a "very beautiful" Negro girl and an "average" white girl. Photographs were taken of the white girl only. "The press wasn't ready for it," said the lovely narcissist. Revlon was waiting for the go-ahead from editorials. The black cover girl on *Glamour*'s August 1968 issue was encouraging, as is the recent use by *Vogue* of black models, and *Mademoiselle* presented "the face of the 70's" with a beaming black all-American cover girl. For ads in *Ebony*, Revlon will use a black model as exotic, expensive and improbable as her white counterpart, but for the national campaign, blacks are not yet safe: they are not yet like everyone else.

Revlon's principal line for men is Braggi,* which corresponds to Ultima II. "Our concept in advertising is man talking to man. The packaging is masculine. Braggi was created by Charles Revson, and Mr. Revson—there's no question about it—he's a man." I laughed. "A real man, I mean," she said hurriedly. "In the ads, he's talking to another man. The approach to the image is an educational one. The audience we want is a Mr. Revson-type man—the distinguished, professional-leader type who's not afraid to use these products."

Selling to men is not yet as easy as selling to women. The traditional male image is a shield against narcissism and hard to wear down. Though men will use women's cosmetics—"Whenever I have a party, if I go to the bathroom after a man, I find my powder all over the place," said a beauty writer for *Town and Country*—the image must not be feminine. "Homosexuals wear women's cos-

---

* Its chief competitors are Aramis (Estée Lauder) and Arden for Men.

metics," Bill Mandel told a reporter from the *Times*, "Men's prod-ucts are just too mild for them. If a man is sexually secure, he will buy male cosmetics."

But since nearly everyone I met in the business affirmed that men often use their wives' creams or lotions, the implication of homo-sexuality is used only to provoke men to buy their own. Although products in the lab are undifferentiated until fragrance is put in, or sometimes not until the label is applied, men's cosmetics are selling spectacularly. They are still mainly bought by women as gifts, but an increasing number of men believe that bronzers, fragrances and such will emphasize their virility and make them look and feel better. Men's cosmetics counters, with emphatically masculine decor, are opening up in large department stores.

Fragrances are the biggest sellers. Revlon's Pub, a cologne, is ad-vertised as "A Hell of a Way to Smell Damn Good," thus dispelling whatever aura of femininity a fragrance might suggest. Pub is for gorgeous brutes who, because they wear Pub and not "Bar" or "Saloon," reveal hidden finesse. A dab of England adds a touch of élan. When the image is to be less emphatically virile, Revlon offers That Man, Monsieur Balmain and Braggi colognes for elegance and chic.

Selling powder, bronzer, face cream or hair color can be difficult, since these suggest vanity (a feminine trait) more than do colognes or after-shaves. But Braggi's face bronzer is the most successful item in the line. "It makes you look healthy and tanned," crooned Revlon's publicity lovely, "and it evens out the skin tone." So does the face powder, but though a man might buy the bronzer to cover up blotches or skin discoloration, "he would never admit it—he says he buys the bronzer to look tanned."

Revlon is fashion leader in cosmetics. The largest company after Avon (and publicly owned), it has created the most luscious images in the beauty business. Its different lines are a network reaching out to all America—every age, race and sex—offering "necessary luxuries" described in such mellifluous gibberish, with such extraordinary pho-tographs that fantasy grows plump with desiring them. Revlon takes in *Vogue* and Paris; when new collections come out, Revlon is ready for them, with colors to match or contrast. A few seasons ago Paris dictated purple, and Revlon immediately brought out three purple lipsticks, in different tones (though Bill Mandel told me it was impossible to match makeup to fashion because a woman remains the same from the neck up and her makeup needs are established by her physiognomy). Revlon ads are often more extreme even than *Vogue*— strange lighting and bizarre shadows thrown on the model's face, clothes that are costumes for anything from a nineteenth-century opening of the Viennese opera to satellite-straddling garb of future lady astronauts. When Revlon offers makeup "to take to the moon" (a campaign Mr. Mandel did not favor), it's to give readers "delusions of grandeur—that they're going to look so marvelous that somebody will want to take them to the moon." Though a skeptic has referred to the Revlon image as "Bronx modern," it goes far beyond that, into surrealism, where time has been altered to prevent death and aging and reality exists in little capsules of heightened, almost terrifying moments of beauty's absolute power.

In preaching what he calls "dames-man-ship" to new employees, Bill Mandel advises his audience to remember that, "no matter who [the woman] is—or what she is, the way she *thinks* she looks is the key to her personality. . . . No matter how plain or cranky she may be early in the day, given the time to put herself together, she is by evening a totally different creature."

Selling to this woman is not easy. One needs, "Explosiveness . . . Elegance . . . Exclusivity . . . Change . . . and Fashion. That's what the Revlon aura is made of. . . . Elegance is the cornerstone of Revlon's longevity—staying power, if you will. And gentlemen, without Elegance you can never build the next important aura quality—Exclusivity." Since Mr. Mandel is speaking to men, he must take notice of their logical minds. Exclusivity may not be the appropriate term to designate products that sell in the millions, but women love the word and the concept. "Let's face it, fellas, it's girly and it's part of the way they think." To maintain exclusivity, Revlon "has exclusive-franchise drugstores, exclusive demos in exclusive department stores. . . . We want [women] to reach *up* to find us. Not physically—emotionally."

Revlon was built on this concept. In the thirties, when nail polish was selling for ten to fifteen cents and Cutex led the market, Charles Revson decided to bring out a nail polish for sixty cents. Cutex was sure there would be no customers, but Revson was vindicated. He then brought out coordinated polish and lipstick. Starting as a small manufacturer in 1932 with a three-hundred-dollar investment, Revson parlayed his company into a three-hundred-million-dollar business, the most far-reaching cosmetics empire in the world, with one thousand outlets in Paris alone. His genius had been to offer hope at a higher price than any of his competitors. He so infuriated the cosmetics queen of America, Helena Rubinstein, that she referred to him only as "that nail-polish man." * (After her death, Charles Revson bought her twenty-nine-room duplex apartment on Park Avenue.)

Once established as an expensive name, Revlon could go on to other elements of its success: explosiveness and fashion. In the fifties, Fire and Ice, a color for lipstick and matching nail polish, was the inspiration for electrifying ads of "fantasy and sex," as Bill Mandel sees them, an image maintained over Cherries in the Snow (girl on a white marble floor reaching luxuriously for a bowl of cherries), through an ad of Jean Shrimpton in frilly lace holding a teddy bear; and now the image persists in the Moon Drops line. Each line has one hundred to three hundred products; fantasy and sex work for the twenty- to thirty-five-year-old market but not for the fashionable Ultima II user and not for young girls. But Revlon's overall image is definitely sophisticated, ignoring the under-sixteen market. "They're too fickle—we let Yardley have that," said Bill Mandel. "There's twelve to fifteen percent of the market we're not interested in." Girls are difficult and hard to pin down. They may buy from different companies each time they want cosmetics. Revlon devotes itself to women because "the only consistency is inconsistency" and they will respond with loyalty to being understood.

"Women have a greater expectancy *from* life than men, . . ." Mr. Mandel told the American Management Association. "This questfulness for living in an atmosphere of elegance and femininity is the cause of woman's restlessness." She wants change, continual change, and therefore has elevated fashion to "our country's unseen government." Mass communication makes this possible and the beauty industry "could take a lesson from Detroit" on how to provide endless variety within constancy. "To understand a woman," he concludes, "you must love her. And when you love her you no longer need to understand her."

Revlon has studied the woman, discovered her secret dreams and sold them to her. *Das ewig weibliche zieht uns hinan* to more and

* This epithet inspired the name for Revlon's "That Man" line.

more products, more dreams, more images. Whether Revlon is created in the image of the woman or vice versa will never be resolved. Whose dreams and whose dishonesty are fooling whom? "All of life is a game," Mr. Mandel told me. "Love is two psychological hangups meeting."

The beauty industry is derivative. Revlon's distinction is created by an advertising image only; its prices are competitive, and its products are essentially the same as those of any other company within that price range. The companies "are just like lemmings," commented an important beauty editor. "One company comes out with a new product, and all others follow like a flock within a few months." Secrecy rages; because so little variation is possible and because the audience is basically the same for all manufacturers, it's among the most suspicious industries of America. A man from Grey Advertising, who handles one of the Revlon accounts—like a furtive miser, cosmetics companies have many accounts, presumably so that no single agency can know too much—said he was sorry but he couldn't meet me or even speak to me on the phone. "My client's policy is not to say anything to anyone," he explained.

"Of course. That's because they don't want you to see how mean they are," said a young woman who once did free-lance copy for them. "Revlon are the meanest people in the world." To work on a cosmetics account paid very well, she said, but you could be fired in a week. Relations between advertising agency and cosmetics company are tenuous and temperamental.

One of the happiest relationships was between Clairol and Shirley Polykoff, the "genius" of Foote, Cone and Belding who claims to receive her inspiration by mixing with common folk on the street or in the subway. Her brilliance made Clairol the top name in hair color, particularly for blondes. Miss Polykoff, who feels that the modern woman wants to see herself as "a wholesome siren," is the inventor of the most famous ad line in America, "Does she . . . or doesn't she?"

When this slogan was first formulated, Clairol approached *Life* magazine with a ten-page color ad. *Life* turned it down, saying the ad was "too suggestive." Clairol, determined to make a big impact in a family magazine, asked *Life* to research the ad among their women employees. Not one admitted to finding a double meaning in the words and the ad was carried, in 1955, to launch a triumphant campaign which, in the wholesome picture of mother and child, gave evidence that even "nice" women could color their hair.

In the thirties, fewer than five percent of women colored their hair; the war and postwar period did not substantially increase the percentage. In the fifties, Clairol was running a campaign to establish a "nice" image for users of their products: "Her looks are exciting, her manner is gentle and that is a lovely thing in a woman," said one ad. Another introduced the mother-and-child theme with, "She's as much fun as a kid and just as fresh-looking." The 1955 campaign continued through the sixties, and was broadened to include blacks (dark-haired models captioned with "Does she . . . or doesn't she?"; lighter-haired models with "If you want to, why not?").

Though Americans are sentimental, the mother-child presentation doesn't work for all products. When Toni developed a home permanent in the forties, they ran their famous "Which twin has the Toni?" ads. By the fifties, other companies had come out with home permanents, and Toni no longer ruled the waves. An apocryphal story goes that they decided their slogan had lost its effectiveness and went on to something else. The new ad showed an adorable little girl somewhere between the ages of three and six and her adorable mother. The slogan said that both were making "a hit with Dad." A large campaign was launched with nationwide coverage, and Toni's sales plummeted.

Distressed, Toni's directors called in a Viennese psychiatrist from a psychologically oriented ad agency, a man who claimed to be one of the seven disciples of Freud directly appointed by the master. He looked at the ads and asked, "You are selling this to whom?"

"Women, of course," answered the Toni people.

"Ah, women," said the Viennese. "They are not understood. You do not understand—the person they hate most in the world is the little daughter who tries to look pretty so she can have her father in bed."

Toni immediately switched back to the reliable twin ads, and sales climbed up again, back to where they had been before the disastrous plunge into Lolita country.

Clairol didn't make the same mistake. The child is merely an accessory and the slogan diverts the woman, consciously or not, from the fact that she is a mother. Instead she sees herself as an exciting, mysterious woman; a mistress but, because a child is in the picture, mistress to her husband only.

"All Clairol hair color advertising—no matter what the product— is built on reassurance rather than fear," said John Mack, vice-president in charge of marketing, "and frankly, each brand's campaign is designed to fill what we believe is an emotional need of that group."

For older women, whose hair is graying and who might feel anxious about aging, there is Loving Care—"Makes your husband feel younger too, just to look at you"—and Look-Alive Gray. An account executive for another company, an attractive woman in her forties with bleached platinum hair, describes the ad as part of a syndrome. "All women identify with young swinging girls. The woman over thirty identifies with the young girl because she's been there, but the young girl doesn't identify with the older woman. . . . Look at that Clairol ad. The woman with gray hair looks about nineteen. Her husband looks fifty, but she's a *young woman*. In the second picture (after the color), you see her husband nuzzling her. She doesn't look any different from the first picture, except her hair's a little brighter. But the women who're going to buy [Look-Alive Gray] don't want to see a regular gray-haired woman. They know what a gray-haired woman looks like—they see her every day in the mirror. They want to identify with a young woman."

For girls between sixteen and twenty-five, concerned about boys and their future, Clairol issues a teasing invitation to the party of life: "Is it true blondes have more fun?"

After the early twenties, women become more cautious. A woman of thirty has responsibilities, perhaps a job or family, and can't afford to be whimsical. "She knows time is fleeting," Mr. Mack points out, "and has by now probably discovered that she may not be immortal. To give her a lift, we are running this exuberant campaign—'If I've only one life, let me live it as a blonde.'"

Clairol emphasizes being "natural" and "individual." With Innocent Blonde, you can "re-blonde your hair back to childhood"; Born Blonde allows you never to leave it. This ad is very effective for America, where twenty-seven percent of women are born blond, only five percent past the age of twenty-one remain blond naturally, but twenty-five percent remain or become blond somehow. "We really believe it," says Shirley Polykoff. "If you look well, you have a greater sense of respect for yourself, especially today when the whole trend is loss of identity."

American women spend more than three-quarter billion dollars on hair coloring a year, and this amount rises vigorously. In 1968 there were one and a half million first-time hair-color users, and sixty percent of Clairol's sales came from items that hadn't been on the market five years earlier. But, though products become more sophisticated, colors range over a spectrum Nature couldn't provide and women in large cities match their hair to their mood, clothes or the season, most of rural America and the Midwest believe, as they did in the fifties, that changing the color of your hair simply isn't "nice." Though the Passport Agency has omitted hair color as an identifying trait—"it's completely unreliable," said an official—women who travel abroad are society's froth. The hair-color business depends on "bread-and-butter colors," as they're known in the trade, the blacks and browns that correspond most closely to the natural color of most women and provide most of the profit.

However, as with makeup and fashion, the outposts of the beauty culture are being educated by Madison Avenue. And most of the cosmetic companies' large advertising budgets are apportioned to print rather than television or radio. The message of "look better to feel better" is daily preached to all America, and we may have faith that the strongholds of conservatism will be weakened, bread-and-butter will change to colors of champagne, smoked salmon and perhaps even crème de menthe.

"Before we have exhausted the women's market, there is always the male of the species to turn to . . ." John Mack assured the Marketing Club of New York. In 1968 Clairol brought out Sudden Summer, the first hair lightener made especially for men ("You can be the he she wants you to be"). It's shampooed in; five minutes brighten, ten minutes give a week, twenty minutes a month, of sun. Men who are not afraid to try this "eye-catching, girl-catching, sunstruck look" are reassured by photographs that they will give the impression of spending their lives on a sailboat, yacht or surfboard. The outdoor look is both virile and "natural," and the Clairol user, whether male or female, regains his identity by being more "himself" and more sexually stereotyped.

While Clairol's major success has been hair color, and particularly blond, it's also an established (1932) cosmetics company. The sun-drenched, mind-bleached look of Clairol girls can be further enhanced by wholesome-siren California Girl products. A Clairol salesgirl explained, with the erudition of a Hollywood starlet, how she advises customers: "Well, you have to first of all get an image of the woman yourself. . . . What kind of feeling tone does she send out? It's relative of course. The obvious things like her skin color, eye color and the shape of her eyes, the shape of her face and of her hair. And all these are obviously obvious things. But I think makeup should be really given to women more philosophically today than physically, as it's mostly portrayed." The philosophy of the California Look seems to be, "Swing with it, baby; tomorrow is something else."

No matter how young and frivolous the Clairol girl, no matter how strong the lure of California to all potential starlets, surfers and hippies, California Girl can never compete with Yardley, the third largest cosmetics company in America (after Avon and Revlon), with a powerful image of Youth and London, composed of Shrimpton, Twiggy, the mod scene, Shakespeare (Romeo and Juliet), Victoriana, and the salable conviction that Yardley is what's happening. Romantic poses, tendrils and lace are part of Yardley's image; so are vinyl-dressed girls and boys with long hair. London as mod capital of the world is used by Yardley for all and more than it's worth, and the old Yardley of lavender and saddle soap is smothered in paper union jacks. A girl in white vinyl on a motorcycle in front of the Tower of London advertises Slicker: "I'm a London girl and I never look alike two times in a row." As Yeats's poem, where "Night walkers' song / After great cathedral gong," contrasts coexisting cultures, so Yardley mixes and matches its metaphors; the Romantic heroine of the nineteenth century and the tough cookie of the future both cover their lids with Eyelighter because, "It wakes up your eyes and you know what that can wake up."

"In over two hundred years there has never been a woman like Jacqui Brandwynne," gushes *Women's Wear Daily*. "As the first female vice-president for Yardley, she has made history in a company that is more than two centuries old." A few months after achieving this honor, Miss Brandwynne became president and chief executive officer of her own company, an ad agency that handles the Yardley account. Miss Brandwynne is very much responsible for the new Yardley. A small redhead with false lashes, dressed modestly in black with a gold belt, a magnifying mirror on her desk and tiles inlaid on the floor, Jacqui Brandwynne spoke with a lilting accent I first took to be Germanic, but later discovered was French Swiss. Talking with her, one feels she is deliberately acting out the part of a charming European woman.

She explained how and why Yardley's image was changed: "Well, in the first place it was a dying company. It was a company that literally was getting very dowdy and old. And unless something definite was done with the company, you know it would have gone on for years and years—but not ever being a major company in America. And they got an arrangement * and Mr. Burr [Donald Burr, the president]. And he got me." At the time, Miss Brandwynne had worked for Helena Rubinstein, done free-lance articles and was working at the teen-age magazine *Ingenue*. "I like teen-agers very much. They seemed to me a very vital force in America, both in fashion and beauty. But really, everybody talked down to them and everybody molested them with pimple products. . . . Treat your pimples, get rid of your pimples—you know—and gave them mountains of pimple products and I didn't believe in it. I didn't believe in this kind of segregation, the pimples and the no-pimples," she confided with a charming smile.

Having decided to emancipate teen-agers from pimple problems, Miss Brandwynne developed for young people with "imagination, creativity, fun" a line that would offer what was psychologically needed by teen-agers as much as it is by adults: security. "Every single woman or every single man who uses toiletries or makeup uses it to feel better," she informed me.

"We decided to do a line for people under twenty, and do it with every fancy, mood, idea, word, picture that has ever been. And we started this idea—old clothes [Victorian]. . . . And we did a great many other things. We did the first psychedelic show, or the first multimedia show four years back [1964]. You see, much before any of these artists who take the credit for it, we started. . . ." They also started a show for department stores, with "a poetic section, a great music section . . . a lot of imagination . . . multimedia . . . films . . . slides . . . and live personalities." And they began a newspaper that now goes out free to one and a half million young people. Called

* They were bought by the British-American Tobacco Company, the world's largest.

Beauty Beat, the paper has a few bits of information on music and fashion, but is mainly a collection of ads for Yardley. Its language seems to be a private code, and I could not understand: "show him how you REALLY are . . . soft, innocent . . . HAPPENING . . . Like it is HAPPENING . . . BIRD!", nor make out the real message behind: "What would you do if . . . a certain H.I.M. named Noel Harrison told Y.O.U. what he liked in H.E.R.S., while smiling with those gorgeous blue eyes?" Miss Brandwynne, editor-in-chief of *Beauty Beat,* seemed proud of her newspaper and convinced that "the kids love it."

Jean Shrimpton was chosen as Yardley's chief model, who traveled throughout America on selling tours, because "she's a person . . . she was much more real than a star." Her prettiness and femininity attracted Miss Brandwynne, who was sure that young girls want exactly those two traits, and not elegance or kookiness. Yardley created a line of Londonderry hair products for Jean Shrimpton, which have been doing well. "They're very nice products, lovely products, but they also have feeling. All our products have soul."

"Apropos soul," I asked, "do you have any products for blacks?"

"Oh certainly we do," Miss Brandwynne assured me. "You see, we have one thing which we do, we make over kids all the time . . . and they can be any color in the world. They're just great. And they're fine for our products and the products are fine for them." Basically, she explained patiently, Yardley was not concerned with any particular look. They use no American models because they are an English company. "We want to keep that English look," she said, but a minute or two later added, "we want to keep that very special look, which is different, you see, from everything else."

I asked Miss Brandwynne if she could define the Yardley image. "It's not any one thing. It's not Shrimpton and its' not Slickers, which become [sic] the number one lipstick in America. It's not our Victorian powders and it's not our next-to-nothing foundation or our newspaper, *Beauty Beat,* or our fashion—but primarily, it's an ensemble. It's the colors, the tone, the mood. We created language." I looked astonished. "I mean, Slicker has become a language. You know, we created many words, many sayings, many images that have impressed literally all of America."

The images recede. Jacqui Brandwynne, editor-in-chief of *Beauty Beat,* is also the author of "Summertime Love," the Slicker theme song:

I knew you once upon a dream
And now that dream is you
Your face shines soft
    Your lips shine soft
Your eyes shine honest too
I love you wild, I love you **mild**
I love the helpless you
But what I really love you for
Each girl is truly you.

Women's Wear Daily reports that Jacqui Brandwynne "is writing lyrics and songs, short stories and her new goal is the movies." Faced with such talent, who could doubt Yardley created language?

But *Vogue*, with its delicious frills of adorable adjectives, might in more justice point out its influence on the English tongue, and Revlon, advertising the "luminesque look" for eyes and "rockcrystal candy-frosted mouthcolor glissers," seems to have definitely upstaged Yardley. But, linguistic pretensions notwithstanding, Yardley has taken over the youth market, enticing first users of cosmetics through cheerful packaging and bonuses, similar to gifts in Cracker Jacks— whistles, chains or little dolls. By bringing toys into the cosmetics industry, Yardley can woo all little girls who received their first make-up kit at six. Costumes on Yardley models conform to dreams of the young (more conservative than Moon Drops users), dreams of faraway lands and fairytale clothes. And Yardley, with its traditional line of men's toiletries, is in an enviable position to capitalize on the growing trend to men's cosmetics. Between saddle soap and slickers, Yardley has created a dual image for men: the staid, trustworthy man of note and the with-it, switched-on tomcat.

The new Yardley has inspired a multitude of cosmetics lines to transform themselves in its image. Love Cosmetics seems directly born of Yardley and had a nationwide campaign in color spreads for months before its products were available. A boy and girl, neither conventionally attractive, are on the grass, presumably of a campus. She wears a frilly blouse and jeans and sits cross-legged. He, in a pale-blue work shirt, is intent and loving, a hand on her arm. They are the kind of kids regularly seen in newspapers and magazines accompanying stories on hippies, student revolts or new sexual mores. On the facing page, bold letters announce: "This is the way Love is in 1969." The copy states: "Love today is different than it's ever been.

It's freer, more natural, more honest—more out in the open." So are girls, the ad continues, and so are complexions. Finally, bending so far backward that only a cosmetics advertiser could do it without breaking his spine, the coda is a litany:

> We're young too.
> And we're on your side.
> We know it's a rough race.
> And we want you to win.

The products are all packaged in shiny containers of a lunar age, and the cologne, called Eau de Love, has an air about it of Oh! de London, Yardley's cologne.

Yardley will probably succeed in destroying completely its former image. Pond's, whose cold cream seems to have been used by everyone's mother and grandmother, is not yet willing to relinquish the days of its glory, when the queens of Spain and Rumania and the loveliest debutantes gave testimonials of its worth.

With Pond's, the hope game changes. Though Yardley and Clairol are not quite so expensive (or "exclusive") as Revlon, they still cost two or three times as much as House of Westmore or Maybelline. Pond's cold cream is one of the cheapest and is generally considered more a toiletry than a cosmetic, more utilitarian than luxurious while still competing (indirectly) with higher-priced brands.

Women who buy makeup from Arden, Max Factor or Revlon may still buy their cream from Pond's because they see it as wholesome, high quality and dependable. Ruth Downing, vice-president and associate creative supervisor of J. Walter Thompson, the agency carrying the Pond's-Chesebrough account, feels "that the advertising of thirty years ago still lingers on." ("She's lovely, she's engaged, she uses Pond's.")

Miss Downing uses Pond's herself. Its appeal, she says, can't be defined—"all the imponderable components"—though she sees it as "a fountain of beauty type cream. . . . it has a do-good quality, unspecified but felt. . . . I think Pond's has a kind of magic to it. Women nonverbally attribute to it a magic that makes their skin look better."

Pond's users are generally in their thirties or older, because younger women, according to Miss Downing, don't really need cream. "Girls under the age of eleven are self-absorbed with themselves as people, not as women. From eleven through the teen years, they develop bad skin and use cover-ups or Noxema. Through the twenties, the average woman's skin tends to be normal, and if she washes with soap and water she's O.K. From the age of thirty, her skin is drying out and she feels older. She starts thinking about creams in a serious way, and that's where Pond's gets in the picture."

However, Pond's is not willing to rest on its eighty-year-old laurels and predictable audience. It joins the crowd of suitors around Youth by presenting a "7-day beauty plan," whereby the wallflower uses Pond's for a week and then gets her man. For its makeup, Pond's ad reads: "Steve and I have been swinging together ever since I started using Angel Face medicated makeup."

Fashion magazines and *Fortune* decree that we are in the grip of a "youthquake" and the beauty business ignores anyone reactionary enough not to be a teen-ager. Women of every age identify with eighteen-year-olds or must be taught to do so. "There's some massive lack of self-confidence in the American woman," said Ruth Downing. "A terrible sense of revulsion of age, aging, letting anyone know how old you are." Even Pond's, a brand name inextricably linked with the product, like Kleenex or Coke, must join in the national dance of youth.

But Pond's remains ambiguous because it seems functional. Miss Downing feels that women abandon it when their income suddenly increases. A truck driver's wife whose husband becomes owner of the trucking firm will ignore Pond's in favor of Revlon or more expensive lines, like Estée Lauder or John Robert Powers. "What she's buying is prestige and her reflection," said Miss Downing. "It's her way of saying publicly, I've arrived . . . I think status is important—the eternal need to look like you matter, like you're significant." So conspicuous consumption comes to the containers and labels of products that should be almost invisible when used.

Some companies sell status, and hope becomes even more expensive than for those who seek only youth and sex. Estée Lauder, called the last queen of the cosmetics industry, presents a line with the mystique of haute couture. Lauder products lead Revlon in ninety-five percent of the stores where they overlap, but Lauder products are sold only where décor will enhance snob appeal. Charles of the Ritz is another such company and like Lauder, sells only through salespeople they have trained. It has merged with Lanvin, owns Yves St. Laurent and Vidal Sassoon and has a loyal, expensive clientèle.

Helena Rubinstein and Elizabeth Arden stand between Revlon and Lauder. Their prices are closer to Revlon, their aura to Lauder. The dead old ladies who began the two firms are ghostly legends of admirable women, both beyond reproach, though their products sometimes had to be recalled for safety reasons: women inspired by ambition and visions, who beautified our mothers and grandmothers and began the cutthroat competition of today's cosmetics industry. The Arden–Rubinstein feud is an American catfight in the Punch and Judy tradition. A plastic surgeon who was once consultant on cosmetics for Helena Rubinstein told me, "The only person in the whole Rubinstein organization that had decent skin was Mrs. Rubinstein herself and she never used any cosmetics." I pointed out that in Helena Rubinstein's autobiography, *My Life for Beauty*, she writes about a cream from Poland that she and her sisters used and that founded the Rubinstein empire. "Yeah," said the doctor, unimpressed. "She invented that cream from Poland . . . Nearly every so-called exotic person comes around with some strange formula that was given them by their old grandfather from Transylvania. . . . Believe me, this gal never knew anything in Poland, all she knew was how to make money and told a good story about it. A rather fascinating character. She could just as well have been in the machine business or any other business and she'd have been a great success. She's a good merchandiser."

Fortune wrote that Elizabeth Arden "has probably earned more money than any other businesswoman in history . . ." The names Arden and Rubinstein lend prestige to products and their advertising emphasizes femininity and graciousness. The "red door" of Arden salons all over the world, unlike the red light of other establishments, has become an emblem of class, and the two Maine Chance beauty farms run by Arden (in Maine and Arizona) are patronized by women in Diors who retrieve their jewels from the safe at dinner time. Rubinstein's ads show "portraits," not crass photographs, of obviously well-born women.

Beauty, bringing in more than seven billion dollars a year, with "glamor shares" on Wall Street consistently growing, and with virtual immunity to recession, is a business that encourages the

American Dream. Fortunes are still to be made, empires can be extended or established. A Candide-like optimism reigns. Since nothing is essential, everything is good and there are no limits on exploitation. Everything in beauty can be sold to the American consumer. He buys through hope or fear, for intangible emotional or psychological satisfaction, and his insecurity is the bottomless cup from which manufacturers and advertisers drink. New companies, based on a single product or a line, are continually born. Polly Bergen's Oil of the Turtle has been expanded to a line of fifty items. Miss Bergen is an actress with beautiful skin, whose advertising slogan ("I have an ugly friend") made women believe that wretched, wrinkled creatures like turtles could provide oils to rejuvenate the facial skin of human females. (Helena Rubinstein vetoed Royal Jelly because "women are not bees. Bees are insects and women are human beings.") Zsa Zsa Gabor and H. L. Hunt opened cosmetics lines. Kenneth, America's top hairdresser, went into cosmetics "for money" and travels across the country giving lecture-demonstrations. But generally, small companies have little chance against the giants. Those, like David, who use their own weapons can succeed, but those that fight Goliath on his terms must buckle under.

That beauty spends more money on advertising than any other industry in America is understandable: competition is strong, the intrinsic value of any item dubious, and the proliferation of new products makes essential the creation of a need for them. We women buy to compete with other women and hold our own in society. We have learned to believe that an ugly girl can become beautiful, that youth and seductiveness reside in jars and bottles. Even those who use no makeup, or very little, believe this and so advertise an aspect of themselves in contradiction to the system. The naked face can be making a religious point (This is how God made me and it would be presumptuous to tamper with His will), be giving a psychological test (Accept me at my worst and then I'll believe you really care for me) or be throwing out an egotistical taunt (I don't give a damn what you bastards think of me). Hippies with mottled hair, scraggly beards or unattended acne use physical appearance as part of their statement against present values and patterns of behavior. Many are not total admirers of America; they don't want to become involved in traditional economic and sexual roles of a middle-class society that bequeathed them bombs, violence, psychoanalysis and enemies and they don't want to be mistaken for acquiescent citizens of that society. But the naked face of social protest has become the "natural look" (which *Glamour* says uses fourteen different products), just as "Black Is Beautiful" was turned into a new selling entrée to the black community.

We know and accept that God helps those who help themselves, and the woman who diligently follows a beauty ritual can expect her reward on earth. "To be born woman is to know—/Although they do not talk of it at school—/That we must labor to be beautiful" wrote Yeats in an early poem. Love traditionally follows a beautiful woman, as it does a powerful or successful man. The concept of love in the Western world since the Middle Ages makes the use of artifice a natural practice for women.

Men, however, believe that they attract through virtues other than physical appearance. Though until the twentieth century men have always been conscious of fashion and were sometimes foppish, these traits were reserved for the gentleman who used them to announce his affluence and taste, not to attract sexual partners. Femininity is associated with curls and lashes, blushing cheeks, alabaster brows and ruby lips, but masculinity is shown by action. While these concepts still have loyal supporters, men do, after all, make up almost half the population, and to ignore them as potential consumers would be a grievous omission of the cosmetics industry. Men are as interested in sex and perhaps even more worried by it than women. Sexual attraction is the greatest selling device in America; if one adds to it dreams of commercial success and reassurance against fears of aging, there is no reason why the American male should be left out of beauty's feast.

So far, this method works. Men are being told that particular products make them appear younger, more dynamic and successful.* Young men are given the sex pitch, the *Playboy* dream of beautiful nymphs imploring their attentions. The photograph of a beautiful woman's orgasmic face in a red light bears the copy: "The whole idea of a man's cologne is to start a kind of fire in a woman. Burley starts the kind of fire a woman can't put out." Hai Karate cologne and after-

---

* *Beauty Fashion* gives a list of adjectives used in ads for men's cosmetics: bold, brash, virile, rugged, commanding, vigorous, brisk, stimulating, potent, exhilarating—all these are sexual. Another group of adjectives emphasizes status and success: debonair, self-assured, persuasive, modern, enlightened, fit, dynamic, sporting, contemporary, robust.

shave offer free lessons in karate so men can defend themselves from the onslaught of women.

Older men are sold more through their fears than hopes. Afraid of retirement, of being usurped in the organization, of women's scorn or of death and illness, these men are given the assurance that a bronzer or face cream will bring the illusion of youth. Dr. Brauer at Revlon's Research Center explained, "A man of sixty-five is on an extended vacation at the twilight of his life. . . . He wants to look better . . . and it's our industry that's going to give it to him."

All mouths will suck at the teats of beauty. The old will appear young, the infantile will be given maturity and this great land will earn its noble title of America, the Beautiful. Advertising encourages the natural progress, but even without effort, the market expands. People live longer, earn more, start consuming earlier. The age for first users of cosmetics mercifully falls every year. Social stigma has been removed from makeup and Grandmother is now free to bead her lashes. A Department of Labor survey showed that expenditures for cosmetics increase sharply as income rises, not only in buying more types of products, but in greater per capita use of individual items. The survey estimated that families with incomes over ten thousand dollars would increase ninety percent between 1965 and 1970; more women would work, more people would move to cities, and the fifteen- to thirty-five-year-old female population (representing the greatest cosmetics expenditures) would increase almost sixteen percent in those five years.*

More affluence and leisure bring more time for dreams and devotions. More old ladies will go to beauty salons and more executives will have their faces lifted. When tangibles have been achieved and reasonably distributed throughout the country (the gaps are insignificant to the industry), then luxuries and diversions become essential. The FDA (Food and Drug Administration) recognizes this, and in its Fact Sheet on cosmetics states realistically: "Beauty is big business in the United States. With confidence that a new shade of nail enamel, an intoxicating scent, or 'covering the gray' may lead to romance, social acceptability, job advancement or other elusive goals, Americans spend billions of dollars every year on cosmetic products." After this fanciful

* U.S. Department of Commerce figures estimated that the fifteen- to twenty-nine-year-old female population would rise thirty-five percent between 1965–70.

flight of language for a government agency, the FDA goes on to say that "federal law—the Food, Drug and Cosmetic Act—does not require that a cosmetic fulfill all the hopes and dreams that may be encouraged by its advertising."

With this lack of discouragement from the federal government agency,* advertisers are free to misguide the consumer as much as they want, so long as no actual false claim is made (that this product cures cancer, for example, or that it will remove wrinkles forever). *Advertising Age* reports that cosmetics ads have kept up with the tempo of America and have even helped to create it. We were formerly a country trapped in the drab ethic of Puritanism, dulled into sober reflection by the Victorian era. But "gradually, with the help of [cosmetics] advertising, twentieth century society began to place greater emphasis on personal appearance in the here and now and on the enjoyment of the 'good life.' "

Our good life is public, and advertising, contrary to claims made for it, is not the vanguard of society. Public schools, public housing, public figures and public opinions have contributed to make privacy a suspiciously un-American trait. American business is conducted with open doors, American love is made in movie houses and on highways, American friendships are in groups and communities and American dreams are displayed on billboards. With motivational research and group therapy, we all become figures on a giant screen. Our habits, functions and emotions are available for perusal and manipulation, especially by an industry that claims to supply our "deep-seated needs."

---

* But the FDA is not totally permissive: "The law does require, however, that a cosmetic be labeled: without false or misleading representations, with informative information about the product, its manufacturer, packer, or distributor, and the quantity of its contents. The law also provides that a cosmetic must be free of substances that may make it injurious, that it be packaged in a safe and non-deceptive container, and that it be produced in a sanitary plant.

The law further states that any article intended to prevent or cure an ailment be labeled a drug; that color additives "be used under safe conditions as established by the Food and Drug Administration"; and that if coal-tar dyes are used in a hair dye, the label must "bear a conspicuous warning," since these dyes are known to cause skin irritations and allergic reactions. Finally, the Fact Sheet states: "The Food, Drug and Cosmetic Act provides the authority to remove from interstate commerce any cosmetic which is shown to be unsafe or otherwise adulterated or misbranded, and any drug which is either unsafe or ineffective." (Note that ineffectiveness is not cause enough to recall a cosmetic.)

Even the private parts are public business. Through the fifties, "Modess because. . . ." was as far as advertisers dared go in suggesting the secretive functions of the body. Mouth and body odors led to copy that reflected the embarrassment of most people, and although the ad would tell you what "even your best friend won't," there was much circumlocution and euphemism. In 1969, vaginal cosmetics were advertised in color spreads—"Unfortunately, the trickiest deodorant problem a girl has *isn't* under her pretty little arms" or, "You don't sleep with a teddy bear anymore . . . you're a big girl now with big girl problems"—and whereas twenty years earlier the Maidenform bra ad was hard to place because it was so "daring," now the ubiquitous use of nudity and relaxed allusions to perspiration make it possible for so prim a magazine as *Seventeen* to carry ads about vaginal smells.

The beauty industry can penetrate the last corner of privacy, where smells once considered erotic are now routed for their blatant, embarrassing intimacy. The guiding motto of the deodorant people must be "divide and conquer." When most adult females in America deodorize their underarms, then males follow and soon the children. Family-type deodorants become popular; new packaging in aerosol cans nearly saturate the market. Surely there must be another outlet for deodorants.

And it is found. *Women's Wear Daily* gives wide coverage to vaginal sprays, a twelve-million-dollar annual business. "What could be more artful than a sweet smelling vagina? . . . Right now, only major drug companies are making vaginal spray but the market is being evaluated as another lucrative beauty spot." Boldly, the article faces reality: "PEOPLE ARE STILL UPTIGHT ABOUT DISCUSSING THE VAGINA EVEN IF IT IS DEODORIZED." However, women's magazines "have been spraying the message of the deodorized vagina" and, though some cosmetics companies are reluctant to enter this "field of clover," Revlon is already "deodorizing the male crotch." With this in hand, what can be far behind?

Larry Gross, social psychologist at the University of Pennsylvania, explained that the first step was teaching people that it's wrong to smell human. "Once you've overcome the resistance for one thing, psychologically there's no longer any reason not to do the rest. And with the dissonance-theory approach, you might even say it doesn't matter on what pretext you get somebody to do it at first; once you've got them, then you can get them going on anything." He believes that "America's definitely a very repressed society in terms of smell," which is "deeply emotionally evocative" and "deeply erotic." Dr. James A. Brussel, psychiatrist, points out that "where sweat is extolled and a positive factor it certainly is an indisputable evidence of a piece of living. Dead people don't sweat. As a matter of fact, very old people don't sweat . . ."

Most of America deodorizes, and only books of beauty advice for the very young or for blacks still talk about the "problem." In *Let's Face It*, a beauty book for black girls, Elsie Archer writes: "There is no excuse for unfeminine body odors. You cannot control your perspiration without some assistance. . . . If your budget will not allow such a purchase [deodorant], don't despair. Plain baking soda, found in your kitchen cupboard, will cut down perspiration and its odors until you can do better."

I asked Margaret Mead why Americans use so much deodorant, and she answered bluntly, "Because they smell if they don't." But, I argued, why should Americans consider smell so offensive when Europeans don't mind and even find it attractive? "In this country," Dr. Mead pointed out, "there were people of different nationalities crushed together. They [ate] different kinds of food, they slept in different kinds of beds, washed with different kinds of soap and they were repugnant to each other. . . . Do you ride in the subway much? Do you really expose yourself?"

"Yes." I agreed it was an olfactory nightmare. "But I've also ridden the Moscow subway in 1959, when everybody smelled of a strongly perfumed, horribly sweet soap, much worse than human smells."

Dr. Mead insisted I was protected, that I never smelled anyone "who hadn't bathed every single day." Also, she accused me of never having been "in any one of these crowds where everybody was farting and smelled of a combination of gardenias and garlic. . . . If you're going to have cross-class and cross-national ethnic associations where you have different customs, deodorants make it practical."

To be American is to avoid as much as possible any uniqueness of race, color or ethnic background. Removing intimations of body functions or states allows you more easily to become a proper citizen. Formality is a necessary adjunct to democracy, since it obscures differences and permits standardization. Cleanliness, grooming and beauty join, and "the beauty people are after the clean, sweet smell of bath success," as *Women's Wear Daily* reports. "The plan is to keep everyone sweet, clean and well-oiled."

Once you've taught people that their own smells are offensive, you sell them products to get rid of the odor, and then other products to supply a different smell. Both body and psyche are explored for hidden recesses that can be aired and then adapted for profit, either financially for manufacturers or psychologically for individuals. Group therapy, mass media, wife swapping, crowded living all emphasize the public and pubic sides of personality. The national obsession with "sincerity," "individuality" and "naturalness" have become the province of the beauty people. But, just as "natural" in the natural look has nothing to do with the real, so sincerity has little connection with honesty. The confessional spirit of Walt Whitman, carried on by Norman Mailer, is the spirit of American conversation. Truth must be apparent, movements of the soul can all be verbalized and self-understanding is the ability to apply society's clichés to oneself. Our personal slogans are no different from advertisers'. "I have an inferiority complex" or "I have ambivalent feelings toward my parents" reveal no more about the human psyche than do "Every woman alive loves Chanel No. 5" or "The real you might be a blonde."

Despite depth interviews and psychological manipulation, advertising is basically a conservative industry, the echo of our own voices. In the vanguard of the beauty business are magazines that, directed to a small, usually sophisticated audience, provide a general aura and have a predictable readership that will not be swayed by a few editorials. Cosmetics advertising must follow *Vogue* and other leaders. Intended for a mass audience and censured by sales records, it can only afford to reflect tendencies. Though ads may direct consumers to desire something they had never heard of or were even antipathetical to, they manipulate only within the realm of acceptance. *Vogue* might conceivably show a man in full makeup; Revlon or Arden wouldn't dare because obvious homosexuality is still taboo. The "revolution" in advertising merely mirrors a "revolution" in society. Nude ads, hints of lesbianism and onanism are possible when movies, songs and general life styles have already incorporated these. The American public and the public American ask for images to reflect a kaleidoscope reality, in which the ingredients never change but are always seen differently. The outspokenness of advertising, the exploitation of dreams have occurred *within* a culture that rejects privacy as segregation.

In frontier times, the community was necessary for survival. Later immigrations left ethnic groups to band together, emphasizing national origin over individuality in order to protect their traditions and values from an unknown culture. Heterogeneity has meant that national bonds were forged through myths and mystiques; hope, not actuality, created the dreams of America. An elderly English peer once told me, "You Americans always think you're right. We know we are." Between these two attitudes, between bravado and smugness, lies the difference between a life led for an audience and a life led for oneself. The American way, of beauty, business, death or life, is to put on a show. Let everyone forget his humble beginnings or his nervous breakdowns; on stage, we can fool others as easily as we fool ourselves. We buy American, dream American and look American.

For one cosmetics company at least, The American Look is serious business. Max Factor, which invented pancake makeup and is traditionally associated with Hollywood, has an Armed Forces Division that provides makeup and demonstrations for servicewomen or the wives and daughters of servicemen. They call their Military Make-up Artists Program "a whole philosophy of service to the military establishment." Their newspaper, *Max Factor Country*, contains gossip and personal news from military bases, information on Military Make-up Artists, reports on the doings of present and former Max Factor employees and such fashion stories as the new design of overcoats for WACs or suits for WAFs. Makeup seems the key to retaining or creating femininity in women associated with the armed forces; it's also a way of selling America to the world. "The American Look is more than an advertising slogan," writes Derek Politi, correspondent and division manager, "It is a symbol of our philosophy of doing business; it is our salute to patriotism and we mean it as a sincere compliment to the Exchange Service and to military dependents everywhere."

Dorothy Dunbar, Chief of Military Make-up Artists, writes that dependents "vote for The American Look. . . . It is their heritage and they wear it with pride. . . . It has become the most admired look in the free world today and we here at Max Factor are proud to salute it."

3

Products and Services

A dermatologist in one of America's largest cosmetics companies told me, "What I hate are cosmetic kooks—you know, those people in the fifties between Third and Lexington. These cosmetics kooks have a patter, they all speak with an accent, they all have a ritual. They can point to twenty celebrities that owe their existence to them. And lastly, and this is the dangerous thing, they actually believe what they're doing is important. . . . What starts out as charlatanism ends up as prostitution."

They cater to the "many people who wake up and have nothing to do. They may have a luncheon engagement, a dinner . . . and that's the sum total of their needs." These people, most of them women and all of them rich, need activity and ritual. If they have a bent for hypochondria, they spend their days in doctors' offices. If they have insufficiently developed vanity or have lost control, they turn to addiction of food, alcohol or drugs. But many are left, particularly in large cities—women with no jobs, few responsibilities or duties, no intense interests and a great sense of loneliness. They have money and perhaps see their husbands in the evenings. Their children are grown or in the care of nannies. Like heroines of Russian plays, they are in mourning for their lives, and attempt to obscure the mourning by devotion to Narcissus.

After the breakfast tray, the exercise salon. A luncheon, the hair-dresser for a set and facial and perhaps a sauna or massage before the beauty bath and preparations for evening. Such a day, led by many New York women, may be vain but is not more vacuous than others. Appointments give a sense of importance, even imperativeness. A date with Erno Laszlo, skin specialist, must be made six months in advance and will simply not be kept if the woman is more than twelve minutes late. Hair accustomed to biweekly salon treatment will impress its owner as "ghastly" if an appointment is missed. If a woman has forgone a facial too long and her eyebrows are in desperate need of plucking and there's not enough time to make up before a cocktail party, she'll get scant pleasure from the occasion.

The beauty business is founded on the firm rock of narcissism. Most people, however, even those dependent on beauty aids for self-confidence, devote only a small portion of their day to grooming. They pay close attention to their image but don't drown in it. They have rituals, of course. Men who otherwise seem unconcerned about personal appearance will spend an hour or more in the bathroom in an inflexible routine of showering or bathing, dusting on talc, shaving with lotions or creams, applying after-shave or cologne, combing and conditioning their hair and examining themselves from different angles, perhaps even grimacing, as a check on their effectiveness. Men concerned with their image will devote time to body building, use creams and makeup on their skin, develop fetishes about hair, wear false pieces, go to men's hair stylists, hair weavers or experts on baldness. They spent time in gyms, steam baths and solaria. Some will take a two-week vacation at a beauty farm for sixteen hundred dollars.

Women's rituals are more obvious and elaborated. Hair must be set, styled, colored, straightened and conditioned. Skin must be soaked, oiled, creamed, powdered and examined. The body must be kept in shape, squeezed in or padded where the shape won't conform to the ideal. And a woman alone with her makeup and mirror is totally devoted, completely self-absorbed. Each woman has her routine and her set of materials. At work, she becomes an artist, believing that through her skill she can transform plainness to pulchritude, re-design her image or so heighten her beauty that it becomes magical. With patience and professionalism, she attacks her task and is the world's undisputed expert. Later, she may doubt the success of her work, but while engrossed in it, she's selfless and serene, thinking only about the production at hand, concerned solely with perfection. It is a moment of peace, when the woman has no rivals and is filled with abstract hope. She is not now concerned directly with getting her man or finding a better job; she concentrates on the eyeliner, knowing a blink could ruin the effect, and her hope is almost religious: if she follows the ritual, she will become better, a transformation will take place, she will come into her own. Even if she knows that after the routine is over she must go to the super- market or clean out the basement, the knowledge doesn't affect her now. This suspended time—two minutes for some women, forty-five for others—is her communion. She is not thinking of herself as a complicated being; she is not, in a sense, thinking of herself at all. The figure confronting her is in need of assistance, and she alone knows what to do. She may be proud of her efforts, but with the pride of a painter. The face is the canvas, she's pleased with her work, but for that span of time the face is lifeless, neither containing nor hiding the person: it's an object she is making.

Beauty rituals are something to do, a way of filling time. They give temporary relief from worries and insecurity by providing something to believe in, or at least follow, and by releasing the person from concern with his own ego. For women, visits to the hairdresser or to consultants on skin problems give an illusion of purpose and a reason for getting out of the house. At the beauty salon or at home, the at- tentions to her appearance are like parental ministrations in a world where all needs—even unreal ones—are being cared for.

These rituals are also an outlet for frustrated creative impulses. The craftsman not only sees but feels the result of his labor. In the pre- occupation with oneself as object, one gets the same pleasure and sense of achievement as in fixing up the car. One tinkers with oneself and beautifies it. The richer people are, the more time they have, the more they need someone to share it with. Beauty practices help the individual maintain a dialogue with himself.

A young woman psychologist told me, "I was once at the airport and there was a whole flock of nuns in the bathroom. . . . The tension of all these women standing in front of mirrors washing their hands and none of them could look in the mirror—incredible!" The brides of God shun vanity (though some working nuns do wear light makeup), but the brides of men often find no brighter light than the one on their mirror.

Not only ad agencies and large cosmetics companies believe that the reason for being is to be beautiful; many individuals dedicated either to beauty or to beauty's profits have devised techniques, products and even mystiques to justify concern with one's own appearance and elevate it to a way of life. Dr. Erno Laszlo has treated the skin of such luminous women that he is able to turn down ninety-nine percent of applicants for his services. Hungarian-born, with a staff of countesses and baronesses, Dr. Laszlo offers a twenty-minute consultation for seventy-five dollars. Applicants are given very long questionnaires to fill out, describing their health, emotions and personality. If, like the Duchess of Windsor, Doris Duke, Greta Garbo or Charlotte Ford Niarchos, they become clients of the great man, women must follow his commandments to the letter. They must wash with sea-mud soap (eight dollars a cake), obey his "Beauty Ritual Instructions" and return regularly for full electronic and cosmetic therapy. "He is to the skin what Mr. Kenneth is to the hair," *Life* magazine pronounced, but since Kenneth's prices are within the range of credibility, this comparison was not possible until Dr. Laszlo opened his institute at Saks Fifth Avenue, where women could buy Laszlo products and advice for use at home.

A Czech acquaintance of mine is not impressed by Laszlo. During one of his talks to a small group of women, she giggled at his pomposity. He turned toward her scowling. "Madam," he said, "you are not serious. You know what will happen to you? You will become an ugly old Czech." So far his prophecy has not been fulfilled.

When a famous woman dress designer went to see Laszlo, it is rumored, the doctor examined her closely and announced, "I will have to put you on a very strict diet." The designer was unhappy, imagining deprivation of meat, alcohol and other necessities of her life. "Yes," he affirmed. "You may not eat any caviar or salted almonds for a month."

Dr. Laszlo, who says, "The skin speaks to me in Hungarian," has become a legend among fashionable women. Those who patronize him are convinced he is the source of whatever beauty they possess and would not dare to experiment by going away from him for even a few months. Those who are skeptical insist his clients would look as they do no matter what, that all are women who have habitually led good lives and taken care of their skin, and that their good complexions are a result of health and diet, not of Dr. Laszlo. The believers (like *Harper's Bazaar*) acclaim his wonders; nonbelievers giggle at his spiel.

Other individuals and companies come out with hormone creams and various "miraculous" ingredients for "rejuvenating" the skin. Royal Jelly (from bees), turtle oil, mink oil, placental substances and extracts from fruits and vegetables have all been acclaimed for mysterious and marvelous effects on the skin. Since federal law does not require cosmetics to be effective, the products are not recalled, though most, after a period of being fashionable, are simply ignored. These creams generally are not harmful, though an overdose of estrogen (a hormone popularly used) may deleteriously affect female organs and has been shown to cause cancer in animals. Still, the danger is usually latent, with unfortunate "accidents" occurring from time to time. These products are extremely and artificially expensive, supposedly because of the esoteric ingredients, and are sold with much pretentiousness. They're bought by women who go to Laszlo, Christine Valmy, Aida Gray or the other priests and priestesses of the skin cult who offer electric massage, oxygenation, computer advice, bizarre products and fanciful, cultish language. Buyers of thirty-dollar and fifty-dollar creams are true believers, whose hope has been so reinforced by the price that it's probably strong enough to accomplish whatever miracle the cream fails to perform.

The tremendous growth of the beauty business in general provides a market for special products and services. Cosmetics lines cater to the under-ten-year-old market, to blacks, to sensitive skins. Elegant dogs, particularly poodles, have a choice of nail polish in "a rainbow of colors," can wear false lashes and choose the most flattering color wig, which is tied under their heads. Dog wigs are available in platinum, red, brunette, green and other shades. If the poodle is a New Yorker, he can stroll into the DogToggery of Saks Fifth Avenue and buy a small bottle of cologne—"Sniffe"—for four dollars. The cologne smells rather like 4711, and is made in Paris "pour les chiens exclusifs."

But fifty percent of the industry's intake comes from services, virtually all of them offered in beauty salons. Since hair is so large a subject, it must be dealt with separately (see pp. 68–105). Centers for skin care exist in most large cities and many department stores, offering diagnosis and cure. Expensive beauty shops and private beauticians give facials, a luxurious massage of the face by hands or machines.

The facial is probably the most sybaritic pleasure in the beauty culture, an hour of which the greatest voluptuary could boast. Scalp, neck, upper back and arms are massaged. Tight muscles rubbed with oils thaw in gratitude. Forehead, temples, eye sockets, nose, chin, cheeks, mouth are caressed into beauty and you drowse for a time in redolence.

My first facial was at Kenneth's, given by a stern, patrician-looking woman named Miss Hills. She had a robust accent, was born in Russia and has been doing facials for twenty-six years. I doubted that I would offer much challenge to her powers. My skin was never a problem. No acned adolescence, no blight of blackheads or pimples ever plagued me. Though my skin is dry, a little cream or oil easily restores it.

Miss Hills peered at me through three rows of spectacles—her own and two sets of magnifying lenses. She asked me to remove my eyelashes (but they were real). She found bumps, crevices, large pores, clogged pores and a whitehead that she attacked immediately, painfully lancing and then squeezing it. She spread hot wax on my eyelids and pulled it off, to tear out scraggly hairs. My eyes ached and burned; she produced tweezers and attended to maverick hairs not already uprooted. With eyes pinched against tears, I asked her how often people come for facials.

"There are people rich and people poor," she informed me, evening the brows. "People rich come once a week—at least once a week. People poor come when they can, but you must come once a month at least."

That job accomplished, she was again studying me through her three rows of glass. "You look like a jeweler," I told her.

She sniffed. "Because I am working on a jewel."

She found blackheads and squeezed them out. She applied a "stimulation cream" to my face and the skin smarted and tightened. Convinced finally that I was a monstrous collection of incrustations and warts, I felt a martyred pleasure from this ordeal by fire. My impurities had been found and routed; now all the evils of the epidermis would be scorched away.

My reward was immediate. Warm oils, smooth creams and lotions were massaged into my face, my neck, my shoulders. Fingers held and stroked the sockets of my eyes and it was the moment of consciousness that an anesthetic is taking effect. I let go, drifted, knew it was hopeless to try arranging my thoughts. Naked under Kenneth's leopard print robe, in subdued light on a contour couch, I was in capable hands, I had nothing to do but lie there, floating on the tide of fantasies and half-dreams, vulnerable and a little in love.

Perhaps my reaction was exaggerated the first time, but much of the feeling came back in later facials. I could understand easily why women with the money and with nothing essential to do would turn to a facial as a fix—a way of forgetting small frustrations and tensions, of entering the drugged world where you are no longer responsible but believe you are safe. This sense of peace and even humor could otherwise come only through a coincidental mingling of sensual pleasures: a spring night with mellow wine, a familiar tune and the rustle of waves—or in sexual exhaustion and gratitude. Surrender is the essence.

To relax the body and keep it in shape, exercise must accompany massage. An exercise salon is expensive, sociable and rigorous. A gym is the same without expense. Jogging and sports can liven up the circulation, but all these take time and initiative. Career girls, executives and others busy on the make need more efficient ways of maintaining *mens sana*. They buy Relaxacizors or Dynatones, machines that stimulate muscles by passing electric shock through them. This routs flabbiness, tightens the skin and brings back the look of youth. Dynatones are sold in department stores for ninety-nine dollars (sixtynine dollars for the facial exerciser). Relaxacizors are sold through newspaper and magazine ads with coupons attached.

You send off the coupon and wait for a salesperson to visit with his lecture-demonstration. The machines cost from one hundred fifty dollars to four hundred dollars, depending partly on how many attachments (belts and pads) you require. Each attachment is meant for a particular body area, but the largest machines hold duplicates so that you can give Relaxacizor parties where host, hostess and up to six guests "turn on" simultaneously. First you rub Moisturizing Gel (a conductor) on the skin, then place the pad over it and let forty shocks per minute enter your system. In demonstrations, people generally lose two to three inches from their heaviest parts. Though machines are most popular with the middle-aged, many young people are now buying them because, the salesman adjudicated, "they are becoming aware of the revealing look of new fashions."

These gadgets are not for people with empty days. Just as housewives will turn down a cake mix that offers "no work at all" because their guilt is aroused at not doing enough in the household—as Vance Packard reports in *The Hidden Persuaders*—so many women won't take the easy way out. Some reject the machines through a justified fear that overuse can break down muscle tissue, but most don't want the machine for the same reason that they refuse massage. They want to be able to *work*, to sweat, to have the satisfaction of physical exertion and the reassurance that they have done something today. I know a pretty young woman editor who goes to an exercise salon three times a week (cost: twenty-one dollars). Returning home, she kicks off her shoes and collapses in a deep armchair. When her husband comes back after his day's work, she tells him, "Darling, *you* fix the drinks tonight. I've been to Carola's and can't possibly move."

Carola Trier runs one of the most fashionable exercise establishments in New York (her chief rival is Kounovsky). Her machines allow the client to do his exercises lying down, thereby keeping a straight spine. Other equipment helps pull and stretch the body (single-minded beds of Procrustes). Some of Miss Trier's clients come for physical rehabilitation after accident or illness; some are dancers who work daily to strengthen their bodies and make them more supple. But housewives, models and working women come too, at least twice a week (Miss Trier won't accept anyone for fewer visits), sometimes commuting from Greenwich or Long Island, for her machines, massage and mystique.

A tiny woman, whose head seems too large for her body, Carola was born in Germany, and her accent is heavy as sauerkraut. She speaks continually, dominates her assistants and clients, moves like a panther and is in total control. At her salon, people "purify the body and clarify the mind"; she urges them to "concentrate on ourselves and not think what happened before or will happen.

"Lie back flat, let your head fall. . . . Just be comfortable, forget about everything else. Feel a little bit like Alice in Wonderland. . . . I will show you a lot of things that you could say with a nicer terminology and without accent. . . ."

Half-hypnotized, the women succumb. They hear that "our forefathers had to make their body into a tool for everyday living," whereas for us, "all our activities are arranged, and therefore we are not as healthy." Miss Trier intends to inculcate exercise as a way of life. "Now, people don't like to think of a hundred in any context. If I would say, 'Let's go down and take a hundred steps'—'What?' you think. 'Nuts.' But if I say, 'Let's go over to 77th Street and look at the new collection of Yves St. Laurent,' you say, 'Great.' "

She teaches walking—"a forward, progressive motion. . . . The only people in the world who move backwards are"—she sweeps out her leg in a large circle and places it behind her—"the lobsters." Her clients must walk with grace and show fine posture. Then they will achieve a better image of themselves and be able to project it, convincing others that they are beautiful. "People come here," she says, "with a very negative outlook to their own bodies," and though people who seek exercise "must somehow like their body," they are inhibited by awareness of the body's faults. After a few months with Carola, a woman "starts liking [her body], looks back and likes her looks."

The change in body image occurs partly through physical conditioning and partly through Miss Trier's relentless evangelism. "I walk to the grocer on Fifth Avenue or wherever you want me," she tells her class, "with the feeling of wearing an evening gown. Because I can't afford to think of myself—I'm a five foot, I don't know, I always lie about it and say five foot two. I'm little, I'm ugly. . . . I must think of myself as if I was tall, beautiful . . . because otherwise they might drive over me. . . . And you, what you have is not the image you have of yourself, but how you're seen by others. So that a long neck is nothing unless you see a long neck the way other people see it, and carry it (proudly). It's the way what you make out of it and not what it is."

She tells women to imagine at all times that they are wearing a deep decolleté, a long dress and bustle; she reminds them that a leg begins at the hip. "If you would come to my house for dinner and I'd give you chicken leg just to here"—she points to where her leotard ends—"you'd say I'll come to her for exercises but I'll have my dinner at Riker's."

Her enthusiasm, her dedication and, mainly, the marvelous show she puts on, pay off. "In summer I'm busy because of the bathing season, in fall I'm busy because of the new fashion. . . . In winter people come here to prepare themselves to go skiing. . . . In spring I'm busy because there are new fashions again. For a gym teacher, I'm *very* well informed about fashion. Before the belts came in, I was having women make their waists smaller."

Miss Trier may know about fashion, but Miss Craig, the former exercise teacher at Elizabeth Arden whose book of exercises is on the best-seller list, is the guru of the gymnasium for many of New York's Beautiful People. Amanda Burden, "Babe" Paley and Jane Engelhard have been her customers. Miss Trier, who admits that Grace Kelly has been one of her clients, will not name others. "That's like saying 'Here sleeps Washington,'" she explains.

While exercise salons can't properly be considered part of a beauty ritual, they are certainly part of a beauty day. Sweat from pliés and knee push-ups washes away the guilt of a regal object who, like Madame Pompadour, sits and succumbs to beautification. After a bout in the gym, the hairdresser is justified; so is a facial, massage or visit to the Eyelash Studio.

The studio, two blocks from Carola Trier on 58th Street, is run by Jean Kane, who applies individual lashes while her clients lie on a contour couch, spotlight aimed at their eyes. She buys human hair from Europe and sends the virgin strands (untouched by chemicals) to a factory for sterilization and shaping into lashes. She offers many colors, though black and brown are most popular. "I always admired pretty eyes and the look," explained the small plump blonde, who ten years ago set up her studio. Though actresses were her first patrons, she now has many nonprofessional clients who are willing to pay ten dollars for a consultation, twenty-five dollars for applying top and bottom lashes (usually twice a month), and fifty dollars or more if they have sparse lashes, spaces between the hairs or desire special effects. When Miss Kane goes to a studio to decorate the eyes of an actress or model, she charges "a couple of hundred dollars.

"I can give them the Oriental Look, the Indian Look, the '39 Look or the '22 Look," she says, mentioning only a portion of her repertoire. A very pretty blond client, a young Ingrid Bergman, was sitting in her new lashes and nodded. "I'm so pleased," she told me. "I'm the outdoor type, but these are so natural." When I had come in, she was writing in a notebook. She confessed it was poetry and, with another glimpse at her long pale lashes, she scribbled on.

The services offered in New York are exceptional because New York is, after all, the capital of the beauty culture. Women can be made up professionally in beauty shops and department stores or have their own makeup man come to the house for twenty-five dollars to prepare them for the evening. Time and money are the only prerequisites for a professional beauty day. In New York, Los Angeles and some other major cities, women are offered a wide enough selection of services to have a busy, varied beauty routine every day of the week. The customer chooses what she wants and has not been led to a particular salon by mass media or glossy advertising. In New York, the style is elegance. Many beauty shops offer "a day of beauty," with sauna, massage, facial, hair styling, manicure, pedicure and makeup for seventy-five to one hundred fifty dollars. New York is fashion-conscious, and beauty services are designed to keep the wealthy client looking as though she inhabited *Vogue*.

In Los Angeles, the style is more health-conscious. Californians have more health-food stores than New Yorkers have bookstores. Los Angeles cafeterias offer safflower oil and sunflower seeds on hamburgers, cigarette and liquor consumption is going down, everyone is encouraged to take sun and sports and, in a land of light clothing the illusion of fashion is secondary to physical fitness. Beauty rituals tie in with health rituals; far more attention than in the East is paid to eating practices and food fetishes. Everything must be "natural" (and the California Look in makeup emphasizes the "unmade-up" face, tanned skin and healthy, sun-bleached hair). In Beverly Hills, Aida Gray restores her customers' skins through oxygen and offers a line of cosmetics made from herbs, fruits and nuts.

Los Angeles has been called America's future, and supports its epithet in decentralized and impersonal city planning, imperviousness to sensuality and the destruction of class lines. Here, more than anywhere else in America, the show goes on and the show is all. Forest Lawn, the cemetery described by Evelyn Waugh in *The Loved One*, tries to destroy distinction between the living and the dead. The flourishing cosmetic-surgery business removes distinctions of age or physical imperfection. Thought cults provide cogitation for the millions and religious or mystical cults remove individual responsibility. Compared to Los Angeles, New York is Europe—a place of such degeneracy that death is practically accepted and fashion elevated to a principal diversion in the game of life.

Between the two cities women and men can decide which life style to emulate or adapt. Between California and New York, those with the prerequisites and inclination for beauty rituals must do it themselves, following editorial advice and advertising's instructions. They can buy *Vogue* or study *Glamour*'s make-overs, which "start with a psychiatrist and end up with cosmetics," according to Alexandra Penney, the makeup editor. They can write to Aida Gray for her masques and balms, or send for a cream made by Ana Maher with "a base of pure cucumber juice."

Most American women buy what they need in drugstores or super-markets. Those with more money and time buy in department stores, cosmetics boutiques and beauty salons. Invalids and recluses can buy from Avon salesladies or through mail order catalogs. They can all buy with assurance that the product is safe. At the Revlon Research Center, Dr. Opdyke showed and explained to me how cosmetics are made.

Most pigments used have existed for thousands of years. A new pigment is tested for two to five years and then is often rejected. The oils and waxes for makeups come from their manufacturers in large barrels bearing code names. A vat of castor oil may be labeled "Sunlight," for instance, to insure secrecy and guard against piratism. Those who put together the ingredients theoretically don't know what they are but only their proportions.

When a product is made, it is tested for safety. No matter what its intended use, the item may somehow come into the eye. As a test, it is sprayed into the eye of a rabbit. "Anything that will impair the rabbit's vision will not be marketed," Dr. Opdyke assured me.

"Another problem is that eighteen-month-old toddlers are forever taking their mothers' bottles." Since ingestion could lead to poisoning, the LD (lethal dose) 50 test is made on rats, animals that can't regurgitate and must either digest or die. A dose that kills fifty percent of them is the standard toxic dose accepted by toxicology all over the world. Revlon sells no product with more than five grams to one kilo of body-weight toxicity without making it emetic. (Toxic items are very rare.)

The new cosmetic is also rubbed on the skin of a rat. After ninety days an autopsy is performed, with blood tests and microscopic examination of each organ for damage. Cancer tests are carried out on mice—particularly susceptible to the disease—over a period of two years. Other tests are done on three generations of animals to determine effects of the product on reproductive organs, milk supply and other sexual functions.

The need for testing is obvious, but one persistent danger is often overlooked: that the cosmetic will be eaten regularly. "Teen-age boys consume more lipstick than anybody else," Dr. Opdyke informed me, and they can be in a state of chronic toxicity. An amorous nibble on the cheek gives a snack of blusher and a passionate lick of the chin coats the tongue with foundation.

In three constant-temperature rooms products are stored in their containers to see how well they age. The heat of Tucson, Arizona, is reproduced in a room kept at one hundred twenty degrees. Bottles and jars are kept there for a minimum of ninety days. If the product separates, emulsifies or otherwise alters, it's sent to the analytical lab for further testing.

A dropping tower tests breakability. Bottles are dropped from different heights to determine when they explode. A weather room, where a weatherometer can be set to reproduce any desired climate (and wind velocity), is the testing lab for cosmetics on people. Revlon can accurately observe how their product will react to an August night in San Francisco or how it will look on a breakfasting Chicago housewife whose pipes have burst in December.

The research center has many cells, each with its specialized job of making or testing creams, lipsticks, deodorants, perfumes, labels, boxes, spray cans or nail polish. In the fragrance lab, men are more reliable testers than machines; they are required to have "analytical noses" and, Norman Grief, head of the lab, is known as "The Nose." In special smelling booths—oversized confessionals with a tiny door for a nose to enter—air can be circulated constantly to test the staying power of a scent. Some smells should be transient (for use in soaps, hair sprays, etc.), but perfume must last for several hours. A pretty "fragrance fountain" sends up small jets of scent in a miniature of what Peter the Great or Louis XIV would have coveted.

The microbiology lab "protects the product from the consumer" instead of the other way round. A protective agent is added to cosmetics to avoid reaction to germs, fungi or whatever else might be on the consumer's skin. If the agent works, the inserted culture can't be detected later; if it doesn't, a new protective is found and the product undergoes all tests again.

A large computer, feeding into another in downtown New York, engineers the translation of a sample to bulk. This job, an extremely complicated one, was originally done by three chemists with slide rules. When all three concurred in their computations, the recipe was adopted. When they didn't, all computations had to begin again.

Livestock is stored in the Bronx lab, one of the few cosmetics labs to have its own animals. Humans are also used, but almost exclusively in the downstairs beauty shop, where human heads subject themselves to products used previously only on dead hair or live animals. The subjects must sign a waiver, similar to the one signed before an operation. Their reward is free bleaching, straightening and all the other beauty shop services.

The Revlon Research Center is exceptional, but all large cosmetic companies have their labs and many smaller companies with expensive lines have theirs. Of companies that sell products for under one dollar, however, ninety percent have those products made by outside suppliers. (This naturally suggests that brand names indicate little more than who pays the advertiser.) The difference in price only marginally reflects a difference in quality.

Drug and Cosmetic Industry estimates the cost of ingredients in any lipstick at about one cent, the manufacturing costs between three cents and five cents; in any cold cream the estimated cost for all ingredients and manufacturing expenses is below forty cents a pound. But a company's principal expenditures are advertising and distribution.

Another major cost is speculation. A company makes many products, but only some will sell. The cost of the chosen few must cover the cost of the failures. Stephen Mayhem, retired head of the Toilet Goods Association, reports that "only twenty percent of the new products find a market at all." (This is a strong statistic in favor of the argument that cosmetics advertising doesn't exploit consumers; it's more manipulated by them than they are by it.) The cosmetics business would be Russian roulette in reverse if companies were not careful to minimize their losses. Large firms often sell doubtful products through private label companies and the consumer pays insurance for items that don't succeed.

So, though the market is secure in general, particular items are unpredictable. Gold dust for eyelids may become the rage or have a glittering premiere in *Vogue* and then be forgotten. Any new cosmetic is like a Broadway play, with a strong chance of flopping, but the possibility of a smash keeps angels hovering and vice-presidents dreaming. Everything is possible in fashion, and everything must be offered. Today's products will be obsolete in the next decade, and chemists are already working on the beautification of our children.

In the immediate future, natural products and aromatics will probably be stressed. The skin can already be treated with oils from the avocado, olive, coconut (ingredients in Ultima II Translucent Wrinkle Cream), other fruits, vegetables, nuts and animals. Mink oil, a craze earlier in the century, is now returning. Bath "baubles" called Mink and Pearls became an instant success in early 1969 and *Mademoiselle* called them "a double helping of luxury, real or implied."

The confusion between "natural" and "healthy" will lead to acceptance of aromatherapy, now practiced in France and England. *The Daily Express* (London) describes this as a "new cult that is really an age-old one. It started with the Chinese, who taught the Egyptians, who taught the Greeks, who passed it on to the Romans." It's the massaging of various "nerve points" in the body with oils distilled from flowers, trees and plants. It claims to cure skin ailments, revitalize aging skin, conquer fatigue and be generally rejuvenating. The aromatherapist supposedly discovers weaknesses in the body by examining the skin and massaging the back. Then he prescribes the appropriate oils—rosewood resin to strengthen weak hair, sandalwood to aid elimination, peppermint essence to calm inflamed skin, angelica to help nerves, seaweed to cure insomnia or patchouli to feel younger.

A computer is already for sale (made by Clinique) to analyze skin problems and prescribe cosmetics (also made by Clinique). Clinique is so proud of itself that it advertises ". . . [makeup] so ahead of the fashion times it could very well change the direction of makeup in the next decade. *Clinique is the future of beauty.* And it's already arrived." Clairol has a computer for hair care, which may be dialed for solution of each woman's special problem.

Hair will become as colorful in the seventies as eyelids were in the early sixties. In a Revlon lab, chemists are working on a dye to be applied for the day or the evening. By about 1973, Revlon will offer women (and perhaps men) the opportunity to match their hair to their clothes—blue one day, green the next, apricot for a summer evening, white for tennis and perhaps gingham for a picnic. Clairol predicts a pill to change hair color and no one will ever again worry about growing gray. Mary Quant, the English dress designer with a successful cosmetics line of her own, announced in October, 1968, "I want to develop pills so you can get up in the morning and take pills so that your complexion is the color you want, your lips are stimulated and your eyelashes grow."

Frank Reckless, chief chemist at Helena Rubinstein's Toronto factory, predicts that people will use injections or pills instead of a depilatory to remove hair, that injections will change hair color and that plastic skin will be available to change or modify the shape of the face—to pad hollows, for instance, or straighten a nose. Mala Rubinstein predicts a fragrance pill to let you "smell sweetly all day," and another pill for sun worshipers to prevent discoloration, burn or coarse lines. This should be available in 1977, she estimates.

Clairol suggests that new devices will be made, and sluggish skin will be cheered by electrical charges or hydrotherapy at home. People will carry an oxygen pack to protect them from smog and stimulate circulation. Makeup will be built into cleansing creams and lubricants, so you can clean your skin and color it too.

The stigma on cosmetic surgery is disappearing and within a few decades people will readily repair to surgeons when any aspect of their bodies offends them. Plastic forms are now available to hide or reshape the body and plastic calves may be ordered by mail from Frederick's of Hollywood. Padding and strapping of the breast will be replaced by inserting or injecting plastics that give the desired shape. Faces will be lifted as a matter of course and a few tucks might be made for special occasions. Baldness has no future in a time of hair weaving and improved hair transplants, though men will probably continue to shave.*

The future is Orwellian. Cosmetics keep pace with the implications of biologists and geneticists, just as they have kept up with politics and ideologies. Embryos are created *in vitro* (though not very successfully yet); new individuals (frogs, so far) have been made from the single cell of a parent, and the Rand Corporation predicts that within fifty years this process, known as "cloning," will be widespread among humans. In only a few years from now, parents will be able to choose the sex of their child, and genetic surgery may be prevalent within twenty-five years. The human being, we learn, is infinitely perfectible and will be perfected by humans to better serve an electrotechnological society.

In the eighteenth century "God said, 'Let Newton be,' and all was light." Two hundred years later God granted man computers, and mystery became a matter of incorrect programming. Scientists and

---

* Though men habitually complain about the chore of shaving, very few take advantage of depilatories advertised in men's fashion magazines. According to Dr. Opdyke, however, depilatories are used by Negro men. Whether this indicates greater sexual security, greater intolerance for a boring task or simple economy is not obvious.

technicians work to control and adapt humanity. Humans will be made to fit needs, certain traits will be programmed in and others will not. The robot is a possibility.

Cosmetics aim not to create but just to modify the individual. In the future of beauty, no one will look old, no one will be unattractive, any eccentricities of the physiognomy will be removed or hidden, and the future American will be able to decide which stereotype of beauty he wants for himself. That is the difference: the world's future will see men made in the image of scientists; the future of cosmetics will allow each man to make himself over in the image he has of himself.

HAIR

'Never shall a young man,
Thrown into despair
By those great honey-coloured
Ramparts at your ear,
Love you for yourself alone
And not your yellow hair.'

'But I can get a hair-dye
And set such colour there,
Brown, or black, or carrot,
That young men in despair
May love me for myself alone
And not my yellow hair.'

'I heard an old religious man
But yesternight declare
That he had found a text to prove
That only God, my dear,
Could love you for yourself alone
And not your yellow hair.'

—YEATS, "For Anne Gregory"

1

The Presentation of Hair

Fifty cents of every beauty dollar are spent at the hairdresser. Hair is the most malleable feature of the human body, the most obvious indicator of class, sexuality, age and fashion. "Every culture does something with hair," Margaret Mead assured me. Hair can be cut, shaped, bleached, dyed, curled or straightened; it can stand up or lie flat; one can cut patterns into it, ornament it with jewelry, ribbons, flowers, birds or cover it with false hair and hide perfume bottles in it. Hair can be limp or stiff, shiny or powdered, and fashion can show infinite variety in dictating any combination of style, color, thickness, texture and length. Not only the most adaptable part of the body, hair is one of the most extraordinary materials anywhere. Both alive and dead, it carries magical associations, survives as long as bones, is replaced every few years, is erotic, romantic and reveals the status of its wearer. When age peppers it with gray, one gets a dye and removes the offense. In America, shades of youth often frame old faces. In the battle against death and aging, hair stands in the front line of attack, and, armed with rinses, toners, "cover-ups" and peroxide, Americans burn or hide the embarrassment of years.

American hair is also a distinguishing racial characteristic. Blacks are woolly, Jews kinky and Orientals straight. An American Indian girl with a permanent can look like "somebody on the other side of the earth," said Margaret Mead, who averred that even congenital malformations can be obscured. One distinguishing feature of Mongolian idiots is a flat back to the head and very fine straight hair— "give them a permanent wave, you can conceal this." Dr. Mead, an advocate of the beauty culture's therapeutic possibilities, went on:

"We have made it possible to stop penalizing people for genetic and general bad looks. And I think it's marvelous."

"Bad looks" are, of course, relative. The Afro is now considered beautiful even by *Vogue*, which devoted whole spreads to the style and its variations. A few years ago such a hairdo was inexcusable except on the heads of African delegates. A generation ago, it was a "golliwog."

The Afro was originally an emphatic statement of *negritude*, the African precursor of Black Is Beautiful. It showed solidarity with African brothers and sisters, repudiation of American values and an open commitment to separation from the white world; it was the potent symbol of a break with Uncle Tomism and slow methods of social reform. The hair stood up high, proud and militant. Its wearer was not ashamed of black history; slavery and persecution give all blacks a chance to claim their suffering and attempt to redress evils of the past by present action. Followers of Malcolm X wore Afros, and then the Black Panthers did.

But mass media allowed the pledge of solidarity to become a fad. Women who had straightened their hair most of their lives now let it grow naturally. Black people could "do their own thing" and no longer emulate the black stars (Lena Horne, Dorothy Dandridge) who were considered beautiful because they closely approximated the national stereotype of Caucasian beauty. A new stereotype was available, the Afro-American look, which is as African as a Jewish delicatessen is Israeli.

Harold Melvin of Casdulan, the Harlem Kenneth's, became an expert on Afros after doing one for Cecily Tyson. Then he did wigs for another entertainer, Abbe Lincoln, and discovered she held strong views on hair. "I think her feeling about the Afro was somewhat political. . . . I think she felt that she had to prove now, after a few years of straightening, that she had suddenly found her bag. And her bag would be to indicate that she is totally black, without trying to emulate the Caucasian in any sense of the word."

As in the youth movement, physical signs of revolt became part of the fashion image. Established dissent, whether political or personal, is part of the American way of life, an effective means for transforming serious antagonism into simple naughtiness or, at best, a "difference of opinion." Young girls more interested in boyfriends than politics let their hair grow in this slighty daring, with-it way. A young black acquaintance of mine abandoned her straight wig for an Afro. A few months later she was wearing her wig again because "everybody was calling me sister. And they all said we should be going to Africa and stuff like that. Strange people were coming up talking to me just cause I wore the Afro. I wasn't having that."

She was working class. An upper middle-class girl and her father walked into the hairdresser's on 57th Street where I was being shampooed. He was black, with kinky hair. The girl, whose mother was white, had pale skin and straight shining hair. She was here to choose a wig, her father's birthday present to her. Young, pretty and high-spirited, she clowned while trying on half a dozen wigs. A long blond fall intrigued her and she pouted under it with an effective Bardot *moue*. But she finally decided for the Afro, a "natural" wig that would be specially made for her, each hair hand sewn, for four hundred to five hundred dollars. The father shrugged, smiled, said he didn't understand kids anymore, and approved.

According to Mr. Melvin, the Afro isn't healthy: "It sometimes causes the hair to break because of the fact that it's not easy to comb through anymore. Now you have to tug and pull, causing a lot of strain and sometimes the hair breaks. And you find that instead of accumulating a lot more hair, you're really losing it faster than you were, you know, with the other [style]."

But the Afro is not chosen because it's healthy, or even because it's natural. Most hair, if left alone, would resemble a nest more than a smooth structure. As much care and as many products are needed to cultivate a "natural" as are needed for the more "artificial" straightened look. The Afro, like the Italian cut of the fifties, is merely the latest rage of the beauty culture. It appeals to urban, sophisticated people (male and female) and there are almost as many whites with Afros (or approximations) in mid-Manhattan and Greenwich Village as there are blacks with them in the ghettos. Most interesting about the style is the false information it conveys. It would seem to, but doesn't, indicate racial separateness. The black airline stewardess with an Afro has been conditioned by the same culture as her curly blond partner. Curls and even frizz are in this year. The rallying cry of "natural" has been brought into service of the unreal. To wear an Afro is not to reject the values of white America; it is only the substitution of one stereotype by another: a game of individuality where real distinctions are lost.

Hair is every man's natural calling card. Color, texture and style announce his race, class, nationality and often, his sexuality. A history of man could be written in terms of hair, showing ways of life, social structure, relations between the sexes, even attitudes to one's gods. Hair is a primary instrument for man's mastery of his fate. Babylonian kings sprinkled gold particles in their hair and beards. Egyptian gods had blue hair, and when mortals emulated them the deepness of shade indicated social rank. The actors of Greece used a black wig for the villain, blond for the hero and red for the clown or fool. Roman ladies aspired to barbaric passion by bleaching their hair, and blondes of the Renaissance were the products of chemicals, floral substances and hats cut open for exposure to the sun. Queen Elizabeth wore a red wig. During the American Reconstruction, the nouveaux riches powdered their hair with gold and silver dust.

English judges proclaim their dignity through wigs, and dictators sentence their people from beneath moustaches. Toupés hide a man's shame, dyes cover signs of age. Beards add intellectuality, maturity and intellect where they are otherwise lacking and blond curls provide a rope to climb society. Throughout history and geography, individuals have been concerned with what's on their head only slightly less than with what's in it.

There's no new hair style under the sun. Every style worn today had its counterpart in history, though hair has never again attained the height and breadth of Marie Antoinette's time, when elegant ladies wore three feet of it piled on their heads, often hiding scent bottles and decorated according to some theme, with miniature models of cities, opera sets or blown glass ships. The epitome of male hair grandeur was reached in England during Queen Anne's reign, when wigs cascaded in curls down the shoulders and chest. Since special servants were required for the maintenance of wigs, these elaborate hairdos disappeared after the French Revolution.

But what one revolution took from the upper class, another gave to the middle class. The French Revolution offered equality and fraternity and the Industrial Revolution provided the devices to achieve them. Hydrogen peroxide was first demonstrated in 1867 and bequeathed the world millions of bottle blondes. In 1872 a French barber waved hair with curling irons, which led to the marcel, and by 1907 Charles Nessler, a German living in London, had developed a way of softening hair with borax and baking curls into it. Cold-wave home permanents appeared in 1934, and Dr. Joseph Kalish, an expert of the industry, claims there have been no real breakthroughs since then.

Styles are cyclical, though they include more wearers with each revolution. But there are traditional attributes of hair: a woman's crowning glory, a man's evidence of virility. Lady Godiva was no hoyden as she rode through the streets in her hair; this natural look spoke of the protective covering given by God or nature to those creatures not strong enough to fight.* Milton—a "trichomaniac" according to Robert Graves—endowed "our first mother" with hair so luxurious that Satan was lured from his depths to her side in Eden, where he began to weave the world's great woe.

> Her unadorned golden tresses wore
> Dishevel'd, but in wanton ringlets wav'd
> As the vine curls her tendrils, which imply'd
> Subjection. . . .

Eve and Shirley Temple, both great innocents, wear golden curls to declare their modesty, weakness and gentleness. Christ, too, usually has long blond hair, though His mother, curiously, is often dark— too pure and proud for bleach. But light hair is usually the wife, heroine, princess, maiden in distress or Doris Day. Dark hair is for evil women or mistresses. Dark men are villains, and many believe that Nixon lost the 1960 election because the shadow of his beard gave too strong an impression of darkness. (He employed a more skillful makeup artist for his 1968 campaign.) Redheads are fiery, peppery or preposterous. Rita Hayworth was America's redhead, Marilyn Monroe our blonde and Elizabeth Taylor our brunette. Marilyn (like Brigitte Bardot and Jayne Mansfield) was a sex goddess because a child's face contrasted with the sensuality of a woman's body and excited licentious Puritans. By contrast, Elizabeth Taylor is completely a woman, assumed to be knowing and probably not nice.

Long hair is sexual. Removing hairpins in movies or paintings is often as erotic as undressing. The upsweep with tendrils at the neck suggests femininity, charm and motherhood. When it's let down, the

---

* In 1968 Vidal Sassoon was selling his wig dress—a long curly wig that covers the body and can be worn alone, with no undergarments.

woman is helplessly female. If she cuts her hair, she repudiates her sex, as the suffragettes and flappers did, as women artists, lesbians and businesswomen seem to and as nuns have to. Except for nuns and Orthodox Jewish brides, hair is not chopped off in America as a sign of subservience to one's master or the Lord; it is shaved in institutions for punishment or to get rid of lice, shaved before a brain operation or cut short by girls themselves as a sign of self-hatred (see p. 184). When models or actresses crop their hair or when fashion decrees a poodle cut (as in the twenties, the early fifties, the late sixties), commentators inevitably point to this as a sign that the division of the sexes is lost, that women are trying to be men, that the age of glamour has ended (Rex Reed, in *Women's Wear Daily*, writes: "Today we're stuck with creeps like Mia Farrow, who looks like a wet wharf rat. . . .") or that sex is dead. Though some might admit short hair is easier to care for or is cooler in the summer than long, most react through uncontrolled sensibilities and regard a woman with short hair, particularly if straight, as mannish or homosexual.

Hair is a far more complicated sexual symbol than breasts, calves or muscles. American women are, ideally, totally hairless except for head and pubis. American men ideally are hairy except for their backs, buttocks and ears. Baldness is a threat to virility, though long hair is effeminate.

Body hair is animal, hairlessness angel. Many American women want to continue being angels. European women, either more realistic in accepting their mortality, or more resigned to nonworshiping males (the Church has claimed them first), rarely shave their legs or underarms (although some German women shave their pubic hair for childlike appeal). American men are shocked—they "go to Europe and just crawl with horror watching Italian girls," Margaret Mead informed me, "appalling." But European men on their first visit to America find the sleek women unsexy. Though hair itself is erotic, the reactions to prevalence, absence or length of hair are culturally conditioned; a culture creates the signs and expressions of individual eroticism.

So the "female animal" of Italy contrasts with the American "statue," the woman on a pedestal. Here, even women who presume equality with men, even those who compete with them professionally, will assiduously remove body hairs—telltale signs of evolution—with razors, depilatories, "epilators" and electrolysis. The beauty culture, like any other, has taboos that must be observed on pain of exorcism. Lesbianism, even onanism can be suggested in beauty magazines but never, ever could one see in *Vogue* or *Mademoiselle* a model with hairy legs. She would be as shocking as a hermaphrodite, and a similar sort of creature. A hairy leg in America means a man's leg. Any American middle-class child by the time he is thirteen knows exactly the limits of hairiness appropriate for each sex. He knows which areas may be hirsute and which not and is aware (consciously or not) of the sexuality implied by a lot of hair in certain places. On the chest, it means a real he-man (unless the back is covered with hair too, and the he-man becomes a hairy monster). On men's arms and legs it's all right, but lower in prestige. Their hairy underarms simply exist and can be deprecated or teased. Young girls can be merciless with another girl who has a few hairs on or between her breasts, and both sexes, by the time they reach sixteen, expect females to have smooth legs, underarms and most everything else. Even the down on a young girl's face may be suspected of unfemininity and removed by electrolysis.

When I was nine, the mother of a friend of mine—another fourth-grader but, unlike me, with remarkable breast development—took me aside discreetly to say that my eyebrows needed plucking. She suggested tweezers, wax or permanent removal. My mother, born in Prague, took the news philosophically. She had never tweezed her eyebrows, but if those extra hairs on my brow were the obstacle between me and assimilation, then tweeze I must. (She did, however, refuse to let me have electrolysis or wax.) Later I was told my hairline needed smoothing out, and again electrolysis was recommended, to give me a perfect line. Assured by now of my nationality, I refused.

My mother has never shaved her underarms (though, paradoxically, she removes hair from her legs) and I suffered mortification through this quirk of hers. I saw the horror on my girlfriends' faces when they first noticed and, between loyalty and embarrassment, I could only nod mutely. Now, even after years of living abroad, I can't bring myself to wear a sleeveless dress without first making my underarms smooth and hairless. I never achieve my objective. Hairless they may be, but smooth, never. The skin is too sensitive and reacts to razor or cream with a furious rash. My vigorous scratching is, I realize, neither ladylike nor sexually alluring, but shave I must. I am an American and must preserve one of the American female's secondary sex characteristics.

No logic explains, no "health" or "sanitation" reasons justify, and female shaving belongs in the incontestable realm of physical sensibilities. That hair should be considered disgusting or unclean when it grows naturally on the legs or under the arms and be seen as beautiful on the head or pubis is a mystery created from the seeds of Puritanism, sprouting in a multimillion-dollar hair-removal industry.

American women go through more effort to proclaim their angel nature by shaving than any other women, and American men, more than any others, have advertised their masculinity by the shortest lengths possible. Long hair is a traditional symbol of femininity (children's drawings often distinguish sex only by length of hair). Eager to show they were real men, Americans kept their hair very short, and the prototype of an American for most of the world is still a man with a crew cut. A man should have little hair on his head and much on his body. The supermale now wears whiskers, beard, sideburns or all three. If a man shaves, he must leave evidence that hair could grow, and depilatories are not popular. Young men start shaving long before they must, to stimulate growth and show impressive stubble. Men ashamed of smooth chests can buy wigs for them.

Hair is sexual and also fashionable. Hairiness for men perseveres, but the former correlative of short hair on the head is no longer in style. A man must not wear a crew cut, regardless of what he wants to say about himself (and crew cut now doesn't mean that you're virile, just square). Longer hair is mandatory. In large cities and hippy centers a boy with a shoulder-length pageboy isn't considered homosexual anymore (though he may be thought "discontented," "dirty" or "Red") and bankers are adding a few millimeters to their locks or letting their sideburns advance slyly down the cheek.

Added length has detractors. "Women in this country are screaming," said Margaret Mead. "They're talking all kinds of nonsense about feminization of men and they won't have it." The fear of male homosexuality is much stronger than of female, Dr. Mead asserted. "The twenties saw a loosening of control of girls, when girls bobbed their hair after World War I and there was an awful lot of uproar.

You know, the fabric of society was going to fall . . . mobs screamed and yelled . . . but we scream much harder about boys than we do about girls."

Dr. Mead, author of *Male and Female*, is an authority on sexual roles and attitudes toward them. She finds the greater fear of male homosexuality "interesting," since with lesbianism, "you're going to get a lot of women who are never going to have any children" and society would be severely threatened. (This argument is untenable, it seems to me, since female homosexuals can always have children —and many want them—while true male homosexuals can't.) "Women are terribly worried about whether men are virile or not," she concluded. "No one's terribly worried about girls."

But hair more often follows fashion than the libido. Long hair on men is shocking in the way Impressionist paintings were: we have not yet been conditioned to the new aesthetic and our sense of propriety is confused. What is now the vanguard will become standard, then old-fashioned, as Madison Avenue revamps the image to inspire sales. Now, the fashion-conscious male must have bright clothes, soft shirts and a full head of hair. He must pay more attention than he ever did to the quality, color and length of his hair. If he's losing it, he can buy a toupé (actors have used them for years). But a toupé is basically an object of derision, if not shame—almost like a merkin (pubic wig), and hair transplants or hairweaving are more modern solutions. Though hair weaving has its problems (men have complained of splitting headaches or said they looked like "monsters" when they came out of the shower),* the ads show happy, youthful men rising from pools, hair wet but luxuriant, their chests hairy and smiles of victory on their faces as though they had just brought down the temple and proved themselves Samsons. Men with enough hair need only worry how long to grow it and whether or not to color it. The executive vice-president of Fabergé occasionally has "a blue rinse to tone down the yellow" in his white hair. Pablo, the beauty direc-

---

* *The New York Times* reported complaints to the city's Department of Consumer Affairs. Commissioner Weisberg asked for help from the state, saying that hair-weaving establishments were springing up with great alacrity. "The bald fact is," the *Times* reported him as saying, "that this thing has taken root all over the country. It deserves a careful brushing-up on someone's part to see if it really does represent an advance." The commissioner then added: "Though it is no concern of mine, if this trend is allowed to go unchecked, it could threaten the market in men's toupés."

tor of Elizabeth Arden, told *Women's Wear Daily*, "I personally would never consider changing the color of my hair because I think I look delicate enough and I am not interested in developing my vanity. I also hate blue rinses and toupés. They are like a padded bra. There is always the problem of what to do with them at night."

But hairdressers in New York report that men are asking for color —nothing extreme, just a way of brightening the hair or covering the gray. Kenneth says that men have colored their hair for a long time, and when he was in the Navy in the South Pacific twenty years ago, "we couldn't keep the peroxide on the shelves." Jerry Spallina, America's most expensive men's stylist, estimates that forty percent of his customers ask for color. Models and actors often change their natural color; other clients want merely to be rid of gray. Though he offers streaking, bleaching, rinses and all other processes of woman's salons ("hair is hair"), Jerry tries to protect his clients from the knowledge that the same products go on their heads as on their wives'.

The sixties brought more men and women to beauty salons than ever before. During this decade men returned to hairdressing as a profession. World War II had placed women in the salons; when the men returned, hairdressing was considered a feminine domain. But now men style and design hair, acquiring the same celebrity as couturiers of Paris. The most famous stylist for men is Jerry, who charges fifty dollars for a haircut and whose clients are generally married to clients of Kenneth. Jerry Spallina and a few others "create" looks for men, then transmitted by *Esquire, Playboy, The New York Times* and men's fashion magazines. The *Ladies' Home Journal* reported to the wives that Jerry suggests subtle dyeing for their husbands: "leave [the hair] lightly flecked with gray."

Little Joe, Los Angeles stylist of many movie stars, told *Men's Bazaar*: "The crew cut is dead. Amen. A man's masculinity will no longer be judged by the length of his hair. . . . The fashion world is in the process of trying to convince one and all that nothing in clothing or styles should be categorized sexually." Sassoon predicts that men's hair will be as important in fashion as women's hair, and he opened a salon for men in London, "because we think men's hair should be cut exactly the same as women's, to suit their bone structure." Richard Stein, who works with Paul Mitchell at Bendel's, is a young, boisterous Englishman with thick sideburns and a heavy mop of hair. He spoke ecstatically: "I feel, I envision, myself [men's] hair will eventually return to the kind of Court of St. Louis—King Louis. Really wild, overdone—as the century tears on, it will get really overdone in a space-age way."

Color, wigs, weaving, transplants, toupés—but all agree the biggest item is false pieces. Bishop Industries, makers of Chapelli wigs, estimates that in the late 1960's eighty percent of Hollywood and television actors wore hairpieces of some kind. Now, when they are sold in men's salons, barber shops, better drugstores, department stores (including Korvette's) and by mail order, men of all ages and professions are buying them. Young men wear them to supplement a lack of fullness, and *The Wall Street Journal* reports that some of its readers buy them to wear at parties, where their drab broker's appearance is transformed into that of a Beau Nash. False pieces give men the impression they're "doing their own thing" and allow men what women have been enjoined to do: put on a different look and become a different self whenever they choose.

The false piece is the great putter-on and putter-off of romance. Her long tendrils and drooping lashes call for candlelight, roses and soufflé au Grand Marnier. His virile moustache and mottled sideburns announce his passionate Latin nature, ready to pounce on the darling woman who repines in suburban boredom awaiting her prince on the 5:18, when she will be ravished by dark, Lawrentian forces. On weekends in Westchester, hundreds of Annas emerge from their bathrooms and dressing tables to confront their Karenins transformed into Vronskys. The props at first suggest a setting for the grand novel but, as the evening unfolds, the mesalliance between fashion and manners becomes material instead for a satirist with a bent for the grotesque.

Stories are told, and reported even in *The New York Times*, of hairpiece mishaps. An elegant gentleman in dinner jacket observes his moustache plop into the martini. A lady who has passed beyond decorum behind the bedroom door comes back into the party with her wig wriggling down her neck, to confront a gay young thing whose lashes are half on, half off. In a garret costing two hundred fifty dollars a month (paid for by the artist's parents), the young lovers claw at each other with abandon until his leonine mane falls behind the couch. The artist's father, meanwhile, is recovering from the shock of diving into the swimming pool before a company of important guests and then bobbing up to display the nylon base placed on his scalp for hairweaving. On the radio is reported the tragic story of a woman separated from her wig box during a transatlantic flight. She had argued with the airline that one's hair must be considered a part of one's person and therefore be allowed to travel in the cabin.

"A wig is like a narcotic for a woman," said Roland Shaefer, president of Fashion Tress, Inc., to *Women's Wear Daily*. "Once she has worn one and been satisfied with it, statistics show that that woman will continue to buy wigs at the rate of two per year." The wig business grew by more than one thousand percent between 1960 and 1970. A complete wig wardrobe (more meager than Queen Elizabeth I's assortment of eighty) is sold in some New York salons for two thousand dollars and a single wig may be over five hundred dollars. Eva Gabor, not to be outdone by her sister Zsa Zsa's venture into cosmetics, has entered the wig franchising business, which is "going to make us all very rich," she says. When asked by a *Women's Wear* reporter if she was wearing a wig, Miss Gabor replied, "Doesn't everybody? Even though I travel with the best hair stylist from Hollywood, I still wear a little one because it saves me so much time."

A wig allows deception without dedication. The bouncy blond party girl is really the dark-haired mother of three. An electric redhead is a pale schoolteacher, cascading curls of an elegant deity in empire gown cover a Mia Farrow cut. And men with bushy sideburns or wild moustaches are clean-shaven tellers on Wall Street. Just as there have always been after-dinner liberals, now there are weekend-evening militants, their politics a by-product of woolly Afros.

False hair, whether worn on head, face or eyelids, is made synthetically or imported in bulk—about five percent from Europe, twenty to thirty percent from India (though in December, 1969, *Women's Wear* reported that Pakistan and Nepal threaten the Indian market) and the rest from other parts of the Orient, often Indonesian now that Chinese hair is under U.S. embargo. It's gathered mainly in convents and temples. In India, hair is offered as a sacrifice by women, men and children, though "an Indian woman loves long hair. That's a sign of something to these Indian women, it's—you know—very symbolic," explained Howard Wagman, importer of human hair. "They have many temples in India where they have many barbers. There's one temple where they have like a hundred barbers. And they shave these people clean. And they're happy about being shaven, you know." Mr. Wagman spoke authoritatively. He is a tall man with the traditionally "distinguished" appearance used in cigarette and liquor ads: pepper-and-salt hair, erect carriage and bronzed skin. His office is decorated with photographs of his family, and he was persistently and conscientiously amused by my questions. He continued: "The temple collects the hair and sells it."

"Do those who sacrifice their hair wear wigs?" I asked.

"No." A smile formed on his sensual lips. "No," he repeated. "You can see women who have been to those temples—carrying a baby and with a husband. All three of them are clean-shaven." The temples support themselves through hair and other offerings, Mr. Wagman told me.

Wig-making is an old business; wigs were worn by ancient Egyptians, Greeks and Chinese. The Orthodox Jewish tradition of shaving a woman's head at marriage still persists, and the wife then wears a sheitel. Mr. Wagman stated that "the people who started in the wig business in this country were what was called sheitel-makers." Wigs not meant for religious purposes were almost exclusively for the theater, not for fashion. The "boom on wigs" began in the late fifties, when Paris designers used chignons and other hairpieces. "Today, that industry's half a billion dollars retail," said Mr. Wagman, mainly because wigs are now accepted consumer items, sold at "reasonable price." Though they are often very expensive, he maintained that "you can get as good a wig at Sears Roebuck for thirty dollars as you can get on Fifth Avenue for two hundred dollars. Really, there's very little difference." Others would strenuously argue the opposite.

Wigs are either hand-tied—each hair individually knotted to the net base—or machine-wefted, where strands of hair are lined up parallel to each other and then stitched together. Hand-tied wigs are often made in Hong Kong or South Korea, where labor costs are extremely low (Mr. Wagman says approximately $\frac{1}{35}$ of U.S. labor costs). The hair is dipped into an acid bath to remove serrations of the individual hair fibers, which facilitates the later job of lining up and sewing hairs, since it no longer matters which end is the root and which the tip. All hair is stripped to some degree and then given one of the seventy or eighty shades of available color. Strongly bleached hair, prepared for pastel shades, is fifty percent weaker than dark hair.

Once sold, the wig must be shaped, styled and often cut to suit the wearer. It should be regularly dry-cleaned and set at a beauty salon. Theoretically, a wig can last a lifetime (or longer). But because initial cost and later upkeep are so expensive, many companies produce synthetic wigs, usually of modacrylic fibers. These can be washed at home and need no setting. Authorities predict that within a few years ninety percent of hairpieces will be synthetic, thereby solving the problem of depletion of natural resources.

Wigs offer freedom to the fashion-conscious woman, who can now swim, ski, travel, even stroll through the rain and still scintillate in the evening. At Zürs, an Austrian ski resort, almost all American women arrive with wig boxes. At an artists' colony in New Hampshire, a woman writer came with three wigs, each a little longer than the other so her hair would seem to be growing naturally during the three months she intended to stay. I've heard a Texan woman opine, "I don't think there's any woman without a wig anymore. I have sixteen and that's not counting false pieces." And her Bostonian friend replied, "You're lucky you still know how many you have. I lost count ages ago."

Though *Cosmopolitan* asks, "Wigs and Romance: Can They Possibly Go Together?" and answers: "Very tough question. . . . If you're going in for more than just a few good-night hugs and kisses, we'd suggest removing the fake hair. (Turn the lights down low first)," most accessories would suffer in the storm of grand passion, and to ask whether any fashionable item is compatible with sexual activity is unmitigated heresy.

American hair, false or real, is part of fashion. In many cultures, hair styles indicate ritualized states of being; here they indicate the present style of personal presentation. Fashion determines which disguise is suitable and, as at a fancy-dress party, all guests are expected to adhere to the theme. The anthropologist Edmund Leach points out (in his article "Magical Hair") that hair is not merely a private symbol of sexuality (or, more specifically, the genitals), but is a prominent feature in self-presentation and a decisive part of the costume for our public performances.

"The mask is our truer self, the self we would like to be," writes Erving Goffman in *The Presentation of Self in Everyday Life*. The mask is created by developing a "front" that employs sign equipment accepted by society as indicating a certain type of person. Goffman quotes Charles Cooley saying that "we train ourselves from the outside inward" and suggests further that "there are many social contexts in which it would be *improper* [my italics] for a woman not to misrepresent herself as being more youthful and sexually attractive than is really the case."

Hair can be a chief sign in establishing a "front," which will then determine "performance." Society will take you for what you pretend to be, but only if the pretense is perfectly executed. Goffman warns that "a single note off key can disrupt the tone of an entire performance," and this applies directly to people of the lower classes who misinterpret signs. There is confusion about how the front should be presented, and when the pale blond of a debutante is emulated by a shopgirl's canary-yellow hair, or a Negro's red-blond, the front will not be accepted. On the contrary, these women reveal their class all the more and are considered garish. Those who correctly interpret the signs, however, can change their racial or national identification, their sexual impact and their social status. They enter fashion, a serious game of the upper middle class.

Though one out of three American women use hair color, the majority of them live in principal urban centers (forty percent of hair color is sold in New York, Chicago and on the West Coast, though only twenty-nine percent of all food and drug sales are made there). The metropolitan middle class arbitrates fashion and the rest of the country approximates the data. With clothes it's easy; they are mass produced and those women who want to retain a personal style must make their own garments, have them made or—more usually—resign themselves to choosing from available alternatives. But hair can't be mass produced, and wigs must be styled, so each woman becomes her own hairdresser. Only those with regular appointments at a beauty shop can keep up with *Vogue*.

"The major hairdo in this country today is still a form of the Italian cut," Kenneth told me. "It's not as soft and pretty as the Italian cut was originally. It's teased, it's sprayed to a fare-thee-well, it is immobile. It is usually yellow-blond or Mercurochrome red, and it's incredible. There's no subtlety to it, there's no—well, I'll be a snob—there's just no class to it."

"Class" is a function of fashion. A woman's hair must complement her and be in style; it's an essential part of her outfit. *Women's Wear Daily* reports that "the hairdresser has become an international celebrity," mentioning Alexandre, Vidal Sassoon and Kenneth. Alexandre styles royal heads in Paris, Sassoon has worked with many famous dress designers on collections and Kenneth was the first hairdresser to win the Coty fashion award.

Kenneth explained he'd won the award because he was "at the right place at the right time." He felt he was not unique. "I think that some hairdresser would have won it at some point anyway because I think hairdressing has contributed to fashion in the last ten years. . . . Hair was not pretty fifteen years ago. It was not pretty as a material, was not pretty as an accessory. That's why people wore hats, to cover their hair up. It didn't flatter. But with the Italian cut and the rollers and the lift of hair, the softness of hair, the freedom of hair, hair became a part of fashion that it was not previously. And I was in the middle of it at that point." Kenneth says he sees the new collections before the public does, carefully watches Paris and *Vogue* and has "a very good knowledge of what's going on . . . in terms of shapes and forms and things like that."

Of Sassoon, he says, "I think he was as original as anybody was . . . he took hairdressing a step further in a very modern idiom, a very contemporary idiom . . . the graphics of what Sassoon did worked very well with Gernreich." Sassoon's famous geometric cut brought him an international reputation and was worn at showings of Courrèges, Ungaro, Mary Quant and other designers. Other hairdressers have since copied or adapted his style.

"Whatever they tell you," said Sassoon, "and you'll hear all sorts of stories, that was our baby. . . . It was a way of cutting hair as if it was a cloth. Making shapes into a woman's bone structure, to suit her bone structure." In his London but no longer Cockney accent, he explained the new art form: "There are many ways. There are many schools of architecture. You've got Henry Moore and you've got Giacometti. You know, you've got different ends. Well, there are many schools of hairdressing. We don't say ours is the right way, but we say it *is* a definite way. . . . So I'm not going to talk about Kenneth or anybody else, because they've got their bag and they do it beautifully."

Whatever the bag, the main parcel is fashion, society's offering. Hair can transform one's appearance and class. It can weave destiny, especially for women. When small-town girls change the color of their hair, they look different and soon become different. The mousy daughter of a plumber can be an exciting redhead in Chicago and marry a businessman. Negro girls wear Afros or straighten their hair and get better jobs. An Idaho farm girl buys a long blond fall and packs up for New York. A radical change in your hair means a transformation of your marital and economic chances, your self-image and your public performance. When I became a platinum blond, I left behind childish things. As a young girl, I had been large, shy and intellectual. I blushed deeply if a boy spoke to me, never went on dates and was convinced of my ugliness. I dreamed of handsome older men, of Clark Gable and my father's business associates; sex was my preoccupation and I formed hopeless crushes on anyone who was kind or complimented my eyes. At thirteen, I was forbidden to wear makeup (and so wore it only at school), but since my parents never mentioned hair color, I surreptitiously bleached a few strands with Light 'n Bright.

By the time I was sixteen my "reddish-blondish-brownish hair" was reported in the high school yearbook. A few months later I entered an Eastern woman's college and felt completely out of place. I was not for groups, had spent most of my life alone or with contemporaries of my parents, I had no *Social Register* beside the bed (in fact, I'd never heard of the book before), no Bible, was considered supernumerary by my pretty, peppy redheaded junior sister and during the college mixers of the first few weeks I remained dourly at the side, telling myself there was a sociological aspect to the scene and feeling unspeakably superior, because I spoke to no one.

During Thanksgiving vacation my father noticed at last the ravages I had perpetrated on my hair and insisted it return to its natural state. I explained this was impossible, that my hair was bleached and only the roots were virgin. He demanded that it become one color and shed its patchwork effect. I complied by going to Helena Rubinstein where Rosemary (who later became chief colorist at Kenneth's) transformed my motley to platinum.

My personality was not instantly changed, though my wardrobe was. Truck drivers whistled, men tried to pick me up and at parties boys encircled me. My makeup was adapted to my hair (gray pencil instead of brown, charcoal mascara and violet shadow). I waited, among my scrubbed and bermuda-shorted classmates, to be recognized for my true self. Results came slowly but noticeably. Teachers told me (I did well in school), "I didn't believe you could be the one who wrote this." Like T. S. Eliot's pride in being mistaken for a bank clerk, my joy was profound at passing for a dumb broad.

Junior year I transferred to Barnard and lived in Manhattan, where taxi drivers offered me steak, Scotch and even more, a police car rushed me to the theater with sirens wailing when I was unable to find a cab and little mementoes from shy men were left outside my door. A Jaguar or Thunderbird carried me off to lunch between classes and boys followed me out of the Columbia library.

My style of life altered. Because I had platinum hair and large breasts, I played the role of bombshell. I was careful to disguise any critical ability I had, tried to reduce my vocabulary, cooed a lot, learned to pout and emitted little noises meant to suggest my kitten-ish nature. For the first few years, I despised any male who was at-tracted by me. Then, when I took the attentions for granted, I became tough, frivolous, sometimes funny and sometimes cynical. I was easily in and out of love. I learned to make jokes about my appearance that would endear me to the more intellectually-minded, and in London, where I went to live after graduation from college, I could combine the sex image with the national tolerance for eccentricity. I was secure in my power and the assurance spread. Eventually I dared reveal my opinions as well as my cleavage and after my first book was published the platinum disappeared.

I used hair to color my destiny. The pale blond was acceptable in the fifties, when frank artificiality was in vogue. At that time, women were still reacting to the earlier stigma on cosmetics, were painting mouths over their real ones and forcing their hair to grow in con-tradiction to laws of gravity. Now, the platinum would be considered cheap. Fashion and beauty emphasize the natural look, a counter-reaction to the last decade. The face is contoured and molded to emphasize best features and obscure others. Hair is bouncy, healthy and, if colored, made to resemble a natural shade. The look should underline, not distort.

But the natural look is open to ambiguity. It can mean natural beauty or the studied effect of naturalness. A client of a New York beauty salon always spent a long time in the ladies' room after she was finished. One day the hairdresser discovered her secret: she had taken the bleach and toner used on her head and was applying it to her pubic hair. "I want it to look natural," she explained in self-defense.

The hairdresser (a woman) then insisted that if this job would be done in any case, it should be done professionally, since the strong chemicals could easily cause damage to such a sensitive area. From then on, the client always had color done in a private room and it was done completely. The hairdresser told me that "quite a number" of women ask for this service, though almost all are Europeans. American women, despite the claims of *Vogue* and *Women's Wear Daily*, have not yet accepted the Total Look.

But natural can also mean clean or pure—the way God intended. Americans wash their hair more than anybody. Men often wash it daily in the shower (and some women do too), and *Seventeen* reports that its readers wash their hair on an average of almost three times a week. A French woman visiting America recently commented: "In France we know about this. If a man wants to take an American woman out in the evening, she's always washing her hair. She can't go out because this is her night to shampoo." She speculated that perhaps the dirt in American cities (she was in New York) caused people to wash their hair so often. I pointed out that the ritual is continued even when the person is in the country or abroad.

One of the great moments in American musicals was Mary Martin in *South Pacific* singing, "I'm gonna wash that man right out of my hair," while lathering her poodle cut. The audience loved it; the song incorporated so much that was American, in outlook and in the glorious activity of shampooing on stage. When your hair is "squeaky" clean, all's right with the world and you regain purity. The sexuality implicit in hair has been watered down.

For most Americans, excessive or obvious attention to hair is a stand for sex or vanity. While city people can even match tresses to their dresses, the country as a whole sees this as interference with God's will. And even if the coloring of women's hair can be accepted (particularly the discreet covering of gray), men's hair must remain in its natural state. Amy Greene of *McCall's* commented: "One of the great things that cost Humphrey the election was that he dyed his hair and everybody knew it. Why did this man have to dye his hair? It's crazy."

I asked if she really thought people had voted against him on that account. "Well, up to a certain point," she maintained. "It bugged them. But Nixon went on with full makeup."

A man is responsible for his face, said Lincoln and Shaw. In modern

America, this leads men to using bronzers, facial masques, powder and perhaps in future other makeup as well. But hair is something different. A man who colors it or wears a wig must take special care to guard his masculinity. He must consider it part of his presentation, a signal to others of his youth, dynamism, prowess and style.

Hair joins makeup for the grand illusion of individuality. As more hair products are made, the consumer must be taught that he can express his true self by using them. For women, hair can carry any theme or motif, as in the days of Marie Antoinette, with the difference that the themes are mass produced. Hairdressers and fashion magazines offer horoscope hairdos (to match your sign), His and Hers styles or Unisex wigs, even animal hairdos. *Women's Wear Daily* reports that Julius Caruso is doing styles "that look like everything from poodles and terriers to his latest—a water buffalo." Hairdos represent moods (sweet, sultry, sophisticated, etc.), temperaments, periods in history; they take inspiration from novels, movies, paintings and they emulate famous people.

Because hair is such an obvious feature, it can be a mark of individuality. Gertrude Stein's cropped hair was not only part of the way she looked, but of her outlook. Hitler's moustache and the sideburns of Francis Joseph were definitely particular. False pieces, however, are made identically for thousands of men. The illusion of individuality takes over as the quality becomes marketable and meaningless. Kenneth says, "What has happened in the area of men in the last five years is absolutely phenomenal. Phenomenal. And it's just beginning." False pieces, which dramatize the phenomenon, are "decoration—that's fantasy. I don't think men have ever disliked illusion or fantasy any less than women. I think the very fact that men like women is a proof of their liking an illusion."

The fantasy is, that by conforming to a relatively new stereotype, one is being original. Revlon sells hair color by showing a beautiful brunette and writing, "Sweden may export blondes. But their brunettes they keep for themselves. Until now. Here they are, re-created by Revlon." Another ad has a gorgeous blonde crawling over rocks, her mouth half open to receive the spray of what one assumes is the sea. "The Blondes of San Pellegrino" is the headline. Underneath: "The Italians consider them the most beautiful women in Italy. Perhaps the world. Now Revlon captures these rare, sun-drenched, healthy-looking blonde shades. For You." At the end of five more paragraphs, one learns: "If ever you wanted to be treasured by a dark, handsome man, now is the time." Why a woman from St. Louis would look Italian if she bleached her hair blond or how a Bostonian looks Swedish if she dyes her hair dark is not explained. The grand illusion is merely furthered: that this product brings out uniqueness, rarity, the single magnificent creation that is you alone. With hair products, more than any others, people are likely to believe the message.

2

Hairdressers

The tall young moustached man caught my eye in the mirror as he arranged a curl to go forward instead of back. "How about it?" he asked in a low voice. "We could even have drinks first."

"No thanks," I answered. He continued working and started to whistle. Good-looking; sexy eyes. "Do you always come on like that?" I asked.

"Well"—he grinned—"I figure I'll get turned down nine out of ten times, but there's always that tenth one and I get a lot of women in the chair." He paused, looked through the mirror at all the clients; his hands left my head a moment and he turned to contemplate them in the flesh. He put both hands on the sides of my head to smooth the hair, brought his mouth close to my ear and said, "Four of them in this room now."

That young man has since left the profession. A coworker of his, an extremely popular stylist with John Barrymore features, moves in and out of hairdressing whenever a woman dismisses him. He is usually tanned, spends a great part of the year out of the country and finds hairdressing a perfect opportunity for gaining the contacts necessary to be a gigolo. Jean-Jacques (not his real name) is genuinely brokenhearted after an affair. "I can't help it," he explains, "I always fall in love with the woman."

A taxi driver who had been a hairdresser at nineteen—"can't tell you about that, the reasons were too personal"—announced as he drove me through Queens, "Guys who go into that [hairdressing], they desire the company of women. They consider themselves lovers. They're not really that. A guy like that, who wants to work with women, to be around women all the time—he's got to have a hangup somewhere." The cabbie insisted all hairdressers were homosexual. I objected and gave examples. He said, "There are fairies and fairies. The guys who swish around, and the others."

His is the common stereotype. A publisher friend of mine explained, "The image of a hairdresser being queer or neuter is made by men who couldn't face the thought of their wives being in the hands of any other men for hours and confiding in them." A hairdresser is often said to take the role of psychoanalyst or priest with a woman, is sanctified into a eunuch, and women, who often disclose far more to their hairdressers than to their husbands or girlfriends, have not chosen to explode the myth.

Vidal Sassoon, who reveals in his book that "amorous clients are an occupational hazard," has certain standards in hiring people for his salons. "There's no question of whether it's a faddy or queeny thing to do. . . . If someone is homosexual, he's got it tough before he starts, without [me] making it harder for him. As long as they behave heterosexually towards the job, as long as it's done in a very gutsy way, fine. Because hairdressing basically—to stand there ten, twelve hours a day—is very gutsy. You've got to stand behind that chair and it drains you. Because clients are using you as an emotional springboard, and you are physically working hard on those haircuts. So as long as somebody stands behind that chair and uses themselves in a heterosexual way, I don't care if they sleep with their pet camel when they leave. That's their bag."

Francesca Ruta, who formerly worked with Kenneth at Lily Daché and now has a salon of her own, explained the "very personal thing between hair stylist and client" by saying, "psychologically, whether the woman realizes it or not, many times she will come because she wants to make a confession of how she feels. . . . I don't say every woman comes into the beauty salon feeling that she is going to tell you what's in her heart or in her mind, but she will do that without being aware. . . ."

Women go to men stylists, said Francesca, simply because there aren't many women stylists. (Curiously, as with cooking, hairdressing is considered to be within the province of all women, but the great hairdressers, like the great chefs, are assumed to be men.) "I find I always have to be masculine in my way of thinking when I'm standing behind that chair," Francesca told me. "She [the client] likes to be flattered, she doesn't like you to be honest; she *would* like you to admit what *can* be done, she would like you to make a suggestion."

"About her life?" I asked.

"About her hair, in associating it with her personal life. Because it depends on how you make *her* feel with *her* hair, which will bring her into a tranquillity. . . . She wants to have cocktails, she wants to go and have dinner. She wants to do all these things, many times her hair is her drawback."

"Is the drawback real or only in her mind?"

"That's how *she* feels. It's a very unrealistic attitude."

Because hair is so pliant and can be used to emphasize or disguise features and even traits, women come to the hairdresser with the feeling of being made over. Away from the screams of children, temper tantrums of the cook, bad humor of the boss or secretary, women relax in an irresponsible world where they literally let their hair down and are taken care of. They enter, remove their clothes, put on a gown usually of pastel (babyish) color, order a coffee perhaps and give themselves over. Their hair is washed and their scalp massaged. Whatever the hair needs, it will get without her asking for it. Then she is brought to the stylist, who perhaps cuts her hair and usually sets it (except for certain styles of Sassoon and followers). They confront each other, woman and hairdresser, but only in the mirror. They rarely see each other face to face. The smooth glass, the feminine atmosphere, the relaxation and knowledge that nothing, short of fire in the building, can get the woman out of here before the stylist is through, gives her the strangers-on-a-train feeling, where everything may be said and nothing will be repeated. She could, of course, simply read a book or magazine while he is working on her, but what woman could resist observing the transformation in progress? Sometimes client and stylist confer on what should be done, occasionally the woman commands (in which case the stylist might refuse to do her) and often he decrees and she accepts. While he works, he must concentrate on what he's doing, measure the strands of hair to make sure the cut is even, collect the hair in setting paper to insure a smooth line afterward, select the exact roller needed for this particular part of the head or decide whether Scotch tape would be preferable to clips for keeping down the bangs. Usually he is too preoccupied to hold his own in conversation or to embark on a monolog. What he can do best is let her drift of words fall over him and respond from time to time with appropriate sympathy, encouragement or indignation. He represents her private world, away from job or family, where she is recognized only as a client, where people know her specific hair problems and where her confidences are kept with almost professional secrecy. She will probably not see the stylist anywhere else. She trusts him, she establishes a firm loyalty and he becomes a special, secret friend whom she rarely thinks about away from the salon, but, once in it, she recognizes him as one of the only people in the world who understands her. She identifies with him as she does with a dress designer; he becomes part of her style, her way of presenting herself. She would not consider going to an important event without first going to him.

For these reasons, it is as difficult to change hairdressers as it is to change doctors. Smart New Yorkers go to a particular stylist at a particular salon. If he moves, she generally follows him. If she decides to change, he will probably hear about it, and when she comes back to him she will be told that her hair is in terrible condition and badly cut. The top salons are like clubs—Kenneth the most powerful and coherent of them—and to transfer loyalty is an act of betrayal.

To go to Kenneth can be an act of faith similar to belonging to the Masons. He is America's top hairdresser and some of his prestige rubs off on women who come to his salon. His prices are competitive with all other well-known New York salons, but his name is magical.

Born Kenneth Battelle in Syracuse, New York, he spent eighteen months in the navy, then attended Syracuse University to study liberal arts. He left for lack of money—his mother was divorced and there were four younger sisters to support. Though Kenneth wanted to do creative work, he realized that money had to be made and went into hairdressing as a compromise. He worked at Helena Rubinstein, where he acquired his most famous client, Jackie Kennedy, and then headed the salon of Lily Daché. After disagreements with the owner, he left to start a salon of his own, sponsored by the Glemby Company, one of the three large firms that own most of the well-known beauty salons in America. Glemby, which is publicly owned, controls about four hundred and fifty salons, with an annual profit of around forty-three million dollars. (A stylist at Kenneth told me, apropos this, "The beauty industry is the biggest monopoly in America.")

The salon on 54th Street has five floors, is opulently decorated in paisley, velvet, leather, gilt and has parquet floors. Kenneth looks dignified and slightly Edwardian, with sideburns and thinning hair. He dresses in conservative colors with a touch of flamboyance in the cut. When I interviewed him, he wore a pin-striped suit tight at the waist and slightly flared at the hips, with a gray dotted tie. First he did my hair, trimming and then setting, never inquiring how I wanted it. But the result was beautiful: my usual style with a few tendrils added at the neck. When I asked how he had known what to do, he remarked nonchalantly, "I was listening to what you said and you told me without your knowing it, you didn't want it a different way." Later, talking about new clients, he said, "You very often have a failure with a woman's hair the first time, or the second time. . . . You've got to feel her . . ."

Kenneth is extremely self-possessed and obviously keeps his own counsel. Though warm and cordial, a raconteur, he is always the observer in his stories, not the participant. He is dignified and intelligent, a wide and probably voracious reader, whose success has obviously come from serious dedication, cleverness and the ability to anticipate implications of what he does. As we talked, I had the impression that Kenneth was someone who would always guard against easy intimacy and seeks neither flattery nor confirmation of his ability, talent or taste. He seemed either not to need, or to be wary of, friendship.

He dismissed my opening questions on the source of his fame. "I don't operate under the premise that I have influence on anybody really." When I suggested that women might come to him for prestige, he said, "I think that's silly. . . . They don't think it has anything to do with social standing as much as the fact that they think I'm going to be able to work with their hair." I insisted that his reputation must attract clients and he finally conceded—"there's no getting away from that"—but insisted this was true for the first time only. "I must tell you that reputation or not, if they don't feel they look good, they don't come back. And the name of the game is that they come back."

He tries to please the client by making a hair style to compliment her particular appearance. Unlike Sassoon, he has no specific look. Though many credit him for having created the Jackie Kennedy style, he says, "That doesn't have so much to do with me as it has to do with her. She looks the way she wants to look." Why, I wanted to know, did he then become so famous, if he had innovated nothing?

"I have innovated things," he admitted, "but they've been very minor things. . . . It's been a very logical, step-by-step thing of one kind of hair look into another kind of hair look. But very, very gently. Because I don't think that anybody should be forced or told—or is comfortable radically changed."

Comparing himself to Sassoon, he said, "I don't see women as graphically as Vidal. I don't see them as cutouts, in a sense. And I don't mean that as a put-down; it's a question of eye."

I went back to the original theme: "You've become a superstar."

"That's part of the time, it's part of communications. It's Marshall McLuhan, you know. It *is*," he insisted, his voice rising for emphasis. "I think I'm part of the whole thing of communications, of people living in a vicarious way by interest in someone else's life, whether it's a professional life or a private life or a political or trade life, or whatever. I think that's what it's all about. . . . It's happened in ten to fifteen years. Cosmetics is going more and more in that direction—of personalities, people. Because we are in a time when people are identifying with one another or trying to identify with somebody. There's a need and a want of individuality and probably less of it than there ever was."

We went on to discuss the changing status of a hairdresser. Sassoon had told me: "Yes, there has been a change. I mean, nobody invites me out today to comb their hair in the evening. If they invite me out, it's because they want me in the company, with whatever's going on." Sassoon gained eminence through his connection with high fashion. His clientele has been bright young women in the arts, entertainment and business. Kenneth's clientele includes some of these, but is most known for socialites. As his clients come into prominence, so does Kenneth. "Nobody twenty-five years ago would write about what a hairdresser was doing," he said sternly. "I have been asked what kind of wine I liked. At which point I said, 'Who the hell cares?' And at this point the reporter said, 'Everybody cares.' And I said, '*Who* cares?' But it's serious, really. I just fall on the floor hysterical."

I suggested that though some years ago his profession would have excluded him from it, he was now in society. "But I must tell you that I am not in society," he corrected. "I mean, I do not go *around*. I am not an extra man. I am not involved in any way in society."

"I mean that you are socially acceptable," I clarified.

"Oh, I don't think that's true at all," he again contradicted. "I would argue that with you right down to the nitty-gritty. I think there are many, many places where I would not be socially acceptable. I've been turned down at three cooperative apartments in New York City because I was a name, a celebrity."

Sassoon, an ebullient young man with a slim, muscular body, is Jewish and Cockney. "I was very Cockney and very East End Cockney lad, you know, always getting into trouble. When I was a kid—eighteen, nineteen, twenty—I had to make up my mind. If I wanted to make it in this business I had to take voice production and elocution lessons."

He is in direct contrast to Kenneth, in work as well as personality. We had said hello to each other over the years, ever since I had lived in London and gone to his Bond Street shop. Now he was in New York, on Madison Avenue, wearing a blue shirt, tight tweed pants and a broad black perforated tie folded in half horizontally and fastened with a pearl pin. When I arrived at ten, he said he could give me only twenty minutes, because he was leaving for London the following day. Forty-five minutes later, he declared me "a doll" and said we could talk until noon. He was affectionate, bubbly and quite open, asked questions about me and seemed eager to establish a kind of friendship. His movements and facial expressions made clear all the time that we were a man and woman talking and that he was aware of his masculine charm.

Sassoon's autobiography, *sorry I kept you waiting, madam,* a book written with some assistance and much high spirits, describes his life in the East End, street fights against anti-Semitic Mosleyites, his beginning in hairdressing, going off to fight in Israel, return and disillusionment, and finally the commitment to hairdressing as a creative and potentially remunerative profession. He had his start as a boy of fourteen, when his mother took him to be apprenticed to a neighborhood hairdresser. The apprenticeship was costly, the Sassoons had no money and Vidal was accepted free of charge because, leaving the establishment, he held the door open for his mother and so impressed the master by this action that he was granted an education.

Paul Mitchell, who formerly worked for Sassoon, remarked that hairdressing in England is "practically a ninety-nine percent Jewish profession." (Mr. Mitchell is not Jewish.) When I repeated this to Sassoon, he let out some definite expletives and then, more calmly, explained: "This is absolute nonsense. First of all, when I came in the craft, in hairdressing, it was very la-di-da. An East Ender had no chance at all. In fact, it was the very reverse of what Paul has told you." He then listed most of the top names in English hairdressing at the time when he entered it, and not one was Jewish. He mentioned his own people and ended the list with "Laurence Taylor, Roger [Thompson], my top stylist in London. He's been with me seven years and is now creative director in London—who by the way isn't Jewish. Frankly, I wouldn't give a damn if he had green stripes, it wouldn't make a scrap of difference. But before our crowd came into the business and made some sort of mark, they were all non-Jewish." He sputtered a bit and then concluded: "And now, I'd like to forget it. Because that is so nonsensical, it's like whites and Negroes and I'm not going through all that rubbish. . . . I don't know why the whole religious thing came up in the first place, because no one even thinks that way nowadays unless they're a bit that way. Because, you know, people are either groovy or they're not, what the hell."

Sassoon is certainly groovy. He married an American actress, Beverly Adams (who formerly dated Elvis Presley and Sandy Koufax), and is an accepted celebrity in America, food for gossip columns, part of the entertainment world, a swinger who could as easily have been a pop singer. He's definitely attractive and has never suffered the stigma of homosexuality. "I've always liked beautiful women. There's no problem there." I told him he put sex into hairdressing, and he accepted the compliment with relish.

His approach to hairdressing is very different from Kenneth's. Like most English boys and many Europeans, he served an apprenticeship and regards his profession primarily as a craft. "If you were lucky, after five years, people recognized you as a reasonable hairdresser—maybe after seven or eight for somebody who was very good. And you very rarely became an innovator. If you did become an innovator before ten years in the craft—there's so much to absorb and learn—you were respected as a craftsman or a tradesman, or a skilled designer, whatever you were. Because you'd given so much time to your art form and you'd studied it."

As in many other fields, the European approach is traditional, based on centuries of guilds, where the quality of a man's work is stressed over the object he creates. The American approach is to stress the commodity. To Sassoon American hairdressing ". . . is very strange, you know. A lot of throwouts from the showbiz world—not throwouts, it's not a nice word—people who couldn't quite make it, looked around and thought, 'Where's the best place I can make money in the easiest, shortest time?' So they went to school for a thousand hours, became hairdressers, and it became a sort of chic, funny thing to do."

Whatever the differences in training and motives, Kenneth operates as though he were rendering a service, while Sassoon is more concerned with creating a work of art. I went into Sassoon's salon one day to have my hair washed and set. The stylist I had been assigned to, a shaggy young man in a bright shirt, his hair curled up below the collar, took one look at me and said he would have to cut my hair off. I refused; he said he would not take me on as a client. I went to Linda, one of the chief stylists, whom I had known in London. "Do yourself a favor," she told me, "forget it. If you want your hair done, come to me." She was, I knew, the only one who would undertake my long, thick, kinky hair. I told her I would be interviewing Sassoon and hoped he would do my hair at that time. "Do yourself a favor," she repeated, and I nodded, understanding perfectly. Despite his charm, despite his artistry, Sassoon could not have done my hair. He is a particular kind of artist and demands particular kinds of material. Hair must be straight (at least initially) and geometric. The client must be passive and submit to the stylist's inspiration. Many women are turned down. In his book, Sassoon reports with pride that he has always refused clients who were unwilling to put their heads entirely in his hands. Kenneth, however, cannot remember ever refusing a client.

Harold Melvin at Casdulan does not send clients away either. His salon is the most prestigious in Harlem. "I think we get the majority of women who have a kind of status," he said, but added: "Of course we deal with women on every level. . . . Mostly black, but not only black." Mr. Melvin has medium skin and very kinky hair worn in a natural. His eyes are intelligent and gentle, he looks younger than his thirty years and is handsome in a more traditional way than Sassoon or Kenneth, like a movie star or Jim Brown football-hero type.

Aloof at the beginning of the interview, he then relaxed into very young eagerness. I asked why his status clients didn't go to Kenneth. "Because Kenneth can't give them the service that I can," he said matter-of-factly. "He can't do what I do. He might be able to do it if he wanted to invest the time. . . . When you're dealing with hair that's really rough, it's like a sheet that's been washed and dried and hasn't been pressed. And you first have to smooth the hair in order to [get] the silkiness that you see in the finished product. The hair has to go through certain stages and Kenneth, or white hairdressers, are not really interested in doing that. I think they're fascinated by the idea, they would be fascinated by the idea of handling kinky hair. But it's a real chore. A real job. And if one doesn't know what one is doing, you can destroy the hair. It's much more important for a Negro woman with kinky hair who uses the heat process to have somebody who really cares about her hair." Mr. Melvin uses both heat and chemicals. Since hair often breaks from chemicals alone, this is an extremely risky and difficult job.

Mr. Melvin cares about Negro hair. "I got involved in beauty," he said, "because I used to look at girls hair-wise. They were home in the kitchen doing their own hair. I had three sisters; one had straight hair and the other two didn't. My father had very straight hair, very coal-black wavy hair. And my sister and only one brother—and there were eight other children in the family—they were the only two who had hair like my father. You would think that out of eleven more than two would have a better quality of hair, but it just didn't happen." Kinky hair doesn't bother Mr. Melvin, "because there's nothing I can do about it." Though he is one of the leading authorities on the Afro, having done this style for national magazines and demonstrated it on television, though he wears a natural himself, he is not an advocate. "I happen to think that there is a thing about straight hair that somehow brightens up the complexion and actually does enhance the look of a person."

Mr. Melvin is not intimidated by slogans or fads. He believes each woman must decide what suits her best in hair and makeup, and not be so influenced by white standards that she either copies or rejects them categorically. "I've always wanted to say, Wake up, America. Let's realize that Negroes are not one hue. Negroes are like a flower garden. There's pink, there's yellow, there's reddish-brown, there's dark brown, there's black, there's—well, they just range from the whitest of white to the blackest of black." The spectrum of skin color is matched by the variety in hair, from the tightest kinks to the straightest silken tresses.

"It amazes me that now people are walking around talking about Black Is Beautiful like it was something that happened yesterday," he went on. "I'm so totally and completely amazed, I can never get over it when someone uses the phrase. . . . What happened to those people? Where were they looking? What kind of mirrors were they passing ten years ago, fifteen years ago, twenty years ago? The only value I can really see in the brainwashing that is going on about this Black Is Beautiful thing is that two years ago if you stood in front of a black person and said, 'You are black' and you were three shades lighter than him, he would have wanted to knock you down. You know. Which to me is fantastic. Therefore, you do get value here. Because it removes the sensitivity that these people had before. . . . yes, even from another Negro. And God forbid a white person should say, 'You are black.' Oh God."

Black beauties at Casdulan have their hair done the way they want it, just as the clients of Kenneth do. Some choose the Afro, which Mr. Melvin thinks became a fad more through Miriam Makeba than Malcolm X. He reminded me that Katherine Dunham and her troupe wore naturals, mainly because they were traveling around the world and could find no hairdressers who would properly manage their hair. "However, the word Afro has to be either said Afro-American or you really can't use it. Because the African woman doesn't wear her hair in that kind of shape that these people are wearing." Many of his clients continue to have their hair straightened. This is not necessarily emulation of white America. In Africa some tribes straighten their hair; in America, women have been busy for decades putting permanent waves into straight hair. Whatever texture you have, you want to change; and fashion, in its generosity, will pick up any human trait and raise it to the highest level. The Afro will ride the wave of fashion until it flattens out again.

"American women need constant change," Francesca Ruta pronounced. "They excel in change—good, bad or indifferent. . . . Woman will never be satisfied. No matter how much she achieves and how much is given to her, materialistically or otherwise, her drive, her obsession to have more can never be fulfilled. . . . Because once she's had that freedom—and we all love it, I mean this is the catch we live in—she doesn't want to give it up. Yet she becomes frustrated because her marriage or her relationship with a man isn't what she wants it to be. She really wants to be feminine. Right now we're in a stage where we're rebelling. I will not give up either, I want both. And after she has both, she still hasn't gotten what she wants." After this harsh assessment, Francesca admitted that appearance, and hair in particular, can give a woman considerable assistance in bridging the gap between conflicting roles or can dramatize the particular role that should predominate.

When I came into the salon, Francesca had been redesigning the hair of an old client, a woman who had spent the past year and a half being breadwinner of the family during her husband's severe illness. She had always worn her hair short and straight. Now, the husband was back on his feet again and she came to Francesca for a more feminine style. When I arrived, she was just being combed out and was delighted with her new curls.

I asked Francesca what she did when a woman asked to look different. "How can you give her what she wants? You probably have to know a hell of a lot about her," I suggested.

"No. No I don't. I have to talk to her. I just can't go into styling the hair without having consultations first. I have to know *what* she wants to change; what she was before and what does she want to be now? Why she feels she needs a change so desperately." Francesca then told me a story of a very young girl who came to her as client five months before, having been recommended by a psychologist. "This child was hiding—from what I didn't know. Her hair was completely long and full, covering her face. The minute I would comb her hair back, she'd shake her head and push it forward. She didn't want to see herself. She didn't like herself. Very confused, disturbed child. So I asked her would she be happy if I just shaped her bangs because she had such a pretty face . . . perhaps we could design a hair style where it would be pleasing to her and myself, since [I feel] I'm an authority on hair. And she said, 'What would you do?' And she's all of twelve, thirteen. I said, 'Well, I would cut the front and expose the best feature you have, which is your eyes. . . .' I said, 'I'd leave the back long and give you a partial cut. And if you feel that you'd like the whole complete look with short hair, you'll tell me.' And sure enough, we started cutting and she liked the way her hair was beginning to shape in. I cut it short enough on the sides to make her eyes most predominant. And as I cut . . . she said, 'I like what you've done. You can cut the whole thing now.'" Since then the child has become a client, and her mother came to praise Francesca. Later the father came, having been told by his daughter, "You must meet this nice lady." He explained that he was separated from the girl's mother and the girl had become "confused," not knowing "what she wants to be" or "where she wants to go." She also had not believed she was pretty. As Francesca told it, the father had said, "You've started her off into a whole new phase of life. . . . Now she loves herself." He gave her a horse and the child went on a diet, supplementing it with exercise to reduce her overweight.

Francesca concluded, "With this child, it [the hair style] gave her inner strength, which she was lacking before." This can happen with mature women also, she assured me. "They get tired of being themselves. This is where it starts out. If they can achieve that new image in a beauty salon, then it goes on into their clothes . . . for a whole complete look."

I had first met Francesca when she was working at Daché, where I went every three or four weeks. There Rosemary, whom I called my second mother because in her hands I had been reborn as a blonde, brought purification by fire. My ghastly roots were stripped and toned. My life then had certain rhythms, dictated by the bleaching. Travel was precarious; I underwent the trials of a saint, struggling to maintain my blondness around the world. In Finland, I couldn't explain anything to the hairdresser; in Russia, the official state colors were of revolutionary garishness; in France, most of my hair fell out.

Only in New York was I safe, but sorely tried. I left the hairdresser with a scarf over my head to mask the faint green color of my hair, a necessary first effect because of the persistent, plaguing red in my pigmentation. My eyes were usually red too, from weeping, and I went straight home to bed. The six-hour process had made my scalp break open many times, I had wept with pain while the acids burned my head and I knew my brains were being bleached along with my hair. Scabs formed the first day and I had to keep from scratching. About five days later the miracle would occur, when my hair "oxidized" enough for the green to be replaced by a wonderful ash. For a week or so I was Cinderella at the ball, utterly beautiful, free of pain, bearing my masterpiece of a head for all to admire. By Week Three, brassiness would show and the roots were beginning to sprout. As this condition progressed, I wore scarves and felt dirty. When I could no longer stand the shame, I went back to face the six-hour ordeal and return to Week One.

It was a precarious life. I could never be sure that the magnificent man I had met during Weeks One or Two would even speak to me during my later weeks. I hated being seen during Week Four, and in refusing a party sorrowfully contemplated my last, lost chance for happiness and love. There was no sympathy for my plight—even women friends considered me slightly mad and wondered why I dedicated myself with such conviction to pain and expense. My platinum hair cost me about fifteen hundred dollars a year, and would cost more now.

I still undergo the pain at Francesca's skilled hands because I insist on having both straightening and "blazing" (a streaking process) in one cataclysmic session. This pain, however, is ignored or belittled— probably because unlike a root canal or other dental violences, bleaching is considered a contribution to nothing but vanity. That may be true, but when acids burn open the scalp and pain shocks the client into tears and silence, there is no thought of vanity. As in all other pain, no thought exists at all. One merely endures, struggling to fasten the mind on something else, to remain dignified throughout the torment. It abates, finally, and is forgotten. Next time, a client comes again in a mood of hopefulness and cheer, unlike the dental patient who approaches the chair as though it might be electric. The pain of bleaching brings a reward: visible, obvious—a transformation of self as emphatic as if produced by drugs or alcohol. One leaves the hairdresser happy, and when scabs form one thinks, not of the ordeal at the beauty salon, but of how beautiful one will be at the next party, at dinner or in bed.

For more than six years, Francesca has been meting out the necessary punishment preliminary to grace. When I first came to her, I was no longer a platinum blonde. I was also a published author and my hair, though certainly not natural, had deepened, in compromise of my will and God's.

I go regularly, as many women do, to the beauty salon, which is institutionalized ritual, the changing-house of our society. There women are made more acceptable by bringing out their "true" (i.e. imagined) selves. A client's intimacy with the hairdresser reflects her interest in the transformation and she becomes dependent on him to the degree that she depends on a front. She enters a conspiracy with him, who has taken over a role she is accustomed to playing herself. Now, in front of the mirror, she is no longer both actor and object as in private beauty rituals at home. He becomes an extension of her—both are seen in the mirror only, but now there are two images, and she is the passive recipient of beauty ministrations.

But the closeness between a woman and her hairdresser is not completely dependent on the confessional situation, where reflecting glass and perhaps a cubicle create formality and allow exposure. Women like hairdressers because hairdressers like women. The profession attracts imaginative, artistic types who extend sympathy to a client because they identify with her or can accept her frame of reference. As a group, hairdressers are probably more interested in women than is any other; regardless of their own sexual proclivities or even of their sex, they offer beautification of the female object and irresponsible friendship. But some remain with their own sex, and men's hairdressers are beginning to replace barbers.

At Jerry's, which, like Kenneth's, is owned by the Glemby Corporation, men with money and fame rest comfortably in beauty-shop chairs, tilt back when they're shampooed (in most barber shops, men's hair is washed forward, allowing the man extreme discomfort, a wet front and soap in his eyes) and are offered the privacy of a London cab by means of sliding walls. If Jerry himself works on them or if they're getting color, they have completely private rooms, where they can also have manicures and facials, their shoes shined and a good round of gossip. Clients are men from the entertainment world, politics and business. "I have rich customers," Jerry says. "They're not millionaires. They got like four, five hundred million."

In the chair, they talk politics and stock market, giving Jerry good tips ("You buy this now and sell in three months"). Or they talk about their private lives, clothes ("You know a good shirtmaker?"), deals or health ("You know a good chiropodist?"). They become friends, they depend on Jerry to give them the front they want. I asked Jerry how he decides to style a new client. "Number one, he has to have hair to begin with." Jerry is small, Sicilian (he began barbering at ten in Sicily) with graying hair that he usually dyes and wears just below his ears. "Now, if he has hair . . . I study his features, the way he dresses, I ask what business he's in." Then he washes the hair, combs it in different ways until satisfied by a look that complements facial shape, disguises thick necks and receding hairlines. "Most of the time they leave it to me." And most are satisfied, coming back every few weeks for a fifty-dollar razor haircut, which Jerry began using in 1949, after seeing it at De Fossé in Paris. "I was familiar with the razor cut, but the French glamorized it," Jerry admitted. He used it because "when I got into the trade, everybody wanted his hair straight à la Valentino."

Since then styles have changed. From straight to wavy (usually done with a comb and hair dryer, rarely through permanent waving), and two years ago back to straight. Jerry disapproves of straightening ("breaks the hair, makes it red and doesn't last long") and is pleased that kinky hair and the natural look are in.

He hardly uses hair spray anymore, though men often ask for it. "I was the first one in the world to use hair spray for men. . . . When I first started using it, I got the name as queer, as fag." Now, when spray is almost a standard item, Jerry prefers the loose, unset look of hair.

In the past fifteen years, said Jerry, the attitude toward male grooming has changed ninety percent. "Twenty-five years from now, men will wear lipstick, beauty marks . . . as they used to." At the moment, however, masculine men confine their beauty practices to hair products, scents, deodorants and bronzers. "There's prosperity in this country—thank God for that. More people are traveling," opined the stylist, who had just returned from a few months on the French Riviera, leaving unoccupied his house in East Hampton. Traveling Americans see European beauty practices and want to imitate them, Jerry feels. "The European male spends more money at the barber shop than women do at the beauty shop . . . in France the man spends more than the woman . . . and this is working-class people, not professionals. The wife washes her own hair, she doesn't spend a dime on herself, but he goes to the barber two or three times a week."

But not all is well in Europe. "In England the men are very cheap when it comes to barbering. . . . The cheapest place to get a haircut is in England. . . . They are far back as far as grooming is concerned." Ivan, the men's stylist on Jermyn Street, doesn't even charge more than a dollar fifty for a cut, though his clients are celebrities.

In America, quality must announce itself through price. When the president of CBS went to Jerry, he told other executives and CBS television stars to follow him. When David Susskind suggested another stylist, the president insisted he not go to "the minor league, just the major league."

Now that men's beauty shops find such man-to-man endorsement, the sweet intimacy between client and hairdresser promises to embrace beauty's second sex.

WHAT A PIECE OF WORK IS MAN

❦

Corinna, pride of Drury-Lane . . .
. . . seated on a three-legg'd chair,
Takes off her artificial hair;
Now picking out a crystal eye,
She wipes it clean, and lays it by.
Her eyebrows from a mouse's hide
Stuck on with art on either side,
Pulls off with care, and first displays 'em,
Then in a play-book smoothly lays 'em.
Now dext'rously her plumpers draws,
That serve to fill her hollow jaws,
Untwists a wire, and from her gums
A set of teeth completely comes;
Pulls out the rags contrived to prop
Her flabby dugs, and down they drop.
Proceeding on, the lovely goddess
Unlaces next her steel-ribb'd bodice,
Which, by the operator's skill,
Press down the lumps, the hollows fill. . . .

—Swift, "A Beautiful Young Nymph
Going to Bed"

1

The Man-Made Woman
and the Man Who Made Her

[1] THE WOMAN

Greenwich Village, five o'clock in the afternoon, the girl from Oklahoma was up, in floral lounging pajamas, hair shining and loose over her shoulders, her makeup perfect and the color TV on. She made herself instant coffee (only food in the place) as preparation for the interview and looked through some clippings she'd saved on plastic surgery. When I arrived, she said she was hungry, and I went down to the corner for a scrambled-egg sandwich. She thanked me. "I always have a scrambled-egg sandwich when I wake up. I get hungry." Her voice was soft and drawling. "Oh no, I never wake up before this. I go discothequing all night. I never go out before midnight."

"Then you never get taken to dinner," I commiserated.

"I never eat anyway. I don't like to. I watch out for my figure." Her body was slim, full-breasted and through the lounging pajamas her movements suggested round and hearty hips.

"It's not healthy," I informed her.

The dark eyes smiled in their beautifully applied shadow. "Oh, I take lots of vitamins."

Susie was the perfect replica of something lifelike and cute. She giggled a lot, her face was smooth, her flesh was a vinyl with all the properties of real skin. Her expression was tidy, pleasant, perfectly arranged to advertise the coolness of Coke or the freedom from discomfort that Tampax offers. I'd come to talk about her operation, and she was bright-eyed with love for the role she was about to play, star of the drama she would create, a tale of knives and stitches, chemicals and silicones. "One thing I had done that I think worked for me very well was this dermabrasion. I had deep wrinkles way on top, very, very deep. And I had it done a year ago. And now I want to go back and have, you know, under the eyes and the cheeks and around the mouth."

She told me about it, happily, the pearls that were her teeth gleaming, the face with a translucent shine so realistic one wondered at the genius of whoever had invented the spray. "You don't have any sort of local anesthetic, you just lie down. They give you an injection to relax you, but it really doesn't take an effect until they're finished, you know. It's a scare brush that rotates at very fast speed, and they take your skin, they spray it with some sort of freezing thing, and then they just take the skin off with this brush. . . . Well, no, you can't really see it. You're aware of what's going on, you know. After that you have to sort of lie there while they absorb all the moisture that comes. You know, bleeding and draining and then they bandage you. And you go home like a mummy." Her lips delectated that word, and she laughed. "You really sting for about a day, twenty-four hours. Then you take it off. And you have to sleep with your head up, you can't lie down or do exercise or move around too much. And then after about five days you start soaking your face. You get a crust over your face and after five days it starts peeling. Very painful, yes, I think that's the worst part. Afterward, it's like any skin. If you press it or touch it, it burns a little bit. It takes seven days to two weeks for the crust to come off. After that the skin is very pink, you know."

"Why did you want to have it done?"

Almost a frown on the lovely face, but no, my imagination, that was just the indication of thought and now all was smooth again. "Because I started getting a very unpleasant expression. I had you know frown lines—I don't know, maybe they're from the family but they have been my characteristic. But it bothered me, I didn't want it."

Sorrow for what had been. Then the little face brightened with remembered glory: "Every doctor I've been to thinks I'm crazy you know." We laughed together, a good joke meaning she knew that I knew she was crazy. Why else would she be talking to me? But we both knew, too, that *crazy* was a term for high spirits and a free soul.

"You know, I say I have this problem. They say, Yours is most minor to most people we get." Now she could bring in the doctor, her co-star, introducing romantic interest in the operating theater. "He's terrific, he's handsome. We're the same age, he keeps saying: 'I can't believe we're the same age.' " Now delicious laughter perks for a while, and Susie, who is forty, cuddles up to her joke, that she fooled the man who did the operation. She can't let it go, it was all too good, too reassuring, too funny: "He said I was the youngest patient he'd ever had for a face-lift—yes, that was before my dermabrasion. But then, you know, he was very pleased. And I became like his star patient. And I'd come into the office and everybody would rush up to see me, like I was . . ." She can't hold it back anymore, the little bubbles burst and force out the laughter, fizz of champagne popping the cork. ". . . I was . . . the star, you know."

The face-lift had been done four years ago. The doctor had advised her to wait, but Susie was a girl who always knew her own mind. "I said, 'What do I want to wait? I want it done now.' He said, 'Maybe we'll just do a little patch and see how it works.' And I said, 'I don't want to fool around with experimenting. I want it done.' "

Mistress of her fate, she knew puffy eyes must be brought down. A friend had told her about a man with big bags under his eyes. "He had these removed. They were you know an heritage of his," and she became interested. Her eyes were getting more and more puffy; she went to a "medical doctor" and was given "medications"; but the doctor said it might be sinuses and it might just be age. Susie was thirty-six then and looked much younger—she knows she always looked very young. Her escorts, frugging till dawn, were younger than herself, and night owls must shine in darkness. "The first thing I had done was eyes. That part is the most marvelous that anyone could ever have. They cut underneath, they make an angle up across and down. And they take out all that fat tissue, they pull all that skin up, they trim it off and they sew it back. You wear stitches for about a week. They take them out, you cover it up with makeup and nobody knows."

"You're allowed to wear makeup?"

"I did. My doctor told me not to." Strong Susie, in whom the spirit of dauntless pioneer women has not yet turned flabby. "They say some of them—you know—sort of get bruised. Mine didn't." Of course not. Sweet girl, peering out so fearlessly from under thick black fringes. Sweet Sue, who keeps her hands under the table (she'd shown me the brown spots, queer little bugs of age that made her flesh creep to look at them), whose meals are pills, furniture fur pillows and morning, night. She talks about her eyes and has the glow of an El Greco saint peering into beauty. "I was so pleased with the effect I mean, I had huge eyes after that. I always had little, bitty teeny-tiny bitty eyes. . . . Suddenly I had big eyes you know. So I was so pleased with that, that was so great, I went back to my doctor and I said, 'I don't want to wait ten years, I want it now. I want to have it now, not later.' " (Who could resist such a plea? Who could refuse to take the knife and cut open the face from the temple down along the ear, behind the lobe and then follow the contour of the scalp?) "They take the skin from the frame and cut the skin from the tissue, you know, of the face, and then they pull it and they trim it out and sew it back on. So he said, 'From all that I did, you'll never age.' "

No photos from medical journals or pamphlets by Norman Oren-treich had prepared me for her. Plastic surgery began its upsurge after World War II, when burned and mutilated bodies were made whole again. Man was restored to his function. Children with withered legs walk, ruined faces are repaired and here's a deathless kitten. Surgeons correct the error of mortality. "They put you to sleep for the face-lift. Mine went very well for me. Because I had it done like on Wednesday and they released me on Friday and Thursday they took my bandages off. They wrap you up like a computer.

"On Friday I got out of the hospital and was walking down the street and I was on television." When she laughs, as she does now, her arms jerk helplessly and have no way of joining the hilarity. "Nobody knew. I was walking down the street and they stopped me in front of [a store] for an interview"—laughter rising—"about a writer" —more laughter—"I'd never heard of"—he-he-he-he-he—"a Swedish writer." The laughter competes too vigorously and Susie is held by it a few minutes before she can speak again. "They never dreamed. See, I have this long hair and like it was all coming down, see. You get bruises in back and in the neck and your face gets puffed. But I got a very cute round face. I liked that face, you know, 'cause it was very round. Very poochy-woochy. I really liked that." Susie's joy is trans-fixing, but I'm not yet taking it like a lady, so I avert my face from the hysteria.

When she's calmer, she tells me about the hospital—how clean and modern it was, with no old people anywhere. The doctors, nurses even the patients were all young, and Susie didn't mind sharing a room with an eighteen-year-old who was having her nose fixed as a birthday present from her family. The girl was "wild about" Susie's doctor; he was so handsome, she said, that if he were her doctor, she'd be sick all the time. The hospital was very expensive, but the doctor's bills were most reasonable. Five hundred dollars for the eyes, five hundred dollars for the face.

I watch the tape running, eating every soft word from those small lips. "So yours was a success story," I say, to come back to journalism. "After those two operations, what did you go on to?"

"Oh, after that I had that dermabrasion on my forehead, then I had a chemical peel. Now that was something else. They burn your skin off with acids"—she's laughing again, spilling over in giggles that will drown the words. "They take an acid and they burn your skin off with acid. No [you're not unconscious]. That hurt. That was very painful because I have overly sensitive skin and it burned. It's supposed to burn like for an hour or thirty minutes. For me it burned four hours, and I was crying."

"Why did you have it done?"

"Because I had a lot of freckles. I had an awful lot of freckles and a lot of that uneven skin color, you know, from too much sun exposure?" The word hovered, she grabbed it. "Blotches," she explained with finality, "on my face. And also I did it because they help wrinkles on the forehead. It just made a better color for my skin. Freckles, sunspots . . . I can show you here. . . ." She pulled down the pajama to the level of her nipples. I saw the swell of large breasts and determined to ask her about them later. "I have it on my chest. . . ." The skin had a few freckles and moles, widely dispersed, some very faint. It was ordinary-looking skin, remarkable neither for its radiance nor its impurity. "You see? See, it's all splotchy. They can't do anything with that, though. My face looked like that too."

"Just a few freckles."

"Well, the doctor saw more than average, you know. I went to him; I was a leprechaun."

Why had she done all this? That was the question, but I couldn't rush the drama. It was hers, to be unfolded inch by inch, meaning subservient to the action.

"Did you feel more beautiful after these operations?"

"Yeah, I did. I've always been a very plain and very ordinary person—looking, I think. Except, I don't know, a lot of my friends say I have an interesting face." A tiny pause. "When I had this done, I didn't think I was going to be beautiful." She laughs, to confess her heresy. She's a model, but insists she never underwent plastic surgery for the sake of her profession. "No. No, it's just that I went through an emotional thing, and I decided to do it because of that, I guess. Once I got into it, you know, I just kept on going. I kept wanting more things, more things.

"There's something I forgot to tell you. I had these implants put in. They're plastic bags, I guess. What they did . . . I don't know, I got myself in such a big mess. It was just like a whim, I called the doctor two days before I was going into the hospital to have my eyes done and asked him to do this. And why, I don't know. But my girl-friend and my sister were interested in doing it. I've been to San Francisco and all those girls out there were doing it. So it seemed the thing everybody was doing at the moment, you know. And I had beautiful breasts, I always had a nice body except I was heavier at one time than I am now. I lost about twenty pounds. So I lost a lot in my bosoms. But it didn't bother me. I like nice, cute little bosoms. I love them, in fact."

Her little loves were distorted, made enormous, propped up on her chest like vicious, giant growths that threatened to devour her cuteness and her class. "A small bosom is nice, a big bosom is just deforming. I wanted to just kill myself. The doctor was feeling sick about it. I guess most girls who have this done just want tremendous bosoms. I don't understand it. He said, 'You know, fashions are going to change and big bosoms will be fashionable again.' And I said, 'No. They won't. Ever. They'll never be fashionable again.' I didn't know I was going to be Jayne Mansfield, I really didn't. I mean, I don't have skinny arms, but here I was, these real big bosoms walking on the street like. . . ." She was defeated by the remembered horror of those twin monsters.

"Didn't men whistle?" I asked, to revive her.

"Didn't they! I was so self-conscious. It was in the summertime, when you wear, you know, little things. And I walked out the door one day and there were these young boys standing there. And they said, 'I don't be-*lieve* it!' Of course it was obvious what they were, you know, talking about. And I went swimming and I had this bikini on. I mean, I wore a top, a cover-up. There were these little teen-age girls there and when I took the top off and these huge bosoms—they just shrieked. They shrieked!"

The implants were taken out and she no longer looks "disfigured," so Susie happily contemplates having more things done. I mentioned a thigh lift—it removes excess fat from the upper thigh, but invariably leaves a scar—and she thought the prospect intriguing. Not for now, though. "I haven't any fat. Last year I exercised religiously for three or four months and I had the most terrific body I've ever had in my whole life. Really, I had a terrific body." But exercise is just the finishing touch, the polish on the beautiful object. Of immediate importance, her hands must be operated on. "All the way back when I was twenty, I always knew I'd have plastic surgery done. Really, we talked about it—me and my girlfriends—we all said we were going to do it. And then after I had it done, the face-lift, the doctors decided it's better to have it done at an early age because you don't get the set lines.

"I said I went through an emotional thing. See, I had this guy that I was with for like, four years and he was ten years younger than I was. And that really was what started me off. We broke up, you know, and I started getting really worried that I was ten years older than he was. . . ."

I suggested that others might have chosen analysis—"Yeah, I'd never do that," she said, laughing—and tried to accept themselves. "But you changed yourself, so it's really the reverse of the same thing."

"You mean the other side of analysis? . . . Except I know that that wouldn't have done me any good. Not as happy, you know?"

That was final, I thought. Susie's elation had faded, the greasy sandwich wrappings were on the floor and the light in the room seemed dimmer than before. Susie was restless, in obvious need of action because the night had begun and somewhere not far from this room jukeboxes were warming up. I packed my tape recorder and reached out my hand. "I don't know," she said, still sitting, her eyes sightlessly sweeping the floor near the crumbs, "My life's moved for me. Except this guy that I was with, you know. We went through this horrible thing together really."

I sat down again and she looked at me. "It was just the personality, but of course at the end it got so bad, we really started fighting and he would say really cutting, evil things to me. He hates terrifically."

"Has he seen you changed?"

"Yeah, but he wouldn't say anything. He used to make awful remarks about my age and the way I look, when we were together. He has a girl now, she's eighteen. Very pretty, with these great big round eyes." Susie was silent a few minutes, struggling. "You know? We were going through this horrible thing. He was saying everything to me and I knew as long as I was with him, I wouldn't be able to do this thing."

"You mean plastic surgery? Did you just start with surgery after you broke up?"

"Uh-huh. In fact, I probably felt like breaking it so I could do it. You understand that?"

[2] THE MAN

In a Manhattan brownstone with mossy carpets and oak walls, two dryads—blond and brunette—were chatting with a blond Adonis. They looked at me with mistrust when I entered so near the switchboard's closing time, but the man smiled, gave me his hand and introduced himself as Dr. B., Susie's plastic surgeon. I looked up at his six foot two or three inches and saw a man so perfect that, for a moment, he was laughable. A Marlboro man, a Hollywood hero—a man conforming so strictly to current standards of male beauty that there was nothing to say, nothing but a helpless feminine shrug of acceptance and acknowledgment that the trick had been pulled off. Upstairs, his office added to the fantasy: a room in the castle transformed into a study, where stern ancestors of present rulers stared from velvet walls and tinkling crystal was suspended from the embossed ceiling over the azure carpet. I gave a small grunt and wished the set would come down so I could speak. My only hope was pretending to be a *Vogue* interviewer who could rely on a photographer to supplement my portrait of this Beautiful Person.

"Do you feel any social stigma because of your profession?" I began awkwardly, in medias res. He looked at me benignly, in silence. "There used to be," I explained. "At least I think so. Do people discriminate against your profession anymore?"

"No." His voice was gentle, drifting up from violet banks and hidden ways. "Well, some of the old general surgeons feel plastic surgeons sort of bastardize their trade, you know. But this is narrowing down now because they need plastic surgeons for a lot of work that they do, that they can't finish because they don't know how. But at a cocktail party, you're a hit. You're a hit. All doors are open to plastic surgeons. Socially, this is an accepted thing and people are delighted to have a plastic surgeon at one of their parties."

"Doesn't the hostess worry that the guests might think she's a patient?"

"There's always that possibility, but you know, I've been the guest of quite a few of my patients and it's never really been brought up. It maybe has, but behind my back."

It was easier now; gods should be silent or speak through their oracles only. He could be put in place: the handsome forester from Oklahoma standing tall in a New York room, with high ceilings, an old-fashioned in his hand, smiling down at trouser-suited young women and their unwrinkled mothers, indifferent to long-haired boys or hash-smoking artists. A figure of elegance and as pure as any menthol-smoking dreamer floating down *Life*'s center fold.

The phone lit up. He swiveled his chair away from me and spoke, "No, I don't think what he gave you could have any effect. I told you it would take a few days. But call your dentist and ask him what was in those pills. . . . The swelling isn't supposed to go down yet. . . . O.K., I'll be speaking to you tomorrow." He turned back, a small smile of self-satisfaction hovered a moment and gave way to seriousness.

"Who are your clients?" I asked. "Are they all women?"

"No. I teach quite a bit. My practice is mostly cosmetic surgery—I would say seventy-five percent. It's taking bags from under eyes, too much skin, doing noses, pinning ears back, doing face-lifts, breast work and sometimes taking off flabby abdomens after people have lost a lot of weight. That type of thing. I have a good percentage of males, not necessarily for face-lifts, but for eyelids, for noses, for ears. I'd say my practice—having been in practice only six years—is not what you'd consider the economically elite. I'm just now getting into the sort of socialite groups. The woman who just called was a baroness. Whatever that means."

"Do you ever do surgery without a fee?"

"Well, my fees are reasonable." But he didn't feel he had answered adequately. In New York City, anyone might be a liberal and you always had the tedious feeling that you had to explain. "My associate I think charges about twice as much for the same operations. . . . Well, I have a lot of nurses too. . . . Or if the nurse in the office needs something, I do it essentially for nothing. Maybe for the insurance."

A responsible man, with a generous knife. Dr. B. looked uncomfortable and often during the interview protested that he probably wasn't giving me what I wanted to hear. He'd shown me his new office-in-progress, a room like a sauna, with wooden walls and a soft dance of light. But he was still young and struggling and not at the top by any means. His youngest patient was a three-month-old with a cleft lip, "my oldest face-lift is eighty. She just talked to me this morning, she wanted to have more work done."

"It seemed to me Susie was very young for a face-lift."

"Well, I procrastinated and argued with her for months before I would do anything."

Did he do some kind of psychological testing before taking on a patient? "Well, I spend a lot more time with my patients than the average person does." That, I thought, might be one reason why they became patients. "I think it's very important to talk to them, try to get to know them the best you can in the first interview. Some patients you can know are going to be problems from the very beginning."

"Do you ever refuse to take someone?"

"Oh yes." A good move, moral stamina has been displayed. Let no one get the wrong impression of plastic surgeons. They're human, money isn't everything, after all: you still have standards.

"On grounds that they may be too unstable?"

"Well, that would be one of the grounds, yes. First of all, you never want a patient who's unhappy with their results. And if you cannot do what they want, it's stupid to operate on them. Because you know you have an unhappy patient on your hands, which is bad for your reputation and headache and it's a bother and it goes on for months and months. But you can't always be sure. You can never. I've had some patients I've been a little skeptical about and they've been very beautiful patients. Others seem *very*, very blasé and very intelligent, very open-minded about the whole thing and it turns out they're doing their surgery for some other reason. Say, breast surgery."

I thought of Susie's twin monsters, now dead and unlamented, and of the hard, heavy breasts I'd seen on topless waitresses, young girls who jerked their flesh around as though trying to rub it off. I remembered Susie talking about them. "The cutest one I saw was built like a boy. She was so cute dancing. I don't know, she was completely out of it, you know. She really had a lot of personality. But the others just sort of looked disfigured really."

"Why do women want that done?" I asked the blond doctor.

"Breast surgery?" He was surprised. "It's the overall American image of what is feminine."

"To have large breasts?" I pursued.

"Larger. I don't think they're concerned about making them like they used to. I think all the surgeons are coming down insofar as making large breasts."

Big breasts with erect nipples thrusting against a sweater: a picture of bliss. Strong American women taking power by the balls, only not quite there. "It's a sex symbol," Dr. B. explained. "That is the difference in males and females."

Fair enough. "Is there surgery for making the penis larger?"

He laughed, good-naturedly, and his complexion became pinker. "No."

"That would go over tremendously."

"Certainly would." He laughed; his face seemed contorted in laughter, but the sound was of choking: air sucked in too rapidly, released through coughing. Then he was calm again. "We have one patient in the clinic who had his nose done with what he considers a good result, but it's thrown him for an absolute loop. He is, he admits, he's prepsychotic now, and tremendously fixated on this. And he's been to see me privately on a number of occasions. He wants his old nose back. And it's all very complicated and involved with his sex image—the penis and the nose. One of the old sayings, when you're going through training is, Beware of a male over thirty who wants his nose changed."

We were both pleased that he'd given me what I wanted to hear. The atmosphere by now was genial; his pink laughter had removed all intimidation through his beauty. "Is that true?" I asked.

"Well, I've had very happy patients over thirty. But I think this has to be really considered. I don't mean they're homosexuals or like that. There's something—their sex image is wrong. Something's wrong with their sex lives. But this is just a sort of cookbook-type rule."

Beware of nose jobs and the breast is easy. But there were so many stories, so many case histories. Husbands bringing in wives who were insufficiently developed, mothers bringing in daughters. A woman executive who'd spent her life compensating for flat breasts with successful ad slogans, had silicone implants at age forty and gave it all up for a husband and child. The patients of Dr. Robert Alan Franklyn described in his book, *On Developing Bosom Beauty*, are women in the arts, politics, athletics and less glamorous professions; a model, the daughter of a famous debutante, a black-leather-clad motorcyclist who had demanded whether or not the doctor fixed flats; a nun's sister, an actress who insisted on being operated at midnight for purposes of secrecy, the Negro wife in an interracial marriage and many others, all documented, all with stories so amazingly simplistic one forgets that breasts are not genitals. These little globes take in the women's worlds, two hemispheres around which life must be shaped. And there was Susie, who had had her breasts enlarged on a whim, and Dr. B., who had performed the operation.

"Well, I don't know Susie. I know Susie as you would know a patient, but I don't know. What did she tell you she's had done?" I told him. "She's a pretty good example of someone who wasn't really sure of what she wanted, I think." The good doctor mumbled on to himself, too softly for me to hear. "Well, I don't know whether I can give you really a succinct analysis of my impression. I knew her for a long time." He got up and searched in his desk, then behind the satin screen for her files. I protested that it wasn't necessary, I didn't want him to violate professional ethics, but he continued his search until he returned to his leather chair, successful, the card in his hand. "You can see from this the number of visits I've had from her. So after doing her breast surgery and she admitted that she wasn't so sure what she wanted to begin with, I tried to talk her out of it. And she insisted on having this removed. Well, when they were removed it would have been a disastrous-looking situation, which nobody would have been happy with. Because there was a lot of loose skin. So something had to be done. So we approached this and then she started in on the face situation and it was a long time before I would ever agree to operate on her. And she realized the amount of improvement that was going to occur was not a tremendous amount. Yet she was willing to go through the expense and effort and discomfort and all the things she had to go through to have it. So far as her motivations for this, of course she wanted to look young. I know she was going out with younger men. She used to come in and tell me little stories—well, she met this guy and he thought she was too young for him and he was only thirty. Little stories like that, so I know that her thing is one about age I think. Why, I don't know. How to analyze it."

"Is this the usual motivation for beauty surgery? To look young?"

"Well, it's said. . . ." the pink is returning and he begins breathing as though walking against a strong wind ". . . that every woman . . ." breathlessly, hardly able to get out the words ". . . wants to get laid." Now he chokes again. "Even the eighty-year-old woman?" I ask, and wait for the fit to be over.

"No. This woman walked into my office and she said, 'Now look.' She's a little tiny thing. 'I want to get rid of this mess here' "—the doctor was tugging at his neck, wrinkling the skin for a crepey effect —" 'I can't stand it. And it's not for vanity reasons.' She said, 'I have a very good job and I want to keep it.' And she really did. It turned out that she has a very good situation. It's not just hit miss—what do you call it?—free-lance type of thing. She's working for a very reputable situation. And she probably wants something else done, because she wanted to know the days I'm going to be available next month. Yes, she was very pleased and she sent her daughter to me. Her daughter was old enough to need a face-lift at this point. I asked her today, I said, 'How's your daughter?' And she said, 'She's very, very happy.' Daughter's a married woman, lives in the suburbs, has a family. It would be hard for me to say exactly why she wanted this done. Maybe she was feeling insecure with her husband. These are the ones you really have to beware of, that come in and say. 'My husband is running around with someone else. And I feel that if I had my nose fixed, or breast tucked up, that I might be able to keep him.' And a lot of people will say, 'I'm in a very good job.' I've had a man come to me and say, 'You know, it's impossible now to get into a new situation in advertising if you're over thirty.' Because you know the emphasis on youth today is phenomenal. There are whole firms that have nobody over thirty. Not that I'm involved with them, but this is things I hear."

Your face is your fortune then. If all men looked like Dr. B., as ageless, perfected, the physiognomy supplying its own retouching materials, then companies could employ septuagenarians and no one would know. Eternally young men with decades of experience could rule with confidence, free of ulcers and competition. "So men have face-lifts."

"Yes, but less frequently than females. I have one interesting guy whose eyelids I did the first year I was in practice. He had the most horrendous bags under his eyes that I've ever seen, at about age forty. He has an antique shop here in New York and he's very involved with antique shows and that type thing. He came back about four years later and he said, 'You know, I spend all of my working time sort of finishing up and making old furniture look good. And I don't know why I should let my face go, why shouldn't I tack this up too?' So I did a face-lift on him and he's been very pleased with it. He just said, 'Why not look better? I don't see the point.' "

The same patient later had his hair transplanted, but not by Dr. B., who finds the operation too tedious. Hair transplants are becoming more and more common in New York and California, though it was Norman Orentreich in New York who probably started this technique of cutting small circles of scalp with living hair from the back of the head, then stitching them into the front. The antique-store owner was very pleased by his transplants, which Dr. B feels resemble cobblestones.

"I wonder how it feels to have so many things done to you."

Dr. B. smiled. "Well, I'll tell you. I had a little plastic surgery, strictly cosmetic surgery, myself. And I'll tell you my approach to it. I looked at myself and I've never been overweight. Not that I've had to watch it. I eat whatever I want to. But I had a double chin. And I started analyzing the situation and I had a receding chin and so the measurement of the tip of my chin to the hyoid bone here was quite short. So this tissue, which has a tendency to ball up, still does as you can see, and it's not because of overweight." (I saw no tissues balling up, but didn't want to interrupt. I had no idea how a balled-up tissue was supposed to look.) "So I had a chin implant. This was just an idea. It's a silicone, preformed little implant that goes in your chin. It's inserted through a little incision here and it fits right over the bone. Usually there's no problem in the chin. So your profile is —" His neck rose like a small periscope, proudly bearing the head with perfect profile. There was a moment of anticipated awe. If Douglas Fairbanks were to have done such a thing in a room alone with a woman, would he later have faced a damages claim? What was I to do if the sense of beauty overpowered me completely? That was all merely anticipation, however. The actual profile in sight, I observed it as coolly as I might a scar after having been told of the original injury six months before. "Did you feel different?" inquired the journalist.

"Well, I can show you the photographs. Quite a remarkable difference in the amount of fat that's here."

"Did you feel like a new man?"

"No, I didn't feel like a new man. I feel it looks better here." He was sitting very straight. "There's been a tremendous change in the public attitude toward cosmetic surgery. Used to be very hush-hush, you know. A woman would never tell anyone she'd had her face lifted. She'd go to her grave with this secret. But now it's discussed openly. Some of them still do come in with a bit of guilt feelings about it. Well, why can't I grow old gracefully? And a lot of them will bring this up: 'Now what do you think, doctor? Do you think I should? And when is the best time?' And I say to them, 'I think the best time to have your face lifted is when you feel it needs it and the doctor agrees that he can do enough to satisfy you.'" He paused, to recollect the many images in his mind. All the supplicants, the petitioners who had come to him pleading, "Doctor, what must I do? How should it be done? When?" And his calm answers. "It will be done when it must; it will be done as it can; it will be done when it wants itself done." To him had come all the suffering, against whom God had committed sins of omission or commission, those whose face showed age though their minds had destroyed it; those whose breasts were small though their femaleness surged through their blood. "I've seen dramatic changes in people, especially girls with the breast implants. They come in little mousy-looking things like this"—he demonstrated by hunching over his chest, trying to imitate a chicken-breasted female—"and you see them after they've been discharged and they've gone out and they have a new wardrobe. Oh, it's not a normal breast, there is a difference. But in clothes you can't tell. Can't tell even in a brassiere. You'd have to palpate it. Amazing thing that happens with a woman who has breast surgery—she loses all modesty. I've seen girls that have had their breasts built up practically show them to you in the elevator. And talk about it as if, you know, they had painted their nails."

"So the breasts take on a life of their own."

"One thing, I think the whole business of the breast as a sexual organ is overrated. For the most part. I know males—being a male and talking to other males—there's not nearly so much interest from the male standpoint in breasts, except for the looks. And a man can be very proud of his wife, it can give him much more pleasure to see her looking beautiful, with a low-cut gown on and nice figure than he'll ever get out of what's in bed. Especially after you know, the initial—the honeymoon." We both laugh; it's all gone splendidly. In the best of all possible worlds, women can be beautiful and men can remain young. Optimism rules. Candide in his brownstone restores the look of innocence. All very reasonable: psyches can be trained, patterns of behavior can be altered; why should faces and bodies be denied at the feast of human adaptiveness?

"But what happens if surgery doesn't work? Or what happens if a woman comes to you expecting her life to change because she'll look different, and then her life doesn't change?" This, I knew, happened to addicts of every kind, the alcoholic who goes on the wagon only to have his wife leave him and he falls off with a thud; or the overweight person who takes off a hundred pounds and finds life in exactly the same messy state it was in before, so shoots himself. A bump on the nose can justify rejection, but without the bump, what has one to fall back on? "Isn't there a danger of depression, even suicidal impulses?"

"Oh absolutely. Absolutely. I never have had one that's gotten to *that* degree, I don't think. Possibly one patient who had an image that she was very much like Zsa Zsa Gabor. But totally different, I mean. But totally different. Basic structures of her face and everything were totally different. With a round face, a short neck—fat neck—and I talked to her longer than I would ordinarily talk to a patient, explaining where the difficulty lay in getting a dramatic, fantastic result with a face-lift. She seemed to be very intelligent about the whole thing, and from the moment I took her dressing off, she started crying. I think that's the only seriously unhappy patient that I've had." I wondered about the poor guy with the perfect nose who admits he's prepsychotic, but I left him to his sex problems.

The need for beauty, an image, the need to "get laid," those were all behind it. But the special fear was growing old. "Don't you think

Americans have a fear of aging that doesn't exist to the same degree anywhere else?" I asked as my last question.

"I don't know about that." He smiled, his eyes were ready with a joke. "I think Hungarian women are the most vain creatures who ever walked on the earth."

"Maybe the standards of beauty could be changed. Perhaps age could be seen to give character. We could start training the population that wrinkles are beautiful."

"I hope not," he said fiercely. "I hope not." Then he showed me to the door.

2

Only Correct

Cosmetic surgery is the fairy godmother of the beauty industry. With her, "all losses are restored and sorrows end." Her wand (a knife) brings youth, sexiness and freedom from blemish. All the promises of cosmetics are mere metaphors compared to surgery's achievements.

"There are two major areas of medical concern in dealing with the plastic-surgery patient," write Jacobson et al.* "One is the *anatomic deformity* existing as a consequence of genetic, infectious, neo-plastic or traumatic processes. The other is the *sense of deformity*, an intense personal experience of the patient." This experience leads men, women and adolescents to change the shape of their noses, breasts, abdomens, thighs and hips; to change the texture of their skin, have their ears pinned back, wrinkles removed, hair grafted from one part of the scalp to another or racial characteristics modified. Surgery, more than anything else, offers the hope of seeming what one has not become. The paper explains further: "Emotional disturbances are not uncommon among patients having plastic surgery. Numerous psychologic issues can be represented by a patient's anatomic concerns."

A person's view of himself is largely a function of society. Deformed children don't recognize their deformity until the age of four or five, when the body image develops. According to Jeffrey Kramer, psychiatrist in charge of the Day Center at New York's Roosevelt Hospital,

* "Psychiatric Contributions to the Clinical Management of Plastic-Surgery Patients," Wayne E. Jacobson, Eugene Meyer, and M. T. Edgerton, *Postgraduate Medicine*; Vol. 29, No. 5; May, 1961.

"people who see themselves only as objects are infants." The object-self can become a substitute for self-knowledge; and the "sense of identity" has become a crucial theme in American literature because lack of privacy has led to fragmentation and objectification of the personality.

"Partly as a result of exposure to advertising propaganda and questionable publicity, many physically normal women develop an almost paralyzing self-consciousness focused on the feeling that they do not have the correct size bosom. Whether one views them as the victims of the attitudes of a crass society, or as uniquely distorted character problems in a psychiatric sense, none-the-less, their lives and often the lives of their husbands and families are made miserable by the development of such conflicts." This was the preliminary finding of Drs. Edgerton and McClary at Johns Hopkins in their study of psychiatric implications of breast enlarging.* Decrease of breast size, they found, is "primarily an anatomical problem" and women can suffer physical pain or discomfort from oversized breasts. The operation is unpleasant. Incisions are made around the base of the breast and up to the nipple. Because the nipple would be pulled down under the breast, it is cut out and then stitched to a higher position. The nipple is then naturally insensitive, and scars usually remain on the breast.

"In contrast," state the authors, "augmentation mammaplasty [breast enlarging] . . . is usually requested by patients with emotional problems and occasionally with no obvious anatomical defects." This operation is relatively new as now performed. Originally, breasts were made larger by cutting fat from the buttocks and reimplanting it through a large incision. The fat would melt, scars would remain and the buttocks had sad depressions. Two erotic areas became disadvantaged instead of one. Then paraffin was tried and later, silicone injections.

Silicone is probably the most controversial product in plastic surgery. It has been used to remove wrinkles, "plump out" aging skin, build up atrophied or withered parts of the body and increase breast size. It's a fine product in its place, but unfortunately it travels.

---

* "Augmentation Mammaplasty—Psychiatric Implications and Surgical Indications," M. T. Edgerton and A. R. McClary, *Plastic and Reconstructive Surgery*; Vol. 21, No. 4; April, 1958.

Tests are now being conducted at New York University in which rats and mice are injected with such extreme doses of silicone that they are incapable of movement. Later autopsies show silicone in the liver, adrenals, kidneys and occasionally other organs. The substance has been made illegal for interstate commerce after two deaths—in France and California—resulting from injections of silicone into the breasts.*

The early topless waitresses and some Hollywood stars were silicone phenomena. In the fifties, plastic sponges began to be used as implants in place of injections. Now the most popular material is an inert silicone foam, placed between the chest wall and breast, forcing out the natural breast and interfering with neither sensitivity nor milk production. During pregnancy, the breasts will expand normally and decrease later. Few women with plastic implants try to nurse their child (I came across only one example in my reading and interviews) and a young surgeon told me, "She's more concerned with the looks than the function," adding: "I don't think I would advise a patient to breast-feed."

Women who have this operation come from every class. Most have been small-breasted since adolescence, though a sizable minority hope to rectify the ravages of childbirth after the postpartum period had shriveled or shrunk their breasts. Some women are remarkably flat-chested, like men; some have small but abnormally drooping breasts; some have marked assymetry and some (like Susie) have normal or even larger than normal breasts. The surgeon generally tries to find a compromise between the hopes of the patient and his sense of aesthetics.

Because America is so mammarian, small-breasted women can become depressed, hysterical and self-hating. Surgery is a way to fulfillment, if not of womanhood, then of its stereotype. In two Johns

---

* The deputy director of the Food and Drug Administration wrote to me: "Under the new drug regulations, a silicone may not be distributed for injection in humans unless the sponsor has accumulated satisfactory evidence of safety in laboratory animals and has filed an acceptable notice of claimed investigational exemption for a new drug, providing for its use." The deputy director also informed me, "There has never been on file a claimed investigational exemption providing for the distribution of silicone intended for tissue augmentation by injection in the mammary area. . . ."

Hopkins studies * of eighty-four women between the ages of seventeen and fifty-two with plastic implants, it was found that the average patient is white, Protestant, married, between twenty-seven and thirty-three years old, middle class and with one or more children. Two-thirds of the patients had a sense of inferiority through breast size since adolescence; one-third felt inferior only since the postpartum period. They were self-conscious about going to beaches, trying on dresses or comparing themselves with another woman (often a sister or mother). Very few showed a desire "to further exhibitionistic tendencies or to exploit sexual attractiveness to men for narcissistic gratification." Most had a history of depressions, brief or lasting. "Superficially, these patients presented themselves as lively and efficient women with accents on feminine attractiveness and easy sociability. This presentation in many cases had qualities of the so-called 'hysterical personality' . . . chronic underlying low self-esteem . . . linkage of depressive feelings and a sense of inadequacy of the breasts. . . ."

They had unhappy childhoods, often with alcoholism or paranoia in the father, anxiety and depression in the mother. ("This," write the authors, "is in sharp and interesting contrast to the average female patient who seeks rhinoplasty [a nose job].") Most have had a lot of surgery. If they are not divorced or separated, their marriages show "intense strain or turbulence." Almost all women were the dominant partners in their marriages.

Despite their desire for larger breasts, they felt they would be turned down by plastic surgeons, that their small breasts were an unalterable "punishment." The authors suggest that "the deepest meaning of the punishment of having no breasts (or small breasts) was related to guilt about affectionate and sexual feelings for their fathers. Despite the commonly held view that a woman's breasts are a direct connection with her femininity and therefore with her mother, our data in this group of patients regularly supports the view that the size of the breasts was felt to be a measure of a father's love—'that something a girl should get from her father.' . . . The phallic sym-

* Edgerton and McClary, *op. cit.*; and "Augmentation Mammaplasty—II. Further Surgical and Psychiatric Evaluation," M. T. Edgerton, E. Meyer and W. E. Jacobson, *Plastic and Reconstructive Surgery*; Vol. 27, No. 3; March, 1961

bolism of the breast has been frequently recognized." Since fathers in this group were generally passive, "it might indeed be femininity that the girl is getting from her father and that his 'phallic' qualities are more gentle and giving than the mother's."

A ten-year survey of adolescent plastic surgery patients* showed that teen-age girls undergoing mammaplasty were similar to adults, also feeling inadequate and unfeminine, showing hysterical and depressive character traits and with a bad family situation. The major difference was that adults came for surgery at a time-of-life crisis (usually marriage), while the girls were mostly concerned with boys and how to get them.

Almost all operations were successful, for both adolescents and adults. Many patients underwent psychiatric care before and after surgery and, whether through the surgeon's or psychiatrist's skill, they seemed able to make a lasting change in their self-image. ". . . the prediction that some other fixation would develop has not been borne out." To the authors' astonishment, "the patients found wiser, more sober and deliberate solutions to problems after the operations. . . ."

A larger bosom feminizes a woman in America, where breast size doesn't represent fertility or maternity, but has become a measure of sexual potency. Breasts are a sex object *per se* and nubile girls compare to see who's bigger. Since sexual roles in America are stereotyped but not standardized (unlike Italy, for example), a woman is often unsure of what her womanhood means or how she should exhibit it. Prudery, anatomy and fashion prevent her from displaying her genitals, so she makes prominent a sexual characteristic that can't be overlooked. If her breasts are enormous, she becomes whistle bait and is constantly reassured that she is an object desired by men. To be desirable, even as object, is better than being overlooked.

Although women of every class and occupation undergo this operation, socialites and professional women don't want gigantic breasts. The dean of women at a large university gained confidence and ease from a breast operation, even though her breasts are still small. Women with social power or confidence in their own abilities don't

---

* "Psychiatric-Surgical Approach to Adolescent Disturbance in Self-Image," Norman J. Knorr, J. E. Hoopes, and Milton T. Edgerton. *Plastic and Reconstructive Surgery*; Vol. 41, No. 3; March, 1968.

want great "boobs" or "tits" advertising their sexual pseudopower. Large breasts are not fashionable and not very nice. Fashion authorities dislike big bosoms and the trend is to de-emphasize them. "The bra is finally a fashion accessory," announces *Women's Wear Daily*.

But millions of women are obsessed with breast size, though relatively few undergo surgery. They may have religious or moral scruples; they may be physically afraid of the operation; perhaps they can't afford it. For them, there is a large bust-developing industry. Padded bras are advertised and sold openly. But, though American men seem more concerned about the illusion of a large bosom than with the actual stuff, women themselves often feel that padding is "phony" or "cheating." A patient in the Johns Hopkins study explained, "One might be in an accident and be found out and feel so ashamed that one couldn't face people again." So padding is sold mainly as an "uplift," not as a substitute. It's the real thing women are after.

Bust developers of at least a dozen varieties are strenuously advertised in magazines and through the mails. Ads rarely reveal what method is used, but almost all promise discretion ("Will be mailed to you in plain wrapper"). The Voluptuous Method advises: "DISCOVER what gives some Special Hollywood, European and Topless waitresses (sic)—their Big, Big Bosom measurements." Discovery lies in a small booklet with badly typed instructions for exercises. The same solution lies behind the London Girl Method. "So you are small busted. You live with it. You tell yourself you are lucky to be small. . . . So who needs to look like a sex image, who indeed. Then it happens again. You see a well endowed girl with inches to spare. Your longing and envy returns to haunt you again and again. . . ."

Some methods offer a gadget to exercise with; best known of these is the Mark Eden, a pink plastic device for $9.95 that resembles a jawbone, with a hard spring and leather strip inside. The ad gives convincing testimony in before-and-after pictures of women who have amply profited.

For the more lazy, there are creams, hormone creams, pills with or without hormones, massage kits, "chemical" treatments (usually bottles containing mainly water), suction devices, electricity, vitamins and breast douches. "Try this amazing new exclusive discovery at once. Contains 40,000 units of estrogenic Hormones." Or: "PRO-FORMA contains no harmful drugs, chemicals or hormones. You have nothing to lose . . . just a lovely, more youthful bosom to gain."

Frenziedly, on the sad quest for feminine potency, millions of American women dedicate themselves to a medically impossible proposition: that anything at all can actually make breasts grow. Breasts have no muscles and can't be increased through exercise (though the muscles around them can be strengthened and perhaps give an illusion of greater fullness by slightly correcting the sag). No pills, creams or any of the other methods have added a centimeter. One can modify breast size only through general weight gain or loss, the hormonal changes of childbirth and lactation and through surgery. But the greatest of these is surgery.

Though many cultures cut into the body to make it more beautiful, breasts are left alone. Margaret Mead pointed out that "what is really peculiar is that breasts are so sexual in America." With no attempt at humor, she said, "Our general handling of breasts, separating the mother from breast feeding . . . is extremely artificial." Breasts stand alone, monuments to the American fallacy that biggest means best.

Other cultures tattoo and scarify. In Bali, children have their teeth painfully filed. Body incisions, like the cutting of hair, are usually part of social ritual and indicate a change of status or major achievement. Our plastic surgery serves another purpose: to enhance the individual as individual, making him more sexually attractive and more acceptable to the society and economy. Whether or not your face is your fortune, you can take steps to prevent its being your misfortune.

Dermabrasions and chemical peel remove warts, wens and wrinkles by taking off the outer layer of skin. If the wrinkles are too deep, they can be fattened through injections. Though a young doctor told me that silicone is losing favor with plastic surgeons, he added: "Orentreich uses it as if this was the answer to every possible problem a woman could have."

Norman Orentreich is a well-known plastic surgeon with a fashionable clientele, who habitually brings out pamphlets reporting progress in his experiments with dogs, rats and aging humans. He offers the standard operations—face-lifts cost between one thousand and five thousand dollars—but specializes in silicone treatments and hair transplants. He is reluctant to do chemical peels because he believes the phenol used can be absorbed by the kidneys. He prefers dermabrasion, which allows control of the depth to which the skin is penetrated, and uses it for acne scars, minor wrinkles, discolorations and brown spots sometimes caused by contraceptive pills.

To correct bony hands, Dr. Orentreich injects silicone. (This is the operation Susie was contemplating next.) Dr. Orentreich also uses silicone for deep facial wrinkles. Other doctors are skeptical. "We've run into a lot of problems that people thought they were correcting with silicone, like putting it in eyelids, and they end up with lumps that have to be dissected out," said a Manhattan surgeon. " 'Course you got a bad problem there. You see a woman whose cheeks are all blown up. Naturally if you fill the cheeks enough, you're going to get rid of the wrinkles, but that's not the approach. The thing's got to go back to where it used to be."

Orentreich's greatest fame probably rests on hair transplants: plugs are cut out of scalp areas where hair is growing and are then stitched, with hair follicles intact, to the bald part. In his many writings, the doctor has suggested a more effective means of retaining hair: "Eunuchs . . . don't become bald, regardless of age or hereditary disposition. If a man is castrated after he has begun to lose hair, the hair loss will be completely arrested." This method is even more unpopular than hair transplants.

On the head, many operations are performed successfully. Scars are rare with eye-lifts, face-lifts, neck-lifts, nose or ear operations (whereas thighs, arms, abdomens usually show bad scarring). The face-lift is queen of cosmetic surgery, the most radical incision (which can go completely around the scalp from temple to temple) and the most popular of all luxury operations. It offers fulfillment of the most serious American dream: never to die and always to be young. Youth means love and success. Men and women have face-lifts for similar reasons though women still emphasize romance, men finance.

Face-lifts cost thousands of dollars, require thousands of stitches and take a month or six weeks to recover from. The operation is usually repeated every few years and is enthusiastically undergone by housewives, salesmen, executives and career women, who all must believe, with *Women's Wear Daily*, that "if you don't conform to the standard of physical beauty communicated by the 'image-makers' in this country, the good life may pass you by." Later in the same *WWD* article on the Institute of Reconstructive Plastic Surgery, one learns: "The whole thing has to do with self-respect and the idea of improving yourself, which is just part of the American way of life."

An unattributed quote, presumably by a surgeon, gives the criterion for success: "If the patient gets married, then we know we were successful," and finally one learns the psychosociological basis for face-lifts: "In our youth-oriented society, age is something that is now associated with economic consequences."

Some Americans might prefer to leave the country, at least for their operations. Abroad, plastic surgery is cheaper, and a European or Asian holiday gives time for the wounds of youth to heal. Tokyo's Jujin Hospital performs one hundred plastic-surgery operations a day, many on foreigners (Americans and South Vietnamese make up forty-five percent of non-Japanese). Breasts are enlarged for two hundred twenty-four dollars; Californians, who come regularly, receive face-lifts, and the most popular operation is on Oriental eyes, giving them a fold with silicone and making them more rounded, more Western. Dr. Umezawa, head of the hospital, says, "Americans . . . bring their friends here and have no inhibitions about their surgical operations. . . . Japanese, on the other hand, are very furtive. . . . They sneak into the hospital through a back door and they would never think of telling anyone about their operation."

But Americans are given no chance for secrecy. "American women's worries show up right in their faces," says "facial-tuck" specialist Dr. Jerome Comet Klein, "and they have lots of them." The doctor finds worries neither beautiful nor sexy and to remove their signs cuts two inches in front of the ear, one inch behind, tucks in excess skin and sends his patients home fifteen minutes later.

Those with more time can try the Ever-Young method controlled by H. Edward Wolf. Patients wear a tape mask for at least forty hours, allowing the outer skin to be dissolved by chemicals. Then the lower layer is given "cellular regeneration," an unspecified process. *Women's Wear Daily* comments favorably on this two-thousand-dollar method, and reports: "Employers and husbands who desire mature minds behind youthful faces have been a factor in the number of women who have taken the treatment and men, in the highly competitive field of American business, must always keep an eye on the younger men coming up behind." (The suggestion of sodomy and a reversed Cyclops was surely unintentional.)

Cosmetics companies are beginning to manufacture "instant" face-lifts and do-it-yourself facial peels. Makeup artists and hairdressers tape chin or hairline to give a lift, and Hollywood's makeup kings hint darkly that they could, if they felt like it, manufacture home face-lifts.

Wherever they go and however they do it, Americans who seek cosmetic surgery without obvious reason are an unbalanced crew. Often, their hopes for surgery are unrealistic. Jacobson et al. explain, "Where the patient's expectations of the surgical results are highly colored by magical and grandiose ideas, it is clearly unwise to undertake elective surgery . . . The surgeon's skillful technical results become lost in the patient's enduring psychopathologic state."

Young people, curiously, are generally realistic. Knorr et al. found that "establishment of self-identity is the formative stages in the adolescent. For this reason, physical changes via cosmetic surgery are more easily integrated into the body image percept by the adolescent, and postoperative emotional disturbances and identity crises are of lesser frequency and severity than those encountered in adults." However, the authors note, very immature adolescents rarely even think of cosmetic surgery. "A certain level of maturity is essential to undertaking serious consideration of changing one's appearance."

The patients who underwent rhinoplasties were the most intelligent and rational of the group. Dermabrasion for acne, on the other hand, was not successful because adolescent patients had unrealistic hopes about the result. The exception to this was socially mobile Negroes with facial scars. According to the authors, these patients felt that others assumed the scars to be from knife fights. Later surgical scars brought these patients "relief of depressive symptoms."

Another study * of patients with minimal deformity showed that sixteen percent were psychotic, twenty percent neurotic and thirty-five percent had some personality-trait disorder. The healthiest group, psychiatrically, were females seeking rhinoplasties. Males showed more serious psychiatric disorders than females, and the strongest depressive reactions were found in patients complaining of minor skin defects.

Patients like Susie, who "kept wanting more things, more things,"

* "Surgical-Psychiatric Study of Patients Seeking Plastic (Cosmetic) Surgery: Ninety-Eight Consecutive Patients With Minimal Deformity," M. T. Edgerton, W. E. Jacobson and E. Meyer, *British Journal of Plastic Surgery*; Vol. XIII, No. 2; July, 1960.

are often ambulatory schizophrenics. A paper entitled "The 'Insatiable' Cosmetic Surgery Patient" * says these people "often present very minimal deformity. Although they may be extremely convincing in describing their feelings of deformity and their need for surgery, the surgeon's judgement of the magnitude of the deformity usually does not correlate well with that of the patient."

Fifty-one percent of surgeons categorically refuse such patients; thirty-six percent wait for psychiatric "clearance" and thirteen percent take them on. These patients are usually male, single, between twenty and thirty-five. They show low self-esteem, hyposexuality and are unable to develop good personal relations. "Failure to make significant and meaningful long-term relationships is equated by patients with their sense of deformity. They may seem a paradox, since the examiner may observe that they can relate to others only via the deformity."

Insatiable patients also have grandiose and unrealistic ambitions, are so extremely obsessed with appearance that they are incapable of any constructive action and are too anxious to be able to tell the surgeon what alteration they desire. With the doctor, they are passive and obsequious unless things are not going the way they intended. Then these patients become aggressive to the point of legal threats. They are vague about what surgery should achieve and are dissatisfied after their postoperative enthusiasm. One surgeon who refuses them explained, "They give me the creeps!" Another tersely offered: "Dynamite! Life is too short!"

Though the authors say some patients actually are helped through the combination of surgery and psychotherapy, they point out that patients who are denied either or both neither deteriorate nor decompensate. "The natural course of their illness [ambulatory schizophrenia] seems to abate in their late thirties. The decreased motivation for surgery at this age might be the result of a 'burning out' process similar to that recognized in the acute, overt schizophrenic at about the same age."

When I mentioned this article to Dr. James A. Brussel, psychiatrist and criminologist, he said, "Oh, nuts. I know a certain very internationally known radio commentator that would argue with that. He's had over twenty-odd plastic operations done: his ears lifted, his nose

* "The 'Insatiable' Cosmetic Surgery Patient," N. J. Knorr, M. T. Edgerton and J. E. Hoopes, *Plastic and Reconstructive Surgery*; Vol. 40, No. 3; September, 1967.

shifted, his teeth up, his brow lowered, his chin fixed. Oh no, he would differ with you on that. . . ."

Inspired by psychosis or vanity, a person comes to plastic surgery with the hope of being physically transformed into the image he has of himself. For some, this means changing an inadequate or too-prominent feature. For many, it means staying or becoming young. Rejuvenation is available in all forms and prices. Thankfully, it is beyond the scope of this book.*

Plastic surgery believes, with nineteenth-century liberalism, that man is perfectible, man is a creature of progress. Man perfects men into the image he has of God. The mold, the standard of beauty is accepted on trust and through conditioning. A beautiful man is tall, muscular and youthful; a beautiful woman is slim, with large breasts, shining hair and taut skin. Cocteau wrote: "A defect of the soul cannot be corrected on the face—but a defect of the face, if you *can* correct it, can correct a soul," and this has become the favorite quotation of Revlon's Bill Mandel. In this best of all possible worlds, man is his own master. The growth of social sciences and medicine have made survival of the fittest obsolete. Every human must be given opportunity to participate in the society, but in return must make himself acceptable to his fellow citizens. Ugly people are weighed down by the sickness of their nonconformity. They will not marry, not find good jobs, not contribute happily to the family of man. They, and old people, are plainly the misfits of America. The great society is also beautiful, and officials know that to rehabilitate personality one must first remove the stigma of ugliness.

Criminals, drug addicts and psychotics are given plastic surgery for the same reason that they are taught makeup, grooming, fashion or body-building. By removing the offending feature—a large nose, a birthmark, scars from the needle—one allows the misfit to regain "self-respect" and become like others. Mary Lindsay, former warden of the Women's House of Detention in New York, said that plastic surgery was available to all inmates who requested it. "We had one

* *The Youth Doctors* (Coward McCann, 1968), by Patrick M. McGrady, discusses and eulogizes doctors, charlatans and clients dedicated to the quest for physical rejuvenation. Since I find this quest hopeless and the techniques, therefore, frivolous, I am very grateful to the author for having written the book. Anyone interested in the subject may read it profitably.

girl who was really just terribly burned. Oh, she was awful. And she was one of the classic cases. They made a movie of the before and after and showed it to the inmates and they were all permitted to come to the chapel to see [it]. And after seeing the movie some of them decided that they would like to have plastic surgery." Those who choose it must wait until their discharge, so that visits to a doctor or hospital will not interfere with the sentence to be served. And results are not often rehabilitating, as seen in the subsequent history of the burned woman: "She came back later [*i.e.*, to serve another term]. She was quite an old woman—old as they get in jail, in her late forties or fifties. And she came back several times, and she was very pleased. She had some sort of innocuous way of supporting herself, not really innocuous, it was partly shoplifting and partially asking on subways. But at her age I guess it was too late for her to do anything else. But she was quite a nice person."

The female prison population is much smaller than the male. Mrs. Lindsay explained that male prisoners resemble the general population in intelligence and "various other characteristics," but female prisoners are below average. "I think there's a very good reason for that. People are very good to women, and they try to keep them out of prison. Now, when they do go to prison, it's because they are completely incorrigible and *not very good-looking* [my italics]. . . . It starts with the complainer [who's] less apt to make a severe case against a woman and an attractive young woman. Then the police are less apt to go after an attractive young woman. . . . All along the way they're very kind to women. It doesn't matter whether the crime is murder or prostitution or shoplifting or armed robbery or whatever it is. When they're not [kind], it's because the woman's record is *so* bad, or because as I say, she is so unattractive, that they don't have the usual male feeling of protection." Mary Lindsay was convinced that unattractiveness encourages criminality.

Plastic surgery, especially when it corrects an obvious deformity, and particularly if done at an early age, can certainly have therapeutic or normalizing effects. For drug addicts, it can remove the evidence of their present or former addiction. At Daytop, a rehabilitation center on Staten Island, cosmetic dentistry is performed. The teeth of drug addicts are generally discolored and partly ruined.

Whether or not defects of the soul can be corrected through transforming the face or body by surgery, any concerted effort to improve a patient or inmate will probably give that person a stronger sense of himself. Mrs. Lindsay talked about a prostitute who was fat, ugly and had a large birthmark discoloring her face. Her clients were mainly bums, and she often "cruised the bull" (picked up a policeman) in order to be arrested. She repeatedly expressed her pleasure at being back again in the Women's House of Detention. "I certainly think it would have meant a great deal to a girl like Agatha if her mother would have decided to care a little bit for her," said Mrs. Lindsay. "I think if somebody had waved a magic wand and said, 'You have plastic surgery,' it would have been something too, even if it can't help at all."

"Just the attention?" I asked.

"Yes."

Among criminals, schizophrenics and juvenile delinquents, the self-image is bad. Such people either distort or disregard themselves and almost invariably feel no pride in who they are or how they look. The director of Start, a home for delinquent girls, told me: "You know how they see themselves? You want to know what they say? 'I'm nothing but shit. I'm a pile of shit.'"

If this self-image is reinforced by others, any antisocial tendencies naturally increase. But the division of the beautiful and ugly, or the acceptable and nonacceptable is not objective. Many people hate the way they look, even though others find them presentable or even attractive. Criminals and mental patients often ignore their external appearances; at the other extreme, models and actresses (or actors) can be totally narcissistic, continually engrossed with their bodies and faces and still dislike their looks. When your physical being is your livelihood, you must be perfect. Attractive girls, and sometimes boys, who decide to become models often invest their initial capital in cosmetic surgery. Makeup can disguise a lot, but not a bump on the nose or a double chin. Marilyn Monroe, the story goes, was just an aspiring starlet with no future until a plastic implant built up her receding chin. Then she became sex goddess of America. Present goddesses and minor deities guard their secrets but a number of prominent breasts, if "palpated," would prove synthetic. Models conform to a different physical type, and big breasts would be a detriment; but their facial features can be—and are—surgically improved.

Since man is infinitely perfectible, there's no reason for anyone to limit his ambitions. If he wants to be a model and his nose is too big, he can have it shortened. If she wants to be an actress and her features are too Negroid for Hollywood, she can have them adapted. There is almost no anatomical feature that cannot be made more perfect. *Vogue* (October, 1969) gave evidence in story and pictures that thighs could be slimmed, bellies removed, buttocks and breasts raised; and that "Body Sculpturing" made possible the attainment of the ideal by anyone with money and no scruples about having herself whittled.

But, though some predict plastic surgery is the future, and a face-lift will become as socially acceptable as lipstick and powder, many are still reluctant to change what God gave them. A lurking Puritanism or sense of propriety inhibits them; they find morally reprehensible or simply dishonest the pretense of being or looking different from what you are. They are outcasts of the beauty culture, denying themselves the terra firma of narcissism and self-doubt. They don't understand that you are what you appear to be; they have not taken literally the dictum that every man is responsible for his face.

Those clustered on the rock of vanity know that looking good means feeling good (and probably being good as well). Nothing in the stars or faith should prevent a man from making the most of himself. A very mild form of schizophrenia should be encouraged, because it beautifies the daily confrontation with oneself in the mirror. We should look young, healthy and fashionable.

Fashion usually allows flexibility. One can choose from the available models and perhaps even adopt one. Breast-enlarging operations are reversible, so that if small breasts become essential in fashion (now they are merely preferable), the implants can be removed. But one operation was specifically invented for what became a passing fad. When pointed shoes were popular, the *Journal of Podiatry* reported that some doctors (particularly on the West Coast) were amputating the small toe of women so they, like Cinderellas, could fit the desired slippers.

"If thy foot offend thee, cut it off," said Christ. As with the moon flight, airplanes or the splitting of the atom, former metaphors are now literal. A nation that can actually land men on the moon can actually make dreams come true. Only, the dreams of being beautiful may prove chimerae and as soon as they are fulfilled breed new ones so that the dreamer becomes a kind of lunatic, jacketed in a fantasy of youth and love on a quest that has no end.

3

Interview with a Star Surgeon

Dr. Robert Alan Franklyn dwells by day in his "Beauty Pavilion," a temple in the round dedicated to plastic surgery, with a spiral staircase, slender arches of windows, deep and omnipresent carpeting. He seems in his fifties (but plastic surgeons, like actresses, stand mute on age), is balding, has dark, intense and clever eyes, a swarthy complexion and narrow lips. He's robust and looks Levantine, almost sexy, but his success and the shrewdness in his face remove spontaneity. Quite a handsome man, who immediately handed me a printed sheet, much like a permission to operate, certifying that the undersigned would treat all information "in a manner favorable both to the subject matter and Dr. Franklyn," and would fully identify the doctor. I signed and was given a copy for my own files. We chatted a bit, I spoke of a producer I had met the night before, and Dr. Franklyn told me, "I used to be a producer. Just three or four films. But then I had to decide where the money was going to come from." His decision was plastic surgery, with film producing reserved as a hobby. "I got into it through one of my clients. She was an actress, but she couldn't read scripts. . . ."

"What do you mean, couldn't read . . . ?"

"Couldn't decide what to make of them, whether they were good for her or not. Though probably she had trouble with the actual reading too, if there were words of more than two syllables. So she brought all scripts in to me and I would advise her whether or not they were good for her. Her name was Marilyn Monroe."

I didn't want to embarrass the doctor by asking him directly if he was responsible for her chin implant.

In order not to misrepresent Dr. Franklyn, and also to give a far more penetrating and individualistic view of plastic surgery than any I could invent, I offer the taped interview, with only minor deletions to avoid repetition.

K.P.: The waiver you asked me to sign, your extreme caution in granting me an interview, suggest that you're besieged by journalists and writers. Why do they all want to talk to you?

Dr. Franklyn: Well, I am pretty well known as the person who does most of the face-lifting, et cetera, for the motion-picture industry and the television industry—so that makes me. . . . Well, I can't talk about personalities, I can talk about the general subject all right, but I can't say I operated on so-and-so and look how much better she is now than she was. You can't violate the patient's confidence, but you can certainly discuss the subject. . . . We have here the only private plastic-surgery clinic in the country. . . . All of our work is done in this building, under the theory that cosmetic plastic surgery, which is my field, is the same nature as cosmetic dentistry. In other words, [you go] to your dentist to get your crooked teeth straightened, et cetera, and why does a patient have to be in a hospital for days, weeks or months when all these operations can be done within fifteen to twenty [minutes]? We're using some Novocain, so they come in under their own steam, go out under their own steam. The only disadvantage of course is some bandages on the face, but most of our patients just either stay at home till they come back for a checkup, or any of the nearby hotels, which they find a lot more pleasant than going to a hospital.

K.P.: It must make a difference to have movie-star clients, people who need the work done for professional reasons.

Dr. Franklyn: Well, I think that improving appearances is the prerogative of anybody, whether they're movie stars or not. It's just because California is the center for motion pictures, television, whatnot and these people depend on their faces as their livelihood. If they're getting older, they want to look younger. If they're young and they have a bad nose or something like that, or a receding chin, then they want to get started in show business. But still, I'd say half our practice out here in Hollywood is just the average housewife. . . .

K.P.: Are more men coming to you now than they did formerly?

Dr. Franklyn: No. I think that our percentage of male patients is still about the same five percent that it's always been through the years. Yeah. . . . Well, no, among the movie stars we have a high percentage. And we are also doing a high percentage of top business executives who want to look good. . . .

K.P.: Face-lifts?

DR. FRANKLYN: Yeah. But I'm talking about the average man in the street. He doesn't care how he looks.

K.P.: But probably if the executive starts having face-lifts, then in ten years the junior . . .

DR. FRANKLYN: Listen, I predict that in the year 2000, there'll be plastic surgeons on every intersection just like there are dentists; and you can go to see your friendly plastic surgeon once a year to get checked up on your wrinkles, your deterioration and so forth and so on. It's like people go for the dental checkups. I think the trouble with plastic surgery is again the movies have made it seem, like since the 1920's, a big procedure where you go to the hospital and they wrap your head up in bandages, and lo and behold, two weeks later there's this great unveiling to see what kind of a face has popped out and that's all a lot of theatrical garbage. From a practical stand-point, most operations take about fifteen minutes to twenty minutes to do and that's all. So it takes less time than going to the dentist. At least out here.

[Some] surgeons still like to schedule cases months in advance for a hospital and make a big production . . . and I think taking these cosmetic or beauty patients into the hospital is all wet just in its basic premise. We don't intend to subject our healthy beauty patients to any kind of necessary evil. We don't want thirteen percent of the cases ruined by infections, by second-rate nurses such as they now have in hospitals because [of] your nursing shortage, and by inade-quate equipment. There isn't a hospital in the whole country that's got a cosmetic-surgery operating room. . . . Somehow or other, med-ical superintendents of hospitals and planning commissions decided their hospital is not for the beauty patient, but to serve the community on more serious illness. And I kinda think they are correct. That's why I'd like to see more plastic surgeons having their own setup. . . .

Here we sort of went overboard and got probably the best archi-tect in the world to design a place that would function for us. Be-cause none of the local architects understood it, we had to go all the way down to Rio de Janeiro, Brazil, to get a hold of a man called

Oscar Niemeyer,* who designed the whole city of Brasília, to come here and design one little building for us. But it is a treasure of a building. It's a circular building, it saves us running around and up and down corridors. The essential core . . . are the operating rooms [which] . . . are round, and they're set up for special kinds of lighting; and they've got big plastic domes over the ceiling because we like to operate by natural light rather than by artificial light. Because under natural light, we don't get the harsh shadows that throw us off in hospital lighting, which would interfere with our treatment of wrinkles and so forth. And a million and a half other little ideas.

K.P.: How do you treat wrinkles now, with the ban on silicone?

DR. FRANKLYN: Well, most wrinkles are still treated by surgery, by tightening faces or removing skin and so forth. . . . When somebody has bad frown lines, we do a little operation inside the corner of the eyebrow and then we get instruments underneath the skin from a little incision, which doesn't show because it's part of the eyebrow, and we loosen up the skin from these frown crevices so there's no adhesions. And we clip the little frown muscles to weaken them, so that people don't go right back in the habit of frowning, and that does the trick. . . . Yeah, that stays. Whereas that silicone injection to fill out frown lines is a temporary thing. It doesn't seem to stay more than a number of months, and they have to get it done over again. Silicones are also used for these what we call nasal-labial lines, which you know are simply lines from the nose to the corner of the mouth, and that will plump that out. But again, that's more or less of a temporizing thing and not permanent.

K.P.: I've heard that Orentreich in New York uses silicone for everything.

DR. FRANKLYN: Well, Norman is a bit of a nut and he wrote to us originally to get the results of our experience with silicones, because I was the first person in this country to do anything with silicone. Matter of fact, the first medical literature articles on silicones was printed by me in some German medical journals—1956 or 7 . . . and then the Japanese, who subscribe to the German journals, read about it and they thought that they found the answer to their lack of ability in surgery. So they jumped on the bandwagon and injected everybody

---

* Oscar Niemeyer is a renowned architect and Communist sympathizer for whom the designing of an American beauty pavilion must have seemed bizarre.

from about 1958 to—I guess it's still going on. . . . for taking out wrinkles and enlarging breasts. . . . And then some American surgeons went over there and sort of rediscovered the thing I wrote about originally and thought they found out something new until I reminded them that we've been through [that]. . . . Yeah, we used the silicones for kids with polio that had thin legs, and building out the legs. We used it for wrinkles in the face, and we did a lot of breast enlarging with it. In fact, the whole business of enlarging the breast I invented in 1950. And before 1950 nobody believed there were any flat-chested women in the United States—at least medically they didn't believe it. And the first five, six years that we did this operation, the other surgeons even doubted that there was such an operation and [thought] I was kidding everybody. So we sort of took the criticism up to about 1960. Then 1960 everybody jumped on the bandwagon and they kind of forgot meanwhile that old Franklyn—matter of fact, the first book on breast enlarging was one that I wrote back in 1959 [*On Developing Bosom Beauty*], which told how to do the operation and before-and-after pictures and all that sort of thing. So this is the Bible of flat chests.

K.P.: Can you use silicone now?

DR. FRANKLYN: We don't use silicone at all for injection of breasts because it's turning out to be a temporary thing. . . . We have to make an incision, get behind the breast and stuff it out.

K.P.: Can you use this with breast-cancer patients?

DR. FRANKLYN: Yeah, but generally you have to wait about five years on these people to see that they're rid of their cancer. Because some of them are not cured even though they've had their breast removed, and then years later you can get into some trouble.

K.P.: What if someone comes to you for surgery—a face-lift, say—expecting her life to change?

DR. FRANKLYN: Oh, I think that's pretty rare. I avoid people who think that the whole world is going to change just because they have some plastic surgery done. I think they must be some sort of mental case and might be better off with a psychoanalyst.

K.P.: Do you ever refuse to take people?

DR. FRANKLYN: Yeah, we get people who are obviously unstable, depressed, so forth and so on and we think that no matter what you do for these people, you can't change their brains. What we like is, in other words, normal people, say—you know: "I'm doing all right but this bump on my nose bothers me." Or: "Now I'm getting these wrinkles, I'm not the pretty girl I used to be." Or: "Gosh, I'm flat-chested and I have an inferiority complex because I'm flat-chested." Well, these are normal requests. It's like you, if your dress didn't fit, you'd go to a dressmaker and get it done. You wouldn't say, "Well, my dress fits, but I'm still the old mess that I always was"—and go out and blow my brains out. So, you know, this is the type of patient that we don't want but of course they're pretty rare. Most of our people, I must say, by and large, are fairly normal people.

K.P.: I interviewed a woman who had undergone many different plastic-surgery operations, and she was exceptionally infantile.

Dr. FRANKLYN: Yeah, well, that's the symptom of a patient that should be under psychiatric care, because if you do something for this type of patient, then the next thing she'll say is, "Well, you fixed my breast, now fix my nose." And you fix the nose. "Well, now fix my ears." And so forth and so on. And they really need their brains altered somehow, or their psychology altered and I doubt that even with these people, if you gave them five to ten years' worth of psycho-therapy, whether they're much improved. I'm not an enthusiast, ac-tually, of any form of analysis.

K.P.: What's generally the motive for, say, a face-lift? Besides pro-fessional reasons.

Dr. FRANKLYN: Oh, fear that the husband is looking at younger women I'd say is one of the strong ones.

K.P.: And suppose she gets her face lifted and he goes off and mar-ries the other woman?

Dr. FRANKLYN: Then she goes off and feels that she's strong enough to contract some other man for herself.

K.P.: So it's generally sex—or security—rather than the fear of growing old?

Dr. FRANKLYN: Well, it comes under the general word of *vanity*, I suppose. Pride in one's appearance. If you feel second-rate . . . If you drive a car that's got a dent in it, car drives just as well but you feel unhappy about the dents, so you get the dents repaired. If you're going to go to a party and you've got a nice dress and it's got a stain on it, even though that stain doesn't bother anybody at the party and I doubt whether they'd even notice it, you wouldn't want to wear it. You'd feel very unhappy about wearing it until you had the thing repaired or cleaned. If your house is a pretty nice house and the paint is peeling off it, you go and get another coat of paint. Somehow or other people are educated to corrective dentistry. If your front teeth are crooked, they [sic] get their teeth braced or wired or [if] teeth are ugly, they're capped, and so forth. Strangely enough, the patient has pretty well accepted improvement of your teeth from a beauty stand-point, now they're beginning to accept improvement of the rest of the person.

K.P.: Do you ever see a change in the patient's personality in a positive direction?

DR. FRANKLYN: Oh, I think that the positive thing is that you've removed the source of irritation and feeling of inferiority. And this allows people to more or less express their own real personality and not be held back.

K.P.: They don't assume a new personality to go with the new body?

DR. FRANKLYN: No.

K.P.: What happens to a woman with new breasts, especially if she never had much bosom before?

DR. FRANKLYN: Well, you know, first they would tend to overcom-pensate a little bit. They'll go to wearing low-cut gowns, bikinis and so forth. They tend to be proud of their figures whereas before they were ashamed and would wear all sorts of padding and whatnot. And it's a great relief to these women to feel that they're not false any-more, that they don't have to have an inferiority complex and they can hold their own. . . . You know, it's like saying to somebody, if you had skinny little bow legs and somebody could wave a magic wand and show you a perfect pair of legs, wouldn't you wave them around and show them off? So I think this is a bit natural.

K.P.: Can't a man tell, fondling these new breasts?

DR. FRANKLYN: No, they're like the real thing.

K.P.: Isn't there a scar under the breast?

DR. FRANKLYN: Well, in our operations we have about an inch-and-a-half incision line, which is—yes, that's all.

K.P.: That's very rare, isn't it? So small an incision?

DR. FRANKLYN: Well, I can't educate the whole world on how to operate, you know. I invented the operation. If everybody else wants to prostitute the operation through lack of inside skill and thought about the surgeon's responsibility to the patient, that's their business.

K.P.: Do men ever ask for breast enlargement?

DR. FRANKLYN: Oh yeah, we get quite a number of requests from these homosexuals, but we turn them down.

K.P.: Are there any cosmetic operations on the penis yet?

DR. FRANKLYN: Well, if there are, I don't do them. . . . Yeah, I'm sure somebody would get interested in that, might be very interesting, but I suppose that would be a field for urologists rather than plastic surgeons.* We have to do what makes us happy. I think we're female-oriented, not male-oriented.

K.P.: Do you do hair transplants?

DR. FRANKLYN: No, we let Orentreich and his mob do that. See, again, that's a dermatology type of thing. Because dermatologists are geared to these long, drawn-out little treatments, whereas cosmetic plastic surgeons, the good ones, want to do something, do it completely, get it over with in ten, fifteen, twenty minutes and that's it. We don't like little piddling things that go on.

K.P.: Is that all it takes for any operation?

DR. FRANKLYN: Well, to enlarge breasts takes about five to six minutes. Nose operations take us about ten to fifteen minutes; face-lifts about twenty to thirty minutes; eye-bag operations about fifteen minutes. So, you know, compared to a lot of the old-fashioned surgeons who like to piddle around for two, three, four hours on each of these operations, why—ridiculous. . . . I don't see any reason to batter a face for three hours when you can get the same results in twenty, thirty minutes with a lot faster healing. Because it's the old story, the more time you spend on an operation, the more swelling you get, the slower the healing and the worse the result. Trick is to do things quickly, skillfully and aid the body to heal up rapidly.

K.P.: Are operations ever not successful?

DR. FRANKLYN: Well, there are certain types of operations that may be only fifty percent successful, let's say—but we don't want any

---

* When I reported this part of the interview with Dr. Franklyn to a social science professor at the University of Pennsylvania, he pointed out that the breast enlargement operation with plastic implants could easily be done on testicles. Like breasts, testicles are round and there are two of them. This operation could correct undescended testicles, make others symmetrical, or simply enlarge them. The professor reminded me that codpieces and other devices were used in the past to call attention to them (more than to the penis), and that today male dancers wear clothing to emphasize and separate their testicles.

part of it. In other words, the only operations that we consider worth-while doing in a beauty-surgery practice must have at least a ninety percent chance of success. And that's the type of surgery we do. Once in a while a new operation comes up and looks like maybe it will work and maybe it won't, and if experience points out that it doesn't work most of the time, or if it only works half the time, or even if it works two-thirds of the time, we don't want any part of it. We want procedures that, within the realm of body vagaries of healing, should work theoretically a hundred percent of the time

K.P.: Do you do thigh lifts or breast reduction operations?

DR. FRANKLYN: No. . . . They're tedious and leave bad scars, and I'm kind of not too impressed with the results. . . . I don't know whether the bad scars are worse than the original condition or not. You know, it's a substitution thing of rob Peter to pay Paul. I don't like that type of surgery.

K.P.: Do you ever have patients who want to change their racial characteristics?

DR. FRANKLYN: Well, we get some Japanese girls who want a fold in their upper eyelid, which is simple to do. We get Negroes, mostly in the entertainment industry, who want their noses made smaller and less flaring nostrils.

K.P.: Can one do this without destroying the symmetry of the face?

DR. FRANKLYN: Yeah, well they look better for it.

K.P.: How about large lips?

DR. FRANKLYN: Yeah. We get a lot of Negroes for instance who have really bad protruding lips to be made smaller.

K.P.: How is that done?

DR. FRANKLYN: Just go inside the lip and take some of their lip out. Too much lip.

K.P.: But that kind of thing can't be popular now with Black Is Beautiful.

DR. FRANKLYN: No, now it would be the reverse. Get yourself big, woolly hairdo and big fat lips and wider nose.

K.P.: It must have been in the fifties that Negroes came for surgery.

DR. FRANKLYN: No, Negroes still come around, the ones in the entertainment industry. They want to look white.

K.P.: Still?

DR. FRANKLYN: Oh yeah. They don't have much sympathy, incidentally, with the mass of Negro agitation. They regard themselves as white and anti-Negro.

K.P.: Do you get requests like hairdressers get? Women who come in and say, "Do my hair like Jackie Kennedy."?

DR. FRANKLYN: Oh yeah, we get people in here with pictures of Elizabeth Taylor and say, "Make me look like Elizabeth Taylor." We had one in this morning said she wanted to look like Zsa Zsa Gabor. Then they come in with pages from *Playboy* magazine, they want their breasts to look just like the girl in the center fold, even though the girl in the center fold is already a product of my operation. It's very funny sometimes.

K.P.: I thought the pictures of Playmates were retouched.

DR. FRANKLYN: Well, we've had God knows how many girls in *Playboy*, especially years ago when the operations were first being done. Matter of fact, I even had a letter from *Playboy* saying, "Please don't mention the fact that you've done so-and-so and so-and-so."

K.P.: How does a girl decide to become a Playmate or *Playboy* bunny if she doesn't have large breasts to start with?

DR. FRANKLYN: Well, I don't think they want big breasts to become a Playmate; I think it's just a by-product. One of the funniest cases we ever had was a shrinking kindergarten teacher who was flat-chested and we did an operation on her and she quit her job and became a stripteaser. And she got a lot of publicity, even *Life* magazine: How a kindergarten teacher becomes a stripteaser. But [they] didn't mention in the *Life* article that she had all this accomplished by Dr. Franklyn, which I thought was an astounding story. It was just as though it was a switch from kindergarten to stripteaser. . . .

K.P.: But then you are some kind of magician, who can turn on the Jekyll and Hyde.

DR. FRANKLYN: Yeah, but that's unusual. What I'm saying is that the average patient is nowheres as flamboyant and doesn't make that big of a change in their life.

K.P.: What I want to explore in this book is how much the outside influences the inside and vice versa.

DR. FRANKLYN: Well, I suppose both, it's a constant feedback business. The outside influences the inside, the inside influences the outside. If the outside registers to people that it's beautiful, the reactions of the exterior people then get reflected to the inner woman, mentally.

K.P.: It might be a lot cheaper than analysis.

DR. FRANKLYN: Oh, we've done I don't know, hundreds upon hundreds of graduates of Beverly Hills psychoanalysis. I don't think a week goes by that we don't operate on somebody who's had some kind of analysis. . . . Twelve years for the psychoanalysis, five times a week, fifty dollars a throw and her big complaint was really she was flat-chested and that was about it. So the psychoanalysis might make her understand why she feels inferior and therefore bolster her ego and make her stronger to go around with these feelings, so that they don't bother her so much. But it's a lot easier in ten minutes to get a new chest than it is to suffer for ten years in analysis.

K.P.: But a woman of thirty-five must have some image of herself. . . .

DR. FRANKLYN: That's right.

K.P.: . . . that was established between thirteen and twenty, and it's not going to change that quickly. If she was flat-chested then, certain things happened to her and even if she. . . .

DR. FRANKLYN: Listen. The interesting thing now is we're doing high school girls of sixteen and seventeen who are flat-chested, because the mothers are bringing them in. The girls raise a big hullabaloo. I can think of one last summer. She wouldn't go to school because they had sort of a community shower for the girls in their physical education. And she wouldn't undress and have the girls see how flat-chested she was. She ran away from school. So the mother, after discussing it with the family doctor, brought her here and we operated on her. Now she spends I think more time in the shower. And we also had—I say "we": the community—a sad case last year where girl twins aged eighteen committed suicide because they were both flat-chested and they both thought that boys wouldn't look at them or go out with them, and didn't know what to do about it. And they just sat in the car and turned on the motor in the garage and both got killed and left notes behind. The newspapers reported that they had this great feeling of inferiority due to their "immaturity," it said, and they killed themselves. Now, if these feelings were brought out to a responsible person who would've gotten them to a plastic surgeon, they'd probably be the two happiest little gals in the world now.

K.P.: So one can really change the body image?

DR. FRANKLYN: Yep.

K.P.: Even late in life?

DR. FRANKLYN: Oh listen. We did a woman sixty-five years of age, gave her a new chest and lifted her face. She went to Miami Beach and sent us back a postcard that she got married ten days after she got to Miami. Which—figure that out. I really enjoyed that. Sixty-five years old.

K.P.: If what you're telling me is true—and I'm not contradicting you—then what are the implications on analysis?

DR. FRANKLYN: Well, analysis is basically an intellectual pursuit with no practical application whatsoever. I don't know of anyone of hundreds and hundreds of people who've gone to psychoanalysis . . . who's been materially benefited by it.* Psychoanalysis, whether you know it or not, is now in a very fast downgrade. I think that it has to be greatly modified or it's going to be as passé as Carter's Little Liver Pills.

K.P.: I meant even more—this practically invalidates a lot of Freud's concepts.

DR. FRANKLYN: Yeah, well, as I say, my opinion of psychoanalysis and classical Freudian psychoanalysis is it's nice to read about for the student, but it's absolutely limited for practical, clinical use.

K.P.: But what about the standard example, men with small genitals who—

DR. FRANKLYN: Oh, I think that the man with the small penis certainly feels feminine or unmasculine.

K.P.: —becomes dictators or conquerors. Hitler, say—

DR. FRANKLYN: But you know, again, so what's the difference in the size of the penis? I think what it all boils down [to is] it isn't the size of the penis that counts, either in life or in sexual relations. It's what's in a man's mind. On the other hand, you see great swagger-

---

* Though Dr. Franklyn so roundly condemns psychoanalysis, he says earlier in the interview (see p. 145) that unstable people "might be better off with a psychoanalyst." The cliché is accepted, though its premise is totally repudiated.

A professor of psychology told me that in some ways Dr. Franklyn is right. It has been shown that psychoanalysis *emphasizes* aspects of personality—and therefore leads to distortion, whether good or bad—and does not actually *integrate* the personality. Dr. Franklyn's standard, however, is material benefit, which may be derived through psychoanalysis, though admittedly in a rather subtle manner.

ing males running around because they say, "I have a bigger penis than you do." Does that make them supermasculine? I don't think so. I think they can just accept their physical—

K.P.: No, I meant the view of oneself—

DR. FRANKLYN: Well, certainly people who are glandularly deficient, especially the big tall men who for some reason or other are tall at the expense of sexual maturity, those fellows are acutely in distress because the women figure, "Oh boy, here's a nice big man," and they turn out to be sadly lacking. And we know a few people like that.

K.P.: Can nothing be done about it? *

DR. FRANKLYN: Not that I know of. There's a field for some fellow to make a couple of billion dollars. . . . And I could sit back now and see the ads. You know: "Come and see Dr. Jones. Thousand dollars an inch. How much would you like added to you?" I can see a millionaire might want to buy thirty-six inches. But I think women are more sensitive to these things because our culture is tuned towards female beauty, whereas men were not supposed to care whether they're good-looking or not, as long as they've achieved financial success. In other words, the way our society is structured, the men are supposed to be rich and the women are supposed to be beautiful.

K.P.: But that's changing now, with unisex, long hair on men. Men are being encouraged to develop their narcissism.

DR. FRANKLYN: Well, I think this is more of a style or a fad and I don't think we're going to see that ten years from today. No, I think these people are swimming upstream instead of downstream.

K.P.: Can't breasts be part of a fad?

DR. FRANKLYN: Well, breasts can get flat-chested again, that's why we've always designed the operation so it could be reversed. So when it goes back, just take it out.

---

* I've given up my line of questioning. I had hoped to make a parallel between flat-chested women and men with small genitals, since both groups view themselves as sexually inadequate. If this is the view of self, then it must condition or influence the personality in some way. Subsequent change of breast or genital size could not, I believe, totally erase previous development. Dr. Franklyn seemed more eager to explain the misconception that size of penis has anything to do with its capacity for enjoyment or giving enjoyment, than to discuss any possible similarity between males and females in this regard. A woman surgeon might argue that size of breasts has nothing to do with their sensitivity or their ability to produce milk. If operations to enlarge the penis are ever performed, perhaps they will have to be done by female surgeons.

K.P.: Doesn't the whole thing drop?

Dr. Franklyn: No, it goes back to where it started from.

K.P.: Can one just pick up the breast without enlarging it?

Dr. Franklyn: No. It's like a flat tire, you have to pump it up.

K.P.: You talk quite a lot about cosmetics in your book [*The Art of Staying Young*]. Can they accomplish some of the aims of cosmetic surgery? Can they aid in maintaining or restoring beauty?

Dr. Franklyn: Cosmetics are, by and large, a lot of nonsense. And if women will just learn to stay out of the sun, they'd be better off.

K.P.: You don't stay out of the sun.

Dr. Franklyn: I'm not worried about wrinkles.

K.P.: One looks better, healthier, for being in the sun.

Dr. Franklyn: One looks like a prune, though. That's how they make prunes. . . .

K.P.: Wouldn't you rather be a happy prune than an unhappy plum?

Dr. Franklyn: I'd rather be a happy plum than a happy prune.

THE OUTSIDE
OF THE INSIDE

≈≋≈

[La] Nature . . . nous dresse pour nous, non
pour autruy; pour estre, non pour sembler.

—M. DE MONTAIGNE, Essais, LIVRE II, chap.
XXXVII.

(Nature forms us for ourselves, not for others;
to be, not to seem.)

1

Body Image

Beauty books often suggest a "long, hard look" in the mirror as starting point for self-improvement. They could as easily suggest a Rorschach. The image is a reflection not of one's visual faculty, but point of view. On a good day, I can see dark brown eyes, long lashes, a sensual mouth, smooth skin and an endearing nose. On a bad day these are eclipsed and only the bags under my eyes, wrinkles, kinky hair, fat lips and a pug nose are visible. On a terrible day, there's almost nothing to see at all except a blur of indefensible humanity as I avert my gaze. And on a glorious day, the beautiful eyes hold me, full of love, humor and intelligence.

"When you're pretty well put together," said Jeffrey Kramer, "you can allow lapses. The technical term for this is regression in service of the ego. When you're not so well put together, you either can't allow lapses or they overwhelm you." The self-image is a shifting reality of half-truths accepted in the dialogue with oneself. It's a profitable lie, a workable assumption, the microcosmology that will hold good in the greatest number of cases. A definition of self or ego is the carrot in front of philosophy and psychology, and though there may be an occasional nibble, the thing is never gotten hold of. Even if it were, it wouldn't be sustaining nourishment. The search for the grail or golden fleece and the quixotic journey are myths of the quest for oneself. Since all quests are basically that one, the mythic or commercial elaborations of the theme are accepted as containing truth. The real you is always on the verge of being discovered, and only by simplifying the self—regarding it as mechanism, object or function—can you form a picture of the physical being who reacts, interacts and attracts.

157

Body image is the picture a person has of himself as seen by others, and is doomed to inaccuracy.

"I had a little tiny mutt and a Great Dane in the house. The little tiny mutt always acted like the Great Dane—it was the only other dog he'd ever seen. And I think this is what happens to us," said Alma Cunningham of The Fashion Group, an organization of women executives in the fashion industry. "We only see ourselves in mirrors, and there is a great distortion in mirrors because of the perspective line." To prove her point, Miss Cunningham conducted an experiment at Simplicity Patterns, where she works. In studying proportion of the body to determine where skirt lengths should be, she asked the women there to describe themselves. "Their judgment in every case, even standing looking in the mirror, was wrong. They see themselves the way they want to." Even women professionally involved with fashion, concerned daily with such crucial issues as hemlines, couldn't tell whether they had short torsos and long legs or long torsos and short legs. The mistakes they made were not consistent and not towards the ideal. "One girl kept saying, 'My stomach sticks out.' She had the flattest stomach in here. . . . [Another] had decided arbitrarily that she had very long legs and a short torso. She thought suits looked best on her. It was actually the opposite. And here's somebody who works with patterns, is concerned with figures. She could look at a model and dress her quite well, but when it got around to judging the proportions of her own torso, she wasn't able to see it."

The experiment continued: "We got some brown paper against the wall and drew their silhouettes. There was not a single person who recognized her own silhouette when they were mixed up. . . . I didn't recognize mine either."

The Fashion Group, which attempts to teach beauty and fashion to mental patients at the Manhattan State Hospital, found that the patients were "not able to take general information and apply it to themselves." Alma Cunningham comments: "I don't think that's different to anybody. I don't think it has to do with their problem. How many times, for instance, have you seen cosmetics written up in magazines: you have a square face or an oval one or a round one, and this is what you do in each case. Nobody knows, individually, whether they have a square, round or oval face. They may think they do, but I don't think they do."

Jean Nidetch, bumptious president of Weight Watchers, found distortion of body image among fat men. She asked them to describe themselves "and almost to a count, every man described what he looked like when he graduated from college: broad shoulders, narrow tapered waist, small hips. . . . He'd say, 'Well, of course my chest is a little bit heavier'—it was a great big fat belly."

A study, "Body Image—Male & Female" by Richard Kurtz, showed that "women tend to value their bodies more than men do; they tend to show more approval of what their full-length mirrors tell them." Thin women liked their bodies more than any other women liked theirs—reflecting the culture's predilection for slim women. Tall, thin men, however, valued their bodies least of all men. Large women, with big breasts and broad hips, saw their bodies as "potent," though among men the mesomorphs (muscular), not eurymorphs (fat), considered themselves most potent. This study indicates that people have learned to regard themselves through the eyes of others, and what they see in a mirror is immediately interpreted through a set of values.

Because the values are so completely accepted, people can believe the interpretation even when it contradicts visual fact. A fat man sees himself at his mesomorphic best, but fat people who lose a lot of weight suffer a memory lag and see themselves as fat or fatter than they ever were. A study reported in *The New York Times* showed that when obese dieters were presented with photographs of themselves, distorted to look thinner or fatter than they were, they invariably picked the fat distortion. The self-image could not keep up with reality.

"You are who you think you are," Pirandello might cheerily have suggested, but for psychological realism one must add: And you are who you think other people think you are. You are what you look like and you look like what you are. Dr. Kramer thinks "there's a crucial interplay between the way a person looks and feels." One can't be separated from the other; the outside is an index to the inside and the inside is conditioned by the outside. All the time I was working on this book, a line from Tolstoy's *Childhood* recurred constantly in my mind: "I am convinced that nothing has so marked an influence on the direction of a man's mind as his appearance . . ." He then qualifies: "and not his appearance itself so much as his conviction that it is attractive or unattractive."

2

The Fat Are Different from Us (They Have More Flesh)

"Take it off, take it off" is the shrill, whining command that continually pierces the tranquillity of fat people. The thin man struggling to get out is generally in foul temper, a sadist who never misses an opportunity to castigate, condemn and belittle. He even convinces his domicile that he exists—a parasite who, if given the chance, will devour his host. Fat people listen to his spiel and are convinced it is the voice of reason. Overweight means greater susceptibility to illness, means premature death, ostracism, lost opportunities, lost love and banishment from the world of fashion. Fat is synonymous with ugliness, and so with loneliness. And the only comfort for this sad state of things is food.

Approximately seventy-nine million Americans are overweight. The weight-reducing industry grosses a billion dollars a year; five thousand doctors devote themselves to overweight and make two hundred and fifty million dollars. Fat is a national obsession, a topic of conversation that often takes precedence over all others, including business and sex. Fat is despised. Instead of signifying affluence (as it still does in poor countries), it is merely a product of it, and now indicates "lack of self-respect." Only a poet could say to someone at a cocktail party (as William Meredith did): "If you're so smart, how come you're not fat?"

Every day, millions of words about reducing are fed to the American public, with before-and-after pictures and "true stories" of beauty queens, housewives or celebrities. A full-page testimonial for Ayds with the headline, "I lived in maternity slacks, until I lost ninety-eight pounds" faces the picture of a starving child with the words, "Hunger is all she has ever known." Bookstores have entire sections devoted to diet books; many different diet magazines are available on most large newsstands. Radio, television—all contact with society— bring constant reminders of the fat fetish. To live properly in America, you must be slim. That's the only way to marry, get a job, be respected, have opinions, communicate, relate and date. Everyone's out to help you—from the makers of soft drinks to social psychologists. American overweight has fattened so many volumes that the subject will be treated here only as a side dish to the main course of beauty.

A short explanation for those mythical people who have never worried about weight: food can become an addiction, and there are more food addicts than any other. Food is comfort, escape, a sensual thrill, an activity, a ritual, reward, friendship, love and euphoria. It leads to guilt, self-hatred, general misanthropy, discomfort, tiredness, aches, sickness and loneliness. For most people, the price of a hot-fudge marshmallow sundae with whipped cream, nuts and a cherry on top is high. It means at least one night of self-abuse. It can lead to such despair over one's own weakness that the only comfort is a whole box of Ritz crackers.

There are many types of fat people: the truly obese, the overweight, the newly fat, the cyclical fat (who go from fatness to thinness and back in a regular pattern), the formerly fat and the normal or even medically underweight person who sees himself as fat. A rare creature is someone who is overweight by American standards—a woman who wears size sixteen, for instance—but doesn't care. In an excellent and serious book called *The Importance of Overweight*, Hilde Bruch points out that obese children typically have overprotective mothers. But "children who are mildly overweight are the victims of so much teasing and abuse that all psychological problems are explained as secondary to obesity." So the fat child develops "personality problems," usually through great insecurity about being loved. As an adult, this insecurity makes him hold on to fat. It is evidence of fealty to mother; it becomes a test of love (if someone can really care for him despite all the fat, then the relationship is valid), or a justification for why one is disliked. Dr. Bruch emphasizes the particularly American concern with overweight, "spoken of as a menace to health and happiness which must be stamped out." Also, "the mechanical emphasis on reducing as a goal in itself . . . by now has reached the proportion of a national obsession." As far as she knows, only the Spartans matched this obsession. They condemned overeating and fat; all citizens ate at a common table and penalties were given to anyone found eating privately; young people were examined naked once a month and those overweight were forced to exercise. But among other peoples, throughout history, "the concept of a maternal woman" has been "a plump and cheerful one." In America, however, "there is an overemphasis on the sexually attractive woman, conceived of as very slim, and a condemnation of the maternal type as being dowdy and even unfeminine."

Therefore, fat women generally have problems about their sexual identity and fat men are afraid of being thought feminine. When I was fat (or felt myself to be), I was disgusted by any man who showed sexual interest in me. A man who would want to touch that unappetizing mass of flesh was at best a fool. A friend of mine slept in the nude when she had lost a few pounds and felt thin, but as soon as she gained them back, she wore a nightgown. She protected her virginity carefully until, at twenty-one, she lost some weight.

I was never obese. At five foot ten you can carry even a six-months embryo without anyone noticing. My measurements were in proportion, and if my waist grew to thirty inches, my breasts still towered over with forty-two inches. I was tall and not skinny; therefore, I was big. My weight went up to one hundred sixty-eight pounds and I thought a lot of God, space, poetry and my own uniqueness. Boys my age were contemptible; older men were more likely to see the soul. In all daydreams I was thin. I hated clothes larger than a size fourteen and adored hideous garments in size twelve. Clothes were supposed to emphasize my breasts, so that the eyes of men would travel no further down.

At eighteen I had a glorious summer in Europe, most of the time on my own. I was very blond, handsome men wanted to try my long-preserved virginity, a Viennese doctor said I had to gain weight and I lunched on gin and tonics. I weighed one hundred thirty-six pounds, read Sartre and was ready to revolutionize the world.

Over the years my weight fluctuated. On my twenty-sixth birthday I weighed one hundred sixty-eight again. I was terribly depressed, spoke to no one, contemplated suicide occasionally, but my mind was more occupied with thoughts of food. At all times I was thinking of what I would like to eat next. I knew this obsession; I had had more than a decade of periodic eating binges, when I devoured anything at all. I drank a can of Hershey Syrup the way others would down a cup of coffee. I ate sugar, unadulterated, straight from the bag. I knew the rumors about Judy Holliday, another compulsive eater, who kept the cupboard bare but, when the fit was on her, devoured all the dog food.

"Obese people," said Larry Gross, a social psychologist working on the problem of overweight, "are insensitive to hunger, but very sensitive to external cues." An ad in the paper, a television commercial, billboards, sounds similar to chewing, the refrigerator, pantry, the memory of a candy bar drive one to eat and eat and eat—sometimes to the point of sickness. For those obsessed with the shape they're in, the world becomes very simple: a cycle of guilt and expiation, guilt renewed with each bite, guilt so permanent that it often needs eating binges to justify it. Expiation in diets, saccharine, the giving up of a potato. I was one of those Hilde Bruch calls "thin fat people": "Although they look slim, they not only continue to have the same adjustment problems as when they were fat, but they often seem to be more insecure, dissatisfied and unproductive." Even when I had lost enough weight to be average for my height, I saw everything in terms of reducing. In this condition, you count the steps you take, hoping to rationalize them into exercise. Sex is a way of losing weight quickly: you weigh yourself before and after, and the more stormy the session, the more you lost. Even grief, if it can be maintained through mealtimes, becomes a device for losing weight. No one who hasn't suffered overweight for a sustained period, and preferably during youth, can know the orgy of self-disgust at the base of every fat teen-ager's life.

Sometimes there is no cure for fatness. Hilde Bruch points out that often the psychological factors that caused overweight in the first place are revealed more glaringly when the person loses weight and may not be able to cope. ". . . For many people overeating and being big is a balancing factor in their adjustment to life." Freud showed that curing a hysterical symptom was not enough; another would develop unless the cause for the original symptom was discovered in the personality. So with weight, which can serve the twin psychological purpose of addiction and deformity. An addict often functions well through his addiction; take it away, and he loses control. Deformity, too, can be a way of adjusting. An ugly nose gives evidence to its owner of why he is disliked. When the nose is remade in the image of Douglas Fairbanks', the person must be disliked for himself.

So overweight can be the outward sign of inner trouble, and a fat person can need his flesh as a rich man needs his money. For such a person to lose weight could be hazardous. But most people are fat through laziness, affluence or boredom. Women are more likely to gain than men, because they're in the house all day and near the refrigerator. Mothers of small children are most liable of all, because they get up in the middle of the night, their sleep is interrupted, the child may be difficult and they comfort both themselves and their babies with food. Teen-agers can be fat because their bodies are changing too rapidly for their minds to accept; their body image, their sense of self, lag behind physical changes, and fatness removes the onus of maturity. Other people gain weight because they're lonely, and food is a reliable comfort, a sensual pleasure, a way of rewarding themselves as they were once rewarded by their mothers. Or you gain weight just because you're growing older and haven't learned to cut down the food to match a more sedentary life. Or you've been ill; or you're past the age of sexual competition and you let yourself go. Old people are often fat, blind people are fat, schizophrenics are fat. Overweight means you've given up the sex-and-power game.

Most people feel the fat is an accident, not what they meant at all. Every ad, every movie, every social situation, every shopping spree is a reminder that fat is unlovely, unfashionable, unsexy and unsocial. Losing weight can become as obsessive as gaining it. You go on crash diets, regular diets, strange diets of only bananas or only eggs, faddish diets of martinis and lobster Newburg, liquid diets, brand-name diets (Metrecal), mad diets of no food at all. You go to doctors and get injections, advice, pills. You go to gyms, saunas and exercise salons. You jog, run, ride a bicycle, swim. You're usually successful, for a few weeks. Then you eat again, lose again, eat again. Everything is in extremes. When you're dieting, you won't take an extra carrot stick. When you're not dieting, you won't eat a carrot at all (because it reminds you of deprivation), but take a cookie instead.

I lost hundreds of pounds on diets. I took diuretic pills to get rid of excess water. I usually lost eight pounds a week eating cottage cheese, black coffee and lean steaks. I could lose five or more pounds in two days by eating six prunes, two hard-boiled eggs and a large steak each day, taking no liquid. I put myself on diets of less than six hundred calories a day (below the hunger level) and hallucinated. The last diet I was ever on was given me by a doctor. I went to him daily for injections, got appetite-depressing pills (amphetamines), ate between five hundred and eight hundred and fifty calories a day of protein food, and paid him an outrageous amount. I lost fourteen pounds the first week, nothing at all for ten days, and then six more. In three weeks I went from one hundred sixty-eight to one hundred forty-eight and in four years have never gained it back. (In fact, I've lost twenty more pounds.) For me, the fee worked as stimulus. I couldn't easily afford it and the sacrifice encouraged my dedication. But a friend of mine who spent fifty dollars a week on a diet doctor gained back every ounce and more. I suspect that her inability to keep off weight has to do with her desire for a baby.

No system can work for everyone, though Dr. Gordon L. Green of Long Island offers mass-produced reducing with twenty-five hundred patients a week (he tape records his advice) and such cheering principles as: you may eat as much as you want, drink as much as you want, forget about exercise and order a banana split if you feel like it. Since patients pay seven dollars a visit, his system is lucrative. He is, however, crude compared to Deborah Bordeaux Szekeley, owner of the Golden Door beauty farm, who has developed a Philosophy of Unfatness. This philosophy points out that diets are usually seen as a form of punishment. One must discard this way of thinking and find joy in life, savoring every bite of cottage cheese, going to concerts and reading novels. Both Dr. Green and Mrs. Szekeley are plump and hefty.

The system that has worked best for most people is Weight Watchers, an organization that adapts the principles of Alcoholics Anonymous to food addicts. A low-calorie, high-protein diet is offered (invented by the New York Board of Health) and Weight Watchers come to regular meetings to give their stories and compare notes. They pay three dollars to join, then two dollars a week for as many sessions as they want to attend. Scholarships are available for those who can't afford the fee. There are millions of Weight Watchers all over the world—men, women and teen-agers. Even starving India has asked for a franchise.

Weight Watchers has its own magazine, with a circulation of almost three hundred fifty thousand. It sells packaged, frozen dinners in supermarkets: its cookbook has sold more than half a million copies; it's a corporation with an annual gross revenue of more than five and a half million dollars.

The whole thing began in Little Neck, Queens, when a plump housewife who baby-sat in bowling alleys and whose husband drove an airline bus decided to lose weight. She went to the New York Board of Health Obesity Clinic, was given their diet and tried to stick to it. But she was a gregarious type and disliked solitude in anything. So she found friends to join her. They worked on each other's morales and lack of self-control. If one woke in the middle of the night craving a chocolate cream pie, she called a friend who convinced her to settle for a stalk of celery. The ladies were successful, and others wanted to join them. From this beginning, Jean Nidetch made an empire.

She rules now from her penthouse suite in a New York hotel, a platinum bombshell with a thick fringe of lashes and a handful of large rings. Photographs of herself adorn the walls, the office is as luxurious and swank as a Hollywood director's. She speaks in the old style of Broadway characters, turning each vowel into a long diphthong, so that "talk" becomes "tawuhk," and "chocolate," the most luxurious of sounds, is "chawklet." Nothing like her has hit New Yawk since Damon Runyon's time. She is the antidote to psychiatrists, a glorious narcissist who has the sense not to drown.

"Not being a psychiatrist or a psychologist, I'm not even a public speaker. I'm not a dietician, I'm not a nutritionist. I'm an ex-fat housewife who lost seventy-two pounds. And I had, as a result of being fat, surrounded myself with fat friends, I married a fat man, I had a fat dog and I was raising two fat children. And that's where I am. So that's all I know.

"The dog died from obesity. This is true. Dogs die from obesity. Let me tell you something, I have a poodle now, who we all love. And I tell my children, and they agree with me, to love somebody you don't feed them every time he does something nice. It's the old habit. Fat people think that food is the great reward. I buy him a toy, I have a box of little squeeze toys. He has ample food. But I'm not going to make him fat so he'll die of obesity. Cruel, to kill a dog with too much food. It really is. People who think that you give a dog a treat —you're doing the same thing you do to your kids. You say to your children, 'If you're very good, you can have two desserts. And if you don't behave you can't have ice cream.' "

"That's the Jewish-mother syndrome," I suggested.

She smiled. I had unwittingly given her the cue for her next soliloquy. "Not Jewish. It has nothing to do with Jewish because the Italian mothers do the same thing. And in London, England, we have obesity. In London, England. Where did that come from? So they eat crumpets, they don't know from chocolate cupcakes. . . . I can tell you this, that I worried about England when I went there last July. In July '68 I visited our franchise in England and I worried: How do you talk to people that don't even sound like you? You know, I know this'll come as a shock to you, but I'm from Brooklyn." Pitching her voice high, Jean shrilled: "How do you relate? Firstly, they don't even lose pounds. They lose stone. They pay pounds to get into the class to lose stone. So that in itself threw me. Then, too, they talk about cucumber sandwiches. I know from halvah sandwiches, having lived in Brooklyn. They talk about crumpets, they talk about teatime. I know from egg cream. So how do you talk to them?" But then she looked out at the sea of faces and recognized them. They were just like at home, this was her family, the family of fats. She saw who was going to succeed on the program, who would fail, who had come to praise and who to bury her. It was like Brooklyn, like Little Neck, and she did her stuff. The English Weight Watcher office, which is near Buckingham Palace, has a large sign reading: "We'll Get You Yet, Queenie!".

But Mrs. Nidetch doesn't believe in proselytizing. The first thing she tells her audience is, "If you want to stay fat, stay fat." For herself, she decided to lose weight because, "I simply was tired of saying, and listening to people say, 'I wish I could, but it must be metabolism.' I don't know where the metabolism is! I don't even know how to spell it. And yet I used the word almost daily. The minute I went shopping for a dress and couldn't squeeze into a size twenty-two and a half, I said to the skinny saleslady who, one, couldn't care less and, two, didn't even know what I was talking about, 'It's my metabolism.' So she agreed with me as she sent me to the fat girl's department. I was so tired of lying. I was so fed up with this monstrous lie that I lived with all my life. When I was younger I said, 'It's baby fat. I'll outgrow it.' Why did I say that? because Grandma said it—

as she gave me a chocolate bunny. But you know something? My sister was thin and she brought her a furry one. When I think back —I missed the childhood! I missed the joy of getting a pink, furry bunny. Me they brought chocolate. Which I naturally ate before the day was over. The next day my sister still had the furry one. I had nothing—but indigestion. . . . And then when somebody said, 'Oh, there's two sisters. She's the heavier one,' I said: 'It's baby fat.' I'm four years older than my sister. Why should I have had the baby fat?

". . . Then I got older and I said, 'It's a large frame.' Believe me, there is no such thing. . . . I lost seventy-two pounds, I couldn't have lost frame. Then I said, 'I must have heavy bones.' Now what was I trying to imply? The implication was that my weight isn't there —nobody sees it. When it's recorded on the scale, it's my bones that are weighing this. . . . Look at the constant lying. Then I would go into a supermarket and I'd follow me—I was never alone—and I would buy cookies. Cookies, all kinds of cookies. And, as I checked through, checking them out, I would say to a checker, who also couldn't care less, 'They're for my children.' One, she really couldn't care, she never even asked me who they're for, and two, the terrible thing is, my kids didn't even like those cookies."

One more story clinched it. I could fairly feel the flesh straining against my clothes. "I was at the stage in 1961 where in a restaurant I very loudly and very proudly said to whoever was sitting near me, 'Would you like my roll? I'm not eating the roll.' Now here I am, two hundred and fourteen pounds, giving away my roll. Firstly, nobody really likes it—and I used to do the same thing with the dessert. The dessert comes. It's part of the dinner, so God forbid you should say, 'No, thank you' or just don't say anthing. But it's this great lie. You're waiting for someone, for whoever it is who's there, to say to you, 'How come you're not eating the roll?' And then you go into your little play. You're not even aware of it, there's no rehearsal, you just do it. You say, 'I really can't eat the roll. I'm too overweight.' (They say): 'If you were thinner, you would be ugly.' One. Two: 'If you lost weight you'd lose your sunny disposition.' Which at this point you really don't have. But now there's the attitude and everyone is agreeing—'I know someone who lost weight—and died.' You know, that sort of thing. It gets that extreme. So now somebody is giving you all the right in the world to eat the roll. But you're not getting ready to eat it. So you say: 'Well, I really should lose weight.

I have a wedding to go to and I can't find a dress.' And then she says: 'I know a place where they make size nines to fit you.' Now you have to think: how are they ever going to do that? But the whole thing is so weird, and you're involved in this terrible nightmare that's prompting you to eat the roll. That's all this whole thing is about. You eat the roll and you've given yourself the rationalization to have done the right thing. But you're not quite sure. So now the dessert comes, and you say to the waiter: 'You don't have cantaloupe for dessert, do you?' He says: 'We do, but we're known for our coconut cream pie.' Well—then you turn to your friend, who just gave you permission on the roll, and you say: 'I'll order it, but you eat it.' And she goes through the same spiel why you should eat it and you've gotten her permission."

Psychiatrists and psychologists have told me that the main impulse behind beautification or joining the beauty culture is sex. We make up, shave, fix our hair, lose weight and wear stylish clothes primarily —and some argue, exclusively—to attract the opposite sex. Jean Nidetch says: "Really and truly I don't believe that's true at all." She gave more pragmatic reasons for losing weight: ". . . walking into a phone booth, closing the door, sitting down, and then there's a sudden panic. You don't know if you can open the door to get out." Or perhaps it's "being seated finally in the back seat of a two-door car. Now you are getting to your destination and you got to get out. The front-seaters get out before you. You're lucky if the front people get out after you because you *can* get out—ungracefully, if nobody sees you. But it's broad daylight and the front people got out and are waiting for you to emerge from this can opener. Well how do you do it gracefully when you weigh two hundred and fourteen pounds? And what's worse, some very well-meaning front-seater will say, 'You pull, I'll push.' And that goes to where you live. And don't tell me you lose weight because of sex. You just got killed. You just got demoralized. That's what makes you lose weight."

I persisted, though. Surely one's libido was somehow linked to one's shape. Surely one had a different view of oneself after losing weight, and this must affect sexuality. Jean looked doubtful, thought for a second and then offered me a sex story, since that was what I wanted.

About five years ago, when Weight Watchers first began, one of the men came up and said he must speak to her urgently. A matter of tremendous importance, he said. She asked him to wait until the class was over. When it had ended, another man came up saying he had something urgent to tell her. She said she had to speak to Jack first, then she'd get to him. Jack reported that he'd lost forty-two pounds, felt marvelous, was playing golf and had never been so fit in his life. However, "I hate to tell you this, Jean—did you hear it from somebody else?—but since I'm on this thing, I have no desire for sex. Is it possible that it's the fish? Or the milk? Or the vegetables? What is it?"

She listened with sympathy and concern, advised him to go to a doctor and said she would check. However, she was sure it was medical. Then she went over to the other man. He was the same age as the first, had lost forty-six pounds and felt magnificent. He asked her, "What's in this diet that makes you so sexy? I'm like nineteen years old. I can't get enough sex. Do you suppose it's the milk?"

Jean opened up her arms. "Hey, Jack," she called to the retreating man, "come over here. I want you two to get together."

If Jean Nidetch has any problems, they're well hidden. I asked if she thought she could retain her present personality even if she regained her former weight. "The only reason that I would gain weight is if I lost my mentality and lost control. . . . The only reason I will not be a blonde is because I no longer can get to the place to get my hair bleached." Like a mermaid who's finally found her rock, Jean is totally content. "I've had a taste of this life and this is great. This is great. This is the life I always dreamed about. I didn't know I could ever be part of it. To think that there's a society where women don't have to say, 'Gee, I wish I could take my girdle off'! This is unbelievable! That I could live a life where I don't have to think: July. Oh my God, July means I have to take my coat off."

3

Outcasts and Outlooks

Behind a barred window high up at Manhattan State Hospital, a former junkie is muscle-building. He watches himself in the mirror (regulation steel, so patients won't cut themselves or each other) and sees flexed biceps, a taut chest sprinkled with wiry brown hair, a navel too large and exerted, sparse pubic hair, legs he calls "bantams." He works out with the weights, his skin flushes, little drops of sweat grow into each other and run in rivulets down his face. He's getting stronger, he's sure, and even his genitals are looking up.

Without the mirror, he can't do anything. His arms won't lift, stupor encases him and the dream is gone. His dream is to be a real he-man, who can punch anyone in the face. Like the man in the Charles Atlas ads, he won't let anyone push him around anymore. People will have to think twice before monkeying with his girl or his job. They'll notice him, they'll see he's superior, they'll know here's a fellow you don't tangle with.

"The manic loves the mirror. Schiz as a rule, does not," says the director of the hospital.

Another psychiatrist says, "Schizophrenics don't care [how they look], because they're the only ones in the world they're in, you see. There is no competition. They don't give a hoot in hell how they look to someone else." This is James A. Brussel, whose specialty is deducing the criminal through the crimes he commits. Dr. Brussel, author of *Casebook of a Crime Psychiatrist*, helped track down the Mad Bomber ("When you find him, chances are he'll be wearing a double-breasted suit. Buttoned."), the Boston Strangler ("He probably has a mane of hair the average girl would envy") and other murderers. Dr.

171

Brussel elaborated on the characteristics of schizophrenics: "They become introspective, they retreat into themselves, they're their own show, their own world; they're God, they're everybody. And whatever they want in their world of fantasy, they just will that way. . . . It isn't a question of becoming unisexual, homosexual or monosexual, there is no other sex. . . . They might masturbate, which is quite common, but that's a token of narcism anyway."

A paranoid personality, on the other hand, takes meticulous care of his looks. Albert DiSalvo, the Boston Strangler, did have "a gorgeous head of hair," which he cared for lovingly as a sign (and perhaps symbol) of his virile attractiveness. George Metesky, the Mad Bomber, was always extremely well groomed. Paranoids are careful to present an outside manner and appearance that is perfectly correct. They have accepted social reality, they know the rules by which people judge them, and fastidiously abide by these, the better to diguise their true reality and hide from those who are out to get them.

Manic depressives may use their outward appearance to announce their inner state; when exuberant, they sometimes wear extravagant clothes and makeup. Women might put on Kewpie-doll makeup: bright red lips, white skin, two painted circles on their cheeks, because the clown is the human embodiment of laughter. A psychologist at the University of Pennsylvania said, "My impression is that one of the manifestations of manic reactions is an overattention to makeup, cosmetics, clothes. . . . It's part of a feeling of almost hysterical well-being, being beautiful. Or," he cautioned, "it may be partially a mask."

The director of a mental hospital explained, "Sometimes the manic may be very meticulously dressed, but sometimes he dresses very bizarrely. The makeup may be considered distorted in the female. . . . The manic is almost the supreme egotist."

Mental illness, as usually defined, means the loss, distortion or fragmentation of self-image. Simply, the mentally ill don't have the same relation with themselves that we have. A pretty psychologist on the staff of Bronx State Hospital insisted that the "tremendous loss of a sense of self . . . cuts across diagnostic categories." Dr. Kramer, at Roosevelt Hospital, spoke of "people whose whole language is body language" as having "no distinction between being and acting."

Since we generally assume that the difference between psychosis and "normalcy" is one of degree, a typical purpose in treatment is the reassimilation of a psychotic into society. Dr. Kramer said sociology is "where it's at in psychiatry," and Dr. Brussel, who might otherwise disagree with that statement, explained: "Mental patients . . . are learning to return to that world they're retreating from, the world we call heterosexuality, which is a world of interpersonal relationships between man and woman." A prominent psychiatrist, who asked not to be named, defined psychosis as "a rejection of reality. . . . the ego goes over in the service of the id. . . . We want to bring [patients] back to reality. After all, that is what we're here for. Otherwise, all we would do would be to lock them up, feed them, see that they're warm and let them go ahead with their delusional systems, let them go ahead with their fantasies."

Instead, therapy is offered—medical, physical, psychiatric and social. The patient has exiled himself from society and must be brought back through his psyche and sociability. He must be made acceptable to himself and to the world around him. He must be politicized, returned to a political and economic entity where he participates as consumer, citizen and, incidentally, believer.

Beauty practices are now widely used as therapy. By bringing the patient into the beauty culture, one hopes to restore his sense of self-respect and give him a public personality that will allow interaction with others and with his private self. Clothes, makeup and grooming offer control over role playing; they permit the patient to put his antic disposition off because he can now be identified as a member of society. He learns something else too, not specified and often repudiated by psychiatrists: to become a consumer.

Entrance into the beauty culture means a belief that certain products and forms of behavior will improve one's appearance and that others care enough about improved appearance to act differently toward you. When you believe that, you've accepted a set of values that lead back to the economy. Fantasy has become big business. By accepting socially approved fantasies, you become socialized. The schizophrenic is a nonconsumer. When he is able to accept beautification, he accepts the beauty industry and, like everyone else, learns to demand what the industry supplies.

Beauty therapy is used for all types of patients. A young woman taught modern dance to a group of catatonics in Washington, D.C. She saw that they reacted most to elaborations of a performance: setting, costumes, makeup. So she demonstrated how dancers apply makeup and encouraged them to try themselves. She gave each (woman) patient a different product; one had lipstick, another pancake, a third, eye makeup. The women were forced to borrow from each other, and they did, speaking to each other for the first time.

Beauty parlors and barber shops are a feature of many hospitals, and often instruction on shaving, makeup and hair styling are given. Speaking of the woman patient, Dr. Brussel said, "this does a lot therapeutically," because, "her interest in her appearance becomes a positive factor to her, an attractive thing to her, an interesting thing to her. Because people seem to pay more attention to her, plus the fact that interest in having *her* develop an interest in herself is fostered by someone else."

At Manhattan State Hospital, The Fashion Group runs a program on beauty and fashion, enthusiastically supported by the hospital directorate: "Working from without, we may be of benefit to build up the self-image of the individual." The program is donated by established members of the beauty and fashion industries and by the women executives who form the group. Each week a talk and demonstration are given to thirty women patients, who are all drugged, many very heavily to prevent them from becoming violent.

"I think through the years nearly every good name in town has been out there," said Alma Cunningham. "They're delighted to go . . . and they've never worked so hard." Kenneth, however, was not wildly enthusiastic. "We gave them rollers and a brush and comb and hair spray and some curlers and bobby pins and clips and things, et cetera, and demonstrated on one person what she could do to herself: how to set her hair, how to cope with it. Really, it's how to cope, I think, that's essential. And then I went around and told people what they could do, and how they could look better and how they should go about it. . . . Some of them were purposely, I felt, messy." Kenneth was depressed by his evening there and doesn't intend to offer his services again.

But The Fashion Group is pleased. "We know that sometimes when they even give us very sick people, we can tell the difference in reactions from the first session to the last one. That's very noticeable." Alma Cunningham spoke happily. ". . . sometimes they're like children, they won't even come to the table to sit with us. They stand off by the wall or they'll peep round a post. And they absolutely refuse to participate." But eventually they join, and benefit. "They've really helped themselves a great deal."

To encourage the patients, the ladies of the group are careful to present themselves in a manner that will be immediately identified with fashion. If they "show up in a very good gray dress . . . [patients] don't respond to that sort of thing," so they wear bright colors, strong patterns, bracelets that jangle and skirts of *Vogue*-approved length. The executives are forced to apply the lesson they're trying to teach: your external appearance informs the world about you and identifies you.

Miss Cunningham assured me the hospital director felt the project was "eighty-five percent effective in the studies of the patients later," but she was unable to specify the criterion for effectiveness or how the figure had been reached. The director himself told me that all types of mental illness were represented, but that the participating patients were "on their way" to recovery. Then he added a seeming contradiction: "We have some that have been here for many, many years. They probably will not get out too soon. We've had to try to see what this would do for them."

In her office, her hair very short and straight, her only makeup a streak of blue shadow, Miss Cunningham told me of the near-miracle that occurred during a makeup class: "All of a sudden, toward the end of the session, which was very quiet and everyone was working [making up the patients], an electric shock ran through that room. And we all looked at one another, we couldn't see what was happening. The session closed, and all the patients said good night and left. The doctors and the therapists all got together and they were *jabbering*. There had been a patient, a woman who for about three years had been a mental case, and she was one of the ones whose faces pull—she made faces all the time. . . . They had treated her with everything they knew to do, the doctors told us later, without any visible result. She continued to [grimace] almost constantly. The minute she picked up a lipstick, put on lipstick, she quit. We didn't notice it but they did. And they were so excited!" The excitement returned for Miss Cunningham, and her light eyes became bluer under the shadow. "We had a real thing for a while: 'Don't underestimate the power of a lipstick.' And as far as I know—she was checked up later—she still hasn't grimaced. She was also still wearing lipstick."

And she was also still in the hospital. But, as the doctor in charge explained: "Even if it were to give them a little more ease for a short period of time, even if they stayed in the hospital—any help we could give was acceptable." He said further: "We're attempting to give just one more point of reference: a) external self, b) reality. That's what we're trying to do."

The help is not consciously directed toward a pragmatic end, like economic advancement or increasing marriageability. The hospital is a closed society with no sexual opportunities, and there is only one chance for mobility: to get out. To become aware of one's external self may be a step toward the acceptance of social values and a means of acquiring the self-consciousness necessary for a dialogue with one-self. A young New York career girl asked me, "What would happen to women if all the mirrors disappeared? You know, that confrontation with oneself?" The psyche must become a kind of mirror, reflecting not only what you think you are but what others think you are, too. Just as the mirror distorts, so the psyche must be willing to deceive.

Psychotics often lack this ability for deception. Because the sense of "other" may be missing, psychotics have no reality censor to forbid literalness. A woman who wants to look like Jackie Kennedy "may just accept the fact that she is Jackie Kennedy," said an eminent New York psychiatrist. "And what reality tells her means nothing. That's why we're trying to bring [psychotics] to reality, but at the same time give them enough change so that they can accept a good body image. I can go to one of them and say, 'No. You are not Jackie Kennedy. You are short, you're fat, you're ugly, you're this, that and the other thing.' This would be very traumatic, right? Instead of that, I say, 'You are not Jackie Kennedy; nevertheless, you are beautiful.'"

Reality means becoming (looking) more like the women on the street outside the hospital. "Why not?" challenged the doctor. "But in a competitive sense. There's no woman who wants to be like all others. There is a certain norm, but each one wants to be just a little bit better in some fashion." He then gave an example: "One of the girls down at the ward wanted to be more noticed as far as her chest was concerned. So she wore tight sweaters and maybe she had somewhere around a forty, but," he added gratuitously, "I'd hate to see that babe undressed. It would be grotesque. That's my own attitude." *

She is probably on her way to recovery, since one of the first signs is interest in appearance. She is beginning to like herself and has learned to deceive. She emphasizes a feature that she and society consider attractive and by doing this plays down whatever less appealing feature she may have. She is repudiating unattractiveness, the badge of outcasts.

In trying to define the beauty culture, one must determine its outer limits. Though many individuals stand outside it, the only groups I found were the mentally ill, the blind and the old. The last two are easily led back to the fold; they have merely strayed. Mental patients, however, are generally recognizable as black sheep, who cannot be assimilated until they change their colors. In America, concern with improving one's looks disappears only when the personality breaks down.

Yet cosmetics ads and beauty copy often seem to imply that everyone's a little bit mad. Revlon offers "lipstick to take to the moon," Yardley poses its models in wildly romantic settings and Clairol asks, "Who's you?", answering: "Maybe the real you is a blonde." Fashion and women's magazines evince the need for becoming someone different this spring, this summer or this evening—presenting the woman as chameleon, able to change her colors, features and looks from situation to situation with no traumatic effect on her personality.

---

* Like many others I interviewed, this psychiatrist asked not to be named. He is an elderly man with considerable power in New York mental hospitals. Interviewing him, I noticed his persistent interest in female erogenous areas. I was wearing a miniskirt and black boots. Here, a fragment of our conversation:

K.P.: The image for beauty is now changing. Men are wearing clothes with a soft look and women are adopting a tough-little-girl look.

Doctor: 'Taint so. 'Taint so. This is pure fantasy. You're absolutely fantasizing in a realistic fashion. You may have the tough babe, slim, hard, wears pants, boots, whatnot, but with the boots, what else do you put on you? You put on tight slacks. Where are the slacks loose? Only in the bell bottoms. The rest are tight. They're snug, aren't they? They emphasize the cuntour [contour] of the pelvic area, don't they? Now, further than that. You put on boots but what else did you do? Raised your skirts. But you raised them to the point where fantasy is still permitted. In other words, a man looks at a woman, sees certain things. He undresses her very rapidly and projects a vision which nine cases out of ten is very false, because she wears things to build up or hold in or what have you.

A housewife prepares for a party by getting into her slinky black, her auburn wig and spider lashes. When she arrives, people react to her outward cues, and she is a siren of the evening. At home, she removes all makeup, puts her hair in curlers and accepts her husband's compliments for "pulling it off" so well.

In large cities, nubile skin is covered with pancake and young faces harden in theatrical exaggeration of adulthood. Fourteen-year-olds with heavy makeup and padded bras offer signs and tokens of a womanhood they have not yet achieved. At lunch hour on the main avenues pass files of women with the same facial expressions. Secretaries, waitresses, aspiring models, housewives all seem to be sisters, with overbleached hair or highly teased hairdos, a long fringe of lashes, pale skins, bright eye shadow, and yet they are not manic. Like prostitutes, they exaggerate features as a form of advertising or as a parody of women, demonstrating the lascivious side of every wife and daughter. The line between "normalcy" and psychosis is often hard to find.

In a study of social classes in New Haven, Hollingshead and Redlich found that certain personality traits were diagnosed as chronic schizophrenia when they occurred in people of the lowest classes. On the next rung of society, people with the same traits were considered acute schizophrenics, and in the wealthy middle class they appeared as interesting cases of neuroses. So, too, when Penelope Tree wears bizarre makeup, she is in the vanguard of fashion; when an inmate of Manhattan State Hospital does the same, she is projecting her illness.

But there is a difference, and it lies in amount of control. One psychiatrist explained that psychosis means "fantasy is entirely divorced from reality. You take the neurotic or the normal—fantasy is still used, but it is in reality setting. And they can return to reality very rapidly, whereas in the psychotic there isn't any." The nonpsychotic accepts (or creates) an image of *beauty*, not of *self*. Cinderella, knowing she must return from the ball at midnight, is able to resume her real life.

"The people who fall for these ads," said Dr. Brussel, talking of ads that promise the moon or stars, "are a lot of frustrated, wishful-thinking people. This goes for men too. . . . [The ads] appeal to the fantasy; the childish wishful thinking of being all and everything and at the same time me. The multiple personality drive. . . ."

Janet Simon, a dark-eyed psychologist with long, shining hair, explained: "One chooses an image. . . . There's a tremendous amount of energy that gets expended in deliberately creating the other self [whereas] in schizophrenia, there's so much going on inside these people that they can't find the energy to expend on an image, or the control to manipulate it. . . . [the distinction] between what's inside and what's outside gets so blurred that it might be hard to self-consciously and very deliberately take on another image, another face; to put on a mask."

The psychotic's fantasies, like the pervert's, are antisocial. The playacting of American men and women in the beauty culture is a nationally approved diversion. Larry Gross, social psychologist, suggested that "one of the immediate consequences of affluence is more attention to aesthetic dimensions . . . and the importance you place on fantasies is how far you stand from realities."

Most people I interviewed were eager to give their definition of beauty or talk about someone, usually with a "beautiful soul." These digressions were never particularly helpful for my purposes. The clichés, truths and truisms of beauty are better investigated by a philosopher than a journalist, and the beauty culture stands a long way from the problem of aesthetics. Just as the American way of death has little to do with the awesome fact, so the American way of beauty maintains only a tenuous relation with the awesome illusion. Beauty practices, like death practices, become a substitute for the thing itself.

Beauty is assumed to be therapy, but usually in a very loose sense. We believe beauty can heal and bring pleasure to the beholder and the beheld. It can resurrect the ego; it is part of love. As children, we learned that the frog becomes a handsome prince through a kiss, and Cinderella was loved by the greatest in the land when she became beautiful. Love is the metamorphosis of everyday life: a homely girl is made beautiful through love and pretty is as pretty does.

But in the beauty culture, the teaching of makeup and grooming as therapy is no fairy godmother's want. It is not a question of becoming beautiful but merely of convincing oneself and others that we are more beautiful or attractive than we or they have thought. Sometimes, it just means becoming presentable or acceptable.

The blind are often neither. Since most people judge another partly by how that person sees them, the blind are inevitably disadvantaged. They don't see us and can't respond to our attractiveness. Further, they don't see themselves and usually make no effort to appeal to someone's visual prejudices. Sightless eyes are often accompanied by overweight, frumpish clothes, lack of grooming and, sometimes, an air of stupidity.

The American Foundation for the Blind discovered that of five hundred activities normally performed every day by sighted people the blind perform only eleven. To increase this figure, Albert Asenjo, rehabilitation director, has launched a program of teaching "personal management," including specific training in grooming skills. An instruction book published in the autumn of 1969 gives techniques for applying eye makeup (eyebrow powder, eye-shadow powder, brush-on mascara), scents, cream and liquid skin cleansers; explains how hair should be shampooed, brushed and combed, with special attention to parting hair; teaches methods of shaving face, legs and underarms and concludes with a discussion of liquid makeup ("liquid rouge . . . is not recommended") and lipstick ("Keep in mind that styles change, so a shade once chosen is not likely to be suitable indefinitely.").

Fifty percent of the blind are over sixty-five; ten percent are children. Studies on self-image have been very inconclusive partly because there are no adequate means of testing. Blind children are usually considered mentally retarded; teen-agers delay sexual maturity; frustration has been built into the lives of most blind people so that their view of themselves and the world contains anger, self-pity and inhibition. Zofya Jastrzembska, a psychologist working at the foundation, explained that the self-image of the blind closely accords with psychotic self-image but is realistic at the same time. The blind live in a world where other people can do things they can't. They are deprived of the eighty-five to ninety percent of information taken in by normal people through their eyes. The blind, she pointed out, are not subject to psychosomatic illness; their infirmity serves the same purpose.

The inner vision of the blind is called "videation," said Mr. Asenjo, "meaning to image, to see in the mind what one looks like or what one should look like, or what one's friend may look like, or a flower or a dog or a horse or a car." Though "the congenitally blind do seek each other out," the adventitious blind often associate with sighted people and are aware of their friends' attractiveness. A blind girl is proud of having a handsome boyfriend. Other people's opinions remain important; the values of a banished world are accepted.

Bonne Bell, a cosmetics company associated with skiers, gives lecture-demonstrations on makeup to blind teen-age girls in department stores around the country. Though this may seem a gratuitous undertaking, Mr. Asenjo and Miss Jastrzembska feel that blind girls who make up receive their reward in the attitudes of other people, gain recognition and improve their job chances.

When Mala Rubinstein, president of Helena Rubinstein, became interested in makeup for the blind, she sent her technician to work with Mr. Asenjo. After a year and a half the products and techniques were tried. Miss Rubinstein sat with the girls and taught them; as they were made prettier, they became more confident. One young girl, blinded in a fire that badly scarred her face, was at first reluctant to be guinea pig. After long persuasion, she agreed, and by the end of the day was "transformed," according to Mr. Asenjo. Though the girl could still feel her scars, she knew they were covered and that the world would see her differently.

Makeup for the blind (and grooming in general) provides more therapy than simple beautification. To master the technique is a challenge, and a blind girl can have a great sense of accomplishment when she's finally able to do her own eyes. The ritual itself gives assurance that she is pursuing a normal activity. The same girl probably reads the braille edition of *Seventeen*. She's entering the world around her, where people see and react to being seen. The question of vanity becomes complicated, though Mr. Asenjo assured me the blind can be vain. If so, the mental image and not the mirror nourishes vanity. The sighted person instructs the mirror to feed back his mental image.

Many of the blind are old, but blindness is a mere cipher in the catalog of handicaps of the aged. They are terribly poor compared to the rest of the country, they are ugly by usual standards, they are useless, their hair doesn't grow and their perspiration has stopped. Their mental faculties decline with the physical. They are helpless. With few exceptions, the prospect is bleak and they offend the young by their smell of death. Except for death, nothing is so feared in America as old age.

To mitigate its effects, old people live in retirement communities, shielded from the young and from normal life. They live as on shipboard, going from one activity to another, imitating a probably nonexistent period in their youth when they had no responsibilities and their parents constantly provided amusements. One such community claims to be the place "where mature adults make the most of their freedom years."

The privileged old can lead a perfect imitation of life in gregarious capsules. Or they can choose to remain in society and compete. With money, they have recourse to plastic surgery, hairdressers, Florida winters, spas, rejuvenation schemes and elegant clothes. They can exhibit what Dr. Brussel calls "the Ponce de Leon reflex complex— eternal youth." He defines this as "the absolute fear of death. . . . The basic fear of all people is the return of the organic to the inorganic."

But most old people have neither the money nor the hopefulness to do anything about aging. Unlike the mentally ill, their self-image may be totally realistic, but nobody's interested. The old are interred in society as soon as they stop contributing to the economy. Their values and ways of life belong to history, and their awareness of fashion might have stopped forty years ago, when no nice woman wore make-up and men didn't reach for the deodorant.

Teaching beauty practices to the old is a way of admitting them to contemporary life. At Riverview, Philadelphia's home for the indigent aged, the three beauty shops have special wheelchairs for invalids so the back needn't bend for the head to enter the basin. All ladies have a standing appointment with the hairdresser and rotate turns. There, I saw a blind woman of about eighty smile as spray was applied to her gleaming blond curls. A thin brunette with matching lipstick and polish was asking to have her eyebrows arched.

In department stores and on dance floors we can see miniskirted grandmothers. Grandfathers with tinted hair recline beside swimming pools. Vanity, like hope, never dies. America and the beauty industry teach that there is no one too old, too infirm or too poor to become more beautiful. Even after death, the hair is styled and rouge applied. Meeting your Maker is like a job interview. When you look your best, you feel good and you act good. Even the outcasts must be given hope that they can return, and it is the attractive (the young) who inherit the kingdom of America.

4

Inside

[1] START

"I have girls that, in terms of beauty, wear bikini underwear. And I have girls that wear long johns," explained Gloria MacFarland, director of Start, a home for delinquent girls on Staten Island. "I have girls that throw away their underwear every time they have their period. I have girls that never learned to throw a Kotex away. You know, wrap it up or stuff like that, flush it in the john. So when you say beauty, I think of self-concept immediately."

The girls are like other sixteen-to-eighteen-year-olds, except they are all serving a prison sentence, are more intelligent than average and most are exceptionally pretty. Anne, a slim blonde with blue eyes and navy eyeliner, lashes drawn below the eye, showed me her paintings. A lion with the compassionate expression of a saint, a child on a hill of flowers, the study of a dying leaf. At first she brought out her paintings with defiance, but they were marvelous and I told her so. Her face softened, she looked more like the picture of herself taken a few years earlier, when she wore no makeup, had a long blond page-boy and posed like a debutante for Richard Avedon. She was here now because of drugs, sex and abortion.

Her roommate Betty, a small, dark girl with discreet makeup, had been brought to court by her parents when she ran away from home to Greenwich Village. Her flight came after six weeks of house arrest, when her parents had imprisoned her in her room with chains at the door. Anne showed me Betty's drawings from that time, electrifying pictures with Beardsley-like curves, eyes peering out from various parts of the contorted, art nouveau design. "She was real mad then," Anne explained. Betty watched me shyly while I examined the drawings. They could be illustrations, I felt, for Blake or *The Inferno*. One was called "A Season in Hell," and though Betty had not read Rimbaud's prose poem, she had heard of it and was delighted when I offered to send it to her. "There's a lot in these, one has to look a long time," Anne admonished me when I flicked through too quickly. I wondered in what college dormitory would the girls be so generous with each other's work.

The third roommate was less glamorous than the others, but with a model's figure. She showed me a terra cotta figure she had made, representing Mrs. MacFarland in the last stages of pregnancy, "a fertility symbol," said Jean. By her chest of drawers hung a sketch she had made of her shoes. "Self-portrait?" I asked. Jean smiled broadly, shaking her head yes.

Rosita, the fourth roommate, was a Puerto Rican foundling, with dark, voluptuous hair. She was the only one not wearing makeup. I commented—the girls knew I was writing a book on beauty—and Rosita apologized: "Someone told me once there's no woman too beautiful not to wear makeup."

"Maybe there's no woman too ugly to have to wear makeup."

"I like that," said Rosita, "I'll have to remember it."

When I asked Rosita for her artistic works, she said that although she could draw from life realistically, she had no feeling for it. She couldn't express herself through art, she felt, and so left it to her roommates, whose talents she admired.

Almost all the girls were carefully dressed, combed and groomed. "If the girls shoplift anything, it'll be cosmetics," said Mrs. MacFarland. On the bureaus of most girls stood many bottles, jars and tubes. Most girls were made up, some rather heavily but without distortion. Hair, however, was sometimes very obviously bleached, with streaks of yellow or gold against a dark background, and was often short.

"They chop their hair a lot, girls," said Mrs. MacFarland. "And I always try to relate it to this thing where they take the prostitutes and shave their hair. You know, kind of like a stigma. A lot of girls will cut their hair off at the beginning of treatment and let it grow as treatment goes on. And then do nice things with it."

Mrs. Vanderbilt, the motivation director, explained: "Lots of these girls don't think they're pretty. And a lot of them are beautiful, they have a lot to go on. But they don't feel pretty. They don't have the confidence. . . . Once they start to understand themselves, they start to feel pretty and they take more of an interest."

The treatment, the way to understanding, lies in nightly group therapy. During the day, the girls go to high school or have jobs as candy-stripers in the nearby mental hospital. A few go to beauty school, where after completing their one thousand hours, they can become licensed beauticians. Coming home from the school, the girls like to mimic their instruction. "You want to hear the line we're supposed to give the customer?" And they break up laughing.

In the evening, the girls discuss themselves and each other. Gloria MacFarland explained the aims of this therapy: "No man stands alone. No woman stands alone. The goal of any kind of treatment is, fundamentally, interpersonal relationships. The belonging, the sense of belonging, is one of the key things. So you can't be an isolated individual. We serve others and, through serving others, discover self."

"Do you expect the girls to discover a real sense of identity?" I asked.

"Never. Never; we don't have it at forty. We don't have it at fifty. It's the idea of being able to become that keeps you young. And it's when the old folks decide there's no more becoming that they go. There was a recent article that people determine when they die. And I believe it. I believe it—ask me something about beauty. I think the human soul is beautiful." My expression must have indicated that this was beside the point. "All right, you want to talk about the mask, you want to talk about the outside, you want to talk about *IT*"—she paused long enough for suspense to build—"the daughter relationship."

Mrs. MacFarland, who is a trained clinical psychologist and worked for many years at the Hudson Training School for Girls, believes that the mother-daughter relationship is the key to a girl's view of herself. The mother serves as "ego model" for the girl, is her fiercest competitor, her idol and even, in a way, her other self. Beautifying oneself is a game, based on "the competitiveness with another female, and the basic relationship with another female. Do women dress for men? Or make up for men? Or for other women? I think there's one of the keys. And how much of the fight with mama are they still fighting as this goes on? And has the mannequin given up the fight? And is she going to be a thing instead of a person?"

We had by now gone beyond the specific relationship of delinquent girls to beauty, and of teen-age girls, and had stepped into the larger picture. Mrs. MacFarland emphasized that the girls at Start were no different from others, except "they feel more inadequate in terms of coping." But the coping has to be done by all women. Though the intensities of the parent-child relationship, and particularly the Oedipal relationship, have been accepted in this culture so religiously that they often become an incantation against anger, shock or disappointment, I had noticed among the women I interviewed a certain pattern of childishness. Women like Susie, who devoted such time and expense to plastic surgery; women who had ritual beauty days, where an appointment with the hairdresser was followed by a facial, followed by a visit to the eyelash salon; women who took many hours to prepare themselves for going out—all were striking in their little-girl behavior. Their interests were those of a thirteen-year-old: boys, clothes, their own bodies and faces. They had been unable to, or had resisted growing up. They were living like fairy princesses in a world where parties, hem lengths, diets and mascara were the only concern. These women could neither get into themselves nor away from themselves. They were neither bad people nor good, but simply undeveloped, and lived without real humor or real seriousness from one mini-event to another. Women whose exclusive concern was their external appearance had no self-respect, though women who took care of their appearance as merely one of their concerns seemed more self-assured than women who paid no attention to how they looked. But the little dolls, the ageless sex kittens, had remained their mothers' little girls, frail creatures whom their mothers would protect and care for and who never dared become a person for fear of contradicting mother.

"Do the girls here idolize certain women?" I asked Gloria Mac-Farland.

"They hate a lot of women."

"But don't they want to be Jane Fonda or Jackie Kennedy?"

"No."

"Who do they have as models?" I persisted.

"Malcolm X."

Later, she elaborated: "The dream behind everything is to become a model. More than a movie star, much more. To become a model."

"But the model has no personality," I pointed out. Though

Penelope Tree or Veruschka might be very strong personalities, the public performance of every model requires only that she pose.

"Because they're very frightened of what they are. They know what they feel like, you see, but they can be a mannequin. . . . It's much easier to be something that's fixed, that people can relate to, than take the responsibility of becoming some *one* for people to relate to."

"But a model's profession is, after all, to be no one. . . ."

"A some thing. A some thing."

Amy Greene, former beauty editor of *Glamour*, discovered through make-overs that the girls "want to look like a model . . . any model." She explains it by the desire to be in print, to be seen and also to make a lot of money. Harold Melvin, the Negro hairdresser in Harlem, said, "Negro girls tend to identify with models." And he felt that they identified with white models, who until recently were almost the only ones they saw. The inmates of the Women's House of Detention, mostly nonwhite, also identify with models.

The girls at Start share the dreams and preoccupations of all girls raised in America. They may have acted out what for other girls remain fantasies; they have engaged in antisocial behavior. As Mrs. MacFarland pointed out: "Delinquency is a legal term. Any hippy, by law, is a delinquent. . . . It means that a parent has not taken them to court to say that they're beyond their control." Most intelligent children, at some time or other, are delinquent, in their feelings and mind, if not in their actions. The girls at Start have been taken to court by their parents (other parents might send their child to a psychiatrist, or send him away to school: a century ago, they might have apprenticed him) and then were chosen by Gloria MacFarland. She chooses only those who can profit by the program and, because it's based on verbal ability, this means the girls are intelligent. They're also attractive. Only one of the twenty girls was very slovenly, and she was also openly hostile. The other nineteen were all pretty, with good figures. I wondered to what extent the director had been influenced in her choice by the looks of the girls. An attractive girl, even with a low opinion of herself, still has greater poise and self-confidence than an unattractive girl. Perhaps pretty girls are easier to rehabilitate because they are more acceptable to most people. Mrs. MacFarland might have chosen the ones she felt were more able to cope. Because Start is largely a self-help program, the girls must take on responsibility for improving themselves. Possibly, attractive girls are more willing to assume that responsibility and are therefore in a better position to be rehabilitated.

In the prison world, as everywhere else, looks are important. Incorrigibles are generally plain or even ugly. Good-looking teen-age girls everywhere in America pay attention to their appearance, and though at Start there may be exaggerations (body tattooing, for instance, which was not encouraged, but also not prohibited when a few girls tried it), the beauty culture is generally accepted. Almost all teen-agers have some difficulty in accepting and liking themselves. If they like the way they look, they're free to concentrate on other things, and are more generous towards other people. When I was about to leave, some of the girls tried to dissuade me. "Stay for dinner," said Rosita, "we have great food."

I protested that I really couldn't, I had to get back to my baby. "Come another time," said Anne, the girl who loved animals but cared less for people, "come back and bring the family. We're not dangerous."

[2] THE WOMEN'S HOUSE OF DETENTION

In the sewing room, girls sat in shapeless uniforms, their hair very short, their naked arms often scarred by rusty needles of a quick fix. All are dark, either Negro or Puerto Rican, and they move like cowboys, in imitation of men or freedom. Cigarettes hang from their lips, they pick up a snatch of material, work on it a few minutes, then interrupt for a few rounds of banter—tough, bawdy, with the quick, straight punch of gallows humor. At three, they crowd into the elevators, shouting, laughing, goosing each other, then lifting up their hands to the correction officers, their faces mocking innocence. The faces are tense, hysteria just below the surface, and for a moment one is afraid, in the small box pressed together with all these girls, that a prison riot is about to begin. There are small, wiry men everywhere— until one looks closer: the hint of swelling on the chest beneath the uniform or, where there is none, up to the hairless cheeks.

"The girls are so hard to handle, because the only way they can make any impact on us is by being perfectly horrible, and that makes it very difficult," said Mary Lindsay, retired warden of the Women's House of Detention.

"They use their appearance sort of as a weapon," said a present correction officer, "to show you how bad they can look."

"Yes," said another, "they do it to bother the officers. And we do get bothered by it. They want to get our attention, they want to know someone cares."

The first added: "They want to thwart you. They want you to come over and say, 'My God, you don't have to look that bad just 'cause you're in jail—'"

"They're saying," interrupted the second, " 'Take me like this or do something about me.' They're provoking you."

In the sewing room, the girls avidly read the few dilapidated fashion magazines and improvise patterns for themselves. The budget of the sewing room is one hundred and twenty-five dollars a year, which must cover all materials used, patterns, buttons, thread, scissors and everything else needed to make clothes. The Women's House of Detention has a census of about five hundred. So improvisation is necessary, and the teacher, a pretty, slim young woman, helps them use up the last snippets of cloth—in a contrasting pocket, perhaps, or sleeves of a different material. The clothes are made to go home in and, chiefly, for the annual fashion show. Any girl who wants to can work in the sewing room daily from seven thirty to eleven, again from one to three. Almost everyone here is an addict, and many are prostitutes. The prostitutes are often more particular about their appearance than the other inmates and sometimes will alter their institution clothes to give them a little more chic.

In the beauty shop, inmates are pressing, washing, waxing the hair of other girls. Every two weeks, a girl is eligible to have her hair done and generally will be allowed to come the day before she goes to court. She is not allowed to change the color of her hair or to have it cut very short—though an Afro is permitted at the discretion of the operators. Wigs are taken away unless the owner is bald. Though the girls are theoretically forbidden to wear masculine styles, many come in with closely cropped hair, and when it grows too long find some desperate method of cutting it. They may break light bulbs and use the sharp glass. Razors and mirrors are not allowed (in men's prisons, razors are handed out for shaving, then collected), but a woman who needs a haircut is as imaginative as a suicide.

The beauty shop was originally part of a program instituted under New York Corrections Commissioner Anna Kross in 1956 and was to include a training course in beauty. Since the course requires one thousand hours before eligibility for a license, it couldn't be offered to detained women and sentenced prisoners were too few. Now, there are more than twice as many detained inmates as sentenced ones; but the detained women may be in prison for up to two years before their case is brought to court. The sentenced women remain for only ninety days, and are then sent up to the New York State prison. Three months isn't enough time for the course, and though two years would be ample, detained prisoners can never know how long they'll be staying.

The beautician's course is offered at the state prison. Sylvia, a very pregnant dark woman with velvet eyes, took that course, studied cosmetology theory, passed all tests but didn't receive her license. She has been convicted of many felonies, and the law states that a license may not be issued to someone with two felonies or more.

She now sat in the beauty shop, having worked all day. "Didn't the law discourage you?" I asked. "Didn't you feel there was no point studying if you couldn't get a license anyway?"

She smiled luxuriously, as women will smile a few days before they deliver a child. "Well, there's hope. Maybe the law will change. They're working on it."

"It's not economical. They're trying to keep you out of prison, right? And the best way they can insure that is by giving you a trade, some way to make money. If they don't give you the license, that means you can't support yourself, and will probably have to go back to whatever you were doing," I pointed out.

Her smile remained and she shrugged. I asked Sylvia if she felt tired, standing all day with her large belly. She assured me she felt fine. The prison was going to take care of the birth, would take her to the hospital by ambulance when the time came. But, she apologized ruefully, she sometimes got worried that the baby would come too fast—this was her fifth—or at night, and then an ambulance might not be ready.

I told her I was writing a book about beauty and asked if she thought the inmates made up or cared about their looks. "Well, the girls don't make up much because the stuff isn't available. The commissary used to have things—I think they were donated by Clairol— but now there's nothing but lipstick and powder. They haven't had eyebrow pencil for three or four months, and the powder isn't the right shade for most people—it's very light."

But a high official told me that inmates generally wear makeup. Though their own cosmetics are taken away, she said, they are able to purchase whatever they like at the commissary. Formerly, the girls were rather desperate and morale was low because no beauty aids were available. They would burn wax paper to melt off the wax and then apply it to their hair. (Many Negro women use wax to straighten the hair or give it gloss.) Or, if they had an eyebrow pencil, they would take grease from their food and make a mixture for use as mascara or eye shadow. "Life in jail is, generally speaking, boring, and to get away from the boresomeness of it, [the inmates] take care of their appearance," said this official.

The girls are very narcissistic, she insisted, and always primping in front of the mirror (there's one in each corridor). They make up more than the staff do because they have more time—after all, what else do they have to do? A plump correction officer agreed: "The inmates look better than we do. They get all primped, their hair's lovely."

All corrections officers I met were Negro. The one who escorted me in was tall and severe, her hair crew cut. The sewing teacher was meticulously groomed and the programing director was a grandmother with irridescent blue eye shadow and reddish-blond hair. Otherwise, the officers were generally dowdy; their uniforms fit only slightly better than the inmates'.

"In solitary," said the programing director, "they don't make up. They're like a sick person, all they think about is getting out."

"But here," she went on, "they care how they look. Often those who dislike themselves are well groomed, they have their hair nice and they put on makeup."

I asked whether this was to attract other women, since homosexuality is a general assumption in prisons. "No. If she is [lesbian], she has her own code." She has special signals with the other woman and almost always remains faithful to a single partner. None are butterflies who flit from one to another; and in any case, the director pointed out, makeup is not what attracts women to each other. The dikes, however, are "most fastidious," said Mary Lindsay. "Although they're dressed in very masculine fashion, they're dressed so to perfection. . . . The ones who are on the make for anybody and everybody really dress," she explained, in contradiction to the present officials. "And although their hair is very short, they have it very well done."

Why make up? I asked the officers. Away from society and away from men, there should be no making up at all, if the purpose is to attract sexually or improve one's social or economic position. The small, sloe-eyed director of the beauty shop said, "Eyes tell the story. Did you ever look at these girls' eyes? You can't hold their eyes long, they'll always drop them. Because no matter how pretty she is, her eyes will give her away. Her eyes are dead. Makeup will camouflage that. If she wears enough makeup on her eyes, she can hide behind it."

Do the girls then wear makeup for disguise? "No," she assured me. Nine out of ten try for a natural look. They just want to emphasize what they have, to look better, not like someone else. Of course the prostitutes will be made up for business on the day they leave.

A social worker told me about a woman in a Boston prison, the mother of five who had contrived to get herself booked on a narcotics charge, though she doesn't use narcotics, in order to get away from family responsibility. She had four children by her husband, a man who drifted in and out from time to time. The middle child, the fifth, was by her lover and was her favorite, though he'd become a problem to society and his mother. Here, the woman could be away from it all, gaining time and strength to go back. After she was in prison a while, she began making up heavily, something she had never done before. The social worker commented: "She had a teen-age daughter who was very pretty and used makeup. I think the mother was using makeup now as a way of getting back to the husband, not the lover."

At the Women's House of Detention, as in other women's prisons, inmates are below average intelligence. This was explained by Mary Lindsay as the result of a selection process—general prejudices of society work in favor of keeping women out of prison. A present official feels that "because the majority are prostitutes and unsuccessful prostitutes, it stands to reason they're not bright." Now, however, they are getting more inmates convicted of major crimes, and the intelligence level will probably alter. "It takes a lot more initiative to commit armed robbery and so we may be getting higher I.Q.s."

Almost all inmates are drug addicts and have had to go through withdrawal. Forty-five were considered overtly psychotic upon entrance in a study made by Dr. Emasue Snow. Sixty percent are between the ages of twenty-five and thirty-five, almost all are under forty, and sixteen percent are adolescent. I would estimate that close to ninety-five percent are nonwhite. They have poor educational backgrounds, generally come from the lower classes and are not trained for any job. Many are tough-looking babes who could pass for boys (and probably do) and many bear physical scars that will automatically dissuade any prospective employer. In this community of hopelessness, one imagines there can be no expectations of a future radically different from the past. Most inmates are repeaters.

When I mentioned that Gloria MacFarland at Start had told me her girls saw themselves as "shit . . . a pile of shit," a high official insisted that W.H.D. girls were not like that. They had a better view of themselves and cared about their looks. "Personality does not break down in the average female prisoner," she asserted. "Even those with a poor self-image, even those who mutilate themselves, use makeup." When, a few minutes later, she said: "Self-love plays a very strong part in making up," I felt she was perhaps not totally reliable.

Another member of the prison staff argued that the purpose of making up was not to attract men, compete with women, or any other complicated motive. The most important reason for beautification, she felt, was just that one has been told to. "All their lives advertising has taught them," and prison bars did not lock out the message.

Kenneth had told me, "I think there's a lot of dishonesty in [cosmetics advertising], but I think that dishonesty starts right in the mind of the consumer."

Mary Lindsay had said: "How can you teach people to live in a free society when you lock them up? It's impossible. You can teach them how to be good prisoners, but that's not going to do them much good on the street."

There's a parallel between the two comments. To be a good prisoner means to accept the prison society, its values, behavior and standards and then conform to its principles. The good prisoner, like the good consumer, is in total agreement with the society that surrounds him. The American consumer, who lives in a much larger world than the Women's House of Detention, is taught not by corrections officers but by print, radio and television to accept patterns of behavior.

The presence of things makes people desire them. Publicity not only calls attention to what's there, but attributes value to it. Though there has been no time or place where people didn't want to enhance their looks, the availability of products and services make Americans spend more and more on beauty, replacing one item with a similar version two months later, or owning ten varieties of the same product just because they are told—and believe—that they must have this. I've seen it in myself, when I buy eye shadow in powder form, even though I have it in stick form, because the ads and salesgirl tell me that it will hold longer or go on better. I, a middle-class consumer, don't want to resist; the inmates, aspiring to middle-class behavior, have no reason to. I asked a few cosmetics companies to send their products to the Women's House of Detention because I was sure the girls would be given some comfort, if not pleasure, in being able to make up in the latest fashion. They were no different "inside" than "on the street"; like me, they had learned to consume beauty as part of a way of life.

Three days later, on a Saturday afternoon, I was back at the prison for their annual fashion show.* The officers were resplendent in earrings, necklaces and hats; their faces were carefully made up and their hair sprayed into a new set. Uniforms had given way to silks and bright colors. Everyone was excited. Into the small, dark tunnel of an auditorium came the "friendly visitors"—people who had donated time or gifts to the prison—and relatives and friends of inmates. Everyone was dressed up, and pomp was granted the occasion by the presence of Commissioner McGrath (New York State Commissioner of Correction) and Mrs. McGrath. The show was about to begin; excitement wove through the audience as though this were a high school play and everyone watching were a mother.

For many weeks, the girls had been designing and making the clothes they would wear today. In the morning, all participants were busy in the beauty shop, where almost universal dispensation was

---

* It is a year since the following was written, and another fashion show has taken place— the last one at the Women's House because a new corrections center on Riker's Island should be ready by late spring or summer 1970. This year's show was like last year's, except many more white girls were taking part and Sylvia, so heavily pregnant the year before, took over for the sewing teacher, who was getting married that day.

given for this exceptional day. Miraculously there appeared products never seen before, and the girls chose among the wigs, hair dyes, false lashes, gold shadow, apricot blusher and navy mascara. Each girl could let her fantasy work to make up a new, shining version of herself, as beautiful as any model.

A variety show preceded the fashion show. A mannish girl, with shirt outside her trousers and cowboy hat on her head, was the gutsy, slick M.C. First, from the side below the stage, a soulful black soprano in a blue robe sang "The Impossible Dream" accompanied by a white man playing a very mediocre piano. But her voice sprinted over false notes, carrying dreams of a quest for unknowable victory, as she dared hope for the hopeless.

The curtain opened; seven girls in men's clothes sat over a bonfire at the WHD Ranch. They sang "Moon River" and many songs after that, together or in harmony or as accompaniment to a solo voice. A few dances, a skit, a square dance, and finally a Southern girl sang soul. She was mannish, unattractive, but with eyes looking into herself, and she sang her way out of that place:

> Walk on, walk on
> With hope in your heart,
> And you'll never walk alone.
> You'll never walk alone.

After silence, applause commanded an encore: she sang "I Believe."

When the audience recovered, the pretty sewing teacher introduced "Fabulous fashions from the House of D." The first, an outfit in gray: pants, shirt and hat. Total cost: one dollar. A green pantsuit was next, with print blouse, worn by a girl whose hair was tinted blue. A suit; dress with contrasting coat; a yellow empire cocktail dress; a long African dress with one sleeve; a pink-and-beige coat with matching dress and hat; a yellow cape, hat, and skirt with black top—all seemingly in leather; green taffeta party dress; lounging pajamas; elegant town dresses. I sat next to a friend from *Vogue*, and we had nothing to say to each other as we watched the girls parade slowly on stage, turn, come down the steps and walk through the aisle.

A beautiful girl walked down, her skin almost black, her hair in a thick Afro tipped with orange. She wore a dress of orange satin, tight over her curves; one shoulder bare, the other wrapped in a long sleeve. Her head was high, a pale smile unhinged her lips; she walked like a Dior model, accepting the stares and admiration, but her eyes seeing a higher world, her face aloof and self-absorbed.

These were the girls I had seen in the sewing room: the tough, swearing cookies with heavily scarred arms. Whenever I saw long sleeves, I wondered what they concealed. But now, in front of these eyes, the girls became women whose every movement is conscious of beauty. The girl in orange satin had paraded through her court. And when all thirty (one white girl) assembled on stage for the finale, their eyes shining as the applause rose ("Eyes tell the story," an officer had said), they were beauty queens but without frigidity, exotic wives of an African potentate. Then they walked down the aisle and out, back to their cells. For a moment, they had been loved and beautiful. The fairy godmother's wand had fabled them and, for a tiny span, the impossible dream had come true.

LIVING DOLLS

. . . *Où est Brigitte, le beau chaton,*
Et Marilyn, la blonde déesse?
Où est Jayne et ses hanches de lion,
Sophia, Zsa Zsa et Grace la princesse?
Où sont les filles d'antan?

(. . . Where is Brigitte, the kitten dear,
And Marilyn, the blonde goddess?
Where is Jayne and her glorious rear,
Sophia, Zsa Zsa and Grace the princess?
Where are the stars of yesteryear?)

1

Models

Now we have Twiggy, Veruschka, Penelope Tree, Naomi Sims and the super Shrimp. "I think you are the cutest and dearest girl I have ever seen. I have no words to express my feelings for you. I love your clothes and your looks," wrote a girl to Twiggy, as Twiggy quotes in *Twiggy*. And Twiggy herself writes: "At school we were all mad about Jean Shrimpton. . . . She was my idol. . . . I always had a picture of her with me." At sixteen, Twiggy was heralded as "The Face of '66," and two years later was considered passé by most people in the business. The great Shrimpton continued to hold her sway, and minor deities reigned for a few months or a year from the covers of *Vogue* and *Harper's Bazaar*, their bodies clothed, painted or nude, their heads showing the latest inspirations of Kenneth or Sassoon or Michel Kazan.

Everywhere in America, girls who have never seen *Vogue* admire the sleek women who came to New York and made it, or were so successful in Europe that New York reached out for them. In high schools, reform schools, in the kitchens of Riker's and Howard Johnson's, on college campuses and in the hidden depths of beauty queens, one desire rules: to be a model. Rich, indolent girls dream of it as a vaguely "creative" job that will make them the public's darling. Middle-class girls want to become models for status and money; lower-class girls see it as a way out of poverty or the ghetto. And handsome boys of every class contemplate it at some time or other. If they live in a large city, they will surely be approached and be made to wonder why not—all that money, and your face distributed nationally. However, the boys haven't much hope of fame. Well-known models are

199

women, and men rarely get credits. Still, all models belong to the "in" world of gorgeous clothes and far-out styles, discotheques, jet planes and Beautiful People. They are the sweethearts of manufacturers and consumers, are enormously rich, can retire at twenty-five (or a little later for a man), meet the famous, travel over the world, lead an exciting sex life, and all they have to do for this is stand in front of a camera.

Models, their admirers know, are real people and movie stars aren't. Movie stars have stock personalities and belong to that decadent world of the fifties when people made a great fetish of sex, everyone had wet dreams and masturbatory fantasies, everyone felt guilty about sex so they took symbols instead of the real thing. Models, on the other hand, are not hung up about sex and are much more swinging. They belong to the East Coast, which is closer to London and is a neurotic, nonconforming kooky place. Movie stars are West Coast, where life isn't neurotic, it's plain crazy and those people who are doing their own thing are light-years away from the entertainment industry.

Models, the myth continues, are like anybody. Twiggy was a cute Cockney kid who had no money and didn't even know how to spell. At sixteen she was out of school and a few months later was dining with nobility. Penelope Tree is upper class, but so wild that she's like anyone. At seventeen, she was discovered by *Vogue* in her own bag and has remained there ever since. Veruschka's a baroness, but she's six foot four and that's a scene. Naomi Sims was born in Pittsburgh and lived in foster homes and is black. Since 1963 the blacks have been getting into the business and now it seems sometimes you just can't get black enough. You don't even have to be beautiful some of the time. Is Penelope Tree? Is Peggy Moffitt? Are half those people on the glossy pages beautiful? Of course not. The girls know how to use makeup and the men—well, ordinary-type men are always needed, because the reader can identify with them.

Ordinary-looking girls, even peculiar-looking girls can make it as big as the beauties. We're interested in personality now, in individuality, and not in some stereotyped doll. So anyone can be a model. It certainly doesn't matter what kind of education you had, or where you come from, and it doesn't even matter much whether you're pretty or not. Attractive, yes, but who under twenty-five isn't? And there's nothing you have to know how to do. You don't even have to act. Just put on the clothes and the makeup and strike poses. Anybody can do that, even little kids.

So the American dream spreads. From nothing to Somebody, from shoelaces to Cadillac and now, from P.S. 7 to *Vogue*. Models are the avant-garde of the new society, where large breasts, tight-fitting clothes and teased hairdos are out, and Freedom is in. Freedom means the world should be delivered from war, America must abandon her competitive, economic system; values of the paramilitaristic complex—or, as Norman Mailer calls it, "Technology land"—are no longer viable, and all authority must be overthrown. God, marriage, the family, distinction between the sexes or races are remainders of a culture of conformity; and the future, which is now, must bring real equality of man, most easily achieved by ignoring distinctions between men. Girls shall not be martyred into marriage, to waste lives in drudgery of Sisyphian household labor. Boys shall not be crucified on the cross of economic responsibility. Sex shall not be used for power, and money will be disregarded as far as possible. Intelligence is not a supreme virtue—consciousness must be expanded through feelings and moods. Structure is illusion, and works of art or intellect constrict the mind.

The important thing is to move, make the scene (wherever it is), be true to yourself (whoever you are), put off the outer appearance of the last generation and remove the chattels of former authority.

A model moves more obviously than anyone else. Her job may be to pose, but her profession is to be a chameleon. Wilhelmina, a former model who now heads one of New York's most successful modeling agencies, said, "A model who is too easily recognized cuts short her professional life. You should have a face that goes from one extreme to the other." Manufacturers and designers don't want their products overshadowed by a star.

Basically, a model is a saleswoman who must subordinate herself to the product she tries to sell. People must remember the dress or the makeup, not the girl. She provides a setting for the dress; she's there to sell *it*, not herself. She should be able to go from sultry temptress to sweet little girl. She's a mimic, not an actress, who can hold a pose long enough, often enough, for the camera to catch the mood. Girls who admire or identify with a model may invest her with personality, but she must be a mannequin able to reflect a kaleidoscopic reality. That is, she must never be "herself," the "real woman"; her job is to offer cues that suggest a role.

She's a quick-change artist, she's like the dolls with many faces, bearing under each a caption—"I am happy today," "I am furious today" and so forth. And she's admired for her incarnation of change. Where once the model was scorned by better society, she's now a celebrity. Jean Shrimpton writes in her book that " . . . in the 30's models had little social standing," and quotes Madame Vera, who then modeled for Captain Molyneux: " 'We were not socially sought after at all. The way the girls modelled was quite superb, but it was exceptional to be fêted outside the salon.' " Though occasionally models were known by name before the late fifties—Jean Patchett, Sunny Harnett—it was Suzy Parker who became the first supermodel in today's sense, and she probably became nationally known only after she had gone into the movies. In the fifties, movie stars were the goddesses of teen-age imaginations, and Suzy Parker, with her curvaceous body and sculptured face ("Every morning I look in the mirror and thank God for my cheekbones," she was reported as saying), became a New York version of a Hollywood star. But until the sixties, most models were considered to be girls "no better than they ought," and Jean Shrimpton, riding the wave of "swinging London" with the Beatles and the Mod revolution, was the first genuine model star to be imitated and adored for her own look, to become a model for her generation in the way that Brigitte Bardot or Marlene Dietrich were models for theirs.

Then Twiggy, for a short span, became the world's public property—"It was always the way people wanted to touch me that frightened me so much, as if I was not a person but a thing," she wrote— and thousands of imitation Twiggys cropped up in all parts of this country.

With these two English girls, a new vogue was set, of the model as public figure. More than a debutante, more than the First Lady, more even than a movie star, the model became the idol and image of youth. Though only five or six models at most are known by name in any crop of many thousands and though their prime is usually six months to a year, they remain holders of the dream. They are sprites of the American economy, girls picked out of nowhere (usually a false impression) to become priestesses of the fashion gospel. Once spread on the pages of *Vogue*, they've made it. Since *Vogue* has a tiny (under half a million) circulation, it seems mysterious that girls in ghettos or delinquent homes should have heard of these models. Jessica Canne, beauty editor of *Vogue*, explained: "[The models] are picked up by other magazines, they become feature material. . . . The big weeklies do stories on them, like *Life, Look.* . . . *Vogue* does make personalities."

So does *Harper's Bazaar*; girls who model in either magazine become hot material. Other magazines ask for them, the news media write about them and advertisers demand them. When Yardley decided to revamp its image and bring out cosmetics for women, a special line was designed for Jean Shrimpton, who advertised it in print and on national tours. Yardley also came out with Twiggy lashes, advertised by Twiggy, and within a few months the company was third largest in the country. When Hazel Bishop hired Penelope Tree to its board of directors, it was trying, like Yardley, to remake the image of a cosmetics company in the image of a model, whose image was created by the fashion bibles.

Though models come in all shapes and sizes, from infants to octogenarians, and pretty female models may be in one of three categories (those who work on Seventh Avenue, couture models and photography models), the idols and stars are all in fashion photography and almost all within the category of "high fashion." Though a junior or teen model may monthly decorate the pages of *Seventeen* and though the pretty, milkshake-drinking looks of Cheryl Tiegs may appear on eight out of twelve *Glamour* covers, the superstars are generally girls with sophisticated, elegant or exotic looks. Twelve-year-old girls recognize Terry Reno as one of their favorite models in *Seventeen*, but, as they read her book of advice (*The Model*), they secretly dream of becoming even more than a junior model, of earning even more than sixty dollars an hour, of appearing in even greater publications than *Seventeen*—of becoming Jean Shrimpton. Ten years ago a girl would not have stopped at Debbie Reynolds if she could have become Elizabeth Taylor; and a boy will not dream of someday running his father's firm if he has any hopes of heading the board of General Motors.

The great models, from the public, not professional, point of view, are those who must be booked by special arrangement only, who appear on a dozen consecutive pages in *Vogue*, who can say, as Twiggy does, "as far as modeling goes I've practically priced myself out of the market" and who have been written about in newspapers and magazines of general interest.

"These girls," said Wilhelmina, "are not what we call the real pros in the business; however, they're stars. . . . The girl who really is the top model in the business is the one who does the editorial bookings, who also is the top money-maker in the business and who is the most professional." The clear, soft voice knows what it's talking about. Wilhelmina, a beautiful woman of six feet, with a light German accent, was herself the top model in America for two and a half years. To do *Vogue* covers, to appear in large spreads for that length of time, wouldn't be possible for a girl whose name and face are as known as a movie star's and who is therefore an advertisement for herself wherever she appears. "People really shouldn't ever know it's the same girl," explained Wilhelmina. "That is a real pro, because she can stay around for at least five years longer than the girl like Jean Shrimpton. Every time Jean does a picture, people remember this. And after two years of seeing Jean, even if she only does one ad for an issue, another girl who's not known and whose face goes from one extreme to the other could have twenty pictures in the magazine."

This is the traditional view. "But," says Wilhelmina, "we have this youth kick. The top models now keep changing. Whereas before a peak would last five years, the peaks lasts now about a year—or two, possibly."

"Of men," she says, "it is a little bit different." Male models can never get the publicity of top female models, and are rarely even given credits. Men are older, and stay around longer than women. The top rate (sixty dollars an hour) is the same and men, like women, receive special rates for special bookings. But so far, there has been no male Shrimpton and no male Twiggy, because none of the men's fashion magazines have the stature and influence of women's. Though American men are returning to a pre-twentieth-century clothes-consciousness, most are not so preoccupied with fashion as women and consider such a preoccupation effeminate. And, though a boy's desire to be a model might be condoned or approved in small sections of large cities where homosexuality isn't feared or hated and people know how lucrative modeling is, still, in most parts of America, a boy would be ostracized even by his family for expressing such an ambition. "People automatically think I'm homosexual," said Ken

Baker, a top Ford Agency model and one of the most handsome in the business. Though young men on the streets of America may wear long hair and ruffles, the *laissez-aller* doesn't apply to models. "We have male models with a little bit longer hair—about half an inch or an inch longer than normal, which we call the 'in-type' look. It's a younger male model as well," Wilhelmina said. "But the actual seventy-five or ninety percent of the industry from the East to the West Coast still buys the manly-looking man."

Individualistic, "kooky" looks aren't acceptable in male models, who do most of their work as accompaniment or backdrop for female models. "Clients like to book somebody who looks like the guy in the street, the boy next door," explained a male model. "And advertising is changing—the handsome, film-star type is going out. They're trying to get a new image. But in high fashion, they still need the good-looking types." Male models are more stereotyped than female ones, probably to remove the suspicion of homosexuality. But the standardly handsome, instantly forgettable Rock Hudson-type men become perhaps even more objectified than the women. They are not in the picture for the reader to identify with. A male model explained to me: "Say they're selling a woman's perfume. They use a man as a prop. The man might be kissing the girl who's using this perfume, and the girl's immediate reaction when she sees this picture is: My boyfriend will love me to wear this. Girls identify with a man that they're with"—not with the man in the ad—"and they see a picture and say, 'Well, if this couple can make out, why not me and my boyfriend? If I wear this perfume.'"

However, when a man sees an ad for men's cologne, he doesn't identify with the man in the picture. "He thinks, 'Wow, this girl looks so great. I must put Hai Karate on, I can get any girl.'" He doesn't see the model as a girl he knows: she represents all the women of his fantasies.

Ken Baker is six foot one, with an athletic body, deep-blue eyes and thick dark hair. He wore a tobacco twill suit hinting of Edwardianism and moved magnificently. He has been voted one of the top male models in the world. In a Cockney accent adulterated by residence in New York and many travels, he told me how he had become a model.

"I was a telephone engineer before, and I came into it through very strange circumstances. We were out dancing one night, my wife and I, in London. And they were giving away prizes: two suits, fifteen shirts and various other prizes for some kind of personality thing. I was dancing around and somebody put a number on my back. And there were forty of us selected to go in for this competition. I did it as a laugh because, you know, the blokes I was with there said, 'Let's go in, let's have a laugh.' . . . It was nothing serious. I won the competition, it was pure chance. And the woman that was organizing it wrote to me: would I like to go and do modeling, full time? And I didn't like the idea, to be honest. No, to be honest, my parents were dead set against it. I always confer with my father on things like this. . . . I was about twenty-six, twenty-seven. I saw my father and I discussed it with him, and he said no, he said this was a Narcissus sort of thing; and he said, 'I don't think it's for you.' And I thought, well, it's not, because I'd heard so many stories from other people about the business: that it was full of homosexuals and lesbians—all these weird stories. And I left it, completely." The woman then kept writing, urging him at least to try. She asked him to have test pictures made and when he explained he couldn't afford them, she paid for the pictures herself. They were good, and she tried to persuade Ken Baker to go into modeling full time. "But I wouldn't take the chance. I used to sort of have days off from work and my Gran used to die two or three times a month." He laughed and clarified: "I used to make out different excuses, you know. And eventually my boss started seeing me around in different things and said, 'Look, how are you able to do these things?' And I told him weekends. And eventually I had to come clean and had to leave. I started working just in London. Then I started going over to Paris and to Hamburg—I've probably worked in over twenty countries now. Been round the world three times in three years."

I asked Mr. Baker how his father now felt about his son's profession. "Well, he's taken a complete reverse view now. He's just telling me to save my money, which is a wise thing."

Ken Baker is "in the business to make money—I feel that I've been blessed with good looks and why not make the most of it while I can?" He bought property in England, is saving money and hopes to retire with his family (his wife and two daughters also model occasionally) in a few years. He likes traveling, meeting people and wearing stylish clothes. He finds his life fast moving and amusing. Unlike female models, Mr. Baker goes through no special preparations for his work. Athletic anyway, he doesn't have to worry about keeping in shape or slimming down. He has never had to wear a wig and normally eschews makeup, which he loathes. Only once was he seriously discomfited: "I was asked to do a cigarette thing in London and they wanted me to be completely silver. They sprayed this silver paint over me, my hair and everywhere. The money involved was, I mean, not to be believed. I mean, it was for one-day booking and I think it was almost three thousand dollars. And you just can't turn that down. . . . It took me three days to get rid of the silver, out of my pores and my hair. I felt like a doll, because I was in the bath every night, pampering myself, trying to get all this stuff off me." But that was an exception, and Mr. Baker is very grateful for "this break in life."

Even though his work is usually anonymous—"you're being made to look like a doll and you're being made to stand there in front of the camera"—Ken Baker has many admirers. Women who see him in ads write to the manufacturer for his name, then send him letters through his agency. He gets far more mail in New York than he ever received anywhere else, and one spread brought him three hundred letters, almost all from women. "They want to go to bed with me, mostly," he explained. "I think they want to try me out."

Such a direct approach is a bit off-putting, and he will try to dissuade the lady. "I just write and I say, 'Look. Thank you for your invitation and it's very nice that you should write in this way. But I'm happily married'—I give some way, I put them off that way." He feels "it's a sorry state of affairs" when girls have to write a magazine and go to such lengths to find a man. Their admiration for Ken Baker would be like crushes on a movie star, except the aphrodisiac of fame is missing. I asked if he thought women treated him like a male call girl. Perhaps, he conceded. "I would say seventy percent of the letters, they just come outright and it's almost, 'Can you come to bed with me?' sort of thing. And one girl that I met and went out to cocktails with I couldn't believe because she was so, you know, forthright. And she said: 'I want to go to bed with you.' And she said: 'I'm not making any bones about it.' And I just got scared, I mean, I'm normal, I feel I'm normal anyway."

He has no contempt for these women and feels sorry for them, he says. They're like sixteen-year-olds with a pop idol, "although they don't know the name. They're just looking at somebody who they just fall in love with by the picture."

I had written to Ken Baker asking to interview him. "To be honest," he said, "I thought you were another one of those."

But male models can't compete in fame with females. At her peak, Twiggy received three thousand fan letters a week, mainly from American teen-agers. Wherever she went she was mobbed to the point of personal danger and had to travel with bodyguards. An aspiring model said, "Twiggy was really a fad. She wasn't that great as a model. But it got into a thing for the whole country about a year or two ago [1967], where they were making Twiggy clothes, Twiggy eyelashes, Twiggy makeup, Twiggy everything."

Fads change, but since then there hasn't been so stormy an entrance and exit of universal celebrity. After Twiggy came Penelope Tree, a seventeen-year-old from a respected family, who possessed neither beauty nor the young-girl prettiness of Twiggy. But Penelope was kooky. She wore makeup so extravagant that one could hardly see the girl beneath; struck bizarre poses and in her private, publicized life, wore clothes so peculiar that she seemed at all times a Kabuki doll in the hands of a madly inventive five-year-old. She was admired in the profession for her sheer wackiness. The beauty editor of *Vogue* explained, "Penelope came through as a great personality, not as a model, really—primarily as a personality. It's Hollywood as it was translated to a personality in the pages of *Vogue*."

Amy Greene, former beauty editor of *Glamour*, now at *McCall's*, said that girls idolize models because "a model represents a personality, much more than a movie star does. I mean, Doris Day. Who in the world can relate to Doris Day? Whereas you could relate to Penelope Tree, who's a kooky lady, and it's—'I wish I could be like her because, you know, gee, why doesn't my mother let me run around town like that?' Well, they don't stop to think it might be an unhappy lady and that it's a magazine's creation. They just know that she's on ten pages of something called 'Vogue.' They don't even know what *Vogue* is, they just pick it up."

Wilhelmina pointed out: "Ten or fifteen years ago you had to be like a Roman sculpture, everything had to be perfect, whereas now you're a human being. It's the difference that instead of being a mannequin, you now are a people."

This applies to Veruschka, another fad created by *Vogue*. She's a six-foot-four German baroness who supposedly had her feet made smaller through surgery because her size thirteen shoe created a problem everywhere in the world. She has a gloriously long body with seemingly endless limbs that the camera usually likes to exaggerate. Hers was the body Giorgio di St. Angelo decorated with his body paint, and she is sometimes clad only in jewels. Claude Lalanne, at the prompting of *Vogue*'s Diana Vreeland, cast significant parts of Veruschka's body in gold. Her abdomen, breasts and lips are available as body jewelry, and Yves St. Laurent clapped Veruschka's gold breasts on his models in Paris for the showing of his collection. She has an expressive, mobile face that can occasionally project the mystery and serenity of Garbo, or look like a forest ranger from Oregon or an Austrian *mädchen*.

These girls, who ten years ago would have been turned down by agencies and magazines as freaks, have created a new era in modeling. Models are the exaggerations of everybody else, but they are individuals, because they don't conform to any stereotype of beauty. Let Hollywood retain its small noses and large breasts. In New York and its neighbor, London, girls are human, weird and lovable. They'd rather live on the moon than next door. They are themselves and at the same time parodies of themselves.

The illusion is individuality, and the millions of girls who copy Twiggy or Jean Shrimpton feel they are "expressing their true selves." Boys can't find an archetype nonconformist among male models and so emulate, in their dress and hair, pop idols from the fields of music or politics. But the illusion is the same: millions of individuals "doing their thing" in the same way, their outside appearance an advertisement for their inner "liberation." Models, whether beautiful or not, are girls like yourself: one example of the individualistic mass.

Black models, who were ignored during the time of stereotyped (Caucasian) beauty, are now popular in all fashion magazines. Naomi Sims, whom her agent calls "my chocolate Veruschka" was the cover story of the LHJ. She was reported to make one thousand dollars a week, and the interview told "how it feels to be black and beautiful." In it, she explains her success: "To achieve the pinnacle, you must have a gimmick. . . . Penelope's was doing the most bizarre, grotesque things she could do to herself. . . . I don't know what Shrimpton's gimmick is, but maybe it is that every woman can relate to her. . . .

Twiggy . . . is a little boy with huge eyes and short hair. . . . The minute I walk in the door people stare at me because they think I'm exotic. I think so, too."

Later in the article, after she has explained her family background (broken home, leading her to foster homes), Miss Sims says, "Success is important to me because of my childhood. It's an obsession to be somebody and to be somebody really important." She now appears in *Vogue* spreads and, with Donyale Luna (also the "exotic" type), is the most successful black model in the business.

Though these two usually stand on a color-blind pinnacle, modeling is still a white world. While black models appeared in fashion magazines before, *Glamour* was first to put one on the cover. "It was the largest-selling issue in the history of *Glamour* magazine," said the editor responsible for it. "We sold out in Detroit in twenty-four hours. We sold out in Boston in two days." Since then (August, 1968), other magazines have followed *Glamour*'s lead.

The black cover girl, who had been made up like any other (pink foundation, gray and beige eye shadow, individual lashes, translucent powder and lip gloss), showed a recognition by Condé-Nast (owner of *Glamour*) that young women were able to identify with any model. "It was a college issue," says the editor. "Therefore, my feeling was that college kids are not as hung up as their parents, and they would just accept it like, you know, I'd get up and drink a Coca-Cola. . . . And my point worked." In addition, *Glamour* gained many black readers, some of whom wrote criticizing letters. They objected to the model's hair, which was not Afro. (But Harold Melvin said women were bringing in the cover, asking to have their hair done like that.) They objected that the girl wasn't pretty enough, that for such a breakthrough one should have chosen the most beautiful of all, Donyale Luna perhaps or the TV star, Diahann Carroll.

A black male model told me he now isn't considered dark enough for many jobs. A few years ago, he said, "They wouldn't have had me for a model. I was not fair enough. You had to be very fair with very straight hair, so that the people who buy the commodities or whatnot would not be offended—it was almost a deceiving factor to use light-skinned models. And today you have the exact same problem, only in the reverse. The dark-skinned girls and the dark-skinned boys are getting all the modeling jobs and the light-skinned girls and the light-skinned boys are out." Blacks have been taken by the leading model agencies since 1963 or '64. In the second half of 1968 a combination of political, economic and cultural considerations brought black models to prominance and superstardom. At the end of 1968 an agency was formed, by whites, for blacks only and is called Black Beauty.

Black or white, "Modeling is built on insecurity," writes Twiggy. "It's a profession where you must prove your worth every day, where there's no guarantee of bookings beyond the present ones, where even the superstars know they can be suddenly dropped in favor of another, perhaps no more beautiful, face."

At the Ford Agency, a woman who worked as booking agent in the men's department switched to the women's. "It's unbelievable," she reported. "I feel a tension at the end of the day that I can't describe. Every girl seems to be so neurotic, so pent-up about what they're doing tomorrow . . . because they just live from day to day on a sort of tightrope." By comparison the men are relaxed and secure. They don't have the same competition, and their jobs are more predictable.

Children, also, have more or less predictable jobs. No minimum age exists in modeling. Babies are needed for some pictures, and a woman of twenty-five can have been a model all her life. Children are signed up with agencies, and perhaps the main difference between child models and adults is the children's sensitivity to cattle calls, when fifteen or twenty children are sent to a casting and only one is chosen. The father of one eight-year-old model won't send his daughter to these. "It's very hard for a child to go there and not be selected. They turn around to you or your wife and say, 'Why didn't I get the job?' I'd rather not do that. I don't want her to get the feeling inside that she's let me down or let my wife down."

A high-fashion model, beautiful and successful, knows her success depends on a demand created by *Vogue* and *Harper's Bazaar*, and that her beauty rests merely with the beholder. "I would say that most of the insecurity among models is . . . that they know that there's always a girl who's more beautiful, more fantastic, coming up," explained Wilhelmina.

On a recent assignment abroad, Ken Baker "was working with a beautiful girl and with a girl who has just a very, very plain look. The very beautiful girl didn't have to do anything. . . . The other girl had to wear wigs and she had to make herself up—maybe took another hour longer to make herself look more beautiful. And there was an insecurity, the girl had a chip on her shoulder, that she should have all these problems. . . ." He concludes: "Only about twenty percent really look beautiful without makeup. And they're the girls I really like. . . ."

However, Wilhelmina pointed out that even the most beautiful girls feel insecure. Because they are so used to minute inspections of their faces, because they are constantly working on the same canvas, they see flaws no one else can see, and "even if the other girl isn't more beautiful, she becomes more beautiful in the other model's eyes."

Dr. Jeffrey Kramer noted that actors were generally more mature than models, who show fragmentation and infantilism. Then he apologized for the generalization, saying that after all, people who came to him for treatment were usually not very mature anyway. His sample was not models as a whole, but models in crisis. Still, they could be compared with actors in the same situation. "Many models who have enough of it and want to make it to a more mature world, don't," the doctor commented.

An American model has a butterfly span of life. Unlike the European model, she can't go through a training period. In Europe are many different fashion magazines—each country has a few—and many photographers. In America "there's no place to be bad," as Wilhelmina says, because there are very few fashion magazines, and only *Vogue* and *Harper's Bazaar* have real influence. A new look is created by the collections first, then editorials. An agency has on hand many different types of girls, and when one is seen who exemplifies the new fashion decrees of European and American designers, she will be made into a star, for however long the vogue lasts. Only one or two models can weather the seasons, and today that model is probably Lauren Hutton, a very pretty American girl whose looks are not so exceptional that they will overpower the clothes, but who has enough beauty to compliment whatever she wears. Lauren Hutton has been popular in *Vogue* for a few seasons now. She was there before Penelope Tree and Veruschka and has remained after them.

There is always fear in modeling. After the hour of greatness, one must return to pedestrian life. "There are some girls who are so weak," says Wilhelmina, "that their values change to such an extent that they'll never be able to live a normal life again. . . . Once in a while you will run into a girl who has become so independent that she will not be able to be happy with a man."

"A model," she continues, "has to psychologically get herself ready. And she starts the moment she starts modeling." This requires a rare sense of proportion. Girls who go into modeling must immediately face the very strong possibility that they will not be chosen. Even if they become great models or stars, their career can only be a stop-gap, an interim of at most five years when, like Cinderella at the ball, she dazzles the eyes of all beholders. Afterward, she must return to the hearth, but without assurance that the prince will come.

Many men are still not attracted by models, who are too thin, too narcissistic and frigid—a rumor perhaps started by models to protect themselves from the earlier assumption that they were prostitutes or call girls. Bill Mandel told me proudly that he has never dated a model and never would. A train conductor from the Bronx confided to me, "If I'd wake up in the morning with one of those models next to me, I'd scream." And men of many professions protest that "the bones would get in the way," "I want something I can hold on to" or "I want a girl with meat on her bones." Many believe that models are stupid, and a model's necessary preoccupation with her looks can often confirm this. In America, where large breasts are still desired or even essential for sexiness, many men don't understand how their wives or daughters could have elevated models to desirable beauty.

Jean Shrimpton suspects that young admirers "like my *Glamour* image, whereas older women like my *Vogue* image." To her, both images are effigies. She points out that people rarely recognize her in the flesh, even when they identify with the girl in the photographs. That girl is like themselves and becomes the model for long blond hair, a casual look and understated makeup. Though the Shrimpton look is a derivative of the Bardot look (hair also long and blond, but tousled; eyes dramatized with makeup, lips pale), the main difference is that in the fifties girls were trying to look like somebody else; in the sixties, they choose someone like themselves to emulate.

In the fifties, emphasis was on sex. The child-woman—Bardot, Monroe, Jayne Mansfield—was a cuddly doll stuffed with passion. She was the little girl trying to look grown up, at a time when girls dressed like their mothers and women could feel protective, men incestuous, about the sex kittens. In the sixties, the hidden sexual fantasies of the middle-aged were being replaced by the candor and casualness of the young. Boys and girls no longer wished to be so conscious of sexual difference, and the boyish model's body is more like everyone else's than is the voluptuous body of the sex siren. (Though some still choose the latter, "swingers" disdain the old image and substitute sexual equality for potency.)

Youth selects the model, and the pop decade coronates her. Models, like pop art, carry their own obsolescence. They exist for momentary pleasure, have no deep meaning and will be replaced almost immediately. Pop is an offshoot of the beats, which is an offshoot of existentialism, and the message on one pop button is: "If it moves, fondle it." Conservatism of the avant-garde preserves the criterion of constant change. Whatever is new must be embraced, if only for a moment. Who could dare predict whether or not it will become a "thing."

Models are beautiful objects, publicly owned. Though they have been invested with *personality*—which seems to mean they have some gimmick—models are not generally desired as women. They are ornaments, idolized in a country where gift wrapping can be called an "art"; and for American girls they represent a way to instant glamour, fame and wealth. Any girl can become a model in this new era of free enterprise in beauty, just as every boy was told he could become a millionaire or President. In England, a new model agency has opened with the name Ugly. Only people who do not conform to stereotyped beauty are accepted, and the agency plans to open in the United States shortly. But Ugly is an anachronism. Scanning the model sheets of leading agencies in New York, one sees that very few girls are typical beauties. Some are even unattractive, and "striking" is the kindest term one could apply.

"The girls who come in who want to be a model," said Wilhelmina, "I hate to admit, usually haven't got one bit of potential. Who truly and honestly are not even pretty. . . . I think what it really amounts to is that they have been told by their mothers and fathers and uncles and aunts, boyfriends and whoever else, that they're pretty—to give them a little bit more security." That little security sends them to New York, to Ford, Stewart, Wilhelmina, Wagner or any of the other agencies. A tiny percentage of the girls is accepted and the others return home, disillusioned, to marry the boy next door or to accept the job they scorned before. Those who remain in New York use up their savings in preparation for jobs—getting photographs made, buying the right clothes, accessories and cosmetics, going to modeling school or having cosmetic surgery done. Of these, a small number becomes models in national magazines. The elite are seen in *Vogue* and between one and five girls reach Parnassus. Because of this, the dream continues: simply to stand there, in beautiful clothes, in a room with a photographer, and then one's image goes out to the country, even to the world. One becomes the model for other women, front horse in the race everyone's watching—the outcome of which will determine what's "in," until the next race is called.

Models, with their blank faces (not only Jean Shrimpton, but most models wouldn't be recognized off the glossy pages), are totally manipulable. Their function is as close to nothing as one can get and still make money: they just stand there, admired for their masks.

In the mid-fifties came the cult of James Dean, a beat-type actor who aroused girls almost to orgasm and who was dead. In the late fifties, women wore the "corpse look"—white makeup, white lips, black eyes. In 1963 the nation convened for a five-day wake over the body of John Kennedy, a glamorous, swinging aristocrat who, in his death, elicited love even from Republicans. The funeral industry grows (see Jessica Mitford's *The American Way of Death*), promising beautiful, lifelike corpses, and in a culture where aging is ignored and feared, death, like wrinkles, is denied dominion. Democracy makes us equal, whether black, white, old, young, male, female, living or dead. Shrimpton says, "I go to work, I do the picture, I don't think about it. It appears on a cover or something. It's a dead image, it's *nothing* to do with me."

The set pose, the blank face, the dead eyes of a model become the mirror held up by many young Americans. In that image is neither sexual passion nor personality. Beauty keeps her lustrous eyes in a never-never land of stereotyped individualism where the human being is frozen in a series of poses connoting freedom. Like the golden nightingale of Yeats's "Byzantium," the model gives a perfect imitation of life.

2

Celebrities

Models may be admired and even adored, but they belong to a small world of fashion, cosmopolitanism and New York. They're in a coterie, almost a conspiracy, against traditional American values of sex, marriage and big breasts. New York, some argue, is not even America: it's the state of mind of a bunch of Europeans. Even though none can deny that the fashion image is made in New York and then disseminated throughout the country, arriving some months later in adapted form, still, New York is too sophisticated, too un-American to provide dream girls for the whole nation. Girls may come to New York from prairies, small towns, mountains or mining country to be models, but except for Jean Shrimpton (and she's not even American), what model has a name like Liz Taylor, Barbra Streisand or Jackie Kennedy Onassis? *Vogue* is an in-group; models for Greater America must come from greater spheres. The Twig, the Tree, even the Shrimp —what are these compared to Garbo and Dietrich and Monroe? New York may, after all, belong to America, but Hollywood belongs to the world.

"Where did they all go," mourns Rex Reed in *Women's Wear Daily*, "those bigger-than-life superstars of the golden age of movies? . . . They carried around their own lightning. They were the American Dream and the whole world dreamed of being just like them. Glamour? It's become a joke. . . ." Today, change is better than ever and dreams have shrunk to mini-size. "Reality" takes the place of heroism; soap operas are filled with social problems instead of the Romantic quest; through television, the world's greatest figures have entered one's living room, bedroom, kitchen and even bathroom; and movie stars aren't the magnificent, unattainable women of erotic fantasy. * Everything and everyone is attainable—in reams of newsprint, on the small and ever-wakeful screen. We're bombarded with new information, new personalities, new fads every day. We're all in this together, we're all alike, nothing should be private anymore, communal living is provided until death and today's Walter Mittys act out their daydreams. If you want to make love to someone, do. If you want to shoot someone, that's easy too. The true end of equality is extermination of privacy and establishment of public selves for everyone, where the facade equals the self and both mystery and fantasy are subversive.

With mass media and mass distribution, there's no reason why we should be denied one detail in the life of, say, Jackie Onassis. We're entitled to know, and are told, what she wears, how she feels, the emotions of her children, their eating habits and her sexual relations with her husband. We are indignant to hear, on the ten o'clock news, November 25, 1968, that a photographer in Peapack, New Jersey, faces charges of trespassing. He was charged by Mrs. Onassis, whom he had been photographing without permission, and who had asked him not to print the pictures because she had on no makeup and hadn't combed her hair. He naturally refused; she had no right to behave like a private person, to insist on her privilege of preparing herself for the public.

The former First Lady was a *ne plus ultra* package of American dreams. Married to the most powerful man on earth, herself rich and with impeccable family background, she was also pretty, talented and had a model's figure. News magazines reported her doings; she was America's greatest export, could soothe anti-Americanism and even inspire the dreams of Charles de Gaulle. Fashion magazines adored her. She had taste, *chic*, was reported to spend fifty thousand dollars a year on clothes, and was young and daring enough to be seen in— and therefore beautify—the latest fashions. Marylin Bender, in *The Beautiful People*, a book about the personalities extolled by *Women's Wear Daily* and *Vogue*, writes: "Jacqueline Kennedy, the superconsumer, redeemed fashion from the Puritan ethic of sin." Movie

---

* For some, television "soap" stars have become idols. *Newsweek* reports a fan letter written to actress Lisa Hughes: "Please tell me where you buy your clothes, how you do your hair, what perfume you use. I want to model my life after you."

magazines featured her on their covers. After her husband's death, she became the world's most desired widow. She was the darling of gossip columnists; young intellectuals tried to skew their careers so they could meet her, and many dreamed of making love to her; fashionable women tried to arrange their appointments at Kenneth so they could catch a glimpse of her, and anyone who knew her became himself newsworthy. When it was rumored that she would marry Lord Harlech, a movie magazine ran a competition for the best wedding-dress design—thereby recognizing, but completely misunderstanding, her indissoluble marriage with fashion. When she actually married Aristotle Onassis, all of America became a Jewish mother: everyone felt that my little girl, my little princess, should never have married such an unworthy foreigner. She has now, hopefully for her, descended from that giddy height where, Minerva-like, she held the scales not of justice but of fashion. She was undoubtedly imitated more than any other woman in America, though a young, upper-class woman told me, "You know, people think she's—well, a little vulgar." The highest reaches of American society dislike makeup, *Vogue* and publicity.

Though Jackie Kennedy was often spoken of as the American queen, she was queen of a pop culture. Young, beautiful—in a recognizable, friendly way—and definitely "in," she was crowned not by Congress or the Church, but by the Establishment of pop: fashion magazines, writers, painters, the jet set. Her image was created as a model's image is, not through her works or words, not for her originality or goodness, but because she was the supreme messenger of the culture's dicta.

Where there are no hidden dreams, glamor is hard to come by. Though the word is often used, it carries little meaning and no longer signifies distance and mystery. Garbo and Dietrich were glamorous and were spoken of with slight awe as bigger than (and different from) life, half-legendary creatures whom one recognized as part of history even though they were young and alive. Today, Garbo maintains her famous privacy in New York and enormous photographs of her adorn walls of young people who have never seen her films. She has been taken up by camp, and her angel's face looks out from the wall alongside Freud, Valentino, Mao and D. H. Lawrence. Dietrich is still performing, singing her old songs with the same body and face she had thirty years ago. Her hair is very blond, her lashes thick, her skin taut, but her hands are old. Her body seems naked under a sheer evening dress. She is propped up in parody of herself, mummified and made ridiculous by her fidelity to the stereotype she created.

When Yvette Gilbert, the famous French chanteuse, was asked to give a performance in her sixties, she appeared on stage as she was, no makeup or wig, and explained to the audience, "Here I am. I'm old, I'm fat, I'm ugly. I can't even sing anymore, because my voice is gone. But you wanted me, and here I am."

Dietrich, on the other hand, has accepted the American insistence on youth. How she preserves her looks is a matter of great interest and conjecture. A beautician suggested Dietrich sprays plastic skin on her face, which hardens and then is removed after the performance. A plastic surgeon argued this was impossible, but that she probably has had face-lifts as well as other surgery. Someone else said she wears a plastic body form. There are rumors that she is a client of Dr. Niehans in Vevey, receiving cellular therapy—a rejuvenation process involving injection of cells from the foetus of a sheep. The closest I came to Dietrich was the second row during her performance. There was obscenity in her perfect imitation of youth, as there is in the picture of a female child naked except for prurient draping of the genitals and nipples. A woman behind me commented, "It's an era." The friend I came with, a very attractive Central European woman old enough to remember Marlene's initial impact, was depressed. "She doesn't have any more nipples," mourned my friend. "She has just an alabaster breast, like a Maillol." Dietrich had stood rigid for most of her songs, her mouth moving irrelevantly to the sound, as though she were badly dubbed. I wished I had never seen her comeback. She belongs to the age of glamour, was once wonderful and should never have been subjected to my criticism.

In the fifties, when movies claimed to be better than ever, when young people belonged to what was later called the Indifferent Generation, when college students were apathetic about politics and virginity was not yet an accusation, we had a profusion of superstars. Every twelve-year-old could identify at least fifty, and the great ones (some carried over from the forties) were: Elizabeth Taylor, Clark Gable, Esther Williams, Marilyn Monroe, Grace Kelly, John Wayne, William Holden, Marlon Brando, Audrey Hepburn, Humphrey Bogart, Gina Lollabrigida, Sophia Loren, Zsa Zsa Gabor, Lauren Bacall, Rock Hudson, Jane Wyman, Judy Holliday, Joan Crawford,

Montgomery Clift, Gloria Swanson, Brigitte Bardot, Tony Curtis, Debbie Reynolds, Doris Day, Bette Davis, Tallulah Bankhead, June Allyson and so on. (Make your own list.) Of these, only Audrey Hepburn remains as a contemporary figure. The only one with a model's body, she has been caught up in the fashion establishment. She models in *Vogue; Women's Wear Daily* reports on her wardrobe and *Glamour* tells its readers: "College and prep school girls still want to wake up on Christmas morning looking like her." Of all the actresses above, she was probably least coveted by men. They acknowledged her prettiness and denied her sex appeal. "But nowadays sex appeal has become a bit of a joke," writes Twiggy, and only the small-breasted, boyish figure is accepted by fashion and advertising. The editor of a well-known intellectual journal explained to me that the beauty and fashion business is "dominated by faggots." They invented the mini, he said, to torture heterosexuals and to denigrate the woman by telling her she's nothing but a little girl who can go around "showing her crotch and panties." Voluptuous bodies have no place in fashion.

The movie stars of today—Julie Christie, Jane Fonda, Dustin Hoffman, Mia Farrow, Katherine Ross, Warren Beatty—aren't as far removed from the worshipful masses as the stars of the fifties. These celebrities are beautiful or "interesting-looking," they can or can't act, but they are not legendary creatures. All beauty editors I spoke to were convinced girls don't try to emulate movie stars. Hairdressers are hardly ever asked to do hair in the style of some actress; the usual request is to copy a model's hairdo from the pages of a magazine. When I asked plastic surgeons if women ever have a picture in mind of whom they want to look like, the only actress mentioned was Zsa Zsa Gabor. Though Veronica Lake and Brigitte Bardot could set a fad in hair styles, actresses today seem to follow fashion, and will emulate a Sassoon style or a creation of Kenneth's, as seen in *Vogue.*

Movie stars are not considered swinging and therefore aren't imitated. But movies themselves, notably *Bonnie and Clyde*, can "create" a look, and then the actors are brought along in the general upheaval. *Bonnie and Clyde*, its story and its fashions, was a complete success. By combining criminality with nostalgia, it appealed to two strong characteristics of the American personality. Girls could dress like Bonnie in a tough, masculine outfit and still be considered sweet, because the clothes were dated. Boys who dressed like Clyde add a swagger to dandyism. Dress designers, cosmetics companies and pop boutiques selling paper objects were madly enthusiastic about Bonnie and Clyde, and for a few months the country was so enamored of these criminals that even Jesse James was outlawed. A lesser vogue followed after *Cleopatra* (mainly eye makeup, the revival of kohl) and *Doctor Zhivago* (a *Vogue* spread on nineteenth centuryish, Russian-type clothes).

Brigitte Bardot was probably the last movie star to create an international look. Varieties of the sex kitten with the famous pout appeared in New York, Paris, Los Angeles, London. Long, tousled blond hair, heavily made-up eyes and pale mouth were the signs of beauty in the late fifties. A buxom figure was expected to accompany the baby face. Bardot was eulogized as the most desirable woman in the world, and Simone de Beauvoir wrote a book about her. Her life was tempestuous and highly publicized. Because of her kittenish behavior, all the scratching, biting, playfulness, she is not even now, past the age of thirty, ignored by reporters. She gives outrageous parties, she marries and divorces with great alacrity and regularly announces to the press many of her piquant and preposterous opinions. In late 1968, an hour-long television spectacular was devoted to her. She wore clothes one could find in boutiques of any American city, the bits and pieces from different civilizations which when assembled on the wearer become an outfit. She walked barefoot often, listened to a guitar player and padded around Saint-Tropez with her *copains*. She was obviously a swinger. No Edith Head dresses for her. (Edith Head has been the most prominent designer of Hollywood for decades of movies.) No Hollywood version of suburban chic. Bardot was showing them like it is, in her own bag, doing her own thing in front of all the NBC cameras. In 1956 she was adored as a sexpot; but the world was changing, and she could become as kooky and as individualistic as anybody else.

Fashion leaders are mainly the Beautiful People described in Marylin Bender's book. Though the title comes from *Vogue*, the cast of characters has been assembled by *Women's Wear Daily*, a trade paper of enormous influence, read by fashion editors as well as designers and manufacturers to discover where some young society woman lunched yesterday, with whom and what both were wearing. One reads about the preparations for fashionable parties weeks before the party's held. The newspaper's coverage of Apollo 11 gave exact accounts of who was wearing what, particularly lady journalists and wives of politicians.

Amanda Burden, Babe Paley, Gloria Cooper and other women of society are darlings of the paper, which is on first-name basis with all of them. Women outside the group can enter these pages if they or their husbands become nationally prominent. Before the Nixon-Humphrey election, readers of *Women's Wear Daily* were asked to send in a vote for First Lady. *WWD* has a streak of monarchism and confers titles on its characters: Her Ladyship was Mrs. Johnson, Her Happiness is Mrs. Rockefeller, Her Goodyness is Mrs. Nixon. Though Jackie Kennedy had been their favorite, she has fallen from favor since her marriage and is referred to only as Jackie O (wife of Daddy O). The paper would be a scandal sheet, except its items are not juicy enough to titillate many readers ("Amanda discovers Ungaro" was a front-page headline). But the women it extols have power in the fashion world; with endless time for the pursuit of beauty, they can "make" a designer or fad. They are the fashion leaders of New York, which is the fashion leader of the country, and what they are wearing now has been or will shortly be seen in *Vogue* and *Harper's Bazaar*, then bought by J. C. Penney's and Korvette's for distribution around the nation. When the Beautiful People lunch at the most expensive and exclusive restaurants in pantsuits, the hot news is carried along the fashion stream until it eventually reaches the backwaters of the Midwest. Women all over America are imitating women they never heard of, and men are imitating their husbands.

The Beautiful People are a small power group made up of nobility, the well-connected rich, the simply rich and the not-so-rich who attend the right parties wearing clothes of "in" designers and who have a gift for publicity. In this group are the Countess Paolozzi who posed in the nude for *Harper's Bazaar* in 1962; the Patiños of Portugal, who gave a party in 1968 that required a year's preparation; the Carter Burdens (millionaires with Kennedy panache), the William Paleys (she is the mother of Amanda Burden, he is chairman of CBS), the Robert Skulls (he owns a taxi fleet and they collect pop art), denizens of the beauty and fashion world—Bill Blass, the Revsons, Estée Lauder— and occasionally an actress, particularly Audrey Hepburn. This group is recognized neither by the public at large nor by America's social elite. While many Beautiful People belong to the upper class, as a whole the upper class frowns on publicity seekers, would rather shop at Peck and Peck than at Yves St. Laurent's boutique, and finds the whole business of jet set and conspicuous fashion consumption rather distasteful.

Young Americans may not realize that when Jackie Kennedy shortened her skirts, "the future of the miniskirt was assured," as *The New York Times* reported, but official sanction from the highest rank of Beautiful People was necessary before manufacturers could risk a massive output of minis. For young people, the "in" group of *Women's Wear Daily*, *Vogue* and *Harper's Bazaar* doesn't exist; they do their own thing and follow pop stars, models, of course, and singers.

In the fifties, when apathy coupled with prurience, Elvis Presley sang and gyrated his way into the libidos of young America. The beat of his songs matched by the grind of his hips were too revolutionary for parents and television. Teen-agers all over the world grooved. In Finland, I read graffiti expressing love for Elvis; in Russia in the late fifties the first question my contemporaries asked me was about him—his age, his Cadillacs or his latest recordings, sold on the black market. He started the tidal wave that brought the Beatles. Elvis came along with the beats and Brando to deliver the message straight from the groin. His hair was long and his clothes were the kind Brando wore in *The Wild One*: tight, black, leather, connoting speed and liberation. Boys copied Elvis, and when the Beatles came with their sweet baby faces and longer hair, the boys copied them. Elvis liberated adolescents to sex, the Beatles liberated them from the older generation. The boys from Liverpool brought the news to their American comrades that youth was in, love was in, there was a solidarity and conspiracy of youth everywhere to remove the bonds of their oppression (for the English, it was the class system; for Americans, the family), and their early songs ("I want to hold your hand," "Roll over, Beethoven," "She's a woman") were simple, with simpleminded lyrics that could appeal to micro- and mini-boppers, an age group left out during the Elvis reign of emphatic heterosexual sex.

Elvis now makes a few million-dollar movies a year, gives concerts at one hundred thousand dollars each, and his influence on style persists among boys of the lower classes. The middle class is faithful to the Beatles and their inheritors; to Bob Dylan (whom they consider a poet) and other singers of social protest; to soul singers like Aretha Franklin, and to some who fit none of these categories. Sonny, the male of Sonny and Cher, says, "Entertainers are a barometer. . . .

What we were doing three years ago has caught on now." From jeans or nudity to actual costumes (Sergeant Pepper), singers present a variety of looks, all anti-Establishment, antibusiness suit, antitraditional entertainer's garb of satin and sequins. Many dust jackets now could be included in fashion magazines, and the pop singers have become the models (particularly for boys) of the entertainment industry. A beauty editor explained, "[The Beatles] had the best sense of humor in the world. They were putting the world on and making reams of money and having a ball. . . . Pomposity has gone out completely, in every way, and also in beauty." She illustrated with an example: "I mean, if you see a lady immaculately coiffed, with the fantastic David Webb jewelry"—David Webb designs very expensive, elaborate, almost rococo jewelry—"and the fantastic tailoring of a Zuckerman or Norell, you fall down kicking and screaming because there's absolutely no touch with reality anymore."

The reality modeled by pop stars is a teleidoscope, distorting the real world for a greater aesthetic kick. "Beautiful" has come to mean the unusual or even the absurd. A "beautiful person" does not mean someone endowed with unusual pulchritude—it means someone with soul, a *mensch*, a person who doesn't give a damn what the world thinks of him, but manages his rebellion in such socially acceptable ways as wearing improbable clothes or letting his hair grow long. To call an anecdote "beautiful" means it has been about an act of absurdity or minor outrage. If a lady says fuck to a priest, it's beautiful. If John Lennon poses naked with Yoko, it's beautiful. Beauty is shock, the unexpected (though within the limits of acceptability), the physically ugly. Though the French have a term, *jolie laide,* they mean a woman who, while not endowed with beautiful features, is charming and flirtatious enough to seem enormously attractive. We mean something else: the beauty of the gargoyle, the beauty of mocking traditional standards. Obscenity is beautiful, incoherence is beautiful and probably most beautiful of all is self-absorption.

All this is up-and-coming America. Actual America still conserves God, prettiness and traditional sexual roles. The quest to find "a girl just like the girl that married dear old Dad" continues, and the high school cheerleader is, for many, the girl of one's dreams.

Though beauty contests are not particularly emphasized in America compared to other countries (in Thailand, the annual choosing of

Miss Thailand dominates all news for a week), they have a different purpose. Most are commercial, choosing a Miss Something-or-other to advertise a product. Variations on the theme of Miss America are concoctions dreamed up by chambers of commerce, pageant corporations, and television stations. Mrs. America, Miss Teen-Age America, Miss Black America, Little Miss America (ages five to ten), Mr. America and many others compete with CBS and Atlantic City's Miss America pageant.

Amy Greene of *McCall's* feels that Miss America, as a symbol of beauty, is "for all the fellows that stand in bars, that don't even have a living room to sit in to watch television." I argued that she must still be some kind of image for the American woman, the woman who dresses up with rhinestones and sprays her hair into an immobile nest.

Miss Greene shook her gray ringlets. "Well, let's talk about Miss America this year. I mean, this lady is incredible. She's eighteen years old and she looks like she's thirty-eight. Her hair is white peroxide hair, it is teased, it is huge. She is twenty pounds overweight."

How, I asked, could such a person become Miss America? "She really won because she jumps around on a trampoline. And this could only happen in America, only happen in America. I mean, if somebody from Mars came down to earth last August and saw the Republican convention, the Democratic convention, went back up, came back down in September and saw the Miss America pageant—I mean, he'd think we were all off our nuts."

Miss America is chosen for a combination of looks, personality and intelligence, a trait determined by Bert Parks, master of ceremonies, asking such questions as, "What does America mean to you?" The winner has a year's reign, during which she travels through the country doing publicity for various companies. She is carefully chaperoned, very busy, often photographed and earns money. According to Miss Greene, "Girls compete in it primarily because it's a way out of whatever life they're living and it's a step into something else . . . either into a big city, or it's a step into modeling or it's a step into show business, or even it's a step into an advertising agency—a better job."

There is ample reason to want to become Miss America, though I met no one who sees her as an ideal of beauty. At the last Miss America contest, girls from the Women's Liberation Movement picketed on the boardwalk with such signs as "Miss America Sells It!";

"Miss America is NOT My Ideal"; "Can Makeup Cover the Wounds of Our Oppression?" For many, the contest is vulgar and pointless. For some, it is merely amusing, and to the more militant, it is threatening.

Whether Miss America is an ideal or not, the concept of choosing a girl to represent the country in beauty has caught on. Miss Black America was organized in protest against an ostensibly representative pageant that includes no Negroes. Harold Melvin said that the contest "should have been as normal as Miss America itself, it should have been the same thing. Yes, it should just be Miss America. And it's unfortunate that one must say Miss Black America. It's unfortunate that people have decided to cut the string down the side because let's face it: we are here. I don't know where we're going, but we are here."

Other groups of females also feel left out. Married women want a chance to compete, and so there is a Mrs. America contest—which, however, emphasizes housewifely virtues more than physical beauty. Mothers are eager to exhibit pretty daughters and possibly make a lot of money through them, so contests are arranged for teen-agers.

Probably the most offensive of all beauty contests is Little Miss America, for five- to ten-year-olds. When I told Jean Shrimpton of its existence, she said, "That's disgusting. I mean that's dreadful, dreadful." A magazine editor reacted with, "That to me is just vulgar and obscene. That is just—ugggh." She gargled her revulsion. And a seven-year-old male informed me, "Little Miss America looks awful. They picked the worst one." In reviewing the televised contest for *The New York Times*, Jack Gould writes: "The cheap and opportunistic exploitation of little girls . . . reached its annual sickening apex last night. . . . With gross condescension and occasional outright bad taste they made puppets of a stage full of little girls who did not have the vaguest comprehension of how they were being abused." After describing the bewilderment of the children and cynical jokes of the participating adults, Mr. Gould concludes: "WPIX and the show-business promoters of the amusement park should return to their senses. Surely, there are ample ways to survive economically without recourse to capitalizing on children."

Beauty contests, whether innocuous or contemptible, make use of women to sell commodities. The girls themselves may compete for publicity, money or social advantage, but the contests are basically insulting. Not necessarily as women militants see the insult—that women are treated as objects—but because the national contest does not judge what it is meant to judge: the fairest in the land. Too many other considerations come in, and if Miss America should be a competition among girls in this country to determine who is most beautiful, it seems apparent that national and racial groups within the country should be represented. If Miss America is chosen for her ability to jump on a trampoline, she is not America's sweetheart and can't feed the dream of love. Traditionally, American men have double standards: a sweet girl with pretty face for wife, a sexy siren for an affair. Miss America appeals to neither fantasy.

The wife type has disappeared, leaving the daughter, who's pretty but too clever and too independent for knitting and baking. The sexy siren was eclipsed in Hollywood and her song adapted for electric guitars. A man now chooses between the lady (who can even pose naked in *Vogue* and still retain elegance) and the female object. Hundreds of magazines for men, some operating for one issue only, offer pages of big tits and big asses solely to titillate and provoke the reader. Pornography (*pornē*—harlot, *graphē*—writing) comes from the ancient tradition of brothel advertising and was literally writings or drawings for the purpose of bringing in customers. The girlie mags offer the come-on but leave the man to his own devices. Except for *Playboy*, the girls' faces are not relevant, and beauty is no consideration. The girls look available, show what they've got and invite masturbation. They are no one's ideal.

Pop stars—models and singers—create the image. Standards of beauty are no longer fixed, naturalness has taken over; you're supposed to look real. Everyone can do it, because reality can never be absolute or static. Each small mirror on the turning globe picks up a reflection, and the only imperative is to keep it turning.

3

Jean Shrimpton

Like the white rabbit, I muttered to myself as I hurried along, "I'm late, I'm late, for a very important date." Only three minutes late, but the date was with the queen of models. It was highly impertinent, I felt, to keep such a lady waiting. She was the chief idol of the modeling world, whose picture Twiggy kept with her always, whom Ken Baker calls the "top model" because she has "true beauty"; the woman young girls want to become and young boys dream of at least meeting. Jacqui Brandwynne, then public-relations director for Yardley, had told me, "We tied her up. Contractually. . . . And then the whole vogue started rolling, and she became the most beautiful model, or the most known model, rather, in the world . . . she has a magnificent look."

I hurried along in the pre-Christmas slush, my mood generally malevolent to match the prevailing atmosphere in New York. Santas on street corners, wailing children, indifferent mothers, indignant fathers all impeded my progress crosstown. But finally I was east of Park Avenue, near her house. The wind was cold and my black boots, brown lamb coat and fur hat didn't give enough protection against the urban chilliness. A cab drew up by the side of the street and a girl stepped out, as tall as I, in black boots, a lamb coat and fur hat. Long blond hair washed her shoulders, and she took large strides to the door. While she searched for her key, I reached her. "Hi," she said. It was obvious, even though she didn't look like Her, the image and the dream. She looked like a very pretty girl with moderate makeup who was late and, despite the cab ride, a little breathless.

We walked up the brownstone to the top apartment, where the

white walls had been faced with wood to look like Ye Olde Englishe Inne—mock Tudor, but the mocking showed a sense of humor. On tabletops and ledges were arranged various collections—one of old pistols, including a miniature no more than an inch long; another of soldiers; another of shells. We took off our coats. I was wearing a black mini and she a black maxi, in velvet with long sleeves and a belt of dark rose velvet. The dress was old, very frazzled, the cuff held onto the sleeve by only a few threads. She said she liked wearing velvet during the day. She was a little girl in grown-up clothes, a nymph imitating mortals, Ondine prepared to have tea with the prince. Her hair, though fine and golden, was in the disarray of knitting wool, strands falling over her face, sometimes getting caught in her lashes, sometimes totally blanketing her features. She picked at it and, somewhat alarmingly, removed long blond tendrils. She scratched her head vigorously. "It's this glue that bothers me. It's just regular glue, and they stick the streaks in, you know. It does come out, it's just that it itches a bit."

I was not yet able to dispel the bad temper and frenzy of Christmas crowds, so Jean gave me a whisky. On the way to the kitchen, we passed a small collage her boyfriend had made for her, with WELCOME TWIGGY! stretched across it. Jean didn't drink. We returned to the living room and she arranged herself on the couch, limbs thrown over all sides of it. She seemed eager to discard her arms and legs, and I wanted to do the same with my body. I felt twice her size (though we're exactly the same height and—as I discovered later—same weight) and realized that research for this book had become precarious for the health of my vanity. A line from Roethke suited her: "Ah, when she moved, she moved more ways than one!" She was careless, even awkward, and yet graceful. We talked a little, in a rambling way, and it was evident that she had no pretenses or conventions. Forthright, sometimes incoherent, she was not a girl for clubs or faculty teas. She was definitely a man's woman ("I'm not a girly girl as such, you know. My friends—mostly men") and it occurred to me that such women are less narcissistic and less infantile than women who see men only as lovers and reserve whatever truthfulness they have for members of their own sex.

I mentioned that models in general and she in particular were idols of the younger generation and asked if she knew why allegiance had switched from movie stars. "I don't know"—her words were never completed. Breathlessly, she lets escape through her lips the first intimation of a word, then cuts it short, to expand as it will in the listener's mind. She talks like a speed reader, offering only the essentials, enough of the word to identify it, but no more. "Models have been so much publicized. I mean, I don't think rightly so. I think it's rather stupid in a way. But I think also, movie stars have become much less star. I mean, they're much more normal people you meet. They're like you, me or the person next door.

"I got publicity because of the timing. This whole emphasis that came on Swinging London and all that, which is very dead now . . . I was part of that simply because . . . I don't know." Her accent is English country, but not very broad. She was born in High Wycombe, Oxfordshire, and grew up on a farm. "I was a model that brought on this natural look, I mean quite inadvertently, wasn't planned; but I met David Bailey, who sort of decided to promote this look, and it happened to take off. I was lucky and . . . also I think people identify with me, they feel I'm like them, I suppose. . . ."

The curls were all unstuck and rested beside her on the table. Her hair still flopped over her face and she removed it from time to time by a shrug or by combing her fingers through. "The emphasis now is on being an individual," I suggested.

"A model's not very individual." She reflected a moment. "Quite anonymous usually."

I protested that she wasn't anonymous, that though young people could admire any model, they had chosen her in particular. "Yeah," she said, offhand. This was because she was associated with people in the news, photographers and movie stars. "So my life had that gilt edge to it. It's never what people think it is, but it looks sort of interesting to them, you know?" She informed me her sister knew the Beatles and "went with" Mick Jagger. "So it was the association . . . that's why they think I have a nice life, I'm interesting." Her explanation was doubtful. "People know very little about your private life," I reminded her.

"Yeah. Because I'm not given to telling about it and I don't give many interviews. It's a drag really." The Garbo of modeling— beautiful, famous and private.

"Don't you get asked questions like 'What do you sleep in?', the kind of questions one asked Marilyn Monroe?"

"Not much, because I don't think I invite that sort of thing, I mean, there's just something about me that's much—you know, people always say I'm cool, which I never think of myself [as], but that sort of question—too tedious and boring, why don't you ask something more interesting?" Luckily, she was addressing unseen interviewers, not the present one. "I mean, when you're Marilyn Monroe, her whole thing was built on sex anyway, that always invites those stupid questions. I never sought publicity and I never went after it. I think that sort of comes through, you know. I don't want a star life or anything. I sort of value my privacy." Apologetically, she continued. "It's so sort of hard, I mean I value it much more now than I did [at] eighteen. Then it seemed more glamorous, and I was very naïve. And it was all new, and it was all an experience; whereas now I like to keep more and more away from everything, you know. I'm very quiet."

Her limbs fell away from her body and back into it again. She couldn't keep still long; she moved existentially, like a telephoning teen-ager during a long conversation in which little is said, much is repeated and the body does an acrobatic dance, unnoticed even by the dancer. Jean Shrimpton was not a Garbo. I had expected that Shrimpton's beauty would be inhibiting. A few days earlier, Norman Mailer had told me, "There's terror in a beautiful woman. She has death in her." Shrimpton didn't behave like a beautiful woman. She is extremely, even excessively, pretty (excessive, because one can't look at her without embarrassment, for fear one is staring), but she is unconscious of her dominion. No imperiousness and no majesty—a girl, not a woman, who is recognizably human and measures neither her words nor a man's fate.

"At the beginning I worked all the time, I did all the housekeeping and shopping. I had dogs and birds galore, you know. I never had a moment to stop and even think what I was going to do tomorrow, it was always planned. . . . I was traveling, and it was just a spot of growing up, you know. I wasn't aware of being somebody's property or public property. Now I hate to go anywhere crowded. I can't stand parties or anything. And I mean I get very stupid about it because, you know, it's just a drag really, being stared at." Yesterday she had gone to buy shoes in an expensive New York department store. People recognized her. "It's awful, you've got big flat feet and everyone's watching you try your shoes on. And you don't want to know, do you? I'd rather try my shoes on in peace than have people looking at me trying my shoes on. That's the drag of it, you know. Who wants to be observed? I don't. I mean, if I fancy somebody, I don't mind him observing me; that's very nice. But generally I don't want to be looked at."

The model is superimposed on the girl, but the girl likes to go off by herself. To be a celebrity gives you an importance you haven't earned. Jean said she was used to working with intelligent people, people who managed her life, told her to shut up when she babbled and would remind her from time to time that she was a child. She doesn't feel pride in her profession—"modeling doesn't give me very much satisfaction"—and envies those who write or paint or have serious ambitions. Her job is mimicry. "You put [on] a frilly dress and bow in your hair and you look like a silly, coy little girl and it's very easy to feel like a silly, coy little girl." Modeling is something you do for a time, without thinking about it ("discussion bores me; I like money"), and afterward you try to piece up your life and go on in a different direction. "I'm very interested in film but not in being in film," she said firmly, "I don't want to act at all. I mean, I did try it but I haven't the right mentality. That's true narcissism. . . . That's exhibitionism of a kind. You never face life, you're always acting."

What she faces is: "I have no talent, none whatsoever, but I'm not stupid either, you see. And the terrible thing of not having the talent and yet being slightly frustrated by not having the talent because you're not stupid. I mean, if you're stupid you're not aware, but I am aware." She broke off and asked me about my book. It was difficult to describe, but I said it would point out the American Way of Beauty.

"It's such a definite way of beauty," she agreed. "Here, they just *crave* for any new thing. They don't know what to do for themselves. I have different concerns, I never think about this, I couldn't give a damn. . . . I'm just not interested in American beauty, not my thing at all. I like natural beauty, but in quotes because that isn't sheer natural, you know, that's helped. They spend a *fortune*, you know." She laughed irrelevantly, a private joke I wanted to share about the comic nature of these people. "You know why? It's that bloody television. . . . You've got to have this, you've got to have that. . . . And they're so insecure *because* of this, you know. There are so many rich widows, rich women, rich divorcees among those. . . .

They've just got too much time and too much money . . . too much television, [they] just turn that bloody box on. And they don't do anything, they don't think—all they think about is what they're going to put on their face. That's bad. They ruin themselves too often."

She had tasks around the house and busied herself for a few minutes sorting laundry. Then she stalked to the phone. Cupping her hand over the speaker, she asked if I would stay for dinner. I thanked her but refused. "What should I have them send?" she whispered furiously. I suggested the standard steak, with perhaps strawberries for dessert. She nodded, ordered those and, as I continued my list of items I found most palatable, she added them to the list. When she hung up and returned to the couch, I wondered whether she had phoned as a matter of simple convenience or whether she always phoned, to avoid going into a store and being recognized. "People don't recognize you," she said—except for some on Fifth Avenue or in the stores carrying *Vogue* fashions. Even people who arrange tours for her fail to meet her at the airport because she looks so unlike a star. "They've run polls, you know, that I come out on top of—which is beyond me why. These women when they vote in polls, they've seen pictures of me in *Vogue*. I could walk into their living room and they wouldn't recognize me. And it's not only an age group [that elects her], it's older women. And I can't think *what* an older woman sees in me because I know when I walk along the street older women think I'm a right freak."

How, I wondered, did men react to her? "I'm not sure that I appeal to men that much. . . . English men can see my type thing," she admitted, "but the American man is still very sort of tits- and ass-oriented. I'm much too skinny, I don't *really* think I'm their type, you know. I'm much more sort of skinny-leg type, which is more a European thing than an American. They like busts and that . . . and they like bottoms, asses."

I suggested that English men probably like them too. "They like smaller ones, I think. I don't really think I'm the American man's, no, not at all." Not the Jayne Mansfield sort, certainly, but there are no sex goddesses anymore. The American businessman must turn to *Playboy* while his wife, daughter and perhaps even son are conniving to project *Vogue* onto the American dream screen. Shrimpton may not be the American man's thing, but he's simply not getting his thing anymore.

She went to sign a photograph for a teen-age boy I know, who now worships it and keeps the picture beside his bed. "I'm concerned with the way I look, obviously," she said, blotting the signature, "I mean, I'm not preoccupied." We walked back to get my coat. "I know it doesn't take very long to look the way I want to look. And I do it and go out and that's that for the day."

"When you became a superstar, didn't you change your relationship with yourself?" I asked.

"Not really, but somebody did write once about me that Jean Shrimpton the model and Jean Shrimpton the girl live side by side in an apartment without getting in each other's way." She laughed happily. "The only thing is," she added, turning serious, "that, having been beautiful, you've got to accommodate the fact that it's going to go away."

"At sixty, you'll still look better than any other sixty-year-olds," I assured her.

"Yeah, exactly. And you know, there's too much in my life. Garbo— she's remarkable. Her looks are modern, that's what's so strange, you see. I mean, she looked of her day and of today. Her looks haven't dated at all. Mine will date, but—"

I smiled and tried to shake by head in refutation. "The only thing is," she said again, "you know, you must miss the adulation. You may think you don't take any notice of it, you know what I mean? You probably get used to it."

UNISEX

We hold these truths to be self-evident,
that all men are created equal . . .

—*Declaration of Independence, 1776*

1

Prettifying the Male

"I don't really think men need cosmetics, to tell you the truth. I think men naturally are beautiful enough to carry their own thing."

—LESLIE OLIVER, young model

"I think men are too insecure to wear makeup."

—KENNETH

"You wouldn't believe men, how vain they are."

—CAROLA TRIER

"We American women have failed them. We failed the male. They have to have external beauty now."

—GLORIA MACFARLAND

"In my profession, I've seen men wear makeup. The men that have worn it have always been homosexuals."

—KEN BAKER

"The male has been more adept at concealing his insecurity. . . . Dr. Brauer has a mirror on the inside of his door. So what? I have a bigger mirror on the inside of my door."

—DR. DONALD OPDYKE

When women started buying clothes for men and could dress them up like dolls, the battle of the sexes took on a new dimension. Successful or beautiful women could become like white liberal nigger-lovers, adoring the sweet, not quite responsible male for his qualities of simplicity, strength and penis possession. As soon as a woman owned a male, she delighted in telling him to have his hair cut, his teeth capped and that blue was the best color for him, bringing out the ruddiness of his complexion. She could give him scents and hair sprays, oils and lotions that she might lovingly massage into his strong, unsophisticated back or could send him, as a special treat, to a beauty farm for a couple of weeks. Having quickly found the boy in every man, this woman likes to nurse him, comfort him, doll him up to show the world what a catch she really has.

The manboy lovers excel in justifying male pseudosuperiority; just as nigger-lovers can extol the Negro ability to dance, box and play basketball, so these find natural and evolutionary justification for male physicality and beauty. Niggers are different from real people, just as children are, and must be humored and admired. Menboys are also not quite like people and nature is called upon to stand up and say to all the world, "This is a man." Otherwise, the world might overlook the fact.

A well-known psychiatrist, who asked not to be named, expressed the reasoning behind manboy love (though a man, he can adopt this ignoble attitude just as Jews can be anti-Semitic or blacks anti-black): "What is the male? The male is the beauty. In the animals, they're the ones with the mane, with the colorful plumage. And the female is drab. The female is attractive to males only at certain times."

This analogy between humans and animals is facile. Responsible scientists and social scientists are wary of making any parallel between the two, even between apes and men. Lower animals may, of course, show traits that also occur among humans, but their connection is observed by a human who interprets through his own experience. Even so, to be meaningful, parallels must be specific, and broad generalizations to humans from the sexual behavior of animals are unjustified. Women are not in heat at certain times of the year; men have no feathers, manes or love calls. The only time when such an analogy become effective is in poetry, where precision of metaphor encapsulates reality.

"It's ridiculous to dress females," Margaret Mead asserted. "Females aren't dressed anywhere in the animal kingdom. It's males who have the beautiful feathers."

Leslie Oliver, a smooth-skinned, oval-faced young model, tried to express her conviction that "as in all nature, the male of the species is more beautiful. Naturally, oh sure. Look at birds, look at animals— always. The male bird is always more colorful and more beautiful than the female bird because . . ." She fell silent, through ecstasy or inarticulateness. Then, after a shrug, she said: "It's the same thing [with humans]. Males are sort of dominant and females are meant to be around them."

Gloria MacFarland, at Start, engaged me in a long conversation on the subject. "I have a beautiful home in the mountains that I never see," she began. "It has Ionic columns in front of it. There's a cardinal that comes to nest. And he is beautiful. He is red and beautiful, and she is gray and ugly." (One wonders whether the male cardinal might not find gray more beautiful than red.) "And what's her role?" Mrs. MacFarland asked, but wanted no answer. "With the pheasant, which one is beautiful? Did you ever see the female pheasant?"

"The little drab female is what he wants to get, in animal life," I suggested.

"Or isn't he what she wished he'd become?" she asked, rather metaphysically, I thought. "The female, when she fuses with a man —in talking about us—isn't what she's doing fusing *her* narcissistic self to make that male something beautiful?" Mrs. MacFarland then informed me that we American women have failed our men. "We don't give them these things, we're in combat with them."

The eminent, unnamed psychiatrist defined present sexual roles differently and in language difficult for a lay person to follow. Among animals, females attract through scent, and "the female, even though attracted by the male, has to be subdued before she . . . submits to [him]. So that we—if you want to use the word *Naked Ape*—we have an entirely different viewpoint between the sexes. The virile type reflects the girl's attraction as far as the man is concerned. It's the muscular, tall male. Now, the woman being passive, does not make an overt pass at the male, but attempts to make herself attractive visually so that the man will make a pass at her. But then she selects the most masculine, shall we say." I was becoming confused. The elderly doctor illustrated with an example: "Did you ever think why do women go to a fight? They shouldn't, should they? But you see, they can very easily project themselves into the middle of the ring where the two men, heavily muscled, very strong, agile men are fighting—for her."

The male, born to be beautiful, needs no additional ornament. Even though our hierarchy is no longer based on physical strength, even though men's invitations to love are success and money, manboy lovers retain their myth. Men are more beautiful and powerful than women. Men are more than equal to women. In a complicated society, where women's preoccupation with beauty has been determined mainly by economics and (the decline of) religion, men should take up that preoccupation for reasons of nature. Though he needs no decoration, man is free to seek it. Women have usurped the male position ("The male is the beauty") and, in order for men to regain their natural position of supremacy, they must indulge in practices employed by the weaker of the species. (Some in the Women's Liberation Movement would abolish all makeup as undignified and have both sexes present themselves with as little subterfuge as possible. In the same way, some black movements would rather change existing values for all America than incorporate themselves within the present culture.)

The soft look in men's clothes, longer hair and the use of cosmetics may be interpreted as a sign of weakness, strength, indifference, vanity or simply the natural consumer evolution. Mary Butler of *Harper's Bazaar* explained that men and women were equally foppish until the Victorian era. Then, men lost their "powder, fake patches and cologne" and "painted women were automatically whores." Women, however, were able to reclaim beauty aids more quickly than men "because historically they had to prove themselves, they had to do something different. And they are, I think, more anxious about their age than men. Because, you know, comes the cut-off physically and they're over the hill. With men it takes longer, doesn't happen quite so quickly and they're productive longer. So this problem never really bothered them quite so severely as women. But now—and I personally can't explain it—it's like men are coming back into their own. It's not that they ever lost it, and yet they were sort of content to be breadwinners or sports heroes or whatever, as opposed to being men."

The pretty, green-eyed beauty editor doesn't think a man proves his sex by physicality. He is shown in American literature and movies as "the hero figure" or "in the gray flannel suit" and both roles became so stereotyped that he "was no glamor figure at all." Now, when women compete for men and, as a young model put it, "men do not go out of their way to court women anymore, like they used to at one time," the image of the American male is changing.

Advertisers of men's cosmetics emphasize that their products will increase the wearer's sexual desirability (whether he is pursuer or pursued). *McCall's* Amy Greene said that formerly advertisers "went along with the status, selling their products to the status-oriented role. Maybe a lot of men have already reached that so-called status and they had to switch their advertising completely around." Where once a man was urged to use cosmetics to appear more affluent than he actually was, now he is told that his cosmetics will elicit female passion. But Amy Greene warned, "Many advertising agencies do not have their finger on the pulse of America, needless to say."

Margaret Mead, who first insisted, "Men have always had to compete for women," a few minutes later announced with no-nonsense authority, "They're not competing for women. Girls are lying around flat on their backs ready for them." The advertising, she said, was "just appealing to his daydreams. There was that marvelous Arrow-collar ad about late 1940's. It was a series of mobile ads that ran in subways. Cavewoman with a club dragging by the hair a man in an Arrow-collar shirt with his arms folded, a look of bliss on his face. But that's just Madison Avenue. Insanity."

Mary Butler suggested that men's cosmetics appeal to the need for looking young, since men "are over the hill at forty, forty-five in a corporate structure." Kenneth, whose copy for women's cosmetics reads: "Women become Kenneth disciples because he makes them look young," agrees. He added, however, "I don't think men are going to wear lipstick and eye makeup."

I argued that there was no reason why they shouldn't, if one followed the reasoning. "Yeah," he said, "there'd be no reason why not, but the whole moral, spiritual, social structure of life would have to change a tremendous amount before this happens."

"The male image has changed very much already," I reminded him.

"Yes. But it's *male* cosmetics. I mean, I believe thoroughly that men will do things to themselves, but they will have to feel that it's separated from the female. It will have to be approached that way. It will have to carry a masculine quality with it."

At the Revlon Research Center there are no special labs for male products. Products are sexless until virilized by scent or packaging. "Men have to be educated," Dr. Opdyke told me. They would not buy an item they think is intended for women.

Ken Baker, who "hates wearing makeup," even though he's a model, says that male models who wear it when not working are homosexual. Yet he admits that some products, especially bronzers, are used by heterosexuals because "a man likes to look well all the year round." Harold Melvin told me that a fair-skinned black friend of his uses bronzer to replace the sallowness in his skin with ruddiness. Mr. Melvin then added tersely that most blacks would not use bronzer because "nine out of ten already have that look." But he also told me of a white boy, a friend of a friend who was "very, very handsome" but still put on "a layer of some kind of blush" and over that another kind of makeup. When Mr. Melvin remarked to his friend, "You said that women are flipping over him. Why does he bother to use makeup?", the friend replied, "I guess he just wants to look prettier." Mr. Melvin then pointed out, "Here's somebody who's already handsome and he's involved with, you know, getting into makeup. So you just have no idea where this whole thing will lead. But I would say also that the day will come when men will wear makeup."

Vidal Sassoon "can't see why a man would want to wear makeup," but adds quickly, "I don't want to be accused of ever being a conservative thinker." So he justifies his approach: "I'm not tuned in, myself, to a man wearing makeup. At the moment, this kind of thing doesn't set me alight." Still, he approves the general change in men's appearance. "Men were beginning to feel dreary in the presence of women. . . . Men are competing to please women. I think this is a very good thing. And, you know, it was a whole American hangup. That to be a man you had to wear baggy trousers, you know, smell of tobacco and look very rugged. Everybody tried to look rugged, which made it ridiculous. And against Europeans, who would look very chic, American men did, until very recently, come up very second best because of their attitude." The English, according to Sassoon, were "*much* hipper, much sooner." Since eccentricity has always been permitted and occasionally fostered in England, a person could dress more or less as he pleased. "Somebody'll walk around in his mother's pink pajamas in London and will be thought [of] as a nut. Quite a strange, funny guy. Over here, he'd immediately be a fag." The American conservatism never permitted any deviation from strict codes of dressing. "That whole Madison Avenue scene, with the thin black tie you know, and the whole sort of unbelievable way of dress, shoes that didn't speak to the trousers—you know the whole scene. An incredible way of dressing, so ugly. *Aesthetically*, it's so ugly."

He and many others want more individuality in dressing, the loosening of controls, permissiveness for taste, personality and humor. Ken Baker likes the new materials for men, the ruffles and flares, "because I would like to have been around at the Renaissance time. They lived a good life in those days and . . . there was less tension, I think, for the persons involved in that period. There was so much fun. If you can sort of envision what went on in those days. I mean, I've read books on that period of time, and I think it was a wonderful time to live and I think it's coming back. Certainly the style is coming back. People are even thinking that way. It would be a wonderful thing if it did come back, *I* think, for one and all."

In recognizing the importance of fashion to men, or vice versa, the twenty-eighth edition of the Best-Dressed List for 1968 included a men's list for the first time. Wyatt Cooper, Prince Philip, Bill Blass, Jean-Claude Killy, George Hamilton and Cecil Beaton were among the winners, as was "an elderly Philadelphia sports figure," George D. Widener, whose comment on this honor was, "How ridiculous."

Tom Wolfe, in addition to being a writer, has become known as an exotic but scrumptious fashion plate. In *Men's Bazaar* he poses in what he calls his "Winter Whites!" and, on the next page, his Green Tweed. Commenting on the state of male fashion today, he points out that "even certified Ivy League kids dress straight army surplus. The Yale campus today looks like an unusually happy, healthy DP camp." He reminisces about the "Old Men's Look!" of Churchill and others and goes on to mourn that "Today, of course, all the old men are lurching around strangled in hip-huggers and English boots and turtleneck jerseys, and their wives have apricot hair. There is not a white-haired woman left in the entire borough of Queens, for example." (This astonishing information is bereft of its needed exclamatory prop.) In conclusion, Wolfe commands, "Onward! Backward! The good old Pretentious Look," which might sit well on one who, imitating Shakespeare, never blots a line, but is not being accepted by those unwilling to commit literature.

Newsweek, in a cover story on men's attire, describes the "new dawn" breaking "over the soft, shapeless waistland of male attire," when Beatles, hippies, student revolts and "a new era of social expression" have allowed men to emerge from "the dark ages of male fashion." Reporting on the elegant, extreme and exhibitionist in men's clothes, the article mentions such items as male handbags, miniskirts, see-through blouses and pants, silk lounging pajamas and vinyl suits. "Seldom has male fashion switched, twitched and disported itself with the urgency of today," it announces, and the cause, according to *Newsweek* analysts, is "money and leisure" and the "pervasive influence" of youth. Media, too, help bolster sales. Women's magazines now feature male fashions, and society columnists report on what men were seen in.

The attention to men's clothes is a revival in fashion, not a revolution. European history shows many eras when men outdid women in finery and elegance, and male drabness in dressing came about through political and economic events of the past three centuries. The French Revolution caused upper-class people, in fear of their lives, to abandon their identifying costumes and put on the clothes of common people. England under Cromwell had already given up primping. In America, the Puritans were dressing functionally: dull colors to hide stains and spots, simple cuts to allow freedom in work.

By the nineteenth century, political ideas of egalitarianism, supplemented by economic mobility, brought common people to power with their old shirts still on their backs. Then Victoria and Albert did what they could to suppress signs of vanity in both sexes. In America, the middle classes chose conservative appearance. Lawrence Langner, in *The Importance of Wearing Clothes,* points out that bankers "set an example of conservative dressing for businessmen. Their clothes, like their bank buildings, say to the public, 'You may safely leave your money in my care. I haven't a vestige of recklessness in my body or soul.'" Langner emphasizes that, "since the middle classes set an example for sobriety and conformity by their dark clothes, these were followed by the clerical office workers or 'white-collar' workers who imitated their superiors to overcome their own feelings of inferiority, and became even more inconspicuous and drab."

Predicting (in 1959) that "we are now witnessing a return to finery for men. . . ." Langner explains that this may in part be caused by increased wages for the lower classes, who then buy clothes "without the restraining influence of the conventional standards of middle-class taste." He suggests that "the rise of the working classes will result in modifying the standard businessman's garb. . . ."

Dr. Jeffrey Kramer gave a supplementary explanation: "Society is moving toward female values." He feels we are now in reaction against "the masculine, industrial tradition," the male society that led to conservatism and traditionalism, and was the context for emancipated women. Women's liberation allowed them to participate in the masculine world. But now "credence in money [and] training is falling apart," and industrialization is being replaced by professionalism. Dr. Kramer pointed out that "boys [are] more related to the Protestant ethic and idea of saving than girls are." Both these concepts have weakened and, "at the moment feminine values, always more now-oriented, are proving more relevant."

Not the feminization of men but the feminization of society leads to interest in the ephemeral. Poets of the Romantic movement, with long locks and soft clothes, lived in the intensity of individual moments ("At a touch, sweet Pleasure melteth") that, like drops of water thrown from the spray, were either becoming or disintegrating. Now in America our culture combines Romanticism (usually born of frenzy or despair) with technology and brings us pop or the Now Generation, an ideal setting for preoccupation with fashion and fads. Fashion is style defined by the moment, and our serious attention to it shows our involvement with the immediate. Monks, living close to eternity, remain faithful to habits of the Middle Ages. Young men just out of high school may change their wardrobes every six months.

For a long time, women have been accepted at face value while men have had to show they're made of sterner stuff. When man is no longer the sole breadwinner and decision maker of the family, when money is no longer the only standard of success and women are promiscuous, there is not only greater equality between the sexes, but greater laxity for both. Femininity means moving from Samson to Delilah, from blind strength to the use of wits.

Beauty is its own excuse, not woman's. The sexes try to attract each other, and logically, the new entrants in the game follow rules established by long-time players. Bill Mandel, addressing the Boston

Fashion Group on the theme, "Will He or Won't He?", makes no attempt to trace reasons for all this fiddle-faddle. He gives a vehement "yes, yes, YES—He WILL" to the question of whether men will wear cosmetics. Suggesting that "man's motivation is to get ready, or be ready, and woman's motivation is to be beautiful—*ready or not,*" Mr. Mandel then reveals, "My view is that man is still a child in his petulant resistance to fashion's efforts to make him a thing of beauty and a joy for as long as a woman will have him around." Still, "the boy is growing bolder," and "There's little doubt that men in significantly big numbers share, or dip into, their wives' night creams; that they use hair dye and hair sprays; that, although the male of the species does not yet have matching lips and fingertips, he doesn't rebel when the manicurist buffs his nails to a shine that rivals that of his shoes."

One need not understand this development, but merely love it. Of course not *all* women will "prefer their men to be cosmetic-oriented . . . any more than all gentlemen prefer blondes." But in interviewing women, Mr. Mandel received many rewarding answers. "Would you encourage a man to look as attractive as possible?" he asked, and was told: "Encourage him? I'd perform plastic surgery." Presumably it was the same woman who answered the next question—"Would you have to convince him that it's manly to buy men's cosmetics?"— with, "Convince him. I'd have to drug him."

Finally, Mr. Mandel concludes: "So, if it's going to be cosmetics for men, it will be because, one, women will want it that way . . . will make it that way . . . will keep it that way and, two, because s-e-x is the great unknown variable of our time."

When Cary Grant was made a director of Fabergé, he said ". . . His and Hers mean nothing to me. I don't know why they try to segregate us so." Believing that everything (a term unequivocally general) should be the same for men and women, he pointed out that "we're both made out of two people. One of us turns out to be a boy and the other a girl. Why should there be such segregation?" These words, spoken in spring, 1968, proved prophetic. Mr. Grant, speaking on the eve of Unisex, was the voice of future (or younger) generations that will surely tread him down.

2

What Is Unisex?

"And the eyes of them both were opened, and they knew that they were naked, and they sewed fig leaves together, and made themselves aprons." Man entered fashion through Unisex. Having lost paradise, our first parents strove to disguise themselves from the sight of the Lord, in whose image they had been created.

Now we have gone back to the original inspiration. Men and women dress alike, in identical clothes of different sizes, the same size or, more traditionally, the same style slightly adapted for the different body shapes. *Women's Wear Daily* has given us the word and concept—"Unisex is the fashion sex"—and enthusiastically sends out reports from the revolution: "Unisex Shop Tries to Change Denver's Button-Down Mind," "All was unisex at Neiman-Marcus' showing . . ." "Unishops Sales Soar for Month," "Aspen's First Unisex Shop Opens," "Unisex Is In at Way In Shop" as well as such related articles as "Unisex on Campus" or "Sex is Alive, Well in Paris."

They report, glowingly, that Gimbel's has set up a dressing room for boys in the junior girls' department,* and Macy's has a girl's dressing room in the boys' department. During the social season in Southampton, "the slightly he-man look for females" was observed, and Barry Sainsbury was "wearing fair long blond curls and a white shirt with blue satin stripes." "In the heart of Texas," we learn, "sexual differences are falling by the wayside." In Paris, boys and girls go shopping together in the same boutiques, "one of the most popular

* In November, 1969, this was converted into a leather boutique.

ways of spending afternoons together," and the head of Cardin's export business announced that "girls today want a man who looks like
a girl and makes love like a boy." Bill Palmer, hairdresser in Beverly
Hills, says that his women customers ask for hair in the same cut
and color as his. "Nothing human is alien to me" seems to be the
recovered motto of the present generation, and while the country as
a whole tries to remove distinctions of race, ethnic background, religion and social class, the fashion gospels, led by the young, supplement liberty by bringing a new flood of clothes and accessories to a
sexually equalized America. "The uptight crowd," ridicules *Women's
Wear Daily*, "snarls, 'You can't tell the boys from the girls.' . . . But
the kids just laugh." *

As in many things, we show British heritage and, as usual, make it
over according to "the American experience." Our Unisex had its
origins in England in the fifties when, though the empire was dying
or dead, the class system was still invincible. One's accent was one's
fate; public schools and Oxbridge prepared the future leaders and
opinion-makers of Britain. The exceptional working-class children
who received scholarships to these citadels of knowledge and prestige
were caught in the dilemma of either acquiring a new, acceptable accent and thereby losing touch with friends, family and origin or maintaining the accent they had and forgoing all chances of future eminence. On this old, established self-perpetuating and self-glorying
scene burst the Angry Young Men, writers from the middle (Amis) or
working (Sillitoe) classes who insisted that England unmade me and
proceeded to show how. Since the Englishman is known all over the
world for his clothes, and male fashions in all respected sections of
European and American urban life were modeled after the English,
clothes became a way out for the ignored classes. But just as "dressing
up" in America means a misreading by the lower classes of upper-

---

* On November 28, 1969, *Women's Wear Daily* announced the death of Unisex, "The
big retailers have agreed: Unisex is dead!" However, the demise is illusory. The name
alone has died; the concept lives on. The Unisex look continues, but incognito—as "The
New Equality" (Morgan of London shirts), "Double Identity" (Paul Harris stores) or
simply in the offerings of boutiques. Moreover, the December 16 issue of *WWD* extolled
the success of a new Unisex shop, with no allusion to the previously announced death.
And on December 26, the news was, "Unisex may be dead in department stores, but it's
just arriving in Washington hairstyling." Whether or not Unisex remains as a manufacturer's or retailer's term, equal opportunities for both sexes in fashion and beauty are
assured.

class fashions, so in England the working-class wardrobe became extravagant but non-U. The hero of *Saturday Night and Sunday Morning* put most of his earnings into clothes, but the result was simply
more pride in himself, not a viable disguise.

Then the mods and rockers exploded on the streets with motor-
cycles and contrasting views on fashion. The leather-jacketed Presley
or Brando look was pitted against Edwardian Teddy Boys and eventually lost. From Liverpool came the sound of the Beatles, resonating
with hope that class was no barrier to success. From mining towns
and the industrial swamp of the Midlands young people with guitars,
dreams and longish hair streamed into London hoping to make good.
They learned to make money and to set themselves apart from the
old, established civilization. By the mid-sixties, after the Keeler-Ward
scandal exposed the seeming propriety of the upper classes, young people had created a subculture so strong and amusing that the fashion
industry had accepted it, and London was mod capital of the world.

In America, young people loved Beatle songs, the Union Jack, miniskirts, costumes, long hair on boys, boots on girls and the sense of
sexual freedom. What had been a social revolution in Britain became
an aesthetic movement in America. Outlandish clothes did not defy
a social system, but parental authority. The world became a costume
party where you dressed as someone you would like to be and then
were free to act as you liked. By the late sixties, the freedom in dressing and grooming became symbolic of political emancipation. Young
Americans could show their disgust with the world their parents had
bequeathed them by advertising a new individuality and conscience
through clothes, hair and makeup that connoted freedom.

"One doesn't even know to begin with whether it's good or bad. I
would guess it was necessary—that the sexes come together before
they can redefine themselves," said Norman Mailer, implying that the
new androgyny was caused by sexual confusion. Certainly sex in America, as those over thirty know it, is passé. Crew-cut boys no longer
grope helplessly on porch settees for blondes with permanent waves.
The old stereotypes have been replaced. Sex, drugs and other forms
of mutual or onanistic intercourse now involve the very young. With
Unisex, we are given the correlative, Uniage. Microboppers start at
nine, children enter political demonstrations, wear clothes adapted
from *Vogue*, use makeup for a natural look, smoke grass, have opinions and choose their own clothes. Grandmothers, after face-lifts or

chemical peels, wander through the boutiques of department stores in miniskirts, trying to overcome their resistance to see-through blouses. All this is good for business; youth is the master and emblems of revolt are transformed by fashion copy and manufacturers into the latest selling gimmick. Media speed the message to all parts of the country, and the traditional American process of homogenization makes possible a mass, middle-class market for mass individuality. A new stereotype is developing that will fuse age, sex and race to produce the American sweetheart, something between a butch and a drag queen. The message, which was originally: *Revolt! Leave the old hangups to the older generation and let's start building a sane world!* has been watered down to: *Buy Young! Let's all kick our hangups and have fun!* "We are in an age where the enormous per capita bulk of communication is met by an ever-thinning stream of total bulk of communication," wrote Norbert Weiner in *The Human Use of Human Beings.* "More and more we must accept a standardized inoffensive and insignificant product which, like the white bread of the bakeries, is made rather for its keeping and selling properties than for its food value."

Whether unisex is "inoffensive" or "insignificant" remains a matter of opinion. Vidal Sassoon says it's very sexy. "It is, actually. Sometimes you see two people walking in a very groovy way. And you see the backs of them, and it might be an England winter, and they've got trousers that are bell-bottom and the same kind of coats on and you just see two shapes and they're both slim. And it's only when they turn round you can see that one's a guy and one's a girl. And yet there's something about their whole silhouette that's very groovy." Sassoon comes from the English working class. Like Ken Baker, another Cockney, he was able to achieve success despite his background. Both men are far from the Oxbridge route, entered professions usually considered homosexual, but then—Sassoon especially—were able to benefit by communications and achieve position and wealth formerly almost impossible for Cockney lads. They are products of the social-fashion revolution. Because they are in fashion, they attain international reputations as the industry becomes a complement to, or metaphor for, life.

Partly because of his background, Sassoon is free of traditional Anglo-Saxon views on sexual roles. He continued his speech above: "I mean, what is a man? A man's got to sort of smell strong and wear ridiculous clothes to prove he's a man? And he's got to always have his crazy shirt and tie on? Which eventually's got to go, because it's strangulation point. We're not in the Brigade of Guards anymore. We've got to get out of it, we really have."

By contrast, Jessica Canne, whose association with *Vogue* makes her look, move and talk like an aristocrat, confessed, "This whole change in sexual roles certainly has me in a great quandary. You'd be surprised the many times I'm getting releases over my desk about a thing called Unisex, which I hate to hear. I refuse to mention." A little later, she reflected sadly, "We're really just becoming more hedonistic and sybaritic as a people. Maybe Mr. Nixon is going to take us back again, I don't know."

Kenneth insists "there's a separation between male and female in spite of unisexual whatever," but he is in the rear guard of an industry that proclaims, "Boys will be girls." The "feminization" of men and "masculinization" of women might be merely the rather slow recognition that we all share traits of both sexes. Women have often appropriated male attire, for comfort (slacks), to announce their liberation (bloomers) or for piquancy (Dietrich's tuxedos). Unisex is, however, the step beyond. Here girls and boys become twins; young couples own clothes collectively. The His-and-Hers towels of suburbia are the unsuspecting progenitors of clothes racks with His-and-Hers pants, shirts and jewelry. It is no longer the approximation by one sex of the other, but an absolute lack of discrimination between the two.

This phenomenon has turned every man into a sociologist. Each has his own explanation: increasing coeducation in schools and colleges, the political or economic liberation of women, the demoralization and capitulation of men or bisexuality. None of these alone accounts for it. Though the agitation for equality of women has led to some amelioration of sexual discrimination in jobs and schools, the few women who actually go to Yale or become executives are not enough to revamp society. Though the Women's Liberation Movement makes itself heard, it has not yet made itself felt. Though men look more feminine, the birth rate increases; and stories of free sexuality seem more a sign of new candor or boastfulness than of new activities.

For every cultural happening, there are many explanations. In an old Jewish story a rabbi tells a young man that life is like a fountain. The young man considers this, then asks, "Why?" The rabbi's expression doesn't change. "Why not?" he counters.

Dr. Donald Opdyke at the Revlon Lab sees that men's fragrances are becoming more feminine, that men's toiletries and cosmetics are bringing in a larger share of profits and concludes that "physical differences of appearance are getting blurred." This has happened because, though our grandfathers worked hard and used their bodies as tools, affluence and leisure have weakened the modern man, who "isn't the hard, physical worker he used to be." In addition, the schools are eliminating sexual discrimination by turning coed and, though this is mainly applicable to Ivy League schools, establishments of the elite, Dr. Opdyke thinks "maybe this elimination of discrimination is coming down to every man's level." He further assumes "these kids today are not turned on about sex. . . . They get bored with sex." In his day, he would hold a girl in his arms while dancing; now, partners can be at opposite ends of the room, each concentrating on his own body and the rhythm. Dr. Opdyke concluded his analysis by saying that we are in a "crisis of authority," wherein everything is challenged, all former values, institutions and structures, including the Church, family, sex, economic and political ideologies and education. Though the young people cry, "Down with Establishment," they often have nothing new to offer. And so the changing or blurring sexual roles are part of the phenomenon of undermining that reflects the recognition of no values. Unisex, to Dr. Opdyke, is part of modern life, signifying nothing—except the rejection of all authority.

Another explanation is historical. In the twenties, the grandmothers of many people today were feminists, suffragettes or merely women who approved the proposed reforms and insisted that all humans are political animals. To force recognition of that fact, women were often willing to forgo, or suspend for a time, their traditional sexual roles of wife, mother or mistress. They devoted themselves to showing that a government for, by and of the people was not valid if it eliminated at least half its citizens on grounds of sex. These liberators allowed women to enjoy a new freedom in appearance and manners as well as civil rights, and women learned to make demands in other spheres of life than politics.

Their daughters became the wives and mothers of World War II, when the men were away and women went out to man the country. Most industries and businesses were forced to open their doors to them and, once the gentle sex had entrenched itself, it could not easily be ousted. Their mothers had gained political liberation for women; now the daughters added economic liberation, or at least involvement in the economy. They were not completely at ease, however, in their new role. Psychoanalysis was showing them that true happiness lay in instinct rather than activity, they were taught to believe that "Man Does, Woman Is" (Robert Graves's title), and that they were unnaturally going against their biological natures. The feminine mystique (as described by Betty Friedan) took hold. Though the doors had opened, they were pushed shut again by girls with college educations trying to convince themselves that whatever they had learned was of no importance. Their mothers (among the fortunate) had gone to college and become doctors, chemists, writers, photographers or college presidents. They had sent their children, boys and girls, to college and then saw their sons enter business, science or the arts while their daughters baked cakes, cleaned the house and read women's magazines printed in large type. Those who went to work accepted the general truism that they were not "real" women.

But some persevered, and the liberation that remained dormant during the apathetic generation of the fifties regained force a decade later, on the wave of new political consciousness. Now women insist on the abolition of all discrimination in jobs and schools. *The New York Times* was forced to end its practice of listing jobs separately for men and women. As in Europe and to some extent America during the Marxist thirties, women are entering politics. They demand the right to participate as equals in all forms of human activity, including sexual.

As this equality increases, men are entering formerly feminine activities. The basic tenets of society are despised, and money is devalued as a token of virility. If the girl has more than the boy, she can pay for both without crises of roles. Men and women are comrades. They reject the competitive way of life and no longer struggle against each other for power. Each has the right of sexual refusal or sexual overture. Both can earn money or not and both are responsible for the child.

Hippies and idealists are setting up communes where all members share duties and beds. No human animal is more equal, and to emphasize this harmony, homogeneity or hodgepodge, they eliminate sexual distinction in dress. In colleges, boys and girls protest together, and psychologists report that women are cursing more vigorously and imaginatively than men. (This was always true in the "culture of poverty," according to Oscar Lewis.) Whereas girls were formerly used as shields against the police, marching ahead or carried aloft, the police are now as sexually undiscriminating as the students and give girls the same treatment as boys, even knocking them unconscious with nightsticks.

In China, Israel and Cuba, unisex is a way of life. Chinese comrades all dress alike; kibbutzim provide nurseries for all children, where a mother can present her offering and then go about her work. Cuban soldiers are as often female as male, and for admirers of Che and Mao, equality is as natural as discrimination was to Dr. Johnson. Perhaps our history leads us to the sexual organization of socialist states.

But Americans are never dead serious. Their sense of play and their perpetual adolescence lets them spread a hard vinyl surface over the depths. Often boys and girls dress alike for no profound reason, but because it's fun, because the older generation is still shockable by this, and because—why not?

A third interpretation of unisex is the increasing vogue of bisexuality. Let no part of the person discriminate, not even his genitals. We've liberated ourselves from Puritanism, virginity, fidelity and marriage. More bright young women are remaining unmarried or having babies without husbands. Effective contraception and the disparagement of Christianity allow both sexes to espouse promiscuity. Magazines offer advice on adultery, how to go about it or how to cope with it. American couples are becoming more hip and more honest, recognizing their sexual boredom and so supplementing it with wife swapping. That, however, is a middle-class suburban game. (Even in 1958, in *New Faces*, Eartha Kitt sang of the "game they call Westport," where "you take the wife of which you're not the husband / And somebody else's husband takes your wife.") The kids now have gone beyond that and in premarital freedom seek partners from any race or sex.

One of the people I interviewed talked about a party he went to with his wife, where people undressed and then began a nondiscriminatory orgy. His wife was Catholic, and he was embarrassed. They both left without participating. Kenneth told me of sitting at a table in a dance palace "with kids who were twenty years my junior. I was talking, just being Big Daddy or whatever, trying not to be and saying [to myself], 'What the hell am I doing here?' And I must tell you it is absolutely fascinating because I realized in the conversations I was listening to that girls and boys and boys and boys and girls and girls . . . were going to bed with one another, together and it didn't mean a thing. There was no involvement about it in the sense of guilt. They didn't care . . . and it's happening, happening, happening all over the country with this particular age group. Well, I found it mesmerizing because in my time"—he laughed at the recollection—"boyoboyoboy nothing."

I asked Kenneth whether he thought this change was happening outside New York also. "I think it is," he said. "I think it's happening in coeducational schools, where young people are congregating. I don't think it's happening where they're still with their families, outside of New York or Chicago or Los Angeles—the big urban areas. But I do think it's happening where the young are congregating together. . . . Yes, this is a good thing. It'll probably go much too far, but it's got to. You know, then something will happen that will make them talk sense in ten years or in fifteen years."

"You realize this is all on tape?" The reel was ending, the interview over.

"Oh, I'll be hauled off to . . ."

To where, brave Kenneth, since the revolution is already launched and the standard is carried in trouser suits, pageboys and chains for both him and her? Who would haul off a fashion superstar for calling the innings of the latest sex game? And beyond that, who would ever believe it's true, except those who are practicing it and should be proud to have such a distinguished commentator?

But nonpractitioners can enter Unisex by way of bisexuality too or, more precisely, infantilism. The mini-dressing of the past few years implies a flaunting of sex, but in the unconscious and unaccountable way a little girl flaunts it. Little dresses, micro-skirts, poor-boy sweaters, knee socks and skimpy coats were all present in childhood. England, a country not synonymous with sexual passion, provided the theme, and America, also not known for passionate ecstasy, took it up: the prenubile girl, the small child who gets cuddly with a doll or with her best girlfriend, loves to pull up her skirt to show the pretty panties and is horrified by the coarseness of a male cheek.

Soft clothes, long hair and cosmetics for men are reminders of the little boy who amused the family by wearing mother's clothes and trying out her makeup. A little boy of three can put on lipstick and look cute; a boy of six is told to wash his face and a twelve-year-old is taken to a psychiatrist. But the man of twenty-five can bring back sunny days of childhood by using a hair lightener (he was once a golden-haired cherub) or face powder, which gives his face the smoothness it had when his mother kissed him good night.

When we were babies, we all looked alike. Passers-by didn't know if we were girls or boys, and it was up to our mothers to reveal or disguise our sex by the clothes she put on us and the length of our hair. After puberty, it's difficult to fool anyone. But we can minimize the differences—flatten breasts, lengthen hair, wear slacks and beads—and still manage to confuse a few old fogies. Margaret Mead explained to me that "the kids know perfectly well which sex is which," implying that because I was ten years out of my teens, I had lost the ability to discriminate.

Unisex is still a limited phenomenon of middle-class urbanites. Some people encounter it only in print or on television, some don't notice and others insist it doesn't exist, even when confronted by it. These rewriters of "The Emperor's New Clothes" will not accept the word or the concept, and when they see two people of different sexes dressed alike will shrug it off with, "Just kids."

But many American kids don't have the sexual surroundings that permit Unisex. They inhabit a world that, in the nineteen fifties, was inhabited even by middle-class urbanites; from it people emerged to commit marriage on each other. Virgins before, they could now use the sex act as the most important weapon in the war of the sexes. After marriage came boredom or promiscuity; men leered at Playmates, and women developed pains. Lubricity swelled behind the girdle of respectability.

This is still true in many parts of America. Virginity is expected and even admired. Girls push away any boy who gets too fresh or goes too far, reserve all events of a date for long telephone conversations with the best friend next day, are assured of their sexual power while unconsciously entering the training for frigidity and dream all the while of a foreigner who might seduce them in Venice—but since this would happen on alien soil with someone who didn't even speak English, it wouldn't count.

Boys try vigorously to get beyond first base, knowing that any girl who lets them isn't worth it. They boast to others of their conquests, extol large breasts even if they are embarrassed by them and tell each other of the fast girls you can have your way with. And when sexual needs increase, a boy's usually left on his own to cope.

The sexes are strange to each other, as they are to the Cosmopolitan Girl and Playboy. A letter in *Co-ed* asks the editor, "Could you tell me what kind of girls boys like, and if it matters whether they're thin, fat, tall, small. Also if boys like girls who like the rain, because I just love to walk in the rain." A blind teen-age girl asked Albert Asenjo of the American Foundation for the Blind at what age boys menstruate.

But things are changing. When they first appeared, the Beatles with their long hair and baby features brought assurance that girls and boys are not so different. Young Americans of both sexes could recognize them as people like themselves. A new way was possible; girls and boys could see that the other guy wasn't a maniac after all. On campuses, camaraderie developed. Everyone was for the same things, the similarities between all young people marked them off from adults, and the differences could be played down.

Girls who will not "go all the way" in a provincial high school may change their minds in college or when they come to a big city. Defenders of the old virtues play bass to the more exciting, improvised sounds of the flashier instruments in front. The background changes slowly, the lower classes lag in fashion behind the upper by a decade or so. Provincials live in a different generation from urbanites. But the pace and power of communications increase constantly, and those who are now in the fifties may jump into the seventies in a couple of years.

The acceptance of Unisex is a result of many established aspects of American life (infantilism, sexual equality, coeducation) combined with revolutionary forces. It is part of the valid criticism that the last generation brought the clear possibility of total annihilation, and by undermining their values, we might conceivably reverse some of the lunacy. It is the promise of a new world where all are equal, sex is no longer dirty or mysterious and privacy is recognized as a fraud. That Unisex spread to older people (though generally in slightly adapted form) was to be expected. The beauty industry depends on narcissism and naturally encourages any fashion or fad that increases it. Unisex brings out the infantile personality, full of self-love; it has no stigma of homosexuality, because it allows both sexes to come together in a fashion image (nonsexual); it is a natural for narcissism and for the market. There are no enclaves in America, mass media embrace all events, opinions and fashions and, as Margaret Mead astutely observed, "We've always Americanized from the outside in." To be American now means achieving Unisex and Uniage.

"We have this terrific emphasis on youth in this country, which very interestingly means we hate youth," Dr. Mead said. "Just hate—of the kids today. If they ask for anything, if they do anything different, they're hated by the middle-aged, who are trying to pretend that they're young." But Dr. Mead also said, "The American middle-class man likes young girls. . . . There's a style of liking young girls. And when his daughter is married, he has a crisis, a breakdown. Cause he discovers that there is no young girl for him anymore." This would be reason enough to encourage his wife to take the daughter's place.

Men and women competing for each other, new opportunities for women that take them out of the house, more understanding between men and women that allows relaxation of roles, the rejection of certain economic and social principles in America, the crisis in authority and evaporation of God—all explain in part the current phenomenon. But perhaps essentially Unisex is accepted in America along with the whole beauty culture just because of the fun involved. To be able to play with life, to cheat death by ignoring it, to remove signs of mortality because, suggesting death, they are not sexy, to make one's entire existence into a cocktail party where the chief values are sociability, attractiveness, endurance and flattery are the American Way. Androgyny is one of many amusing ways of passing the time at this crazy party that most of us could be invited to if we will only dedicate ourselves to the belief that fashion (in thought, manners, faith and appearance) is the *ne plus ultra*, the Chivas Regal, of the whole blast.

BEAUTY RETREAT

❧❦❧

Now a lady whose shoulders are beautiful feels
certain that all the young men will be swept off
their feet and are bound to repeat as she passes
near them, "Oh, what magnificent shoulders!"
without bothering to look closely at her face, her
hair, her nose, or her forehead. And even if they
did notice them, they'd see them as things having
no connection with her whatsoever.

—GOGOL, *Dead Souls*

In February, 1969, I went to The Golden Door, in Escondido, California, one of America's most expensive and luxurious beauty cloisters, where women tired of the world, their bodies or husbands could make a retreat and return refreshed. The nuns and priestesses of beauty provide a haven (at eight hundred dollars a week) for those seeking the peace that comes through continual attention to the body. I chose The Golden Door because the other establishments were too grand. At Elizabeth Arden's Maine Chance or Neiman-Marcus's Greenhouse, clients wore Diors and emeralds. The Duchess of Windsor had gone to the Greenhouse in May, 1968, on her first vacation without her husband, and was reported to be pleased.

Once at those beauty farms, I was sure I would be evicted as an interloper, possessing neither the years, nor the wardrobe, nor the class for assimilation. The Golden Door called for casual clothes, was in the promised land to one shivering through an eastern winter and its brochure was "haikued" and sensitively photographed.

> "The peony receives
> the morning moon,
> the morning sun"

captioned a picture of a girl swimming in radiance. The brochure promised that "Serenity takes you by the hand, leading to moments of heavenly stillness" and, later: "Our Golden Door plays rare tricks with time. The young catch glimpses of a rich maturity. The mature feel deliciously close to their youth." For men, there was a photograph

261

of a lonely tuba player in a web of deep forest with the words: "The world is but a single dewdrop/set trembling upon a stem/and yet . . . and yet . . ." Afterward came assurance that "Hardheaded businessmen adore soft-living while shaping up, function more brilliantly for months after an incomparable Golden Door Interlude."

This spa is patronized by the Gabor sisters and owned by Deborah Bordeaux Szekeley, wife of a man with an inundation of titles, honors and illustrious ancestors. She offers luxury and an accompanying philosophy. To study the faiths and rituals of the beauty culture, there was no place more apt.

I kept a journal, not as secretly as I'd hoped because I can't write by hand for any sustained length, and the typewriter's tut-tuts at night were heard by my neighbors. The journal began before I arrived and ended a few days after I left. For me, the trip was like an anthropologist's journey, and I wanted to keep a frame of reference. I had been afraid I would be unacceptable at five foot ten, weighing less than one hundred twenty-five pounds. I didn't want to lose weight and finally gave as reason for being at the retreat that I was run-down, exhausted and underweight.

THURSDAY, JANUARY 30

In three days, I'll be there, after eight months of anticipating, seeing myself naked on a plush couch in a fragrant room, my body being massaged with Lawrentian oils. Here I'm cold and nervous. I imagine the hands working over me—to loaf and invite my soul!

But it's almost time. Alternate ways of spending the money plead in my mind. I'm horrified at the prospect of being incarcerated an entire week with unspeakable women. Who would spend eight hundred dollars a week to be fussed over? A severe neurotic, at least; probably someone vacuous and infantile, useless to herself, with nothing to occupy her day and thoughts. Daughter-types, caring only about their appearance, intent on becoming dolls to remain mama's darling. A week with them! And then, too, the planned day: from seven in the morning charging relentlessly and not so much as a drink (or more) to post the evening.

I'm still afraid, as I've always been, of tightly contained societies: the moment of panic when you board ship, knowing you'll be locked in the middle of the ocean for five days with no chance of escape. Shipboard romance, dancing, drinking, white moon on black waters and you in a new silk, schools of dolphin—all are nothing against that bald fact of captivity. I was afraid of going away to college and later, of all the little communities I then went to and worked in, happier than at any other times in my life. But I need my priestlike freedom to move, I can't be contained, and freedom means using geography as part of your personality.

Now this beauty farm—a strange country.

SUNDAY, FEBRUARY 2—On the United flight to Los Angeles

Flat land. Flat for hours, flat land will be at least half, if not two-thirds of the trip. Now it's completely white beneath, probably Nebraska, white squares with occasional dark spots indicating houses. The Platte River winds along with us, cutting an enormous bed on both sides, like long fingers, arteries, veins and skeletons of giant leaves. Most of it uninhabited, probably uninhabitable.

A minute and farther west. Squares of brownish-gray, others dusted by snow like sugar. Demarcations of the squares sometimes appear as roads. The perfect pattern is often angrily and beautifully disrupted by branches of the leaf skeletons on a white, two-dimensional tree. The pattern is becoming more and more aesthetic—a Mondrian with dark, lighter, light squares of different sizes, sometimes striped, sometimes etched with swirls or lines to suggest contour. Small squares inside larger ones cut into the next square.

This flatness is America, and I've never thought about it before. How genuine can our ideals be, formed in the East by people from a geography of contrasts, with ocean, mountains, skyscrapers and parks? The self-made man, Yankee ingenuity, independence or anarchy aren't relevant here. This flatness is China, people are expendable, values interchangeable. All's smoothed down—no peaks, depths or complexities. A country of white squares produces people like white bread: bland, unnourishing, unimaginative. Imagination here would be too close to madness, stretching indefinitely, nothing to stop it. Each man a survivor, and domesticity, family security and coziness must be the supreme virtues. This is no tiny island of concrete where vision is blocked and freed of formlessness.

A dangerous country. With all this flatness, why isn't it a dictatorship? Some figure or at least system should be strong enough to contain (and reassure) the Plains dwellers.

Plain: that's the word. Plain cooking, plain emotions, plain characters. New York and rugged New England should secede from the Union and leave America's heartland to its steady, uncomplicated, predictable beat, where God is a necessity and so are virginity, fidelity, cordiality and neighborliness. The Golden Rule belongs here—in New York it's, "do unto others before they do it to you." That's all right for a neurotic, Jewish society. But the psychotic Christian heart of America is close to violence, dangerous lunacy, huge, incomprehensible loneliness.

Still flat.

Rockies: an incurable condition of the earth.

Grand Canyon area. Dry wrinkled mud capped with small snowy bumps—an unmade bed, sheets bulky and creased. Where mud is gray and dusty, you see veins on an old, almost dead hand. To be set down here would be death: alone in the isolation of a planet not the earth. Now snowy, with pebbly texture. Small gorges and grooves. No people.

Extravaganza of death, all this gray, black white ribbed desolation. No nerves here, just projections without peaks and nothing small. Nothing for the mind to appropriate, no room for humans.

Now over the Great Basin, a dull gray-pink (dirty flesh color of topographical maps) with the contours of a soggy Kleenex that dried. . . . The Mojave Desert: pink roads cut like a razor on matting paper and lead nowhere, come from nowhere.

Landing now. It's true, the cliché that no one walks in Los Angeles. We're close to the ground, cars so near you can tell their make, but not one person. How could an enemy pilot have compassion, no matter how low down he was flying? A city without people. Who would care about blasting little metal cars and concrete houses?

FEBRUARY 2—ARRIVAL

The limousine was late at San Diego airport, but then I rode the approximately thirty miles with Joan something from Little Rock. The lady wore a beige trouser suit of light wool, many enamel and diamond bracelets (David Webb design), white gloves and round earrings. She was accompanied by four large, blond, matching pieces of luggage. (On the road to Bath, with a few carriages and the servants well-starched.) Mother and stepmother of eight, grandmother of ten, madame looks no older than forty. This is her first trip to The Golden Door, though she's familiar with the area because she and her husband attend the races at La Jolla. She liked Maine Chance, where she had her facial scheduled as first appointment so that if she tarried in bed awhile she would miss nothing essential for her body. The Greenhouse had better food, but was too citified. Joan has now left her youngest, a five-year-old daughter ("she's cute"), in the care of a white governess. ("It's hard to get white help. She's very good and she gets on well with my colored help. Which is important, you know.") We engaged in a few minutes of nice patter about the difficulty of finding servants these days, comparing prices in New York ("shocking") and Arkansas, commiserating with her daughter-in-law whose nanny had just left.

Neither unattractive nor unaffectionate, the woman touched me at times during our conversation to emphasize a point or call my attention. Her hair was a perfect glistening pageboy and I imagined she must have a standing appointment with a Little Rock hairdresser at least twice a week. This evening, she was in short, curly hair. Her black patent wig box is enormous.

The place is a Mexican hacienda in Hollywood. Inconspicuous from the road, ranch-type, it opens up in back around a courtyard with a pool at the center, white statuary, cacti, flowers, pebbles and doves in a cage. Each room is different, mine probably one of the most extravagant. It's Louis XVI, with a picture of *le roi* in an ornate gilt frame, escorted by Marie Antoinette in a twin frame. Two chandeliers glitter below the high, gabled ceiling. The bed has a gold canopy and showy headboard and at either side two antique marble night tables hold lamps made of a trio of cupids, pruriently shielding their genitals with marble draping. Also in the room: wall-to-wall beige carpeting, pink brocade satin chaise longue, a couch of gilt and red velvet, matching chairs, marble coffee table and end tables. Behind heavy red double drapes, I can part the wall of glass and step out on my patio to recline in the deck chair or take breakfast at the wooden table. My bathroom is prefaced by a small dressing room with open closet and mirrored vanity. The light is strong and the mirror tray bears Golden Door cosmetics: lip gloss, moisturizer, herbal cream for deep cleansing, wrinkle oil, cleansing oil and night oil. Also a flacon of bath oil, to be replaced daily. A pink undershirt, sweat shirt, sweat pants, bermudas and terry bandanna were prepared for tomorrow. But I got into the white terry robe to go to the gym for weighing and measuring.

Ellen Roy, who runs the Golden Door, was supervising the pounds and inches. A blond, tanned woman from Zurich, full of temperament and charm with a slight dash of schmaltz, she was enchanted by my knowledge of German and all was well. I am to have a large breakfast, though the others get only tea or coffee and perhaps a half grapefruit. Also, I was absolved from the 6:45 call for the early morning walk.

Cocktails: a frothy concoction looking like a Margarita, tasting rather tart and good, accompanied by a large tray of vegetable hors d'oeuvres. At dinner I was granted water though the others must wait for liquids until they've finished eating. I ate my chicken and courgettes with cheese sauce, couldn't finish and was oppressed seeing my neighbor devour her green salad with a gob of cottage cheese. This is her sixth or seventh visit, she's been here a week already this time and told me the Door is "an inspiration." (She confided, though, that she's lonesome. On all previous sojourns she and a friend shared the only double room, but this time she has a room to herself.)

The guests are a middle assortment, and nobody's quality. They're all here to lose, but most aren't obviously overweight. A young girl, maybe eighteen years old, is the fattest but one, with long dark hair and a pout on her baby face. She goes barefoot and displays much of her ample figure.

Next to her, a plump woman with false lashes in a gold hostess gown. Joan has a friend, also from Arkansas, who is the *Ladies' Home Journal's* love of an American housewife: rangy, with a simple, wholesome face. A dumpy blonde in brown-and-gold brocade looks like a lesbian teacher, her face much too harsh, eyebrows too straight and low over her eyes, bleached hair lying flat on her head with one curl on either side.

Conversation is slow. I have nothing to say. Ellen gives me the encouraging half-smiles I never got from my second-grade teacher. She announces to all her guests that tomorrow she will ingest nothing but orange juice, and for the next eight days will give up meat entirely, eating only yogurt, fruit and juices. She's slim, but habitually embarks on these diets to "purify the system." "I have been eating a lot of no-good food," she tells us, doughnuts and such that she buys for the staff. She's full of verve, self-satisfaction, and one sees in her the makings of either a great fanatic or a great businesswoman. In the course of conversation she told one guest, "Last July you weighed one hundred and twenty-nine pounds."

After dinner, Ellen gave us a short lecture. "Welcome to the Golden Door. Leave your troubles behind and enter, with your large hearts and small bodies." She gave a small rundown of the activities offered and reminded us that we were now exiled from responsibility. Thoughts of home, job or children would vanish here where you are concerned only with yourself. "Two years ago my little boy went to the hospital for the first time. And I only realized at the end of the day that I hadn't thought about him once. . . . I'm too busy caring about myself and my guests."

At the end of the lecture, someone asked about Zsa Zsa. Ellen said, "I know her very well, she's an old friend," and reported she had been unable to find scars or other signs of face-lifting. "Still," said the old friend, "I think she does something." But loyally, Ellen insisted that all the Gabors are beautiful, have wonderful skin they take wonderful care of (never allowing the sun to reach it) and large hips.

I returned to my room and my ionizer, a small machine near the bed that releases negative ions to help induce sleep and clear the air (particularly necessary, we were told, for people like me, who muck up their air with smoke).

. . . our gold-printed stationery arrives tomorrow.

. . . lunch may be taken by the pool. Just pick up the telephone, tell the girl at reception where you are and lunch is brought. Use the white telephone. The gray one, in the dressing room, is only for emergencies.

. . . The cook, who's also the dietician, is a three-hundred-pound bearded jovial Negro called Harmony. Everybody simply adores him.

. . . for guests who may experience some trouble with their elimination, an herbal tea is offered in the evening after the movie. It works as a mild laxative.

. . . It's a beautiful place, glorious air, and female company might even be relaxing. I look forward to exercise. In her lecture, Ellen described the usual American life in the same terms as Carola Trier: "We don't exercise. . . . We go down to the garage, we don't even have to go outside. We push a button to open the door, we push a button to close the door. Our cars are air-conditioned, so we get no oxygen. This is very bad. This is why we have headaches." She motioned toward Joan, who had complained of one since I met her in the car. Probably a hangover; she told me she'd been partying too much last night.

. . . the women seem undistinguished. No one is eager for privacy.

FEBRUARY 3

"Tighten your popsies," Ellen trilled at the wake-up exercises. "You have a gold coin in there. Hold tight. . . . Release. Now we open our windows and let in the fresh air."

In the steam room, a woman who's been here before (most guests have) said she came to lose weight and tighten her body. She leads a sedentary life, she said, now that her daughter's away at school. Formerly, she drove the girl to a local school every day, and this apparently served for exercise. Her husband works hard, comes home and flops on the sofa to watch TV. They used to go dancing, but not anymore. After he walks forty thousand feet through the factory all day, his wife said, he doesn't ever want to take a walk.

A skinny, haggard woman with jaundiced complexion is here for spot reducing. The last time, she came to gain weight.

In Da Vinci, a rousing exercise session to pop music, we frugged, kicked and twisted while doggedly retaining the grimace of jauntiness.

Herbal wrap is committed in a room with couches, something between a hospital room and a bordello. You steam or sauna first; then the naked body is wrapped in hot towels redolent of peppermint, eucalyptus or lemon. You lie, bound like a mummy, sweating for half an hour. Then a cold shower or "scotch mist" (a technique obviously borrowed from Alabama cops: a hose is trained on you, and the rush of cold water either massages or pulps your body). The herbal wrap is not advised for people with heart conditions. I found it all amazing; finally, I was in a Roman spa and being treated like a grand lady, not like a phys.-ed. dropout.

The fattest woman here weighed in at two hundred and forty-three (I sneaked a look in the book of numbers). After her husband died, she mourned her way through magnificent pastries prepared by her consoling housekeeper. She said her life is exactly as Ellen described —you push a button for the garage door to open, another for it to close.

My facial was superb—first, hands and feet were creamed, covered with plastic gloves or socks and heating pads over them. Then the massage—so expertly loving I fell asleep. At the end, my arms and legs were massaged too, the melted cream rubbed in and up, oiling my limbs. This must be what a geisha offers a man: all tiredness goes, you are feted for existing; you are precious and wonderful.

It occurs to me we're too quick to see all pleasure as sexual. You love food, not as substitute for sex—that's another time. Similarly this., Why be exclusively genital, when you can also be polymorphously perverse?

The baby-faced, barefoot girl is twenty-one. "Without my makeup I look about thirteen," she says, and it's true. She studied cooking after dropping out of a very inferior college, and gained thirty pounds in three weeks. When she came home, her parents said, "You've got to go someplace. Unless you take that off and look like you did in high school, you're no daughter of ours." She was sent to the Golden Door, because her father said the Greenhouse was for women who wanted to get away from their husbands. How did he know? "My father knows everything."

Baba Jensen hadn't wanted to come, afraid that the people would be too old, "and I'd have to talk about art and all that stuff that I don't know anything about at all." She was quite pleased by the actuality. There's another young girl here, and though I'm the only one in the twenty-five-to-thirty-five age group, most women look reasonably young and are in their forties. Miss Jensen admitted she has forty pounds to lose. The boys she goes out with are so mad at her for gaining weight they don't want to be with her. That gets her so furious she just stomps home to eat.

When she finishes her stay at the Golden Door (a Valentine present from her father), Miss Jensen will have to busy herself with something for a few months before her extended trip to Europe. The other young girl, who lives in Brussels, came to California just to walk through the Golden Door.

The women here are generally relaxed and pleased to be exclusively among women. I hadn't realized, with all the equality that usually surrounds me, what relief there is in being with your own sex. (Many tribal societies have separate houses for men and women; in India and Africa the sexes are often segregated; in English country houses the sexes are still separated after dinner and in America colleges were meant for one sex or the other.) Equality puts pressure on us to be self-conscious and sex-conscious, aware of appearance and audience. With the opposite sex, you tighten up, and vanity comes in aid of awkwardness.

Here in this woman's world, there's no vanity or shame and women can be generous with each other when competition is useless. They help each other and are more ready with praise (even for effort, if results don't merit it) than men would be. I've never felt so beautiful as I do here. The women ask why on earth I came, with my perfection of slimness. One shows me off to another. Women who haven't said a word to me before come up with, "You look just great," or, "I'd give anything to have your weight and measurements."

This isn't any beauty parlor. Muscles ache, you're driven through strenuous, exhausting exercises. This is body building, Kennedyism and the Roman way—*mens sana in corpore sano*. The aim is tightening muscles, the return to well-being, increment of energy and physical fitness to aid in resisting disease, and the rejuvenation of the body so it's more able to cope with the life one leads. Without men, the body's an instrument to make work (and play) in different ways. Or it's the production of an artist—part of him, certainly, but he has full control over it and can shape it any way he likes.

We played volleyball in the water today, one of the chief sports that studded me with traumas in high school, where, being tall, I was expected to be good and was as hopeless in that as in all other physical activities. But today in the pool Ellen said I was "the best."

Before cocktails we stood around the gym in towels and "pinkies" waiting for the nurse to take blood pressure and ask questions. The rangy Arkansan told an incident from four years ago when she was here. A girl was being measured on the first day with extraordinary thoroughness—wrists, ankles, thighs, hips, back, breasts, shoulders—everything except her earlobes, according to the narrator. "Well, I think that's it," said the person taking measurements. Then she remembered: "No, I haven't measured your diaphragm." The girl, most consternated, confessed, "I forgot to bring it with me."

Much glee was shown by all. The Arkansan, pleased to be at the center of such happy conviviality, drew out the story: "That was four years ago, that was before the Pill." Everyone was in high spirits; later the narrator told me she was here to escape from her seventeen-year-old daughter. A daughter, she said, was an awful thing to have—"she's so nitty-bitty, always picking on you."

As a rule, though, the women don't talk about their families. Neither willing nor unwilling to mention husbands and children, they will do so in passing, if relevant. No one so far has said what job she has or work she does. No word has been exchanged on an abstract subject. Talk is about how one feels, how much one has lost or wants to lose, but no idea, book or event is referred to. The guests don't seem frustrated, give an impression of independence and, for the most part, have a generous and catholic sense of humor. Every woman I mentioned liquor to has a secret store (as I do) but is still unsure whether or not she'll drink it.

FEBRUARY 4

No claims are made for breast development. When I told Ellen I wanted to increase my bustline, she said the only way was by surgery. In gym, the girl instructing me laughed. Indicating her small breasts, she said, "If you find out how to do it, let me know."

This morning Ellen was all in pink. She chooses a different color every day to match her mood and then wears everything in that color—underclothes, leotard, bathing suit, shoes and the ubiquitous nylon hat, a fluff of improbable blooms that decorate many heads here. It's sold in the shop for ten dollars and is meant to disguise our greasy hair, which was oiled the first day and won't be washed until Saturday. Pink Ellen was soothing and inspirational in the exercises. At the end, we all lay on our backs with eyes shut while Ellen chanted: "Now in-hale. . . . Ex-hale. You are peeking through the branches and see the beautiful blue sky. Oh how beautiful.

"In-hale. . . . Ex-hale. You see a white flower. Its petals are shining in the sun. You smell the wonderful smell of the white flower.

"In-hale. . . . Ex-hale." More of the same, which I can't remember. Then: "You count your blessings. You think of someone you love very much and send a big wish. In-hale. . . . Ex-hale."

In Beauty, Phyllis, with the loving touch, told me she gives men the same treatment as women. The only difference is in hair oil—

slightly scented for women, unscented for men. Guests during men's weeks are mainly executives—many from Ampex, the Californian electronics company—sent down by the firm for two weeks as a health measure. Some of these admit having resisted before they came, but once at the Door were delighted.

The women who come, said Phyllis, don't have "class, just money." Though some are executives (mainly from the garment industry) and some stockbrokers, the majority are housewives. At Maine Chance, women are older, dress elegantly every night, go to cocktail parties and concentrate on beauty. "You get old wealth there," she said. Many are divorcées or widows, lonely women who come every month or so. Clients of the Golden Door come less often—every year, every six months or, occasionally, every three months. Phyllis said that some women choose a beauty farm over analysis. Overweight can be—and often is—tied to emotional problems, and women feel they can work these out here. Some succeed, if only because they've been away for a while. Or they "get enough of a lift" to be able to face the problems when they return. Coming here for two weeks, Phyllis calculated, was cheaper than regular visits to a doctor.

My weight seems to be everyone's concern and preoccupation. Guests and staff ask me about it every few minutes. I've lost two and a half pounds. For lunch today I had a hamburger on toast with ketchup and onions; for dinner I'll have spaghetti. The ladies encourage me to go into the kitchen and ask for anything I want. I shouldn't bother about sitting next to them with piles of food on my plate—good for the character, they insist, and once they go home they'll have to live with temptation all the time. All this sympathy is fine, but the absence of liquor drives me crazy. I've always eaten a lot, but also oiled my way into dinner with Scotch or gin. And not many gobs of food have gone down my throat without a little wave of wine chasing them along. For years, I've never considered a meal anything more than a snack unless wine accompanied it.

Anything for my art or research, I keep telling myself, but natural hedonism is as powerful a drive as murder. I've got to have wine. Joan sympathized with my problem and told me I should demand wine. "For sixteen hundred dollars" (she's staying two weeks), "they can give you what you want." I agreed, and have managed to provide for a bottle to be brought me, on condition that I dine alone in my room. Small price for civilization.

Naked in the solarium, our bodies gleaming with avocado oil, I talked with Marsha, the attractive Hungarian. She's been to La Puerta, the Mexican spa owned by the Szekeleys. It's much cheaper than here and much larger. A hotel offers usual amenities (real food, liquor) and men and women go there together. The facilities of a beauty farm are available free, except for special services like facial, massage or herbal wrap. Minimum price is about fourteen to sixteen dollars a day. Marsha said I must visit and write a novel about it (everyone knows I write), that it's a place where people lose weight, country and self. From "secretary to senator" they go there, hoping to escape their lives and unburden themselves. Here, says Marsha, are not the simple stories of frustrated housewives; they are sagas of madness, murder, incest. Each newcomer is appraised by something like a psychoanalyst, who's interested in gestalt and uncovering their body image.

This Mexican Valhalla is a great money-making proposition. American prices are charged to American customers; Mexican wages are paid to Mexican workers. The Szekeleys grow their own vegetables, have a vineyard and produce the herbs that go into their cosmetics. The staff live on the grounds as a cooperative, and because American girls married to Mexicans have no status, they are employed without wages in return for being able to live there.

Marsha says she would never take her husband. The sight of all that blubber, she said, would turn any man queer. But another woman here, tiny, huge-breasted midwestern woman, who could pose for the Montgomery Ward catalog in floral prints, said she went for a weekend with her husband, and they both enjoyed La Puerta very much.

The ranch is owned and run by "the professor," Mr. Szekeley. Marsha refers to all his credentials (listed in the Golden Door Beauty Book placed in every room) with scorn. "He's as Jewish as they come." (Though he claims as ancestors a pope, some kings, a few bishops and others.) "He has more degrees than Einstein, than anybody. He comes here and tells idiotic stories about Diogenes and Alexander and everyone 'simply *adores* it.' He's the biggest phony there ever was." And Marsha assures me, he must weigh "eight hundred pounds, at least."

The Golden Door was a present to his wife, the prestige, luxury showcase that probably doesn't show a profit. Fifty staff members service twenty guests. The gym is full of intricate spot-reducing machines. The rooms are ornate and extravagant, and the grounds are continually being polished like silverware. The services and deluxe accommodations would cost more separately than they do here.

Marsha's attractive, loves her husband, leads a busy social and cultural life at home and is most like a lady of anyone here. She has a good body, moves with ease (why do European women all know they're women and Americans don't?) and told me she has the tendency, whenever depressed or under pressure to take another drink, eat chocolate or hot dogs (her favorite food) and put on fifteen pounds. When she goes up to one hundred forty, her husband says she looks deformed. So she comes to the Golden Door to initiate a regime she can then more effectively follow at home. She will never stay more than a week; she misses her husband and gets oppressed by the artificiality. I told her I had expected a different class of people here, and that in Europe, after all, spas were frequented by the grand people. She said no. "In Carlsbad, which is the best, you find the most terrible people too."

After the solarium, a dance class. Perfection of torture, provided by an archetypal California girl with platinum hair, blue eyes, a hard little face, thin, tough body and natural vulgarity composed of gutsiness, cheerleaderism and exhibitionism. "Come on, everybody. SMILE." We frugged—an absurd gangulation of overweight women in "pinkies," pugnaciously imitating the narcissistic movements of the very young. We were taught one dance slowly, step by step. A small Jewish woman, New York cabbie type, commented, "Oh goodie, now we have a routine we can do when we get home. My mummy will be so pleased."

When we did pelvic pushes, the better to frug by, she asked the instructor, "What are these exercises for?"

"We exercise everything at the Golden Door." (Good-humoredly.)

A bleached blonde with a southern drawl suggested, "We could call them sexercises."

" 'Sexercises,' " repeated the instructor, with slow sarcasm, "how cute."

Someone else carried the ball: "Then everybody would be asking, When do we get the sexercises?"

When this was exhausted, the cabbie asked, "At what speed should we do them, do you recommend?"

We were urged to "do our own thing." The only reason adults

can't do these exercises, said the hard little sunshine girl, can be summed up in one word: inhibition. So we gyrated more, in front of the wall-to-wall mirror, the cruelty accepted by all women with good humor and even gratitude. There they all were, feeling ten times larger than life, as bulky and awkward as a rhinoceros. Thinness didn't help as I was forced to watch myself engaging in hands off masturbation, my legs like stilts below the pink Bermudas, my arms twitching like a dissected frog.

Then, happily, massage. The stout, efficient Virginia led me to my room after a sauna, the massage table set up, drapes drawn. She said I should gain ten pounds. She comes from a small town in California and grew up poor. Her work here is strenuous. "After a day of working on fat ladies, you can get pretty tired. If they were all skinny like you, it wouldn't be so hard." She snaps out tenseness in the muscles, is like a head nurse, a no-nonsense woman with a strong body and a kind, indifferent maternal attitude toward her "patients." Joan told Virginia she brought greetings from a friend in Texas, a habitué of the Golden Door who was unable to come now because she was preparing for her daughter's debut, after which the girl was going to Acapulco; and the mother had to make sure she had the right clothes. "Of course," nodded Virginia, "these things, graduations and so forth, they're important."

. . . Masie, a small redhead with large bags under her eyes, is a very rich woman whose husband died a few years ago. Loneliness drove her to immediate remarriage with a younger man who forged her checks and used up all her money. Now she's alone again.

. . . Bertha is a stockbroker from Duluth. She's divorced and will not go out with a man, because "what would the children think?" The children are twenty-eight and thirty.

The ladies are doing papier-mâché tonight, while I write this in my gold-and-silver dressing gown. Going into the activity room, the little midwesterner with huge breasts told Marsha and me that she takes classes at home. "All the girls said they couldn't do it and didn't have any talent, but the teacher said, 'Never say that. You'd be surprised what you can do.' And they all turned out the cutest things you ever saw. . . . I made the wise men, you know, the three wise men for Christmas. I made them small and then I asked him how to make them large. So I made them this high"—almost to her shoulders —"and they look really great in my front entrance. . . . I made a lion and a vulture. A real cute vulture, with a tear coming down his cheek. My husband said, 'Why do you want to make anything as gory as a vulture?' And I said: 'You just wait and see, you'll think it's real cute.' And it was, the cutest thing you ever saw." Smiling cheerily, she disappeared into the room with paper napkins.

"Why," I said hopelessly to Marsha, "do they come here?"

"They're very lonely. They want something to do. They have good middle-class marriages, the husband comes home in the evening, has his three martinis and watches television. The women come here to feel better, look better."

"To get a new man?" I asked.

Marsha shook her head. "For other women. For other women."

She's right, I think. This group is insipid, not mean, and trails sad boredom. The faces suddenly become naked, the smile is ripped off and the woman looks about to cry. Or there's the other extreme, of exhibitionism/narcissism. Ellen, for instance, always watches herself in the mirror while teaching a class, rarely looks at her pupils. And a couple of women are always ready to crack a joke. The big-hearted, funny prostitute types with tough humor they can turn on themselves. Everything's good for a laugh, and you wonder what happens when the drinks wear off. Except they haven't had any drinks.

Marsha is my only friend now. She was surprised that we get on so well. "Usually, if you put two European women together, they won't get on at all."

"But I'm a born New Yorker," I reminded her.

"I don't care if you were born on top of the Statue of Liberty, you're still a European."

Maybe I am, and hopelessly decadent, imagining that words could ever be solace for the spirit, holding the ridiculous delusion that man has a spirit, and woman too. I should let in more of the outdoors and submerge myself utterly in the perfect and convivial surface of things.

FEBRUARY 5

I fell asleep at 3 A.M.—no particular reason, just didn't feel sleepy, despite the Scotch I drank. All this exercise is too exhilarating. This morning was gray, for the first time. I got corn flakes for breakfast, read about oil seepage in the Los Angeles *Times* and felt very stiff. The wake-up exercises were impossible. What willpower these women have, who are all twenty years older and many pounds heavier than I! Curses on the seedy urban life.

In Beauty today, Phyllis was off (everyone is off two days each week) and Irene gave me the facial. She said my scalp was loose—a good thing in a woman. Men, she said, relax much more easily than women. "My husband comes home, has his dinner, takes the paper and falls asleep. . . . I sometimes get kinda annoyed at him."

Maybe American women age faster than their husbands because, though endowed with more energy and endurance (being child-bearers), they have too much time to worry in, worry being a greater bringer-on of age than work. Their days are fragmented, always show gaps, and they rely more than men on their emotional life, every twist and turn of feeling.

Ellen was in black and white today because the sun is partly in and partly out. Her relaxation theme at the end of wake-up exercises was the ocean: blue waves moving back and forward (in-hale, ex-hale). Smell the water lilies. "You count your blessings and you send a great big wish to someone you love." (In-hale, ex-hale.)

My neighbor of the first evening, the woman lonely in her single room, asked Ellen: "What do I need these muscles for, honey? I don't need leg muscles for picking up a cocktail glass. You're getting me ready for a life I'll never lead, honey."

But it's Wednesday, day of "letdown," when everyone feels sore, tired and disillusioned. Marilyn, the young girl from Brussels, has recovered from her fever of yesterday. She had completely stopped eating, increased her exercises and was totally dehydrated. She had lost eleven pounds, six of which she put back this morning by drinking water.

Sybaritism: being massaged with fragrant oils in my Louis XVI room while drinking a milkshake so thick the spoon stood up in it.

In the pool, I chatted with Lucy, the bumptious blonde whose "baby" is twenty-two years old. She's a show-biz type, obviously rich, and looks no older than forty. She comes here regularly, has already spent four weeks this time and plans to spend two more. When she came, she weighed one hundred fifty pounds, considerable for her height of five foot two. Once, when she weighed one hundred seventy, she stayed three months. "Oh, it *costs* a hell of a lot," she admitted, "had to scrap my Christmas shopping that year." (Estimated cost then, before the rates went up: seven thousand dollars.) We talked about liquor. "You just have your drink but don't let them know about it. . . . When Eva [Gabor] was here, we used to have drinks before dinner, champagne. . . . For me, one's not enough. I could use a couple of martinis right now. . . . There's a woman, comes four times a year. She drinks all the time at home, drinks so much she doesn't eat, so she gets skinny. She comes here, gains fifteen pounds, goes back and knocks them off again. . . . Now I'm just a butterball, but other times when I didn't have so much to lose I'd have a couple. Not now though, baby."

A few minutes later we were called to join the group in water exercises. The instructor ordered, "Turn around and face the bar." "Fine," said Lucy. "Make it a double martini." (Earlier, Joan had stripped in the sauna to the old joke—"Now to get out of these wet clothes and into a dry martini.")

Ellen's story: Against parental opposition she married a U.S. Air Force man. "I knew the day after I got married that it was a mistake." Still, she stayed around long enough to have three children. Now, "I support myself, I take care of the children, I don't need anything from him. . . . I made the mistake of marrying a man without money." She works hard, sometimes outrageously long hours, and I asked when she thought she would be able to have a life of her own. "When I meet the right man. Then I throw the whole thing over. I get out as quick as I came in. But not now."

Somebody figured out that among the eighteen guests were forty-five husbands. One guest (I don't know which) has been married six times.

. . . Things are fitting into place. Someone said she'd bought her bathing suit in Palm Springs. This is the set described by Stephen Birmingham in *The Right People*: those who live outside the class structure, oblivious or scornful of it, creating their own aristocracy of money. (In Thomas Hinde's novel, *High*, the German professor explains that in Europe one would never expect subtle or intellectual conversation from a butcher. At an American cocktail party, one must remember that everyone there is a butcher, but a very rich one.) These women belong to richness as nebulously as many city Jews belong to Jewry. There's no accepted way of speaking or dressing, no proper vocabulary (U and non-U) or accent; no unacceptable professions, schools, architecture (their houses) or places to visit. It's the whole span of the middle class, without constrictions or refinements.

But if you have the money and your husband bores you and there's no ritualized way out of the boredom (going to the Riviera, cruising on a yacht), why not come here? Is it ever necessary to come? No. Can it do you good? Yes.

Yoga this afternoon: a small, extremely lithe woman with a dark braid down her back and El Greco eyes taught in a church-hushed voice. We concentrated on parts of the body, tensing and relaxing; we concentrated on our breath, on the sound of a fountain outside, but still, that gentle voice and cat body made it acceptable. Remembering our dance instructor, strident, made up, a militant of the "life's a ball" school, I found this woman tremendously appealing with her peace and quietude.

Our last class for the day was Happy Feet, a preposterous exercise of massaging feet because all nerves end there and you're thereby massaging the entire body. Rubbing the little toe will relieve headaches. A class taught seriously by Peggy Jo, with her fluff of platinum hair, long fake lashes and her story of getting drunk with her seventy-five-year-old mother. A charming class, because utterly absurd, and leading naturally to the question posed by one foot-rubber: "Where are the sex organs?" (At the back of the heel.)

For drinks tonight, which were accompanied by a fashion show (modeled by the staff, clothes from the boutique), I wore a Nefertiti look, makeup emphasizing cheekbones and a gold cone over my hair. I was greatly admired, even whistled at. Peggy Jo asked, "How many years did you model in New York? Or was it Europe?" Turning to address the assembled ladies, she demanded, "Doesn't she look like a European model?" I was encouraged to wear no bra beneath my see-through blouse. When dinner was announced, I returned to my room and my wine. I ate and drank too much, then went in search of Marsha, found her in the boutique and we both tried on clothes. The ladies there acted as audience; I was star model in this fashion show and eventually bought a gold bikini because of general insistence. Never has my narcissism been so carefully tended as here. I want to remain in this nest, the only place where I will ever be Aphrodite.

FEBRUARY 6

This morning in Beauty, Phyllis told me again about the woman Lucy had mentioned in the pool. She's an alcoholic, married to a man who excels in cruelty. She comes here for three weeks at a time, needing the Door because she's pampered and babied. At home, she's cowering; here, she comes into her own. (Phyllis has visited her at home.) She won't leave her husband because of his money. "Women don't come here just to lose weight," Phyllis told me. "They come for other reasons." She massaged silently, then said, "I hope my husband doesn't get rich. I don't want him to be too ambitious. The women here, with rich husbands, are so unhappy. I don't want him to be rich so I would become the type of women who comes here."

The Golden Door, said Phyllis, originally had far more alcoholics coming for a cure than now, when an alcoholic is rare. The age has also gone down from a former average of about fifty. The youngest clients are fourteen, sent by their parents "who don't even think about the psychological reasons for the fat, but just notice that the girl is fat and want a quick way to get rid of it." The Door once had a ten-year-old client, but she came with her mother. They stayed seven weeks.

The novelty today was makeup, given only once a week. One by one, we went to the boutique where Betty, the makeup artist, worked on each face. She told me I had a "fascinating" one. After I applied mascara under her direction—too heavily, I felt—she and other women in the shop expressed amazement that my lashes were real. This reporting of compliments, this total self-indulgence, shows what's been happening to me here. I've gotten matier with everyone, forgetting whether or not I like them, going back to college days when we shared a dorm. Or army mentality: we're all in this together, no harm done joking about it. The permanent attention focused on one's body and looks, the persistent comments from staff and guests, put me in the no means unpleasant role of belle. I'm not the youngest, but the two girls are not yet women and their awkwardness and problems come through. I'm the one with the best figure, and the women protect me, idealize me, are concerned with my progress. Much more than I would ever be in a world of men, I'm adored. The most flattering form of adoration, because the women see me naked, because women notice every detail of anatomy, skin, hair, dress or makeup and are willing to comment on it. There are no men around, and so no cattiness, no competition, nothing to be afraid of (I live far away, love my husband and have a small baby), and meticulous admiration is offered, which would not be possible from a man. He could only admire *me*, not picayune effects of long thighs, good skin, gold toenails (they were painted to match my bikini and look horrendous) or whatever. But here, in addition to the physical well-being I'm beginning to acquire (which gives self-assurance), I also get praise. No compliment is so powerful as one from your own sex, someone who wishes she were you and says so. No man could ever want to be me; at most, he could want to have me—but in that there's already a failure of generosity. His acquisitiveness carries innuendos that are not flattering. If he needs me, or feels he does, then a double deterioration sets in: my physical being, the outside, becomes only a means of entry; and his need must distort who I am. Needing me, he no longer recognizes me. He looks for what he wants, finds or improvises it, and stops there. Objective appraisal can come only from someone who wants nothing of you. A man looks at a women to see if she has those traits he wants (just as a woman looks at a man). But a woman looks to discover wherein the possible appeal of the other woman lies. A man sees the cross eyes, a woman the flawless skin. The vision reverses, however, as soon as the man chooses that woman (despite her cross eyes). Then, women wonder what he could possibly see in such a horror.

Here, I'm safe. At a cocktail party, if I were talking intimately to someone else's husband, I would be seen as too tall, my hair would be too kinky, my breasts too small, my mouth too thick. Without the cocktail party, I'm perfect.

At dinner, we talked about the transformations wrought by make-up. Betty had told me that Golden Door guests vary in amount of makeup they normally use. Those from the "old-fashioned" states—the Midwest—use none or very little. The two Washington State ladies had been made up discreetly, though with the same number of cosmetics used on me. They said they both make up at home, but only in the evenings. One was wearing false eyelashes, which she said women at home wore, but "only young girls wear them during the day." Both customarily wear red lipstick, a fashion of the fifties that may be returning.

Bertha the stockbroker never wears any makeup at all. She was fascinated by the artist's handiwork and, like a little girl, shylv asked to try various cosmetics.

There was general agreement that the rest of the country is behind New York in beauty and fashion. A Bostonian said that the Ritz had a sign forbidding miniskirts on everyone but children. Boston was hopelessly old-fashioned, she said, "Even the chic people have the chic of a year ago. . . . They go down to New York shopping, all right, but they come back with last year's fashion." High society, like the Saltonstalls or Cabots, she described as "Shabby. The furs they wear, you couldn't find in the Salvation Army. The opening of the opera is the most incredible thing you could imagine."

Peggy Jo offered her recollections: "At Ohio State University, in 1947, you could always tell the New York girls. We were all wearing our dresses this short" (to the knee) "and gold-rimmed glasses. They were wearing their skirts down to here" (low calf) "and horn-rimmed glasses. A year later, all of us were wearing long skirts and horn-rimmed glasses."

Someone else informed us that "Hawaii is six months or a year behind." No one suggested New York was too far ahead; all assumed that New York is equivalent to Fashion and that the rest of America stands at various removes.

FEBRUARY 7

Today for the first time I took the early morning walk and really needed it, with my legs stiff as frozen taffy. The walk brought chumminess. One said, "I weighed one hundred and thirty-six pounds" (she's five foot one) "and I called up here and wanted to come. They said they had no room, but I could come in two weeks. I said what a shame, but all right. Between then and when I got here I gained twelve pounds. I kept telling myself, You're going to the Golden Door, so why not have that pie, or whatever?"

Later, she told me: "I went to a psychiatrist after my first marriage. But I weighed one hundred and eighty and forced myself to lose twenty pounds before I could go to him."

The cowboy from Washington State, a lanky, big-boned, homey

woman told me that she and her friend had planned to go to Tahiti together. That fell through and they came here instead. She enjoys it, but, though she had strictly kept the diet and followed the regime, she hasn't lost any weight. (It was hard to see why she should, a large woman without a bit of extra fat.) At home she plays tennis often and, when the weather's good, flies a plane. Her husband is a tree farmer.

. . . when Lucy came here four weeks ago, her waist was forty inches (she claims). It's between twenty-six and twenty-seven inches today.

I wore my gold bikini to water exercise, and a moment of silence was asked for when I entered the pool. My gold toenails are really sick-making. The gold polish is necessary in the beauty shop for the toenails of men during their week. It's put on while they're sleeping and provides a harmony of joking for the next day or two. Many men, according to Phyllis, don't remove it when they go home, since it's such an effective conversation piece.

A terrible, marvelous story: One of the guests, who had first come to the Door some years ago, was so pleased that she sent her husband here as a Christmas present. "He felt so good after he came back, he looked around, saw the old bag he was married to and went off with an eighteen-year-old."

Catherine, the Philadelphian, likes being here. A recent personal tragedy so upset her that "it was either this or a sanatorium, and this is cheaper." Here, she enjoys the total lack of serious talk, the simple feminine life that offers nothing more serious than Bingo. "It's a camp for the overprivileged," she says. Catherine was fat all her life, and since the age of twelve her large, pendulous breasts have bothered her. Some years ago she went to a plastic surgeon, hoping to have them cut down, but once she heard what the operation was, decided instead to live with them. "Nothing's been so good for me as that steam room," she said happily. "I realize everyone looks like me."

Marsha: "Isn't that worth the whole price?"

FEBRUARY 8

Phyllis: At Maine Chance, where most women are rich divorcées, there was a woman who seemed to have less money than the others. She didn't dress and act the way they did. Also, she was shy and obviously out of place. One evening at dinner, she picked up the wrong utensil. The hostess leaned toward her and said loudly enough for the whole table to hear, "And that's another thing we'll teach you here—proper table manners."

Marilyn, who's been living in Brussels but was born in Georgia, says the Negro problem at home is resolved, because they know their place. She loves her mammy as much as her real mother. Catherine took in this news with a certain detachment. "Yeah, but would you take your mammy to the country club?"

"I would if she wanted to go."

"Maybe she does; you ever ask her?"

"She doesn't. She knows her place."

This morning came the great weigh-in. Total loss: sixty-one and three-quarter pounds. Catherine lost thirty-four inches in two weeks, Miss Jensen lost twenty in one week, and Marsha lost fourteen. I'm the same weight I was, gained three and a half inches in bust, arms and other places, lost one and three-quarter inches in my waist, upper hip and diaphragm.

Naked, lunching in the solarium. Joan was looking through V*ogue*. Catherine leaned over, saw pictures of the beautiful black model (Donyale Luna) and said, "Isn't she marvelous!"

"Who, the colored girl?"

"Yes. This one. Look at that neck."

"Well"—this was Arkansas, the drawl curling like smoke, drifting over our heads—"I don't know. They're putting these girls in magazines all the time now. It just seems to me they're trying too hard. Poor girls."

Later, in the beauty parlor, I pointed out to Catherine that I have Negroid features and was able to "pass" at times. I said I wished I'd told Joan I was black. After scorning me for pusillanimity, Catherine agreed to go back and suggest this. After a few minutes, she returned with the report:

CATHERINE: I'd like to ask you something. What do you think of that girl Perutz?

JOAN: Well, she certainly looks very Negroid.

CATHERINE: That's what I was wondering about. I'm having my hair done now, and if you'd see the kind of hair she's got, it's going to take a while.

JOAN: Well, I live in Arkansas and I've seen them in all shapes and sizes. Marsha says she's European. But I know a Nigra when I see one. . . . It's an intrusion of privacy, that's what it is, and they shouldn't let somebody like that in here.

Phyllis listened while setting my hair. I looked at her in the mirror. "What's a nice girl like you doing in a place like this?"

"I'm leaving soon. I was beginning to be not nice."

After that, depression. What had started as a sociological experiment ended by sucking me in. Catherine reported that other women in the solarium admitted to "suspecting" me all along. What bitches! They've turned me black, and I hate them all. I'm furious, sick with it, all I want is to get out of here.

But it's Saturday night, the last supper, champagne and boisterous spirits. Barbecued steak and baked potato (for the others, just the peel). All of us decked out, made up, hair gleaming. Lucy, who should know, said this group was exceptional because everyone is so attractive. (Makes you think, and then stop thinking.) Lucy was animated and bubbled continuously through dinner. "I don't collect jewels and furs—"

"But they sort of stick to you."

"—but I have quite a number of jewels and furs. But if I have anything valuable, I keep it in the safe anyway. . . . We have three safes at home and keep them open all the time. Because who cares? Take it, just leave us in peace. . . . Not a day goes by when I don't compliment my husband. And he feels just great. . . ."

Lucy is a friend of the famous and is delighted to tell us all little details about her closest pals. Lucy has a fine marriage. "Every birthday, or Christmas, or Valentine's Day, or whatever, my husband asks me what I want: bonds or money."

After dinner, I retired to my room for a moment of sustaining privacy before joining the small group of five who had refused to go to the theater in San Diego (on the invitation of Mrs. Szekeley). Lucy phoned, and in a voice that must have mastered many conspiracies, invited me to her room for drinks after cards. "But I'm not telling those other stupids," she informed me.

What have I learned during this week? At the Parnassus of the beauty culture is a kindergarten. You come here, are pampered, each whim is taken care of, and your body is constantly attended. Catherine insists it's "back to mommy and daddy," and that's the whole point of such a place. Probably true. All women here are overweight (by their standards or society's) and some are also alcoholics. Addictions (to food or liquor), as magazines report ad nauseam, arise in people with dominating mothers. The case histories in Hilde Bruch's book on overweight *all* showed a possessive mother. Obesity was the sign of a much greater than normal dependency.

So this might be a key. Fat women, alcoholics, people recovering from personal tragedy all need a strong woman. Ellen is aggressive, so are most of the other instructors. Mommy was strong, but she also pampered us. Here we can have the whole scene over again.

By day, we're marched from one activity to another and told what to do or that we should relax and have things done to us. Evening, we're offered vacuous attractions—movies (all second rate), Bingo, arts and crafts. Fun for little girls. We've all grown up too fast in America, we date before puberty and it's natural that we want to be children again (or hang onto whatever childishness we have). Rich women can remain womb-tight all their lives. From daddy to hubby, servants for the house and children, all needs and whims met. Time and money can be spent on keeping the little girl beautiful and slim, and one can live in perpetual childhood, with no responsibility, busily perfecting one's narcissism. Money is a cuddly, sexy cushion, and you can playact behind it. But when these women start growing old, when crow's feet and sagging chins deflect the rich eyes of their husbands to daughters and daughters' friends, then desperation comes. Not only have these women been surrounded by expensive objects all their lives, they themselves have become the most expensive, most precious object in their husband's collection. When they show signs of deterioration, the husbands may lose interest.

> Men grow cold
> As girls grow old
> and we all lose our shape in the end.
> But square-shaped
> or pear-shaped,
> those rocks don't lose their shape,
> Diamonds are a girl's best friend.

As the jewels become less desirable, they become more anxious. Nothing to turn to (you need training for almost everything), nothing to rely on (because all your life you relied on what God gave you, and now He's taking it away), they're lost and easily become addicts. Alcohol is always available, and it makes you fat.

FEBRUARY 9

During exercises this last morning Joan was very glum. She has been looking apprehensive all week, her frown lines wrinkling up to give her the appearance of a rabbit during a hunt, but today she was decidedly depressed. She left class to phone her husband—"my daddy," she called him.

Daddies haven't changed much since the twenties, though now most of them legalize their situation. But divorce is common enough, especially among the moneyed, to make these marriages not considerably more serious than the working arrangements were then. All Americans want money. Men strive to make it, women to make the men. He needs a wife to achieve or maintain his position and certainly needs an heir.

The Oklahoma blonde advised Catherine not to get married again. "Are you married?" Catherine asked.

"Yes. That's why I say it. . . . I've been married three times and I don't think people should get married." She's in New York every month, accompanying her husband on business trips and going shopping. Her husband is constantly away on business. They have three children. Two weeks ago, while he was gone, the blonde decided to come to the Golden Door. When he returned it took him a few days to locate her. He had spoken to her the evening before to announce his departure today for Nassau.

A grandmother here, who's married to a dentist, owns shares of Du Pont, Ford and similar concerns, given by her father. She needs about an hour to dress in the morning, changes her clothes four or five times a day (to be appropriately chic for each of her engagements), and owns a number of false eyelashes, favoring the "light, feathery ones" for daytime wear. Before leaving, she invited us all to come visit her.

A woman who was here last week had a perfect figure, even though she's sixty-three. Her husband is an executive who returns home every afternoon at four or four-thirty, when he and his wife do Yoga together. Much of their time is devoted to improving their bodies. (So spake Lucy.) How do you like your Americans, Mr. Death?

Another guest last week was a twenty-nine-year-old girl, recently married, with a fourteen-month-old adopted baby. Lucy said the girl did nothing but primp, stared at herself fixedly in the mirror, and asked everyone who would listen about the effectiveness of individual lashes or the forward curl in her hair. She was rather thin, with breasts drooping "like a seventy-year-old woman," and large buttocks that continued their mass down the thighs. She didn't want to return home and tried convincing Lucy to come to La Puerta with her.

This week, says Lucy, everybody's great. Often, you get real dogs. Peggy Jo said this week all the guests were ladies and that wasn't usually true.

I left with Marsha after hugging the remaining guests and staff. Lucy and I have the same birthday. Joan said it was real swell to have met me. Tonight the new group will assemble at dinner, all dogs to begin with and dolls at the end. The Golden Door color postcard carries a mesage: "The Golden Door is located 5 miles north of Escondido, Southern California, on Highway 395. Small, serene, select, this golden domain really exists in no charted country. Rather it is a secret abyss of bliss where a buoyant Good Life blends with luxurious repose. Just outside the golden doors, the world stops . . . waits . . . for those favored few 20 guests to clamber back once more."

FEBRUARY 10

Finally out of there. My bill was nine hundred and eighty-four dollars (gold bikini included).

Yesterday I arrived in Los Angeles and registered at the Beverly Wilshire, filling out as best I could the card asking for my name and address, company name and address, names of accompanying children, maids and valets. In my room a large basket of fruit awaited me, a welcoming card (in Spanish!) and black matchbooks with my name sketched in gold. This city is the future, even of the beauty culture. Those representatives of the movie colony I saw no longer drink. They smoke pot instead, with self-righteousness. Those (like me) still stuck in the alcohol era reveal that they come from another generation, show their squareness, ruin their health and are slightly despicable.

The city is a Brasília—not a city, but a wide page punctuated by large, glittering buildings rising from nowhere, surrounded by nothing (the Continental Plaza, the Temple of the Latter-Day Saints) to accommodate, I suppose, those who can't live among their fellow men. Otherwise, it's a sprawling suburbia. Sunset Strip is more bleak than the main street of Great Neck. After dinner, the topless place (I wanted to see silicone breasts) provided girls dressed only in G-strings, their pubic hair covered but their buttocks free. Mechanically, they gyrated to music, their faces oblivious to the movements their bodies were undergoing. Men at the bar, at tables, yawned, looked away, fixed a hypnotic stare on them (television viewers, supermarket shoppers) or tried to catch their eyes. Tomorrow is amateur night on Sunset Strip, when housewives from the Hills can show their topless talents. It's as sexy as a bad sculpture.

This is no country for me. This stark inhumanity, the painted dolls, the emphasis on health and body building, the drab suntanned blondes with guarantees of immunity to all experience stamped on their faces are too close to Nazism for me to shake off the oppression. Here dwells mass-life, love is just a shabby little spurt of feeling that might arise before orgasm; value is a term applicable only to goods.

The frenzy, frustration, even desperation of New York seem civilized by contrast. Downstairs at the bar of this very expensive hotel, the waitress was dressed like a forest nymph and immediately gave her first name. The bar is supposed to resemble the Oak Bar at the Plaza, where waiters in tuxedos expect to be summoned by the word "Waiter!" But here we're all the same; there's no reserve, no integrity, no privacy. It's all out in the open. Freedom!

How does all this apply to beauty? This land is a new Sybaris, because no lasting values hold; but the hedonism is so joyless. It's not a new Sybaris, because the decadence has a twist: everybody's a little kid, existing before the personality has developed to any recognizable state. Money is the substitute for everything—character, beauty, talent, morality, intelligence, humor—and life is lived *in utero*. Through the Golden Door to Hollywood, from playpen to playpen. Death's the con man who'll put something over on you unless you outsmart him. You'll never grow old. The trick: you'll never live, and so you won't be able to deteriorate. The Los Angeles *Times* is full of ads offering computer dating and scientific matching to people of all ages. "Divorced?" asks one ad, "It's not your fault! With no compatibility, divorce follows." It promises scientific mating. Other ads promise you will meet more compatible people within the next few months (if you clip the coupon) than you have met during your entire life. Or they promise marriage. One ad offers to teach you to love yourself, the prime requisite, it insists, for loving anyone else. You fill out questionnaires that reveal to you who you are—then you are sent the name of your mate, guaranteed to be equally enlightened about himself.

Pets are more important here than anywhere else. Their psychology and diet are discussed. A column advises on illness, telling you what to do when your dog catches cold. (Marvelous coming-together of the American fetish about health and medicine with the fetish about animals.) In the lost-and-found column one item has fascinated me all week: "Lost 1 falcon with leash & bells, Reward." Further down the page, under Legal Notices, more women than men advertise "Not responsible for any debts but my own."

Poor people! But they're so hateful—blank and narcissistic and nonsensual. The body. Diet foods, exercise, tans. A hard body for both men and women, developed by surfing and barbells, a body with power. Body and face (peeled, cut or scraped to maintain youth), objects going to the highest bidder. What are little girls made of? (They're all little girls.) Marshmallow on the inside, plastic foam-covered lead outside.

To be more beautiful—for what? To be fucked. Why? To look more beautiful. Why? That way lies money. Alimony stands between man and happiness. Here, the race endures its span of life, dedicated to objectifying itself, to achieving total nondistinction among all creatures. Death, say the poets, is the great equalizer. In the Golden West we've become smarter and made life itself the great equalizer. Nobody must weep alone; there's pot and orgies and crowds and cults. Find a clique, paint your face, harden your body, marry and divorce, make money, move up, up, up; no closer to God, but to His envoy, who has the same face: The Great Producer. Death is for living, let the soul begin to die at birth and the body harden at puberty into lifetime rage.

FEBRUARY 11 ON THE UNITED FLIGHT TO PHILADELPHIA

From Arizona into Colorado, flat land with little wrinkled mounds rising, like shivering nipples. Dried river beds in every state from unmade to deliberately, viciously crumpled.

What's the whole beauty industry for? For *money*. The deep, dark perverse secret of America. We want to look as good as we can—why? Not to get fucked, not to fulfill the dream and become the princess who gets her prince, but for money. Plain old filthy money that we (especially the ladies) don't talk about, any more than we would digress upon shit. But look good and you'll be taken out; money will be spent on you, you'll be seen in the right places and more fat, soft men with tiny phalluses and roaming eyes will call and take you out. If you're lucky, you get passed from one potbelly to another, moving up the fecal ladder to the hardest, biggest shit of all. And you get him to marry you.

Beauty is truth. And the truth of this country is greed, lust, the undying and impenetrable ambition to have money. Nothing else fires the mind, involves the energies, blocks every generous impulse that might inadvertently be still hanging around from babyhood, as money does. Money and power. Power's bought by money. So is sex—a pushover for the money guys, the chief aim of women. Why? Because they have it ass-backwards, do women. Through sex to power and money. But the big boys, the supershits, know it's the other way around. Money is God, immortality, the end-all and be-all. You can always buy another hole to put it into, and only a silly cunt would individualize (or try to brand) a prick.

LIFE IN THE
BEAUTY CULTURE

❦

This above all, to thine own self be true.
—SHAKESPEARE, *Hamlet*

1

Prepare a Face to Meet
the Faces That You Meet

Plump Dorabel and her lashes were sitting on the apple-green couch near the replica, in marble, of a genuine bacchante. The jazz was cool but very loud, for greater psychedelic significance. In the tiny kitchen, two dabs of cottage cheese peered up from melba toast toward a half-finished can of Tab. The dietetic peaches had turned pale waiting to be devoured. In the bathroom, jars, bottles, tubes and boxes held the remainder of their contents, leftovers from a Rabelaisian feast of cosmetics.

Plump Dorabel loves her lashes. "I wouldn't be caught dead without them," she says passionately. "I have them on all night. I take baths instead of showers so therefore the steam isn't that strong. I reglue them when they're coming off." She speaks softly, like someone accustomed to have a listening ear always close by. "I'd give up lipstick, makeup, but not lashes. I love lashes."

Dorabel, who knows more about beauty than the interviewer will ever learn, is not interested in questions. She wants to talk about the new gleamers, blushers, iridescences, transparencies, wetnesses and naturalness. She turns down the music and rhapsodizes alone. "I believe in the creams," she says fervently. "An ugly girl can become beautiful. Makeup can change a personality tremendously. You can be anyone you want to be with makeup."

She's never sure, at any given moment, who she wants to be. She has two full wardrobes of clothes, one in size eight, the other in sixteen. During every year, there will be a time for going to one closet and a time for going to the other. The size eights are all expensive clothes, designer dresses. The sixteens are cheaper. "They don't make anything for people larger than a size twelve," she explains. "The eights, they're all so cute and chic, but the larger sizes, they never look good. Everything's out of proportion."

Dorabel is in her large period now, with hips fastened onto her like great wads of silly putty. When she walks, she has some difficulty managing the lower part of herself, which tends to move slower than the upper. Getting fat was a way she had of extricating herself from social embarrassment. "I get fat when I want to rid of someone," she confided. "Trouble is, ones I want to keep go too." She smiles ruefully, accustomed to the hard ways of men, priding herself on the honesty that never let her down.

Dorabel is an authority on men as well as on beauty. She used to favor homosexuals, but now finds them "too bitchy." "Men are the vainest creatures in the world," she has discovered, and the worst are Greeks. They're terrible because they like fat women, and everyone knows that the only reason to have a fat women is to show your superiority over her. Much better are the men who will drop Dorabel as soon as she gains weight. Those who remain while her weight ascends must be viewed with suspicion. "How can you like somebody who likes somebody like that?" Men have tremendous egos and choose women they can show off. If she's not going to arouse envy in other men, what's the point of dating her? Wise women know this, and this might be a reason why Dorabel says, "I don't think fat people have a jollier disposition, I think they're meaner."

Dorabel has done free-lance advertising copy for cosmetics companies ("Revlon are the meanest people in the world") and beauty copy for magazines. She is extremely well informed on all gossip within the industry, records with glee the roller-coaster careers of executives on the ride down, knows the interior decoration of the most famous bedrooms in the beauty hierarchy, and would be a wonderful character in a modern *School for Scandal*. She is a true believer, whose faith in superficiality is constantly reinforced by the messages she receives from magazines, television and, more subtly, by the practices of those she sees in discotheques, on Manhattan's East Side and at Kenneth's.

She believes that beauty is fashion and fashion is life. We have been given the Word: Change, and by adherence to it can escape the problems and frustrations that beset us. Aspects of oneself, whether good and evil, spirit and body, man and woman or less emphatic antithesis, can all be given voice through that "self-expression" that reveals itself by individual variations within acceptable fashion styles. "Fashion," wrote Edward Sapir, the eminent anthropologist, "is a custom in the guise of departure from custom. Most normal individuals . . . wish somehow to legitimize their personal deviation without laying themselves open to the charge of insensitiveness to good taste or good manners. Fashion is the discreet solution of the subtle conflict."

He explains: "The slight changes from the established in dress or other forms of behavior seem for the moment to give the victory to the individual, while the fact that one's fellows revolt in the same direction gives one a feeling of adventurous safety." Your hair can be arranged in any style, with any texture or color you desire. Your makeup can give you the face you choose. Daily, even hourly, changes of outfit allow you to be all things to all people. As a true believer in the beauty culture, you are engaged in the psychodrama of everyday life.

"Fashion reflects our lives and is in turn influenced by society, by culture, and even by the economy" reveals *Women's Wear Daily* in a front-page article on "The Conservative Backlash." The end gives a warning: "People get too serious about fashion. . . . Fashion reflects life. But a few clothes-horses aside, it is not life."

Fashion and beauty are twin sisters born of democracy and self-determination. Everyone can be beautiful or attractive, we believe, as long as they're willing to work at it. "We've made it possible for people to be attractive," said Margaret Mead, who strongly approves the beauty culture, makes little use of it herself and suggests it hasn't gone far enough: "I think it shouldn't exist that men be over six foot four. It's too rough on men. We should stop it. We'll probably stop it one of these days."

There are no superior beings; if God's plan is evident in what He bestows on us at birth, then we must assume He was careless in His choice of architect. No matter what you are born with, you can present yourself in whatever way you like. Dr. Milton T. Edgerton, professor of plastic surgery at Johns Hopkins, wrote in a letter to me: "There is certainly no reason for any man or woman to feel apologetic about the desire for physical beauty." It is up to you (and perhaps an expert) to carve your destiny. Hard work pays off. The ancestor of modern beauty for the masses was Protestantism, and Calvinism in particular. Your salvation is in your own works, and so is your success. To choose beauty as a goal is not very different from choosing wealth. Diligence pays off; you learn the rules of the game, apply them conscientiously and achieve your desires. Optimism is in all cosmetics and beauty copy: your skin can be radiant if you will use the proper products, your hair will gleam if you brush it a certain number of times a day, condition it, take it regularly to the hairdresser. Your eyes will become seductive orbs if you eat the correct foods, sleep many hours and learn how to apply makeup. Beauty is not a mystery; it is simply a human state, and humans have discovered how to reach it. It can be taught as language is, from a very early age, according to rules of acceptability.

Sol Worth, professor at the Annenberg School of Communications, said that nobody has studied beauty as a "way of classifying culture levels" or "aspiration levels" because it's "like grammar, it's too ingrained. We've had grammar as prescriptive rules for a long time, just as you have prescriptive rules for beauty." Structural linguistics is a new field, and perhaps someday structural beauty will also become an area of interest for psychologists and anthropologists. But now beauty, like good speech, is a quality anyone may achieve with proper instruction.

With mass media as envoys of democracy and optimism, messages are quickly relayed from New York or Hollywood to all citizens. Communications is no respecter of tradition or of social conservatism. The preservation of values is anathema to the great god of data, whose pleasure it is to spit out most of the information received before digesting it. Only the new is newsworthy, and the new is by nature better than the old. Last year's eye was pretty, *Cosmopolitan* admits, but it will no longer serve. To gaze with an outdated eye is as bad as praising last year's pop singer. To appear at a college reunion as the same self who graduated would be tasteless and would indicate to others that you are "alienated."

The success of such "programed obsolescence" has its firm roots in common fears. Most people are, to some extent, unsure or unresolved about themselves. If this self-doubt can become a function of personal appearance, the beauty culture can cure it. When I was overweight, all unhappiness was caused by fat. I disliked myself intensely and could find good reason, since I so flagrantly refused to conform to the standard ideal.

The beauty culture offers a way out for those who dislike them-selves. You can either become someone else or "bring out the hidden you," a self presumably hidden even to yourself. However, should the hidden reality become manifest, optimism promises it will be beautiful. "I think that it is human to play roles," said Kenneth with his well-groomed Edwardian sideburns. "I think it is human to want to escape what you dislike about yourself." When a woman is making up, "she feels she's bringing herself out and making the best of it."

"Oneself" is invariably a distortion and not to be confused with the old art of makeup, whereby a woman dramatized her position in society by using herself as the standard and emphasizing her strongest characteristics. I suggested to Kenneth that Cleopatra wore makeup to be more Cleopatra. "Well, yes," he answered, "but Cleopatra *was* somebody. Today—again because of communications and because of the way we live—there are many women in the world who are house-hold words more than the queen of Egypt was. Maybe they're a friend of Andy Warhol's, you know, or the mistress of a musician. Obscure, in comparison with former times. I don't think that a woman in Duluth who has a family and husband thinks any differently than Princess Grace, if you like. From the standpoint or fact that she would like to be as attractive as possible."

Dawn, a young model who is supporting herself until the big break by selling cosmetics, said: "I think every woman inside of her has a hidden desire to be a siren. You know, and at the same time be soft and Katharine Hepburn." Dawn then continued in jargon all her own: "Even though she may not have explored or clearly have all these feeling tones she would like to think of herself as. And sometimes women take out one particular feeling and try to portray that all the time."

Dawn is a lanky girl with round gray eyes and nervous shoulders. At first, her face is almost mysterious, simply because the well-scrubbed California look is interrupted by gaunt cheeks, more evocative of smoky Parisian boîtes than the Big Surf. She seems per-fectly natural, bearing the face God gave her, but closer inspection produces a catalog of human intervention: gold powder on the eye-lids, gray pencil, taupe shadow, individual lashes, blusher, highlighter, transparent foundation, lip gloss and brownish lipstick, false nails. She has sculptured her face with Renaissance considerations of how it will look at every angle. The globe gleams, catches light, is a harmony of proportions with no feature predominating. "There are so many women around and at the same time there are so many good-looking guys around that there is, you know, almost an overabundance of it." Her voice is surprisingly nasal and, like a foghorn, pierces the din. Other people in the restaurant look up a moment and back to their hamburgers. "There's not a special pretty girl anymore. Everybody's pretty, because of makeup. And if a woman doesn't wear makeup, and she's not as pretty as the next one, there's going to be a girl right there to take the guy she may want to go out with."

Out West, where she was born, Dawn dreamed of coming to New York. When she arrived three years ago, with a large mauve patent-leather hatbox, she was not disappointed. "This is like the center of creativity in America, one of the biggest centers in the world today is New York City. Any time you're involved with that much going on, I think you're automatically involved with an image. . . ." Intrigued by the pace and professionalism of New York, Dawn is not intimidated. She has a firm sense of herself, she knows how to handle her face, she eats health foods and is rewarded with a strong and supple body; and her voice rends the miasma of songs, minor flirtations and futile contracts. She arranges herself for a profile view and delivers a monologue on herself, also a center of creativity: "I've talked to so many men in these last years since I've been here in New York, and I have found very few of them masculine enough to be even put up with. Course I'm a very strong person anyway. This is me. . . . I'm sure many of these men would do any normal girl a world of good; I mean, the average girl's looking to get married and have a family and a husband and a home and all this. But for myself, I want much more than that. I'm tremendously aggre—I used to think that was what I wanted, but not anymore. I have a very strong feeling of, I could not live with anyone less than practically a creative genius. . . . It turns me off to go out with a guy who's interesting to talk to for maybe five minutes and tells you a few interesting little tidbits and that's it. You know. And maybe he's affectionate and romantic and caters to you—those things don't mean anything at all. . . . Because you can get so much more satisfaction out of being part of a person's life who is tremendously creative. To me that's much more of a satisfaction than having my every little whim met. You see, I'm not the average female."

She shares this sense of uniqueness with millions of other women.

Everyone's an individual; the Great American Lie spreads like ink on the blotter, wasting the substance that could be used for expression. Everyone's an individual; every reader of this book has chosen, in his American heritage of free will and individualism, to read it. He is as convinced of his individualism as the author is of hers.

"If you can explain to people how to cut through the phenomenon of categorizing, how to cut through the social steps or whatever," Kenneth advised me, "if you can say to them: 'You think you're an individual, but baby, you're not'—if you can fit that in somewhere, I think that's a great contribution."

Individuals choose what type of house they will live in, what kind of books they will read, what foods they will eat, what cars they will buy and how they wish to present themselves. Aziza offers twenty-five eyes to choose from; other companies present scents, lashes and lipsticks for every type of woman. Young girls who spurn all beauty aids as artificial and bourgeois are as indistinguishable a group as models. With individualism the panacea of the masses, one is free to choose which kind of individualism suits one best. A professor in his fifties who wears a beard and moustache said, "I wear hair on my face because I like it. I have it for a long time. But why haven't I taken it off? Suppose that conservatives wore long hair. I would take it off, I would take my beard off, I really would. I could not stand the identification with a group that I didn't want. But since I know that it's identified with sort of artistic, off-beat, hippy, et cetera, I will accept that identification."

Dr. James A. Brussel, psychiatrist, anticipated my question: "Now you might say why'd I grow a beard? It's not even a year old yet. I grew a beard because I was afraid of foreign water. We go around the world a lot. The minute I get into the Orient—I got an absolute abhorrence of their so-called 'safe' water. I won't even shave; and I grow a beard. This time, on my way to the barber shop, I stopped off [at my publisher]. . . . The publicity director [said], 'Don't take it off. It's a great ad.' That's why I got the beard. I don't like it. I don't wear a beard. But I can't help myself. You see, there is what you'd call a business reason. There's nothing cosmetic. At my age. I should worry about how the hell I look. I mean I got four gorgeous granddaughters."

One prepares the face that is expected. A deb eschews eye makeup, a shopgirl bleaches her hair blond, a New York intellectual wears his hair long and a Hollywood agent uses bronzer. The beauty industry offers the piquancy of volte-face: false hairpieces for Wall Street executives, the natural look for actresses, bright red dye for house-wives. Kenneth, whose makeup artists generally use the same products on all women, said, "I'm always rather amused by—and again, it's part of the lie—that they love to say Miss So-and-so or Mrs. So-and-so is a very high-powered dingdongdingding executive lady. But when she goes home at night she's just all fluffy and feminine and everything else. And you know something? That's the biggest bunch of hogwash in the world, because the woman is just as strong at home. . . . No-body can turn it on and turn it off like that." He became agitated and almost evangelistic as he delivered a final condemnation of the lie: "I think we keep putting labels on people and we keep putting labels on things and we keep saying, well, if she does this, then ob-viously she has to do that, or, if she does that, then she must be so-and-so. I think we have made and try to live by rules in all social classes, in all economic classes, that simply should not—nobody should be forced even to think about. Because I think they ruin marriages, I think they ruin relationships. . . . But people like to categorize. You see, it's so safe, somehow. . . . I'm grossly against Betty Friedan and her whole world. You ever read *The Feminine Mystique*? I mean, I'm grossly against what this woman says because she's categorizing. And she's saying, arm yourselves. Go, baby. . . . But we've had that extremism, you know."

But everyone arms himself. One's clothes, walk, words, hair and face all present a front, a calling card, a way of announcing oneself. Sol Worth feels that a woman makes up "to avoid contact, or to achieve ritual contact [*i.e.*, wolf whistles]. You want to prescribe safe, correct situations." Another professor of communications pointed out that a woman who makes love happily every night with her husband or lover will not wear makeup to bed. She will, however, apply it in the morning before going to work. At her job, she maintains formal contact; in her bed, she has no need to announce herself.

You prepare a face for all uncertain encounters. There is a face for job application, another for a party. The church-going face is different from the boutique-shopping face. Each face looks for reassurance. Paul Mitchell, the mustachioed hairdresser born in Scotland, believes that women groom themselves for men. "It's obviously a two-way conditioning. Women want to look the way they do and men want them to look the way they do, 'cause if they didn't look good they wouldn't get their man and they'd obviously be unhappy and wouldn't continue that way."

Mary Butler of *Harper's Bazaar* feels that "the general thing, if you could wrap it up in a general phrase, is the attraction of the sexes. . . . Then, when you take the different categories or types of people or life styles, then you can subdivide it. If it is a career woman, then she's got to look well for her business because so many people are standing behind her."

Miss Butler believes that beauty must be part of one's whole life, reflecting interests, personality and status. A woman must look in the mirror, "see what she is, what she's got to work with, and then relate it to the kind of life she lives." This analysis "requires on the part of the woman a desire and commitment to work with herself." Most "mistakes" in beauty are made "because women go out and try to copy the ideal." Mary Butler thinks that the working girl is most guilty of this mistake. "The housewife has to please her husband and she's afraid of the new. . . . But this is the housewife, the great unknown, because there really isn't such a thing as a normal common housewife."

Francesca, who is small, green-eyed, of Italian extraction and efficient, wears makeup "because I have problem-type skin. And women would not look at me and associate me with the beauty business unless they saw that I was properly groomed. I wish I didn't have to." People in general make up because "all is vanity. I think every woman is [vain], whether she admits it, rebels or resists it. Now the thing that has become most vivid to the public is that *man* is first revealing that he has the same problem."

Revlon's Bill Mandel says simply, "If women didn't make up, they'd drink."

Jessica Canne sees making up as "an exercise in self-expression. It's kind of a joyful thing to do."

Vanity, narcissism, addiction, self-expression and playfulness are all part of the game. Someone who is depressed will pay less attention to improving his looks (he may try to look worse) than someone ebullient. Preoccupation with one's appearance is heavily determined by the circumstances of one's life—social class, economic level, age and marital status, where one lives and whether or not there has been any recent trauma. So Tommy, for example, is using makeup for the first time in her life at age thirty-two.

Tommy was Deb of the Year in 1955. When she graduated from Mount Holyoke, her parents gave her a small M.G. (which her mother drove all the way from Short Hills while her father came in the old Bentley). Five months later, Tommy married Chris under the watchful eye of *The New York Times*, which noticed her loose hair style, pale face powder and red lipstick. All wedding guests agreed that the young couple was "really attractive." After the ceremony, Tommy washed her face and changed into her going-away suit from Peck and Peck.

Now Tommy goes to a psychiatrist four times a week, works at Haryou and has regular facials. Since the divorce, her children are left in the almost exclusive care of a Venezuelan girl, the eighth child of a respectable, middle-class family. Tommy goes out every night, shops at Lord & Taylor and has a full line of Germaine Monteil cosmetics on her dressing table. She has a standing appointment with the hairdresser every week and owns two expensive wigs but no wig box. When she goes to parties given by college friends, Tommy is often the only woman wearing makeup.

"For the first time in my life," Tommy is happy to say, "I realize I'm a woman." Chris had never been able to commit love on his respectable wife, and Tommy, whose natural ebullience made her affectionate, was first upset, then guilty and later afraid of sex. Right after the divorce, she thought a man could prove his love only by not touching her. Now, with the help of her psychiatrist, with the assurance gained by having a job and many admirers, Tommy is letting her class down and loving it. She's curious about men, interested in them and advertises her liberation through a new face.

As a divorcée in New York, she has made new friends. One is Sally, the wife of a sociologist at NYU. Sally's hair is often in a pony tail, her clothes are from Mexico or India, and she wears no makeup. Sally reads long books and says "fuck" frequently. She and her husband have been dallying with the idea of going to orgies, but, with inhibiting foresight, each feels, "It would be O.K. for me, but I'd hate to watch the other." When Sally and Tommy meet, they talk about city politics, race and sex.

Alix, another new friend, works at a fashion magazine. She is a sleek brunette of twenty-four whose words seem to be italicized in her mind. At her desk, she will write down key words or numbers and, as the conversation progresses, underline when she gets to one of them. Last year she was too fat and spent fifty dollars a week on her diet doctor. She goes to Kenneth's at least once a week (fifteen dollars) and to an exercise salon three times a week (twenty-one dollars). She likes to buy objects that move, particularly if they have mirrors, and generally enjoys spending money, but not on clothes. She is proud to find an old fur for twenty-five dollars or an imperfect pair of lounging pajamas that she then wears to the theater. She is efficient, impatient and often funny.

In the chair, watching herself in the mirror while Kenneth's Mr. John combed out her hair, Alix said she spends "lots and lots" on cosmetics. "I know I spend more on beauty than the average women, but many women spend a lot more than I do. Some take four hours to make up—they devote their whole day every day to beauty. I'm not a real devotee."

To illustrate, she spoke of an acquaintance of hers, "one of the Beautiful People, I suppose you would call her. She has a marvelous Park Avenue apartment, and everything is decorated according to the books. You know—lime green has to go with sunshine yellow, and everything in the room has to follow the color scheme, even the paintings. She has an excellent cook, who whips up a soufflé and makes her own Sauce Béarnaise. There are marvelous wines and very old cognacs. This friend—I can't tell you her name—takes forever making up. For her to appear without her face on—her *maquillage* on —would be like appearing naked. She wants everything to be beautiful, herself, the furniture, plants—whatever she sees. Her profession is beauty; she's very serious about it."

Alix nodded at her reflection. She looked the way she wanted to. Hugging John, she said she "must dash" because she had an interview that afternoon, was already late and wouldn't be able to stay long because of the dinner party tonight. Unlike other women, she did not rearrange her hair downstairs before leaving the salon.

Alix was right. Considering her profession, she was relaxed about beauty. When she goes to the country, she wears no makeup at all and ties her hair back with a rubber band or ribbon. In the city, she attends to her appearance as a matter of duty, just as a car salesman must clean and polish his car. She must reflect the image expected of her.

To understand what the image is can require an imaginative leap. People from the lower classes or from a culture of poverty may not know how to present themselves to middle-class America. A girl from the ghetto is often condemned to remain there unless she learns the rules of another class, dictating how people should look. Too much makeup, or makeup from another decade or no makeup at all can prejudice prospective employers.

"The most fascinating thing, when you get out there—wherever it is and I don't know where it begins—whether it's on 23rd Street or just the other side of the Hudson, or the East River, or I don't know where, where it begins, but it is amazing that people look older than they ought to. Because of what they do to themselves. Makeup, hair-wise and dresswise as well. First of all, nobody buys anything that fits them. It's either too small or too big." On 54th Street, east of Fifth, the most "in" hairdresser of America sadly contemplated the un-educated fashion wasteland stretching in all directions from where he sits. Those in it lack self-perception: "I don't think they see themselves at all. And it's what everybody else is doing. Men. *Men* buy without fail a suit, always, that's one or two sizes too big. All over this country."

Out there is where you "dress up," a term not used by those who are "in." It's for children, who dress up to maturity, and the lower classes, who dress up toward status. But they do it badly. Each class has its own taste and can't understand the taste of others. Upper-class Americans traditionally look healthy, sporty and natural. Their clothes are of common fabrics, in solid colors, plaids or very subdued prints, and are not necessarily well fitting. Makeup is non-existent or not visible; hair is clean, but little attention is paid to style. The Queen of England exemplifies the upper-class look, and though her fashion-consciousness has improved recently, she'd never be asked to model for *Vogue*.

But the Duchess of Windsor would be. Queen of the Best Dressed List, she represents what is generally accepted as elegance. She is one of the Beautiful People, who pay attention to their looks and have the money to "create" their style. Beautiful People are extroverts, whose tastes strongly influence what buyers will select for their stores and what *Vogue* or *Harper's Bazaar* will feature. Mainly people of power in society, they will occasionally take in others from the arts, politics, fashion or the international set. Their clothes must fit perfectly, be sophisticated and individual, come from designers already approved by the group, be different from last year's and probably in colors not worn for a long time. Beautiful People may wear basic black, or they appear in transparent pajamas, but whatever they wear must emphasize fashion and not sex. Their makeup will be discreet (with occasional fantasy looks reserved for special occasions) and their hair is well groomed, shining, shaped and styled with no roots showing. They may go weekly to the hairdresser or, like Babe Paley, three times a day ("before lunch, after lunch and again in the evening," *Women's Wear Daily* reports).

These people establish taste for the middle classes, who may have no time, money or inclination to follow the high standards but accept them nonetheless. The middle class finds aristocratic indifference to fashion dowdy and the fashion habits of the lower class vulgar.

Vulgarity, however, is a relative term dependent on one's training in aesthetic sensibilities. It's probably best defined as incongruity. A bright sport shirt worn in church is vulgar; obvious rouge on an old woman or sequins and rosebuds on her granddaughter are vulgar. But few people accuse themselves of vulgarity; the only ones who would are middle-class people purposely dressing in lower-class style (a too-tight vampish dress, for instance, or a suit made of shiny material). For others, strongly bleached hair, heavy makeup, rhinestones and fussy hats are beautiful or even stylish. A middle-class man who sees a girl with white, cottony hair, a sweater tight as skin, bright lips, black eyes and very high heels will dismiss her as a prostitute. She is, he's sure, interested only in sex. When he sees her with a young man in a shiny leather jacket and greasy hair, he decides they're right for each other and neither of them is much good. They can't possibly have a relationship as he knows it; all they care about is sex.

But the mother of the girl thinks her beautiful and the boy handsome. For a special Saturday night dance, the mother might get herself up in a chartreuse dress with baubles sewn on, her hair might be dyed blue and she'll wear her largest rhinestone necklace with matching earrings. She's put on her face, she's dressed herself up and she's beautiful. Her husband, her friends and the neighbors come by to admire. A Beautiful Person averts his face when he passes her on the street, even though his wife's new two-thousand-dollar evening dress (from Mila Schoen in Milan) is chartreuse and has baubles sewn on it.

"Dressing up," owning "fancy" clothes or Sunday best is a way of approximating the message of another class. In the fifties hair was high, lips were bright and heels were precarious. Fifteen years later, girls still try to be fashionable by covering their skin with pancake, pushing out their breasts and teasing their hair in high beehives. A few years ago, a girl died mysteriously. After her death, it was discovered she had a nest of spiders in her hair and had died of spiders' bites. Her hair, in emulation of the bouffant look, had been teased and sprayed daily and not washed for many months, to keep the effect.

Many of us dressed up when we were younger. Gloria Steinem, an attractive, intelligent journalist who now lives in New York and is always in fashion, told me: "I went to high school and junior high school in Toledo, Ohio, the wrong side of the tracks. You know, where everybody left school when they were sixteen years old." I had gone to similar schools in Queens. "They all get very dressed up every day to go to school because it's the big social event in their lives. And even if there's a tiny party, like a Halloween party, and even if you're in the seventh grade, you wear high heels and grown-up dresses and jewelry. It's still going on," she insisted. Miss Steinem then went to Smith—"everybody's in Peck and Peck dresses and if they put on lipstick they're ready for the Inaugural Ball or something." Miss Steinem now goes to neither extreme. She wears makeup but not obviously, her clothes are *Vogue*ish but not exaggerated and her deep brown hair is worn long and loose with two streaks of blond framing her face.

"There is a notion of what is the right way to look, within this culture," said Sol Worth. "The poor kid in the ghetto who has to learn 'good grooming' to earn two thousand dollars a year more is not very different from the rich middle-class lady who sees that she's getting fat, sees that her hair is maybe not right. . . . Essentially he is convinced there is a right way to look."

Margaret Mead explained that the beauty culture Americanized and democratized its followers. "The most dramatic democratizer in this country was the mass production of clothes, so that you could get things to fit you." We are in advance of England, where "right through World War II, all the gentlemen and ladies had their clothes custom-made. And utility clothes in England were small, middle-sized and large, while we were making nines, elevens, tens, twelves —and little women and big women and fat women and everything. If you were poor [in England] you wore ill-fitting clothes. Hence this is fantastic, the difference between our garment industry and theirs. Now hair is another aspect, and makeup is another aspect in England still. The makeup that's used by the lower classes is perfectly definitive."

Dr. Mead didn't suggest this was true in America. But "out there" are many subcultures, and within each the members are recognizable to each other, though outsiders make mistakes. In addition to "definitive" lower-class appearance, such groups as hippies, nice Jewish girls, midwestern high school girls, young stockbrokers, southern school-teachers and black militants can identify each other by grooming habits. A professor at the University of Pennsylvania explained how misunderstandings arise when cues are not read correctly: "I've seen young faculty from the Middle West who have never seen women who didn't have makeup on think [the women here] were plain Janes. Maybe in that small town the very prissy girls didn't wear makeup. So, for example, you couldn't say 'fuck' to a girl without lipstick. Whereas in New York or Philadelphia it would be the reverse —these would be the girls that would curse like crazy, and the others would be much more conventional."

"Out there" starts at the borders of your own group, and is always an uncomfortable place to find yourself. Though flexibility and individuality are permitted and even encouraged in dress and grooming, they must remain within the rules set for the group. Until recently, airline stewardesses were not permitted to wear Afros or eyeliner. The girls were expected to look "natural" in a strongly defined way, with friendliness predominating over sexiness, good grooming over exoticism, and the plan was to make all girls look like the soda-sipping sweetheart back home in the local candy store. Now there are no longer limitations on the use of eye makeup, and even false lashes are allowed. However, the girls must not be too short (under five foot two) nor too tall (over five foot nine). Their hair should be either quite long, reaching to mid-back and tied, or chin length. In-between length, to the shoulder, is not allowed because it will be too messy.

Offices are not as precise in their requirements, but employers want "a pleasant, clean, neat, orderly look," in the opinion of Harold Melvin, who, with Diahann Carroll, offered a course in grooming to women in Harlem. The purpose was teaching lower-class women to appeal to middle-class tastes, thereby making them eligible for jobs. In teaching beauty, they were teaching a way out of the ghetto. "Some of these girls, not having had a lot of money, didn't know what to do with themselves to make themselves look more presentable," Mr.

Melvin explained. "They needed little hints on how to groom without getting involved with spending money that they didn't have to spend." These hints, it was hoped, would then help them "looking for work or just in everyday living, even if it's for [their] husband."

The first class was announced; both Miss Carroll and Mr. Melvin would be talking about beauty. A black militant came to the meeting and was about to deliver a long harangue when Miss Carroll asked him to be still, to first listen and then, if he had any questions, they would be happily answered. "The interesting thing is," said Mr. Melvin, "that he was actually checking out whether we were going to destroy the image, again, of the natural look or the black woman. Which was so ridiculous. . . . I had already indicated that it was a class on grooming, no matter what kind of grooming. And he got up and he said, 'Why do you keep referring to "our hair"?' or something like that. . . . I then had to get into a thing of explaining that I don't care if these girls all want to cut their hair off and all want to wear it natural, because I'm involved with every phase of beauty culture . . . the head and the face and so on and so forth, and I really don't care what they do with it, as long as it comes off as an overall clean, neat, orderly look. That's all I'm interested in."

Later, musing on this incident, Mr. Melvin shook his head. "I think Negroes who are more militant and even some people who are not, seem to think that the whole thing of beauty from the Negro woman's standpoint is a matter of emulating the white woman. And I disagree with that." Until recently, he said, Negro women were forced to identify with whites because magazines, ads and television all showed white women. This is no longer true. Furthermore, make-up has never been the exclusive province of whites. In Africa now, and for centuries, people have been making up extravagantly, beautifully and almost psychedelically. "So I don't know who has decided that making up one's face or doing one's hair had to do only with white people. I don't know where that thing has come from."

We discussed this theme further. I suggested that all American women, of whatever color, have grown up with the same inundation of mass media, and all have been given the same message. "Absolutely," said Mr. Melvin. I then went on to propose that the African ritual is formal, representing a ceremony or role, whereas the American one is supposedly inspired by "doing your own thing." The young hairdresser nodded. "That's very true."

"Once you have this individuality pitch, it doesn't matter what color you are," I finished the argument.

"Right. Absolutely," said Harold Melvin. "And this [business] of black women emulating white women really should be straightened out."

Fuzzy or straight, the beauty message is to discover yourself and be yourself. The discovery and existence must, however, conform to established rules. If you discover that you are a cannibal, no cosmetics company will help you express yourself. If, as a minister's wife, you discover you are a belly dancer, the parishioners will exert considerable pressure to make you take up again the false front.

Self-analysis is a good selling point for an industry founded on personal doubts, narcissism and fears of ostracism. "Know thyself" is a brilliant motto for any line of products, particularly if one can add the assurance that this knowledge will pay off directly in romantic and social success. But even those who have accepted that Eden's tree of good and evil and the fountain of youth are metaphors retain appalling literalness (or innocence?) about the beauty industry's redemptive powers. Beauty may be truth or goodness, but beauty techniques can at best be only comments on these virtues. Yet *Glamour* magazine emblazons its cover with "How to Find Your Beauty Identity" and inside, urges the reader to "join the first group analysis make-overs." Eleven "case histories" are presented, with before-and-after-pictures to add testimony to a text of simplistic jargon, telling how each girl was able to change her "personality image."

The intellectual vulgarity of this article is staggering. We are told that the girls met in a group with a psychologist "to study the nature of themselves and to determine their essential features and their relations. . . ." The psychologist is not mentioned by name, but each girl is pictured with name, profession and often some biography. We are informed of the psychological tension particular with each and then told the resolution: "To blush up her pale olive skin, our beauty editor used a sheer tawny base, a full pink blusher on the cheekbones, and even pink eye shadow" or: "For the shadows, she was given a pale highlighter that not only helps cover them but opens up the entire eye area when blended all over the socket." Because the problem of each girl is so general and one-dimensional—this one doesn't want to grow up, another doesn't like groups—they show the same insight into personality offered by fortune-telling cards in weight machines. Though it is undoubtedly true to say that a person's view of himself will be reflected in his external appearance, once this view is reduced to a mere peek, the hypothesis becomes absurd and the make-over becomes like all other make-overs, which refashion the girl in the image of the beauty editor.

In the attempt to stress individualism, *Glamour* paradoxically achieves the opposite. Not only do all girls have the same look (not one wears eyeliner, all have gleaming, unpowdered skin, each one is "natural" and there's not a vamp in the lot), but their psychological quirks are so indistinguishable that all merge into one friendly, non-reflecting twenty-two-year-old American girl. The makeup becomes protective covering, allowing the girl to be more easily assimilated into a group of middle-class young female urbanites. The moral seems to be that privacy and originality lead only to unhappiness, and the feast of life has become a masked ball where all guests are given the same disguises. Made over, the girls are now free to act like everyone else; they project an expected image and it is assumed that any identifying marks of personality will be erased or covered up.

This is antithetical to the view of feminine nature set forth by Ortega y Gasset in *On Love*. "The woman possesses a theatrical exterior and a circumspect interior," he writes, "while in the man it is the interior that is theatrical." This being so, "a woman's vanity is more ostentatious than a man's, precisely because it concerns itself only with externals: it is born, lives and dies in that external surface of her life to which I have referred; but *it does not generally affect her inner reality.*" (My italics.)

Between the two contrasting opinions is room for study and observation of the relation between external appearance and view of self. J. W. Kinch, in a paper called "A Formalized Theory of the Self-Concept," tells of graduate students in social psychology who decided to conduct an experiment showing that by systematically manipulating one's response to another person, it was possible to change "that person's self-concept and in turn his behavior." They chose as subject the one girl in their group, "a very plain girl who seemed to fit the stereotype (usually erroneous) that many have of graduate student females." The boys decided to respond to her as though she were the best-looking girl on campus. "They agreed to work into it naturally so that she would not be aware of what they were up to. They drew lots to see who would be the first to date her. The loser, under pressure of the others, asked her to go out. Although he found the situation quite unpleasant, he was a good actor, and by continually saying to himself 'she's beautiful, she's beautiful . . .' he got through the evening." Then the next boy dated her, and the third, always reinforcing the image of beauty. "In a matter of a few short weeks the results began to show. At first it was simply a matter of more care in her appearance; her hair was combed more often and her dresses were more neatly pressed, but before long she had been to the beauty parlor to have her hair styled, and was spending her hard-earned money on the latest fashions in women's campus wear. By the time the fourth man was taking his turn dating the young lady, the job that had once been undesirable was now quite a pleasant task. And when the last man in the conspiracy asked her out, he was informed that she was pretty well booked up for some time in the future. It seems there were more desirable males around than those 'plain' graduate students." *

What had not been predicted at the beginning of the experiment was that both the "victim" and the manipulators would change. As the girl's confidence increased, her appearance improved; this in turn reinforced her confidence, and it was now she, not the boys, who was manipulating. Her self-concept made it possible for her to convince others that she was desirable.

Mary Butler, whose profession is beauty, feels that "if a girl, a man, anybody is brought up from the time they're born with the idea that they are attractive, they are 'beautiful,' they project a confidence of beauty whether they are acceptably beautiful or not."

To believe in one's own beauty is much more difficult, even, than becoming acceptably beautiful. There can be nothing intrinsically right or wrong in employing aids to convince oneself and others that one is attractive. Every culture, society and subculture has standards for beauty, which most members accept. It is then left to the individual to decide how well he conforms. A model who appears dazzlingly beautiful to others may be convinced that her pores are too large, her feet too flat and her nose too long. All other girls at a party seem to her more attractive than she is. A plump, middle-aged woman, on the other hand, might know that she has wonderful hands and ex-

* I. G. Manis and B. N. Meltzer, *Symbolic Interaction*.

pressive eyes, and she assumes that everyone else sees only those traits.

Young people are generally less likely to have a firm self-concept than older people. For some period between the ages of thirteen and eighteen most boys and girls go through extreme self-doubt, which often veers from castigation to adulation. It's very difficult to present a front believable to yourself when you are aware that you don't know who you are, but have not yet recognized that the problem may not be crucial.

In the 1910's, my great-uncle in Vienna told my grandmother to have my father's ears pinned back. "Terrible," he said, "to have ears that stick out so. You can't let the boy run around like that, his schoolmates will laugh at him." My grandmother didn't act on her brother's advice, but until he was adult, my father always posed in profile for photographs. He also sucked in his lips, because someone (probably the same uncle) told him they were too thick.

My husband always had a large nose. As a young boy, believing that strange, wonderful things could happen during the night, he taped up his nose with band-aids but each morning found it as distressingly large as ever. Both men have since been amply complimented on their looks.

I was and still am very unsure about my appearance; I depend on the reactions of an audience. When I went to interview Vidal Sassoon, I realized he was attractive and knew it. His wife, whose full-page photograph is the last word in his book, is a glamorous actress. We were talking about her; Sassoon said that though he loved women to wear makeup, he found his wife incredibly beautiful when she woke up in the morning with no makeup at all. "She's a marvelous-looking bird," he said, and I was intimidated. Then, looking closely at my face, Sassoon asked: "You don't wear much makeup, do you?"

"Oh, I'm wearing *masses* of it now," I replied, hoping that he would wish to see my naked face.

"Well, you've done it very cleverly."

"My husband hates me to wear makeup," I insisted, to prolong the praise and, hopefully, to receive benediction from an authority I could later refer to.

"You've got an incredible look, by the way," said the dear man. "It's a very definite, strong look. I like it."

"That's my face," I explained apologetically.

"Yeah, I mean it. Yes, yes, it's good. . . ."

"I can't help it. . . ."

"But you're happy with it, aren't you?"

"No. I have bags under my eyes, my nose is too small and broad and my lips are too thick. . . ."

"Yes, but you see it all goes up to make a definite look, which is appealing. It's a good look. I'd never let it hang you up."

I was happy all afternoon.

Beauty, like cleverness, humor or goodness, depends on dialogue. The presentation of self must be accepted; the frame of reference must be clear to both. There is no beauty that has not been recognized as such. Whether beauty is in paintings, a river bed, a child's face or a Gothic cathedral, it is left to the onlooker's taste and sense of mystery to find it. Norman Mailer feels that beauty always includes terror. A man knows that death surrounds a beautiful woman, and he seeks her out through his courage. He knows that he can never possess her completely, that he can never be sure of her, and so she brings out his guilt. A man with a plain wife shows his lack of courage and his need for security. Only a brave man attempts to get a beautiful woman.

Poe felt that the most poetical thing of all was the death of a beautiful woman. The formality of such beauty is a long way from the cosmetics industry. It is shocking, a reminder of our insufficiency, a touch of the supernatural. The beauty that is truth or its own excuse for being is a quality of soul or mind, an intimation of mortality. Lesser beauties surround us, and we have been taught, by our backgrounds, which to appreciate. We perceive the universe through our life style and critical faculties. When we are told that "everyone can be beautiful," then the word has been devalued, relegated to the limbo of disembodied syllables whose sounds may continue to give assurance even though they are merely echoes from long-dead concepts.

For most people, beauty remains elusive, sexual, mysterious. A friend of mine returned daily to see a Gauguin painting of a Tahitian woman, the most beautiful woman he had ever seen. Only later did he realize she had the same eyes, with the same expression, as his mother.

The most beautiful woman I ever knew was Diana, a dusky Brazilian. I was a child, and she seemed an angel, with her soft voice, smooth skin and black, deep eyes. When I was twelve, I asked her how to make men fall in love with you. "Compliment their hands," she said gently. "Look at their hands, hold them, say they're beautiful."

"And if they're not?" I asked, with childish insistence on veracity.

She smiled. "Find something else then. Their hair, their tie, anything. As long as you make them believe you think it's beautiful."

I was in love with Diana; she had probably found something to praise about me. I was in love with other grown-up ladies too. They were the hope of what I could become, the splendid incarnation that I, still a tadpole, worshiped and did not quite understand.

Of all people one has known, no one was ever so beautiful as one's mother when she bent for the good-night kiss or brought her redemptive voice into the dark room full of witches, or smelled wonderful in the evening as she embarked on the treachery of going out with her husband. Beauty came in through the senses. A few years later, she had crow's feet, a sagging chin and flaring nostrils. One was forced to love her for what she was, and that was often an ordeal. We learned to distinguish between her various looks and when she returned from the hairdresser or wore a new dress, we told her she looked beautiful. We began to judge, not through our own needs, but through the eyes of our culture. And so we became socialized, chose our ideal among movie stars, models, pin-ups or famous people. By the time we bought our first deodorant, we had become consumers in the beauty culture, and we bought the message along with the product. Beauty had long since removed itself from morality or goodness, become an instrument for gaining pleasure, and we were already well-trained as Sybarites.

"The endless rediscovery of the self becomes a mild obsession of the normal individual in any society in which the individual has ceased to be a measure of the society itself," wrote Edward Sapir. The "rediscovery" may be imaginary. Whenever I asked upper-class young women why they didn't wear makeup, the answer always stressed individuality: "I just don't like it," "I think it's unnatural, somehow" or, "It really doesn't look good on me." The girls thought they were expressing their uniqueness, even though they had been trained to regard makeup as vulgar, and using it would mean giving a false impression of themselves. These girls, however, are a measure of society.

For others, the rediscovery of self can help to reevaluate or liberate oneself from the expected type into new possibilities of behavior. A professor of psychology explained: "Individuals in our society are cut off from other members of society and so have to discover who they're going to be."

The quest is quixotic. Chimerae of potential selves smile up from glossy pages with the teasing message, "This could be you." Revolts and personal deviations have been incorporated into the system. According to what group you belong to (*i.e.*, a combination of class, age, geography, economic standard and profession), you have a certain range in which to experiment. If you move out of your group, you enter the national beauty culture, where your choices are still circumscribed. Vidal Sassoon, who believes that beauty is "part of a way of life, like eating, going to bed, getting up, doing your thing," observes the American way from his English vantage point. The American woman, "from very early childhood through the teen-ager going on to a young woman [is] fed on commercials that tell her to use this, that and the other. I don't think that many of them use it for cabaret [i.e., disguise]. I think there's only certain people that give themselves a complete face-lift every time they make up and in this way don't recognize themselves, become a masquerade, something quite different, and [can] act according to their makeup. I think this is very rare behavior. I don't think the majority have the imagination to behave in this way; in fact, I'm convinced they don't. They wouldn't even give it a thought. As far as they're concerned, a TV ad has told them that so-and-so is going to be good for them, and they're going to give it a try. And they see themselves as they always were and always are. Because this type of imagination goes with very, very few people: the dreamers, the nonbelievers, people who aren't realists, people that want to see change, possibly see it through themselves. This is something that's fantasy. And it would be lovely if more people would fantasize. It would be very, very beautiful. . . ."

He believes the absence of self-expression through makeup coincides with general inhibitions. Young women choose marriage or security as goals in life before they have attempted to discover themselves. "And many of the things that they could have done, which are very exciting and real, are lost. Are lost with the sham and the real unreal, if you know what I mean."

2

The Real Unreal

Mircea Eliade described the sacred as the "really real." The nonsacred can be seen as the real unreal, its reality based on rituals and details that give a seeming order and seriousness to the fundamental concept, which is unreal. Beauty practices, ritualistic but not sacred, can be part of liturgy or ceremony and thereby have a function within a cosmology. Or they can serve to classify members of society. What is unique about American beauty practices reflects and is part of what is unique about American society.

To summarize, it is:

A giddy belief in democracy as the great equalizer that will turn everyone into a young, slim, white middle-class American.

Faith in free will by which each man can control or at least influence his destiny.

Tremendous fear of death and panic at the thought of death, and the correlated obsession with maintaining youth.

Acceptance of an economy that can create needs to fit the supply and that incorporates obsolescence as a spur to consuming.

Sexual irresolution, the interminable conflict between Puritanism and licentiousness or hedonism, which superimposes ideals of masculinity and feminity that lead to suspicion and resentment.

Belief that the good life is for sale.

Reliance on communications as the chief means of producing community; but, since communications present no order or morality, this becomes a source of fragmentation and loss of relationships.

Above all, it adulates the individual as an end in himself, and this unbearable responsibility leaves man with a sense of reality more ephemeral than the dust on rose leaves.

America's other assumptions, political, economic or racial, do not so directly involve the beauty culture or are functions more of history and power than of national idiosyncracies. The factors above are not independent. An American is cut off from community and family, must make his own way and "prove himself" through success, usually measured in money, which becomes the only measure of his worth when no religious or political orthodoxy expects anything of him. The title of V. Gordon Childe's book, *Man Makes Himself*, could describe life in America where, possessing no tragic view, the individual can have no comic one either and must substitute a sense of fun. The quality of life then turns adolescent. Everything is promised: self-indulgence becomes a national pastime approved by manufacturers and advertising companies. "I thing that most Americans feel that anything they spend on themselves is a sign of a strong ego," said Sol Worth. The beauty industry, more than any other, appeals to this tendency.

It also offers hope in a readily understandable way: to spend a lot of money on beautifying (improving) yourself shows faith in yourself and may pay off immediately with attentions or love. Adolescents search for love more avidly than anyone else, and have the hardest time achieving it. Concerned with themselves, they lack the security and generosity to connect with others. But they want to be noticed, they want proof that they exist. Existence is a pretty butterfly that commands attention but must never be caught because it would die.

The beauty culture is part of the pop culture, which believes in the inexorable truth of change. Change, not as a mutating force, but as fashion. Truth is whatever is in vogue. Truth is Oldenburg's giant hamburger, an object taken out of context to shock us by a super-reality that has nothing in common with the real thing. Truth is teleidoscopic, the image of an image. Truth is fashion, the aesthetic resolution of variety and banality. Truth is beauty, or whatever will pass for beauty that season or at that party.

We are placed here to enjoy ourselves for the duration. We smile at everything; we smile when we sell deodorants, we smile when we say good-bye, we smile when we dislike someone, when we are happy, despondent or in love. We smile, because our intention is pleasure. The ancient Sybarites, living in the wealthiest city of its day (destroyed in 510 B.C.), also lived for pleasure. By law, women could be invited to a public celebration only if given a year's notice, so they would have time to arrange their dresses and finery. Sybarites invented chamberpots that could be taken to banquets so the party-goer would not have to miss a moment of fun. In Sybaris, roads were covered to provide shade, cooks registered their delicacies for copyright and rude or untimely noises (like the crowing of a cock) were banned. The townspeople so despised manual labor that even the sight of it made them ill. The Roman historian Diodorus Siculus (80-10 B.C.) reports that one Sybarite told his friend he had seen men digging in a field and had suffered a rupture watching them. His friend was sympathetic: "For I, at the mere hearing of it, have suffered a stitch in my side."

No one wanted to leave Sybaris; no one who shared the life of luxury and leisure could imagine any other form of existence. The city was destroyed by soldiers from neighboring Croton, and remains in the world's imagination as nothing more than a metaphor or, at best, a parable. Sybarites were not Americans or even New Yorkers, but we should still know the word sybaritism, just in case anyone accuses us of it.

"At a time when the normal condition of the citizen is a state of anxiety, euphoria spreads over our culture like the broad smile of an idiot," wrote the late Robert Warshow in "The Gangster as Tragic Hero." National euphoria has a way of assuming the characteristics of psychoses. In the fifties, it was catatonia and now, hysteria. The beat is fast, the mood psychedelic and the sound so loud that we have an increase in the number of hard-of-hearing adolescents. We drown out the voices of doom, we are blind to death and the pace gets faster, hotter until the question of who we are no longer matters.

In a gentle way, Norbert Weiner agitated for the human use of human beings. He meant Americans, and admonished us for our lack of depth: "In the myths and fairy tales that we read as children we learned a few of the simpler and more obvious truths of life, such as that when a djinnee is found in a bottle, it had better be left there; that the fisherman who craves a boon from heaven too many times on behalf of his wife will end up exactly where he started; that if you are given three wishes, you must be very careful what you wish for. These simple and obvious truths represent the childish equivalent of the tragic view of life which the Greeks and many modern Europeans possess, and which is somehow missing in this land of plenty."

So the search for beauty is not to be condemned as mere vanity. Beauty will make us feel better and give us a kind of leverage in a world of make-believe where even a frog can become a prince. Our success stories are similar to that one, or to Cinderella or Pygmalion. Beauty is part of our system of beliefs, and the practitioner is freed from doubt through ritualized behavior. "The [beauty] industry provides only instruments for the ritual," said Sol Worth. "They support it, but the ritual is deep in this culture and almost all-powerful."

Like breathing, the ritual is an unconscious dance. Not to join means you are following another, stronger rhythm. The schizophrenic makes his own music and at times the artist does too. While working, it's hard to maintain one's usual sense of identity or the front that corresponds to social reality.

A young woman novelist forgets the ritual when she's writing. She wears no makeup, leaves her hair as it is and puts on whatever article of clothing is nearest her bed. In summer she wears no underclothes; in winter, the jeans get more and more filthy. But when she's not working, she's very conscious of how she appears to others. At seventeen she became a platinum blonde and disliked the boys who liked her. She hoped to disguise her unfeminine trait of intelligence but was unhappy if successful. She was usually fat, about to be fat or thinking of herself as fat. She had two firm goals in life: to be thin and to write well. The second allowed her to rationalize that misfits and unattractive people were often geniuses, and so between the extremes of berating and adulating herself, she occasionally settled into an approximation of sanity. Overweight, poetry and sex were her main obsessions.

She wore makeup at fourteen, long earrings and clothes too old for her. When she visited London, the whores of Piccadilly and Curzon Street thought she was trying to horn in on their territory, so she stuck to her mother. At sixteen, she wore black and announced, "I am in mourning for my life." She hadn't yet accomplished anything, wasn't married, didn't even have a boyfriend and no poet had eulogized her.

Now she's a presentable woman. She's tall (five foot ten) and slim enough to stop worrying about fat. But the worry is a habit with her, and for a long time after she attained her ideal weight she didn't believe it, continued to see herself as overweight and selected clothes many sizes too large. She's published four novels and has just written a book about the beauty culture, which she often condemns. Last night she went out with her husband. Her hair was freshly washed, her skirt was micro, she was well made up and he complimented her throughout the evening. He's a good-looking Englishman who likes her best when she has on no makeup at all, lets the hair grow under her arms and on her legs, and wears no bra. But she can't comply; she feels too ugly. She tells him, "Accept me as I am" and means by that: Accept me in the image I have of what I could appear. She must wear eye makeup to emphasize her best feature (brown eyes, long lashes) and to distract attention from the bags under her eyes. She has her hair straightened regularly and streaks of color put in. Her hair remains a big problem, though she's no longer a platinum blonde—it's too kinky and thick, too dry and brown if left alone. Whenever she shampoos, she needs many hours and sets it with a special lotion from Kenneth's. When her hair looks terrible (her husband doesn't notice), she refuses to go out.

She was once busty and proud of it. While making caustic remarks about the breast fetish of Americans, she stuck her chest out and wore revealing clothes. After the birth of her baby, her weight went down and her breasts shrank. She now wears padded bras (he hates them) so that she can at least seem busty in clothes. Last night her husband asked her not to wear padding; she argued that this was impossible, and the only way she could avoid it was by having breast surgery. She was serious (more about the rubber than the surgery); for him, there was a sudden chasm between them and he wondered whom he'd married. This had happened before; the woman who could quote reams of poetry and reenter with him the innocence of his boyhood was also a strange creature who actually knew and took seriously the lyrics of pop songs, who shielded her breasts because they were "too floppy" and "too small" (he thought they were fine, and repeatedly told her that) and who accepted the rituals and artifice of the beauty culture at face value.

She says, "Accept me as I am." He says, "I do—that's exactly what I want to do," and she shakes her head. What she is isn't the unretouched picture he has of her. She's a "creation," of herself and America, who wants to wear the latest fashions, appear younger than she is and cover her naked face so strangers on the street or in passing cars will find her recognizable.

She's hooked on beauty. She needs her rituals and gets nervous if she's interrupted while making up. A strict order must be kept: first the blusher, then erase, white shadow, line over the eye and in the hollow, mascara, lip gloss, lipstick. She must have certain products, sometimes foreign, and believes that expensive ones are better than cheap ones. She's often funny and outgoing, but she has to feel safe. Sometimes she's terribly afraid of being ugly and of death. When that happens, she can't believe that anyone loves her, and even if they do, their love isn't worth anything. She then has long thoughts on life and literature; she's ready to destroy everything around her; she loses humor and becomes self-pitying. Her only hope of rescue is to cheat the mirror and deceive some people into believing, and telling her, that she is beautiful.

The wishes of human vanity endure. Beauty is the hope for salvation, for Pandora's box, which offers treasures most desired by men, but should never be opened and the contents never examined, to keep the hope. The search for beauty is one of the great quests, and if in America we seek it in ourselves, this is because we seek everything in ourselves, even God. Maimonides wrote: "If not I for myself, then who? And being for myself, what am I? And if not now, when?"

These are questions the beauty culture hopes to answer. In early Renaissance terms, the Rock of Narcissism may save us from the Sea of Despair. In our terms, you do your own thing. If the reward isn't self-knowledge, at least you've played the game for all it's worth. The worth increases daily, the game reaches out to more players, and America is studded with ornamental humans who challenge the authority of their deaths through their advocate, beauty.

Index

Adams, Beverly, 97
Advertising, 22, 25, 30–33, 38, 41, 43–
  45, 47, 62, 88–89, 131, 177, 178,
  193, 203, 205, 241, 296
Advertising Age, 44
Afro (hair style), 70–71, 85, 99, 100
Afro-American look, 70
Aged, beauty culture and the, 181–182
Alexandre, 84
Allyson, June, 220
American Foundation for the Blind,
  180
American Girl, 9
American Way of Death, The (Mit-
  ford), 215
Aramis, 26 fn.
Archer, Elsie, 46
Arden, Elizabeth, 23, 38, 40, 47, 57,
  78, 261
Arden for Men, 26 fn.
Aromatherapy, 63
Art of Staying Young, The (Frank-
  lyn), 154
Asenjo, Albert, 180–181, 257
Avon, 27, 34, 60
Ayds, 160
Aziza, 301

Bacall, Lauren, 219
Bailey, David, 230
Baker, Ken, 204–208, 211–212, 228,
  237, 242, 243, 250
Baldness, 64, 74, 133
Bankhead, Tallulah, 220
Barbie dolls, 10

Bardot, Brigitte, 73, 202, 213, 220,
  221
Beards, 72
Beatles, 223, 224, 230, 244, 249, 257
Beaton, Cecil, 243
Beatty, Warren, 220
Beautiful People, 217, 221–223, 305,
  306–307
Beautiful People, The (Bender), 217,
  221
Beauty Beat, 36
Beauty contests, 224–227
Beauty Fashion, 42 fn.
Beauty retreat, 261–291
Beauty therapy, 173, 179
Beauvoir, Simone de, 221
Bendel's Beauty Salon, 13
Bender, Marylin, 217, 221
Bergen, Polly, 41
Bergman, Ingrid, 58
Birmingham, Stephen, 278
Bishop, Hazel, 203
Bishop Industries, 79
Black Beauty (agency), 211
Blacks, 26, 36, 46, 53, 64 fn., 69, 70–
  71, 83, 85, 98–100, 135, 149–150,
  191, 200, 209–211, 226, 238, 242,
  309–311
Blass, Bill, 222, 243
Bleaching, 102–103
Blind people, beauty culture and, 179–
  181
Body image, 157–159
Bogart, Humphrey, 219
Bonnie and Clyde, 220

Bonne Bell, 181
Braggi, 26, 27
Brando, Marlon, 219, 223
Brandwynne, Jacqui, 34–37, 228
Brauer, Earle, 22, 43
Breast implants, 114, 120, 127–129, 140
Breast surgery, 109–154, 119–124
British-American Tobacco Company, 35 fn.
Brown, Helen Gurley, 16, 18
Bruch, Hilde, 161, 163, 286
Brussel, James A., 46, 136, 171–174, 178, 182, 301
Burden, Amanda, 57, 222
Burden, Mr. and Mrs. Carter, 222
Burley, 42
Burr, Donald, 35
Business, cosmetic, 22–48
Butler, Mary, 19, 21, 240, 241, 302, 313

California Girl products, 34
Canne, Jessica, 19, 21, 203, 251, 302
Carroll, Diahann, 210, 309–310
Caruso, Julius, 88
Casdulan, 98–100
Celebrities, 216–217
Charles of the Ritz, 39
Chemical peel, 113, 132
Childe, V. Gordon, 319
Christie, Julie, 220
Churchill, Winston S., 243
Clairol, 30–34, 38, 63, 64, 177, 190
Cleopatra, 221
Clift, Montgomery, 220
Clinique, 63
"Cloning," 64
Cocteau, Jean, 137
Codpieces, 148 fn.
Condé-Nast, 210
Contests, beauty, 224–227
Cooley, Charles, 83
Cooper, Gloria, 222
Cooper, Wyatt, 243
Cosmetic surgery, 107–154
Cosmetics, 5–65; men's, 26–27, 42–43; testing of, 60–61
Cosmetics: Trick or Treat? (Stabile), 22

Cosmopolitan, 9, 15, 16–18, 19, 82, 298
Courrèges, 84
Craig, Miss, 57
Crawford, Joan, 219
Crimpers, The, 13
Cunningham, Alma, 158, 174–175
Curtis, Tony, 220
Cutex, 28

Daché, Lily, 91, 93, 102
Dandridge, Dorothy, 70
Davis, Bette, 220
Day, Doris, 73, 208, 220
Dean, James, 215
De Fossé (Paris), 104
Dentistry, cosmetic, 138, 142, 147
Deodorants, 45–47
Depilatories, 64 fn.
Dermabrasion, 110–111, 113, 132, 135
Diet, reducing and, 160–170
Dietrich, Marlene, 202, 216, 218–219, 251
Dior, Christian, 24
DiSalvo, Albert, 172
Doctor Zhivago (movie), 221
Downing, Ruth, 38–39
Drug and Cosmetic Industry, 62
Dunbar, Dorothy, 48
Dunham, Katherine, 100
Dylan, Bob, 223
Dynatones, 55

Eau de Love, 38
Ebony, 26
Edgerton, M. T., 127, 129 fn., 135 fn., 136 fn., 297
Electrolysis, 75
Eliade, Mircea, 318
Elizabeth I, Queen, 72, 80
Engelhard, Jane, 57
Esquire, 78
Ever-Young method, 134
Exercise salons, 55, 56–58
Expenditures, for cosmetics, 43
Eyelash Studio, 58

Fabergé, 77, 246
Face-lifting, 109–125, 132–135, 142, 143, 146, 148

Facials, 53–55
Factor, Max, 38, 48
Fantasy, 178–179
Farrow, Mia, 74, 220
Fashion Group, 158, 174–175
Fashion Tress, Inc., 80
Fashions: children and, 11–12; teen-agers and, 13
Fatness, *see* Obesity
Fire and Ice, 29
Fonda, Jane, 220
Food and Drug Administration, 43–44, 128 fn.
Food, Drug and Cosmetic Act, 44
Foote, Cone and Belding, 30
Ford Agency, 205, 211, 214
Form, beauty, 261–291
Fortune, 39, 40
Franklin, Aretha, 223
Franklyn, Robert Alan, 120, 141–154
Frederick's of Hollywood, 64
Freeman, Erika, 23
Freud, Sigmund, 152, 163
Friedan, Betty, 253, 302

Gable, Clark, 219
Gabor, Eva, 80, 262, 278
Gabor, Zsa Zsa, 41, 80, 150, 219, 220, 262, 267
Garbo, Greta, 216, 218, 234
Gaulle, Charles de, 217
Gernreich, Rudi, 84
Giacometti, Alberto, 84
Gilbert, Yvette, 219
Gimbel's, 247
Glamour, 14, 15, 19, 20, 26, 42, 59, 203, 208, 210, 213, 220, 311, 312
Goffman, Erving, 82, 83
Golden Door beauty farm, 165, 261–288
Gould, Jack, 226
Grant, Cary, 246
Graves, Robert, 73, 253
Gray, Aida, 53, 59
Green, Gordon L., 165
Greene, Amy, 14, 19, 87, 187, 208, 225, 241
Greenhouse, 261, 265, 269
Grey Advertising, 30
Grief, Norman, 61

Gross, Larry, 45, 163, 179
Group therapy, 185

Hai Karate, 205
Hair, 67–105; men's, 76–79, 88, 104–105
Hair coloring, 30–33
Hair transplants, 122, 132, 133
Hair weaving, 77
Hairdressers, 78, 83–84, 90–105
Hamilton, George, 243
Harlech, Lord, 218
Harnett, Sunny, 202
Harper's Bazaar, 12, 18, 21, 52, 199, 203, 211, 212, 222, 223, 240, 306
Hayworth, Rita, 73
Head, Edith, 221
Hepburn, Audrey, 219, 220, 222
Hepburn, Katherine, 299
Hidden Persuaders, The (Packard), 55
High (Hinde), 278
Hills, Miss, 54
Hinde, Thomas, 278
Hitler, Adolf, 88, 152
Hoffman, Dustin, 220
Holden, William, 219
Holliday, Judy, 163, 219
Hollingshead, A. B., 178
Homosexuals: female, 191–192; male, 26–27, 76–77, 91, 148, 204–206, 237, 242, 296
Hoopes, J. E., 130 fn., 136 fn.
Horne, Lena, 70
House of Westmore, 38
Hudson, Rock, 219
Hughes, Lisa, 217 fn.
Human Use of Human Beings, The (Weiner), 250
Humphrey, Hubert, 87
Hunt, H. L., 41
Hutton, Lauren, 212

Image, *see also* Self-image, 7–21; body, 157–159
Importance of Overweight, The (Bruch), 161
Importance of Wearing Clothes, The (Langner), 244
Ingenue, 9, 35
Ivan, 105

Jacobson, Wayne E., 126, 129 fn., 135, 135 fn.
Jagger, Mick, 230
Jastrzembska, Zofya, 180–181
Jensen, Baba, 269
Jerry's, 104–105
Jogging, 55
John, Mr., 305
Johnson, Mrs. Lyndon, 222
Journal of Podiatry, 140
Jujin Hospital (Tokyo), 134

Kalish, Joseph, 23, 73
Kane, Jean, 58
Kazan, Michel, 199
Kelly, Grace, 58, 219
Kennedy, Jackie, *see* Onassis, Jackie Kennedy
Kennedy, John, 215
Kenneth, Mr., 41, 52, 54, 78, 84, 85, 88, 91, 93–99, 104, 174, 193, 199, 218, 220, 237, 241, 251, 255, 296, 299, 301, 302, 305
Killy, Jean-Claude, 243
Kinch, J. W., 312
Kitt, Eartha, 254
Klein, Jerome Comet, 134
Knorr, Norman J., 130 fn., 135 fn., 136 fn.
Koufax, Sandy, 97
Kounovsky, 56
Kramer, Jeffrey, 126, 157, 159, 172–173, 212, 245
Kross, Anna, 189
Kurtz, Richard, 159

Ladies' Home Journal, 78, 209, 266
Lake, Veronica, 220
Lalanne, Claude, 209
Langner, Lawrence, 244–245
Lanvin, 40
Laszlo, Erno, 50, 51–52, 53
Lauder, Estée, 26 fn., 39–40, 222
Leach, Edmund, 82
Lennon, John, 224
Let's Face It (Archer), 46
Lewis, Oscar, 254
Life magazine, 30, 52, 150, 203

Light 'n Bright, 85
Lincoln, Abbe, 70
Linda, 98
Lindsay, Mary, 137–139, 188, 192, 193
Little Joe, 78
Little Miss America, 225, 226
Lollabrigida, Gina, 219
Look-Alive Gray, 32
Look, 203
Loren, Sophia, 219
Los Angeles Times, 290
Love Cosmetics, 37
Loving Care, 32
Luna, Donyale, 210, 284

MacFarland, Gloria, 183–187, 193, 237, 239
Mack, John, 32, 33
Macy's, 247
Mademoiselle, 14, 15, 26, 63, 75
Maher, Ana, 59
Mailer, Norman, 201, 231, 249, 315
Maine Chance, 261, 265, 272, 283
Makeba, Miriam, 100
Make-overs, 14–15, 59, 187
Make-up, 5–65, 295–317
Make-up kits, toy, 10
Malcolm X, 100
Male and Female (Mead), 77
Mammaplasty, augmentation, 127
Man Makes Himself (Childe), 319
Mandel, William, 24–25, 27–30, 137, 213, 245–246, 302
Manhattan State Hospital, 158
Manic depressives, characteristics of, 172
Manis, I. G., 313 fn.
Mansfield, Jayne, 73, 213
Martin, Mary, 87
Maury, Madame Marguerite, 63
Max Factor Country, 48
Maybelline, 38
Mayhem, Stephen, 62
McCall's, 14, 19, 208
McClary, A. R., 127, 129 fn.
McGrady, Patrick M., 137 fn.
McGrath, New York State Commissioner of Correction, 194

Mead, Margaret, 46, 69, 74, 76, 77, 132, 239, 241, 256, 258, 297, 308–309
Meltzer, B. N., 313 fn.
Melvin, Harold, 70, 71, 98–100, 187, 210, 226, 242, 309–311
Men: cosmetics for, 26–27, 42–43; fashions and, 238–246
Men's Bazaar, 78, 243
Mental illness, 172–178
Merkin, 77
Metesky, George, 172
Meyer, E., 129 fn., 135 fn.
Military Make-up Artists Program, 48
Milton, John, 73
Miniskirts, 223
Mink oil, 52
Miss America, 225–227
Miss Black America, 225, 226
Miss Teen-Age America, 225, 226
Miss Thailand, 225
Mitchell, Paul, 13, 96–97, 302
Mitford, Jessica, 215
Model, The (Reno), 203
Models, 186–187, 199–215, 228–234; child, 211; male, 204–211
Moffitt, Peggy, 200
Molyneux, Captain, 202
Monroe, Marilyn, 73, 139, 141, 213, 216, 219, 230, 231
Moon Drops, 25, 26, 29, 37
Moore, Henry, 84
Mother-daughter relationship, 185–186
Moustaches, 72, 79, 80, 88
Movie stars, *see also* Celebrities, 200, 202, 208, 230

Natural look, 86
Natural Wonder, 25
Neiman-Marcus, 261
Nessler, Charles, 72
New York Times, The, 78, 79, 159, 223, 253
Newsweek, 217 fn., 244
Nidetch, Jean, 159, 166–170
Niehans, Dr., 219
Niemeyer, Oscar, 144
Nixon, Richard, 73, 87, 251

Nixon, Mrs. Richard, 222
Noxema, 39

Obesity, 160–170
Old age, beauty culture and, 181–182
Oliver, Leslie, 237, 239
On Developing Bosom Beauty (Franklyn), 120, 145
Onassis, Aristotle, 218, 222
Onassis, Jackie Kennedy, 150, 176, 216, 217–218, 222, 223
Opdyke, Donald, 23, 60, 64 fn., 237, 242, 252
Orentreich, Norman, 112, 122, 132–133, 144, 148
Ortega y Gasset, José, 213
Overweight, *see* Obesity

Pablo, 77
Packard, Vance, 55
Paley, "Babe," 57, 222, 307
Paley, William, 222
Palmer, Bill, 248
Palmer, Lisa, 14
Paolozzi, Countess, 222
Parker, Suzy, 202
Parks, Bert, 225
Patchett, Jean, 202
Patiños of Portugal, 222
Penis, size of, 152–153
Penney, Alexandra, 59
Philip, Prince, 243
Plastic surgery, 107–154
Playboy, 9, 15, 16, 18, 42, 78, 150, 233
Poe, Edgar Allan, 315
Politi, Derek, 48
Polykoff, Shirley, 30, 32
Ponce de Leon reflex complex, 182
Pond's, 38–39
Powers, John Robert, 39
Presentation of Self in Everyday Life, The (Goffman), 82
Presley, Elvis, 97, 223
Prices, cosmetic, 23–24, 38
Promiscuity, 254
Psychoanalysis, 151, 152, 252
Psychotics, 176

Quant, Mary, 63, 84

Rand Corporation, 64
Reckless, Frank, 63
Redlich, F. C., 178
Reducing, 160–170
Reed, Rex, 74, 216
Relaxacizors, 55
Reno, Terry, 203
Research, 22–23, 60–62
Retreat, beauty, 261–291
Revlon, 22–30, 34, 38, 39, 40, 43, 45, 47, 88, 177, 296; Research Center, 60–62, 63, 242
Revson, Charles, 25, 26, 28–29, 222
Reynolds, Debbie, 220
Rhinoplasties, 135
Right People, The (Birmingham), 278
Rituals, beauty, 50–52, 59
Rockefeller, Mrs. Nelson, 222
Rosemary, 85, 102
Ross, Katherine, 220
Roy, Ellen, 266–268, 270, 271, 278, 286
Royal Jelly, 41, 52
Rubinstein, Helena, 29, 35, 40, 41, 63, 85, 181
Rubinstein, Mala, 64, 181
Ruta, Francesca, 91, 100–103

Sainsbury, Barry, 247
St. Angelo, Giorgio di, 209, 247
St. Laurent, Yves, 209, 223
Saks Fifth Avenue, 52, 53
Sapir, Edward, 297, 316
Sassoon, Vidal, 13 fn., 22, 40, 73 fn., 78, 84, 91, 92, 94–98, 199, 220, 242–243, 250–251, 314, 317
Schizophrenics, characteristics of, 172
Schoen, Mila, 307
Self-analysis, 311
Self-image, 139, 151–153, 157–159; blindness and, 180; mental illness and, 172; old age and, 182
Seventeen, 9, 10, 12–14, 20, 45, 87, 181, 203
Sex and the Single Girl (Brown), 16
Shaefer, Roland, 80
Sheppard, Eugenia, 18
Shrimpton, Jean, 29, 36, 199, 202, 203, 204, 209, 213, 215, 216, 226, 228–234

Sideburns, 79, 80
Silicone, 127–128, 132, 133, 144–145
Simon, Janet, 179
Simplicity Patterns, 158
Sims, Naomi, 199, 200, 209–210
Sixteen, 9
Skull, Mr. and Mrs. Robert, 222
Slicker, 34, 36
Snow, Emasue, 193
Sonny and Cher, 223
Sorry I kept you waiting, madam (Sassoon), 96
Spallina, Jerry, 78
Stabile, Toni, 22
Start (home for delinquent girls), 183–188
Stein, Gertrude, 88
Steinem, Gloria, 308
Streisand, Barbra, 216
Sudden Summer, 33
"Summertime Love," 36–37
Susskind, David, 105
Swanson, Gloria, 220
Sybaris, 320–321
Szekeley, Deborah Bordeaux, 165, 262, 273

Taylor, Elizabeth, 73, 150, 216, 219
Taylor, Laurence, 97
Teen Miss, 9
Temple, Shirley, 73
Thalidomide, 23
Therapy: beauty, 173, 179; group, 185
Thompson, J. Walter, 38
Thompson, Roger, 97
Tiegs, Cheryl, 14, 203
Toni, 31
Total Look, 87
Toupés, 72, 77, 78
Town and Country, 26
Tree, Penelope, 178, 187, 199, 200, 203, 208, 209, 212, 216
Trier, Carola, 56–58, 237, 267
Turtle oil, 52
Twiggy, 199, 200, 202, 203, 208, 209, 210, 211, 216, 220, 228, 229
Tyson, Cecily, 70

Ultima II, 25, 26, 29, 62
Umezawa, Dr., 134

Ungaro, 84
Unisex, 18, 247–258

Vaginal sprays, 45
Valmy, Christine, 53
Vanderbilt, Mrs., 184
Vera, Madame, 202
Veruschka, 187, 199, 200, 209, 212
"Videation," 180
Vogue, 12, 13, 15, 18–21, 26, 27, 28,
    37, 47, 59, 62, 70, 75, 83, 84, 87,
    140, 199–204, 208–213, 215–218,
    220, 221, 222, 223, 227, 233, 284,
    306
Vreeland, Diana, 18, 209

Wagman, Howard, 80–81
Walking, 56–57
Wall Street Journal, 79
Warshow, Robert, 320
Waugh, Evelyn, 59
Wayne, John, 219
Webb, David, 224, 264
Weight Watchers, 159, 165–170

Weiner, Norbert, 250, 320
White, Nancy, 18
Widener, George D., 243
Wife swapping, 254
Wigs, 71, 72, 80–82
Wilhelmina, 201, 204, 205, 208, 212,
    214
Williams, Esther, 219
Windsor, Duchess of, 261, 306
Wolf, H. Edward, 134
Wolfe, Tom, 243
Women's House of Detention, 137–
    139, 187, 188–196
Women's Liberation Movement, 225,
    240, 251
Women's Wear Daily, 11, 13, 18, 19,
    34, 37, 45, 47, 74, 78, 80, 83, 87,
    88, 131, 133, 134, 216, 217, 220–
    223, 247, 248, 297, 307
Worth, Sol, 298, 302, 308, 319, 321
Wyman, Jane, 219

Yardley, 25, 29, 34–38, 177, 203
Yoko Ono, 224